IMAM KHOMEINI'S VIEWS ON ACADEMIC INSTITUTIONS AND ACADEMICIANS

Edited by

Dr. Hamza Aziz

Book Title: Imam Khomeini's views on Academic Institutions and Academicians

Editor: Dr. Hamza Aziz

Graphics: Dr. Fatima Reza

Year: 2021

ISBN: 978-1-7330284-8-6

CONTENTS

SECTION 7

PURSUING HIGHER EDUCATION ABROAD

SECTION 8

SEMINARIES (*Howzeh*) AND UNIVERSITIES

PREFACE

Imam Khomeini pioneered a new era in world politics, however, it is not widely appreciated that he was also a great academician. Though he was a theologian, he had unique, modern and revolutionary vision of education from primary school to higher education, role of universities and religious seminaries and responsibilities of teachers, university faculty members and scholars. His ten years of exceptional politico-academic leadership in building new Iran based on resistance against global hegemony and principles of Islamic teachings, transformed the entire education system of country after the success of Islamic Revolution in 1979.

Imam emphasized key role of self-purification and self-reconstruction before acquisition of knowledge, education and training together, character building and acquisition of knowledge and skills side-by-side and ethical development with professional development. According to him, teachers, both from the schools, colleges and universities and the Islamic seminaries are the builders of a nation. They have important and heavy task not only to nurture and train intellectuals but also develop highly skilled human beings who in future, will build society, serve the poor, needy and downtrodden and will also play key role in the future leadership, management and politics of country at different levels.

Another important point that is clearly seen in the speeches and writings of Imam Khomeini is the pivotal role of universities. According to him, all the changes in any society originate from universities. Universities are the factories of manufacturing human beings and universities can make a nation successful. On the other hand, universities with corrupted education and culture can destroy the entire nation and bring the country to its knees.

According to him, the greatest dangers to universities is penetration by individuals, faculty members, intellectuals and scholars with deviant, western influenced thinking and lifestyle. This leads to bad education, training and moral upbringing of young students and distorted notion of education and service of fellow human beings, society and country in their minds. Such individuals especially instructors can make their students neglectful towards self-building and service to society. In addition west-toxication of their souls and lifestyle leads to spread of different types of moral and ideological corruption in the society. A highly educated but distorted young intellectual is more dangerous than an ignorant individual.

Finally, Imam Khomeini being a theologian, emphasizes divine aspects of education and training. According to him the profession of teachers and faculty members is similar to the mission of all the prophets. The divinely sent prophets purified human souls and educated them and reformed whole society – freeing it of corruption and oppression. Similarly, teachers educate and train students and shape their character so that they make progress in their careers and develop into not only successful professionals of but also virtuous servants of God and humble supporters of their fellow human beings in a society.

This book was compiled from the Persian version with the help of *Sahifa of Imam Khomeini* in English. Extensive editing was carried out to make it suitable for English speaking readers. I thank my student Mahdieh who really worked hard in preparing this book. Thanks also to Dr. Fatima Reza for her help in converting it to final book form.

I hope this book will enlighten readers in the field of education and training.

Dr. Hamza Aziz

SECTION I

THE GREAT VALUE OF KNOWLEDGE

The Aim of Education and Training[1]

The profession of teaching is similar to the mission of the Prophets

By virtue of being teachers, you have been entrusted with another noble task, the responsibility of which is as great as its nobleness. Your occupation deals with molding human beings. A teacher produces human beings just as the prophets did. The prophets- every prophet from the first one to the last- came only for the job of molding people and training them. The teaching profession is the same (in aim) as that of the prophets. The Noble Prophet (s) is the teacher of the whole of humanity. After him, it was Hazrat Amir (a) who was also humanity's teacher. They were the teachers of humanity in its entirety, whereas you are the teachers of a part of it. But the task is the same; that is, the sphere is the same; the job is the same. While their range of activity was broad, ours is limited. Therefore, this occupation of yours is very noble one, but bearing a great responsibility, just as the responsibility of the prophets was great. Their responsibility was as grave as the task of molding human beings. They, however, accomplished their mission and the tasks with which they had been entrusted. Your occupation is very honorable and the same as that of the prophets, and the responsibility is also the same.

Date: June 11, 1979/Khordad 12, 1358 SH/Rajab 61, 1399 AH.

Place: Qum

Subject: The beginning of offspring from the viewpoint of Islam

Audience: Female teachers of Dezful

Reaping the benefits of spirituality and *tawhid* (unity) from science

It is only to a small extent- what we seek in the sciences taught in our universities and the ones taught in the old *madrasahs* (schools of theology) is not that as appears outwardly now and with which our scholars are busy. Their work, though highly respected, is not what Islam is after.

What Islam wants and aims for is that all the sciences, whether the natural sciences or the other ones, be moored to the divine sciences and to move on to *tawhid*. It wants every field of science to possess the aspect of divinity. That is to say that when we observe nature, when we observe the physical world and all the things that exist, we should perceive God in them. Islam has come to take all the things that exist in nature to the position of divinity, and all the natural sciences to the divine science. And this is desired of the universities; not merely in the matter of medicine. Of course, medical

---

[1] A separate book on Imam Khomeini's views on 'Basic Principles and Aims of Education and Training' has been published in Persian.

science, natural science and curing physical ailments are all necessary. But the important thing is that center of gravity which is *tawhid*. All these (sciences) must proceed to that divine aspect.

Date: Afternoon, July 4, 1979/Tir 31, 1358 SH/Sha'ban 9, 1399 AH.

Place: Qum

Subject: The differences between a Western university and an Islamic one

Audience: Tehran University professors

Purification as the prerequisite in teaching the Scripture and Wisdom

The secret behind the Noble Messenger's prophetic mission is purification as well as the teaching and training of the nation, a teaching that includes all the aspects of teaching whereas the Book and Divine Wisdom qualify all the aspects of education. After mentioning teaching and training, it points out the pseudo-*'ulama'*, i.e. those who have learned knowledge but do not practice on that learning and have been denounced in the worst possible terms: "*The likeness of those who are entrusted with the Law of Moses, yet apply it not, is as the likeness of the ass carrying books.*" (Qur'an, 62:5). The story of those who possessed the knowledge of the Torah but practiced otherwise is likened in saying, to a donkey bearing books on its back but does not understand what they are and does not benefit from them. The example of those who have become learned but the learning has not left its effect in them, is likened to a donkey which is loaded with books! If knowledge does not leave its effect on man and does not make a human being of a man, no matter if he carries those books in his heart or carries it on his back! The example of such people is likened to those people or rather to the animal, a donkey that has books on its back. Just as a book is of no use to that animal, so is that knowledge which is not followed by commitment or is not practiced and is not followed by mental development, or is not applied to guide people. This is just of the same sort of man who has books on his back, just as if an animal, a donkey, is carrying books.

Radio-Television Message

Date: August 24, 1979/Shahrivar 2, 1358 SH/Shawwal 1, 1399 AH.

Place: Qum

Subject: Islam is a political religion

Occasion: The auspicious 'Id al-Fitr

Audience: The Muslim nation of Iran

Enlightenment

Both the clergy and the academicians are charged with the responsibility of enlightenment, if they perform their duties within the constraints set for the purpose. The fact is that, your job as teachers is one and the same as that of the prophets sent by the Almighty God. It is no secret that the reason for the appointment of prophets was intended to enlighten people and the holy Qur'an is an enlightening book.

Date: May 24, 1979/Khordad 3, 1358 SH/Jamadi ath-Thani 27, 1399 AH.

Place: Qum

Subject: Profession of clerics and academicians; creation of discord between the seminary and university; role of culture in the declination and amelioration of the society

Audience: Ali Shari'atmadari, (Minister of Culture and Higher Education), chancellors of universities and institutions of higher education

The need for all deeds to be divine in purpose

Man should think about the things that are useful in training, teaching and coaching people, and should orient his actions accordingly. If the universities are not given direction, they will be the same as the ones existing for the people, and which produce destructive forces. But if they be given (the necessary) direction they will accomplish what the machine guns cannot. They can render service to humanity, which no one can do to that extent. The main thing is the direction and moving in it. The Qur'an says: "*Read: In the name of thy Lord who createth*" (Qur'an, 96:1). Read, but not for its own sake. Learn, but not just for the sake of learning. Acquire knowledge, but not knowledge for its own sake nor its acquisition for its own sake. Knowledge and education must have a purpose, a direction. The direction is the name of the Lord. God is the object of attention. It is for Him and His creatures. If the pens of the world start writing to serve God and His creatures, the machine guns will be kept away. Otherwise, they will become machine-guns. The destructive tools of mankind have been created by the writers and the scholars of all the universities. All the progress that man has made, has been made possible by the scholars and their writings and speeches. Try to give a direction to this education that you give the people.

Date: December 27, 1980/Dey 6, 1359 SH/Safar 19, 1401 AH.

Place: Jamaran, Tehran

Subject: The importance of knowledge and learning in Islam, and the need for education to be accompanied by training

Audience: The authorities responsible for the countrywide literacy campaign and those participating in the seminar on the literacy campaign

The priority of training over education

The issue of training is more important than that of education. In the noble verse in question, God speaks the education and training first. Afterwards He says: "Refine them". From this verse, it can be construed that purification of self and soul is more important than teaching the Book and Wisdom. The purpose of this prelude is that the Book and Wisdom be embedded in his inner being. If man becomes refined and gets trained under the training of the prophets (a), which they brought as a gift to mankind, then after his edification, the Book and Wisdom in their real sense will become imprinted within him and he will attain the pinnacle of perfection. Hence, the Qur'an mentions another verse: "*The likeness of those who are entrusted of those with the Law of Moses, yet apply it not, is as the likeness of the ass carrying books* (which he does not understand, nor benefit by them)" (Qur'an, 62:5). It wants to point out that knowledge in itself is of no use. Knowledge without training and refinement is useless knowledge. It is similar to an ass or a donkey carrying a load of books of whatever kind- books on monotheism, jurisprudence, anthropology or whatever- on its back. They cannot be of any use to the ass. It will not benefit by them. In the same way, the people who have a store of knowledge of all things- of all the industries, for example- and have all the specializations, but have not been trained and have not undergone refinement, will not benefit by that knowledge. In fact, it is harmful on many occasions. Many a time, the knowledge of the one who is a scholar and knows everything but has not been refined, purified nor received divine training, turns out to be the means of dragging humanity to destruction. How often had scholars brought mankind the gift of destruction. Such people are worse than the ignorant ones. And how often do the experts bring about death and destruction for human beings. They are worse than those that are illiterate. The harm they do is more. They are the same people about whom the Qur'an mentions as being "*like a donkey*." they are even worse than a donkey because they harm others.

Date/Time: Before noon, January 8, 1981/Dey 18, 1359 SH/Rabi' al-Awwal 1, 1401 AH.

Place: Jamaran, Tehran

Subject: The importance of education and training. Priority of training over education

Audience: A group of students from the Teacher's Training Centers in Shiraz, Isfahan, Arak and Yazd

Necessity of urging piety alongside learning

All the Prophets came to teach perfection of moral behavior.[2] The Prophets came in order to teach piety and train human beings. Now these Friday prayer leaders have taken over this noble occupation of the Prophets, which was the Friday prayer, and recitation of the mandatory prayers in the rest of the places. They should endeavor to train the people in piety; invite them to piety. Mention of piety and stating the history of piety is not enough in the Friday prayer; they must call upon the people to become pious and urge them to piety. They must give importance to this divine commandment for which the Prophets arrived and you teachers must give importance to the subject of piety. The students also must give importance to it. The university professors and professors of the seminaries must also give special importance to this aspect that if knowledge is isolated from piety- even if it is knowledge of monotheism, even if it is knowledge of religions- it has no value in that world. If the loss from unaccompanied knowledge on nations and on Islam would not have been greater than its benefits- which it is- then it must be mentioned that an impious person can destroy a country, destroy human beings and the person who is more learned can corrupt the people better. Thus, together with this education, there should also be education of piety. If there are children, teach the children piety to the extent that they can absorb; and likewise the adolescents. The adolescents should not be under the impression that they no longer need or the time is past; the time does pass. It is better for a person in all circumstances to know something than not to know

Date/Time: Morning, December 26, 1982/Dey 5, 1361 SH/Rabi' al-Awwal 01, 1403 AH.

Place: Husayniyyah Jamaran, Tehran

Subject: Roots of differences of values in the world

Audience: Muhsin Qara'ati (representative of the Imam and head of the Literacy Movement), Ghayouri (representative of the Imam in the Red Crescent Society) and teaching staff of the Literacy Movement, employees of the Red Crescent Society from all over the country.

Encouragement to Acquire Knowledge

The young clergymen and university students must continue with the acquisition of knowledge each in their own sphere. The recent very vexing rumors among some of the youth that there is no use in studying is a deviant matter that surely is either because of ignorance and lack of information, or evil-intentioned arising from devilish suggestions in order to deter the theology students from studying Islamic sciences so that Islamic precepts are consigned to oblivion and the obliteration of religion becomes

---

2 بُعِثْتُ لِأُتَمِّمَ مَكَارِمَ الاخلاق "I am sent to teach prefect moral character." (*Wasael al-Shia*, 174, 12).

7

a reality by our own actions. It is also meant to bring up our university youths as parasites dependent on the expansionists so that everyone be "imported", so to speak, like everything else, and the need for foreigners, in all the spheres and subjects of learning, to keep on increasing. This poses a great danger that will push the country backward to the greatest extent. If Islamic science did not have professionals, the vestiges of religion would have been effaced by now. If it does not have them subsequently, this immense bulwark against the aliens will be destroyed, fully opening the way for the expansionists. If the universities become devoid of the scientists and professionals, foreigners seeking gain will spread like a cancer throughout the country, taking control of our economic and technological affairs, and bringing everything under their supervision. Our youth should fight this erroneous thought on the part of the expansionists, and the best and most effective way of fighting them is to get equipped with the weapons of knowledge of religion and of the world. Vacating this stronghold and asking people to lay down those weapons is treachery to Islam and the Islamic country.

Date: February 31, 1978/Bahman 24, 1365 SH/Rabi' al-Awwal 5, 1398 AH.

Place: Najaf, Iraq

Subject: The duties of Muslim intellectuals

Addressees: The Union of Islamic Students Association in Europe

If an Islamic government is set up, it will not wish to see the symbols of civilization destroyed. Islamic government does not oppose universities; it does not oppose science. The Qur'an is replete with commentaries on science and so many of our hadiths speak highly of science and scientists. This being the case, how can we oppose such things?

No, we do not oppose these things; we oppose this scientific method that you have adopted, this method of education and instruction through which you seek to educate us. These are what we oppose. We oppose those manifestations of civilization which corrupt our children, which keep them in a state of backwardness; we do not oppose the principle of civilization nor wish to take the people back to the age of whatever

Date: December 22, 1978/Dey 1, 1357 SH/Muharram 12, 1399 AH.

Place: Neauphle-le-Chateau, Paris, France

Subject: Helping those on strike and giving shelter to deserter soldiers an incumbency upon the nation; colonial culture of Pahlavi dynasty

Addressees: A group of Iranian students and residents abroad

My beloved children! Now you should take greater efforts in order to irrigate this sapling of the country's freedom and independence. Your future ahead is onerous. If you are fully armed with strong Islamic and revolutionary knowledge, piety and wisdom, you will be assured of a certain victory. And if, God forbid, at this stage, you prove to be negligent, you will be held responsible for it. Never allow a coterie rule over you as in the past bitter days of tyranny. Do not forget the Islamic principle of democracy…I consider myself fortunate that the circumstances have totally shifted in favor of our oppressed nation. The same responsibility and commitment that had necessitated your staging strikes and demonstrations during the past months now make it expedient for you to resume your educational task with complete seriousness in a peaceful environment

Date: February 19, 1979/Bahman 03, 1357 SH/Rabi' al-Awwal 12, 1399 AH.

Place: Alawi School, Tehran

Subject: Class attendance and the necessity of changes in the educational system

Occasion: Schools' re-opening after the Revolution's victory

Addressees: Education Ministry officials and school students

The teachers are not limited to the people who go to the universities, the secondary schools or all the other places (of instruction). And the students, too, are not limited to those who go to the universities. The whole world is a university in which the prophets, the saints and those trained by them are the teachers, while the rest of humanity comprises the students; and it ought to be so. The world; the entire world should consist of two classes: one class, the teachers and professors; and the other class, the students and learners. The teachers' duty is to guide society towards God while the students' duty is to learn.

Date/Time: Morning, August 29, 1980/Shahrivar 9, 1359 SH/Shawwal 02, 1400 AH.

Place: Jamaran Husayniyyah, Tehran

Subject: Training and educating people according to the teachings of the prophets

Addressees: Pakistani students and Iranian teachers

God the Blessed and Exalted, looks upon (the acquisition of) knowledge as one of the great acts of worship provided that it has a direction which is that same; "*Read: In the name of thy Lord*" (Qur'an, 96:1). In no nation is knowledge commended as commended in Islam. In many of its passages, Holy Qur'an commends knowledge, scholars and

9

attention to knowledge…. "*Acquiring knowledge is compulsory.*"[3] According to this "hadith" God, the Blessed and Exalted, has said through the Noble Messenger that seeking knowledge is a duty. As it is stated in some of the narrations: "*Acquiring knowledge is obligatory upon every Muslim man and Muslim woman.*"[4] It is only through knowledge that mankind can secure its prosperity in the world and the hereafter. It is only by imparting knowledge that one can train the youths so that they are able to protect their own interests in this world and the next. No power can rule over our country if the people acquire knowledge and culture and learn what the purpose of knowledge is and the direction in which they must move. All the troubles that we had in the course of our history resulted from the undue advantage that was taken of the ignorance of the people. They used the people's ignorance as a tool to make them act against their own interests. If the people had possessed knowledge, goal-oriented knowledge, it would not have been possible for the destroyers to compel them to pursue a course contrary to the nation's. It is knowledge and education with a purpose in mind that can keep the nation safe from all troubles. Those who want to disrupt this movement, this Islamic movement, will not succeed in doing so. They cannot bear to see Islam being implemented in this country. it is knowledge that is able to stop all these corrupt practices. Nobody will be able to commit aggression against you if our people acquire knowledge, goal-oriented knowledge, and if they are trained. There ought to be training to accompany knowledge and alongside knowledge; religious training, divine training, human training plus knowledge. You ought to possess these two weapons so that nobody will be able to bring back the despotism (that once existed).

Date: December 27, 1980/Dey 6, 1359 SH/Safar 19, 1401 AH.

Place: Jamaran, Tehran

Subject: The importance of knowledge and learning in Islam, and the need for education to be accompanied by training

Audience: The authorities responsible for the countrywide literacy campaign and those participating in the seminar on the literacy campaign

Great importance of knowledge and learning in Islam

One of our problems is that the moment there is any talk of "Islamizing" a certain center, there are people who start raising a hue and cry, believing it to imply the elimination of expertise! As a matter of fact, the aim of such people is to tell the world that Islam is against knowledge and expertise, whereas there are a number of verses in

---

[3] *Al-Bidayah wa al-Nihayah*, v.11, p.322.
[4] *Bihar al-Anwar*, v.67, p.68.

the Holy Qur'an that clearly emphasize the importance of knowledge and learning, perhaps more than any other book does. The fact of the matter is that Islam completely approves of knowledge, but the kind of knowledge that can be at the service of the nation and at the service of the interests of the Muslims. They spread propaganda against us claiming that we are against expertise and that when the Muslims speak of a "cultural revolution" in the universities and say that the universities must get Islamized, they mean that the universities now do not need doctors or medical experts or advanced engineering experts. And that the universities should only impart Islamic studies and practical laws! This is a kind of mischief that some individuals and groups indulge in against Islam, the Islamic associations, and the Cultural Revolution. However, what these people do not understand is that when we say that all the organizations and institutions, and particularly the universities, which are the centers of learning and the think-tanks of society should be Islamized, we are in no way suggesting that we do not need any experts and expertise. Islam has emphasized the importance of experts and expertise to such an extent- both in the area of practical as well as religious laws- that it has emphasized trusting the judgment and verdict of the most knowledgeable expert.

Time/Date: Morning, May 25, 1981/Khordad 4, 1360 SH/Rajab 02, 1401 AH.

Place: Jamaran, Tehran

Subject: Importance of knowledge in Islam; responsibility of the university in an Islamic society; duties of the Islamic associations of the universities

Audience: Members of the Islamic Association and the Jihad of the 'Ilm va San'at (Science and Technology) University; members of the Organization for Scientific and Industrial Research and a group of inventors and innovators

Universities should ensure independence of the country and be at the service of the nation

Islam approves of expertise. Islam comes first among all religions that have extolled the value of knowledge and expertise and it has invited people to pursue knowledge. It has asked people to gain knowledge even if it entails going to other places and acquiring it from non-believers. However, Islam emphasizes that knowledge should be at the service of Islam and the Islamic country rather than for use against one's own country.

Time/Date: Morning, May 25, 1981/Khordad 4, 1360 SH/Rajab 02, 1401 AH.

Place: Jamaran, Tehran

Subject: Importance of knowledge in Islam; responsibility of the university in an Islamic society; duties of the Islamic associations of the universities

Audience: Members of the Islamic Association and the Jihad of the 'Ilm va San'at (Science and Technology) University; members of the Organization for Scientific and Industrial Research; and a group of inventors and innovators

Independence of the country depends upon the independence of its cultural centers

The importance that Islam gives to knowledge is probably not given by any other school. The importance that Islam gives to scholars is probably not given by any other school. Islam gives the utmost importance to knowledge but not the kind of knowledge that drags us to ruin and not the kind of scholars that drag us into the arms of the East and the West. Islam strives to foster knowledge within independent minds and minds that serve Islam. Such independence can ensure the independence of our country.

Date: Morning, June 31, 1981/Khordad 23, 1360 SH/Sha'ban 01, 1401 AH.

Place: Jamaran Husayniyyah, Tehran

Subject: Importance of the role of the university in the independence or lack of independence of a country

Occasion: Anniversary of the establishment of the Ad Hoc Committee for the Cultural Revolution

Addressees: The members of the Ad Hoc Committee for the Cultural Revolution and the Supreme Council of the Jihad of the Universities of Tehran and other cities

The present generation must take on training the next generation. They cannot change the minds of the present generation. They insist on the reopening of the universities under the pretext of a shortage of expertise and by claiming that we are against knowledge. Has any other school spoken about the importance knowledge in the way the Qur'an has?

Date: Morning, June 23, 1981/Tir 2, 1360 SH/Sha'ban 02, 1401 AH.

Place: Jamaran Husayniyyah, Tehran

Subject: Freedom from cultural dependence and the impact of the press on the culture of a nation

Audience: Karroubi (The Imam's representative and Head of the Martyr's Foundation), the family of Martyr Ali Mazandarani, and the editorial board and the employees of the monthly, "Shahid"

The issue of knowledge is obvious and all know that knowledge is a noble pursuit that everyone desires to acquire. Seeking knowledge is ingrained in man's primordial nature. If you acquire all material and spiritual knowledge but hear that in a given place there is more knowledge, then you are bound to seek that knowledge. The desire for acquiring knowledge is unceasing. The significance of knowledge is an issue that everybody knows and is evident to all.

Date: September 19, 1982/Shahrivar 28, 1361 SH/Dhul-Hijjah 1, 1402 AH.

Place: Husayniyyah Jamaran, Tehran

Subject: Two main pillars of education

Audience: Muhammad-Taqi Misbah Yazdi, Muhsin Qara'ati (Imam's representative in the literacy campaign), Ali-Akbar Parvaresh (Education Minister), Muhammad-'Ali Najafi (Minister of Culture and Higher Education), members of the office for coordination of theological seminaries and universities and the educationists

A human being is in need of knowledge as well as education and training until the end of his life. There is no person who can do without knowledge and who can do without education and training. It is not correct if some persons think that the time for their learning is past then. Learning does not have a specific period; knowledge does not have a specific time. As has been narrated that knowledge is to be attained from the cradle to the grave it is better for a person to learn a single word at the time of death rather than to die an ignorant.

Date/Time: Morning, December 26, 1982/Dey 5, 1361 SH/Rabi' al-Awwal 01, 1403 AH.

Place: Husayniyyah Jamaran, Tehran

Subject: Roots of differences of values in the world

Audience: Muhsin Qara'ati (Representative of the Imam and head of the Literacy Movement) Ghayouri (representative of the Imam in the Red Crescent Society), teaching staff of the Literacy Movement, employees of the Red Crescent Society from all over the country

Today, when the country enjoys efficient independence and the university has been rid of the bonds of the east and the west and easternized and westernized elements, the dear university students should try ever more to acquire sciences and techniques for prosperity their dear country, decisively prevent devious elements affiliated with the right and the left from infiltrating the university and not allow the sacred university environment to be polluted by selfish motives of deviants affiliated with aliens.

Letter

Time: August 03, 1983/Shahrivar 8, 1362 SH/Dhul-Qa'dah 12, 1403 AH.

Place: Jamaran, Tehran

Subject: Reshuffling the Cultural Revolution Board

Addressees: Sayyid Ali Khamenei (then President)

Knowledge and Faith - Belief and Professional Expertise

The condemned knowledge and the beneficial knowledge

You should know that many of the sciences, from a certain aspect, fall under one of the categories mentioned by the Noble Messenger (s).[5] For instance, the sciences of medicine, anatomy, astronomy, astrology and the like, when looked upon as Divine signs and symbols, and the science of history and the like, when looked upon as a means for drawing lesson, are included in *ayatun mukhamah,* for by their means the knowledge of God or the knowledge of Resurrection is attained or confirmed. At times, the learning of the sciences falls under *faridatun 'adilah* and at times under *sunnatun qa'imah.* But if their pursuit should be for their own sake or for other purposes and if they should lead us to neglect the *'ulum* of the Hereafter, they become blame worthy by accident (*madhmum bi al-'arad*) on account of this neglect. Otherwise, (in themselves) they are neither beneficial nor harmful, as pointed out by the Noble Messenger (s). Thus, all the sciences are divisible into three kinds: first, those sciences, which are beneficial to man in view of the other stages of existence, success wherein is the ultimate purpose of creation. This is the category, which the ultimate Prophet has considered as *'ilm,* dividing it into three parts. The second kind consists of those which are harmful for man and lead him to neglect his essential duties. This kind consists of the blameworthy sciences-such as magic, jugglery, alchemy and the like- and one must refrain from their pursuit. Thirdly, there are those which are neither harmful nor beneficial, like those which one pursues in his hours of leisure for amusement's sake, such as mathematics, geometry, astronomy and the like. It would be much better if one could relate the pursuit of these sciences to the threefold *'ulum* (mentioned by the Prophet), otherwise it is better to refrain from, them as far as is possible. That is because when a sensible person knows that he cannot acquire all the sciences and achieve all the excellences due to shortness of life, scarcity of time and abundance of obstacles and accidents, he would reflect about the sciences and devote himself to the acquisition of. those which are more beneficial for him. Of course, amongst the sciences that which is better than all the rest is that which is beneficial for man's eternal

---

[5] The Prophet (s) said: "Verily, knowledge consists of these three: the firm sign, the just duty and the established sunnah. All else is superfluous." (*Al-Kafi*, v.1, p.32. hadith # 1)

and everlasting life and that is the science which the prophets (A) have commanded and encouraged man to seek. That science consists of the threefold *'ulum,* as mentioned.

Reference: Imam Khomeini (ra), *Forty Hadithes,* Chapter 24: The Classification of Sciences, p. 437-38

All the branches of knowledge are divisible into two main categories

The sciences are absolutely divisible into two kinds. One of these is the worldly sciences, whose ultimate purpose is to achieve worldly aims. The other is the sciences of the Hereafter, whose ultimate purpose is attainment of *malakuti* stations and degrees and reaching the otherworldly stations. Earlier it was pointed out that the distinction between these two kinds of sciences depends for the most part on the distinction between intentions and purposes (behind their pursuit), although they in themselves are divisible into the two kinds. From the viewpoint of appropriateness, the effects described in the noble tradition in relation to the pursuit of knowledge and the learned evidently correspond to the second type of knowledge, the knowledge of the Hereafter.

It was also mentioned earlier that all the sciences of the Hereafter are included in three categories. They either pertain to the knowledge of God and doctrines (*ma'arif*), or to spiritual instruction and wayfaring towards God, or to the laws and precepts of servitude.

Reference: Imam Khomeini (ra), *Forty Hadithes,* Chapter 26: The Pursuit of Knowledge, p. 451-52

You should begin from now to meet this responsibility; these young sixteen-year-old men, these twenty-year-old men who are studying in the religious schools, in all schools, should begin from now, in accordance with the will of God, in accordance with the divine commands. They should be such that for each step they take for the acquisition of knowledge, they take one for self-reform and moral purification. If, God forbid, there is an *'alim* who has not reformed himself, not purified himself; if, God forbid, there is an *'alim* who is not as Islam requires him to be, then this is more of a loss than a benefit. All the false religions which have been invented or created were founded by educated people, people who were educated in the religious schools but who had not purified themselves. If you take note, you will see that all the heads of false religions are from amongst those who have studied, who are clergymen, but those who have not purified themselves.

Date: November 14, 1965/Aban 23, 1344 SH/Rajab 02, 1385 AH.

Place: Shaykh Ansari Mosque, Najaf, Iraq

Subject: Duty of the heads of Muslim countries and the responsibility of the *'ulama* in introducing Islamic programs

Occasion: Commencement of Imam Khomeini's classes in Najaf Religious Seminary

Audience: *'Ulama'*, scholars and students of Najaf Religious Seminary

Responsibility of the seminary students

The burden of knowledge is a heavy burden which is upon your shoulders. Not only is it your responsibility to learn a handful of terms and their meanings, but you have also been given the responsibility for preserving Islam and its precepts. You are the trustees of a divine revelation, and you must purify your souls while at the same time acquiring knowledge. And as you propagate your knowledge to others, you must also ameliorate your soul.

Date: December 13, 1971/Dey 01, 1350 SH/Dhu'l-Qa'dah 21, 1391 AH.

Place: Shaykh Ansari Mosque, Najaf, Iraq

Subject: The necessity of preserving the religious seminaries

Addressees: Clergy, seminary students and Iranians residing in Iraq

The nation needs you young people, but first there is one thing which you must do, you must reform yourselves. You must strive to reform yourselves to prevent yourselves from turning into traitors. He who goes into a shop or department store here abroad and is crooked, (God forbid), and steals something using the logic that they have been stealing from us so we can steal from them, is a traitor. Such a person is of no use to us. Reform yourselves. He who does not put his affairs right with God cannot handle the affairs of the people. You must put your affairs right with God first. We need young people who can be trained in human education- that is, Islamic education- who can become true human beings. We are not indifferent, we do not want just anyone and whatever he turns out to be like, dissolute and I don't know what else, it won't matter. We want a country which is an Islamic country. Islamic means like a human being.

Date: December 13, 1978/Dey 01, 1357 SH/Safar 1, 1399 AH.

Place: Neauphle-le-Chateau, Paris, France

Subject: Unrighteous Pahlavi government; righteous nation needs a righteous ruler

Addressees: A group of Iranian students and residents abroad

If you suppose, or we think that science makes up the foundation of human happiness, no matter what that science is, we are committing some extremely crass mistake. It is an open secret that science on many occasions has been the source of some horrible atrocities. Hakim Sana'i says, "A burglar with a torch in hand would steal more selectively." So, if a cleric is knowledgeable but lacks faith and his way is not that of the prophets, he would be the source for numerous corrupt practices, and corruption would be ever more promoted. Clergies of this type have promoted most of the baseless and superstitious beliefs. The kind of clergies, who think science by itself is everything, never take the path that the prophets followed. Similarly, if academicians insist on only instilling sciences into the minds of Iranian children and fill their heads with scientific ways, this will not help the promotion of our people's happiness, in fact it would be detrimental to the people's welfare for that matter. A depraved academician is different from a depraved businessman, or a depraved farmer or laborer for that matter. The latter, if corrupted, will not be promoting evil practices on a mass scale. On the other hand, a morally bad university teacher spreads his evil ways among large groups who will then take charge of running a country. Corruption as such would lead to disaster for a whole nation. In the same breath, the immorality of a cleric does not stay limited to his person and translates into the immorality of the people of a whole country. It is because of such great responsibilities that you two groups must serve and save the country, and if your approaches are not correctly formulated, the fate of the country would suffer the inevitable damages.

Date: May 24, 1979/Khordad 3, 1358 SH/Jamadi ath-Thani 27, 1399 AH.

Place: Qum

Subject: Profession of clerics and academicians; creation of discord between the seminary and university; role of culture in the declination and amelioration of the society

Audience: Ali Shari'atmadari (Minister of Culture and Higher Education), chancellors of universities and institutions of higher education

"A corrupted intellectual corrupts the whole world."[6] The scholar we are talking about does not encompass me alone. It is you, all of us. You, too, are among the scholars. If, God forbid, you were corrupt, you would spread corruptive practices all over the world. On the other hand, if you are morally good, the whole world shall benefit from your goodness. Both the good and the evil in societies are in the hands of those in charge of teaching those societies. You are the teachers, while the clerics are different kinds of teachers, but both of you enlighten the whole society.

---

[6] *Ghurar al-Hikam wa Durar al-Kalim*, p.738, hadith #45

If the purpose was scientific knowledge alone, and lets says, you wanted to train a medical doctor but it didn't matter whether he was moral and ethical or not, well, this man would become a business minded doctor in future, the kind that would let his patients wait because he wants to raise his fees. He may be a very good doctor indeed and even a great specialist, but just because he lacks morality and he is an irreligious individual who does not believe in God, he makes his patients wait. He writes a prescription and while he is in collusion with the pharmacist to charge the patient as much as he can. He corrupts the poor pharmacist too. The prescription he has written may not worth much, because he wants the patient to refer to him again, so on and so forth. All right, this was an example of a medical doctor from a scientific point of view; you may want to train an engineer and a great one for all he is worth. But, if this engineer is asked to present a design, his approach to the design in question, is replete with every aspect of clever tricks to make more money for himself but worthless as a whole. If we even take a clergy, and let us suppose he is good and knowledgeable, as he understands the Holy Book and the tradition of the Prophet well enough. However, if he does not know the first thing about morality, his religious knowledge will cause people to follow the wrong ways. He teaches the ways of the prophet and the Holy Book in extremely distorted ways to corrupt people.

Date: May 24, 1979/Khordad 3, 1358 SH/Jamadi ath-Thani 27, 1399 AH.

Place: Qum

Subject: Profession of clerics and academicians; creation of discord between the seminary and university; role of culture in the declination and amelioration of the society

Audience: Ali Shari'atmadari (Minister of Culture and Higher Education), chancellors of universities and institutions of higher education

The source of all blessings and all progress, both in material and in spiritual ways, is faith alone. You and we should chip in our efforts to create faith for those future generations who will be responsible for the fate of this country. You would let pious people graduate from your universities, and we would send pious clerics out of the schools. Neither scholars nor scientists for their own sakes are any good in the absence of faith. As a matter of fact, piety by itself would not be very effective, as there are many pious people around, but when a scholar is pious and he is also faithful, then he will be the source of many blessings and contributions in safeguarding the country.

Date: May 24, 1979/Khordad 3, 1358 SH/Jamadi ath-Thani 27, 1399 AH.

Place: Qum

Subject: Profession of clerics and academicians; creation of discord between the seminary and university; role of culture in the declination and amelioration of the society

Audience: Ali Shari'atmadari (Minister of Culture and Higher Education), chancellors of universities and institutions of higher education

Spirituality is important. Strive to attain spirituality. Knowledge alone is useless; knowledge combined with spirituality is knowledge. Culture alone is of no use; culture with spirituality is culture. It is spirituality that insures the salvation of mankind; and you should strive for the attainment of spirituality. Universities should seek spirituality; schools should seek spirituality; classical schools should seek spirituality; so that God willing, they attain salvation. May God make all of you blissful.

May God's peace, mercy, and blessings be upon you.

Date: May 29, 1979/Khordad 8, 1358 SH/Rajab 3, 1399 AH.

Place: Qum

Subject: Molding human beings: main objective of the mission of the prophets

Audience: Women from Southern Tehran and the Wali 'Asr Old School (Revolutionary Guards); inhabitants of the outskirts of Moghan plains

Just as the gentlemen are diligent in gaining knowledge, they should also be diligent in refining their morals, their actions, their beliefs and their moral virtues, because knowledge without) good (deeds and without piety is harmful in many instances. An *'alim* (a learned person) ought to be pious and have God, the Blessed and Exalted, in his thoughts so that he is able to train the community. He ought to be trained himself in order to train the community.

Date: June 26, 1979/Tir 5, 1358 SH/Sha'ban 1, 1399 AH.

Place: Qum

Subject: The grave duty of the clergy in the Islamic Republic

Audience: The *'ulama* and clergymen of Isfahan

The harmfulness of an unrefined scholar

What is important about the universities, the teachers' college, and the centers for training teachers and students is that people should be trained to be human beings along with teaching and learning. People have often reached the pinnacle of knowledge but without being trained to be human beings. The harm accruing to the country, the nation and Islam from such persons is more than that from the others. One who has knowledge which is not associated with moral refinement and spiritual training is more detrimental to the nation and the country than the ones who lack knowledge. The knowledge of such a person is like a sword in his hands. And it is possible that he will use that sword of knowledge to cut off the root of the country and so destroy it.

Date: June 27, 1979/Tir 6, 1358 SH/Sha'ban 2, 1399 AH.

Place: Qum

Subject: The role of the unity of the seminary and the university; the issue of factionalism and party politics

Audience: Students of the Islamic Association of the Teachers' Training University, Tehran

There are many individuals who are educated- intellectuals indeed- but since they lack an Islamic training, they are often harmful for both the country and Islam. The difference here is not whether they are educated in the traditional knowledge or modern knowledge; or, whether the learned men of Islam and the clergies. Or, whether it is your university students and the universities or other classes who intend to enter the arena of teaching and learning content. This depends on the way we all act, in particular the university students population, the members of university faculties, the college instructors, and those young generation who look after training and education, the students who want to be useful for their country in the future.

Training and education

If you are only after learning and this learning does not accompany a correct nurturing and the purification of one's soul, and taking steps in a correct manner, is only storage of knowledge. Or, in Sa'di's words being an interpretation of the Qur'an, "*The likeness of those who are entrusted with the Law of Moses, yet apply it not, is as the likeness of the ass carrying books.*"(Qur'an, 62:5) he is one who learns but his learning is a mere accumulation of learning without putting it into use and thus is not following a human way of learning. In the exegesis of the Holy Qur'an, the receiver of such learning is likened to an animal, a donkey, which is laden with books. Now, it would not make a difference whether or not these books are loaded on someone's back, or, whether they are in his mind and thought. Rather, he who has books in his mind and thought and has knowledge in his mind and thought, but has not acquired this learning in a humane way, that learning will be harmful for the society- it would not make a difference whether this happens on your part or ours- whether it happens to the Islamic sciences and the divine philosophy or whether it is natural sciences or anything related to the nature. If these are not accompanied by teaching of knowledge and are not accompanied by the acquisition of knowledge and a humane training, in this case a human being is likened to an animal that is storage of knowledge. In fact, he is literally an animal who has a lot of knowledge, and not a human being who has the knowledge.

The dangers of knowledge void of self-purification and training

At times the harm inflicted on Islam and on the country by this social stratum is greater than that inflicted by other strata. Most of those false religions that have been fabricated, they have been fabricated by the learned men. No other than learned men have fabricated any religion. It is the learned men who have been fabricating religions. And most of these betrays of our country, comes from these very educated ones. It was the educated that helped the regime and then you had the "doctors," and the like. They were the ones who helped the regime and destroyed our country. If the universities are not improved and our schools are not improved, there is no hope that we will find an Islamic Republic. If these two strata are educated in a way that Islam wants it; if they are educated in a humane way, then on the one hand our country will become safe from the possession of the evils and it will revolve round her own pivot and without being dependent on the foreigners and without the domestic treasons. And progress will result for you as well. The importance about being a university student, an associate professor, a full professor and a pupil- in both education and science- is that there exists a proper way that accompanies the science and education; the learned man who is educated in a humane way which is the same as Islamic teaching.

Time/Date: Morning, July 7, 1979/Tir 17, 1358 SH/Sha'ban 31, 1399 AH.

Place: Qum

Subject: The role of reform and self-purification in training and education

Audience: Students of Ahwaz

Education with training

Education alone is not effective. Training must be placed beside education. This means that when the youth go to the universities and centers of learning for education, if it is purely education, then sometimes it can perhaps also be harmful for the country. Many of the losses that have been inflicted on our country are from these same educated people. Many of the plans that are incompatible with our country have been designed by this same educated class- the educated that had the knowledge but did not have the training; the educated that had only their own personal interests in mind.

An individual who does not have the right training, even if we assume he has the right education; he is educated at the highest level, he is more harmful for the country than the ordinary people. The ordinary people cannot inflict harm upon the country the way he can. It is these educated ones that can design plans for the utility of others. Those who were around this father and son[7] were from the educated class who were educated in Europe and America; but it was only education. They did not have Islamic training and human development. Therefore, the harm that was inflicted upon our country by the educated ones of this country was not inflicted by others. Even the SAVAK did not inflict as much harm as they did. They corrupted the minds. They corrupted our youth.

For this reason, cultural training must be imparted alongside education. It should not be only in the name "education and training." It should be real- it should be both education at the highest level and be complemented with training. Our youth should be trained in human development; an Islamic training that is the same human development. If they are trained in human development our youth shall no longer betray their country; they shall no longer put together plans to hand over the interests of our country to others.

Date: July 14, 1979/Tir 23, 1358 SH/Sha'ban 19, 1399 AH.

Place: Qum

Subject: The need to complement education with training and cultural independence

Audience: Teachers of the town of Shahreza

If the Self (mind) is not purged or purified outcome of the corrupt qualities; the knowledge, the science, the lore will have a negative impact. All the wrong faiths and wrong religions are invented and introduced by scholars because knowledge existed in a place which had no coaching. So, scholars invented a religion their fancy framed. As such the presence of knowledge in the absence of purification, a scholar bearing that knowledge while he is not purified becomes dangerous. It makes no difference for the society whether the scholars are in universities or in a religious institute. Such scholars are like a store. God says: *"The likeness of those who are entrusted with the Law of Moses, yet apply it not, is as the likeness of the ass carrying books."*(Qur'an, 62:5). A scholar might be having knowledge of monotheism, manners and religion but the Self in him is not purged, then he is a being, a creature, an entity perilous to the society. A University is a place where students (youths) go and learn. But if the training and coaching is not a correct one, it is of no use at all. Even if the most correct one occurs, but the students' heart is unpurified, then such youth or student who has gained knowledge with an impure heart shall create corruption in the society. God forbid that the corruption originates from a scholar with an impure heart. There are several narrations and sayings

---

[7] Imam (ra) points to Reza Shah and his son Mohammad Reza Shah.

of the Prophet that in hell the dwellers are in a great torture by the putrid smell of an unpurified scholar.[8]

Time: Morning, July 2, 1980/Tir 01, 1359 SH/Sha'ban 18, 1400 AH.

Place: Jamaran, Tehran

Subject: Education/training from the Qur'an's view, the position of culture in the Pahlavi regime. The need for basic changes there

Audience: The heads of education throughout the country, the Islamic Association members, the Home Ministry workers and the provincial workers

When knowledge enters into a sick heart, it is like the rain in a salty land. It will increase the filth. The rain created a good fragrance somewhere else. The scholar, who is not purified, is more dangerous than an ignorant man. An ignorant remains corrupt for himself. But a scholar not only is himself corrupt, he also corrupts the whole world. He drags a country to corruption. Purification is prior to education. The Prophet came to purify and then to educate. He came to prepare the self. Afterwards he teaches the Book and the Wisdom.[9] If the Book and the Wisdom was not twin to training, the output will be the same as existed before the Revolution in the Senate and the Parliament.

The universities and the seminaries, together with the clergy, can constitute two centers for the country's progress and development. They can also be two centers of all deviations and perversions. It is from the university that committed intellectuals graduate. If the university be a university, if it is really a university and Islamic in nature; that is; together with the actual education, there is dedication and edification as well, then such people (the university graduates) will be able to lead the country to prosperity. Also, if the centers of theology be refined and committed, they will be able to save the country. Knowledge alone is of no use even if it is not detrimental. When we look extensively at the whole world and all the universities that are in it, we will find that the roots of all these misfortunes that have befallen humankind, lie in the universities. The roots lie in the specialization courses of the universities. All these tools of humankind's ruination and all these advances which they think lie in the implements of war, have been basically due to the scientists who graduated from the universities; universities that lacked the ethics and edification to go along with the education given. All the corruption that has been found in a nation, or nations, has

---

[8] The Prophet of God said: "Certainly, the dwellers of hell will be in torture because of putrid smell of a scholar who didn't act on his knowledge." (*Al-Kafi*, v.1, p.55)

[9] *"It is He who has sent among the unlettered a Messenger from themselves reciting to them His verses and purifying them and teaching them the Book and wisdom - although they were before in clear error."* (Qur'an, 62:2)

sprung from the theological centers that lacked commitment to Islamic injunctions. All these fabricated religions have originated from the scholars and the *'ulama*. The university where knowledge has not been accompanied with ethics, edification and commitment to Islam, has dragged the world into corruption. Likewise, the university takes the world towards betterment. If the universities all over the world are able to observe human principles, morals and whatever (good) there is in human nature, side by side with imparting education and training, the world will become an enlightened place. All the woes that emerge in the world are due to those very intellectuals and specialists that are produced by the universities in which specialization and knowledge are divorced from ethics, cultural refinement human awareness and dedication. These two centers, which are the centers of knowledge, could be the centers of all of humanity's problems, and could also be centers of spiritual and material progress. Knowledge and practice, knowledge and commitment are like two wings which, in tandem, can reach the heights of progress and excellence. You have seen for fifty years that this tyrannical government had universities and university professors, and that these same universities and university professors dragged our country into the lap of the superpowers. It was tragic for our nation that the tools of knowledge lay in the hands of those that lacked commitment and were unmindful of themselves. It is a tragedy that the instruments of knowledge be possessed by people who are not committed and lack Islamic morality. There is no difference between the university and the theological center. The only thing is that if there is commitment and purification of the soul together with knowledge, they can then save their country, their homeland by means of these two devices of knowledge and morality, and the practice thereof. They can save it from the clutches of those who want to plunder everything of ours. But if knowledge alone is imparted by the universities and the seminaries, such knowledge, then, will lead man to ruination. All of a country's problems can stem from the university and the centers of theology, and so also its material prosperity and spiritual bliss. The grand design of infiltrating the universities and giving our youths a kind of training that went against our country's interests was for the purpose of corrupting the country which would be the case if the university became corrupted. If the aim of the university was solely to impart knowledge, and assuming that the university taught well- which was not the case- and that teaching our youths the arts and sciences, etc. was carried out in the best manner, alongside all this, however, was the propaganda by which this very learning became the means to bring about decadence in a country.

Date: Before noon, December 18, 1980/Azar 27, 1359 SH/Safar 01, 1401 AH.

Place: Jamaran, Tehran

Subject: The importance of the roles of the seminary and the university; stating the duties of these two institutions of learning

Occasion: The day of unity between the seminary and the university

Audience: Teachers and students of Qum Theological Center; the student members of the office for the consolidation of unity between the seminary and the university

Those who have love for this country and this nation; those who are not dependent and do not serve the superpowers, ought to make efforts to turn the university into a center of knowledge and edification so that all the specializations be in the service of the country. It should not be that a person becomes a specialist and then drags us into the lap of America or uses his expertise to harm our country; the higher the specialization, the worse being the result.

The one who has not become refined, and one who has not felt that he exists for this country, that he has benefited by it and so ought to give back to it the educational benefit that he has derived should know that in the absence of such a feeling and such a conviction, the university will prove to be the worst kind of center as it will drag us towards ruination. But if such a feeling arises, and these university professors- those that are dedicated, who care and who used to worry about this country in the past- mobilize themselves to ensure that the sons of the soil be committed to serving Iran, the university, then, will be the highest institution that will bring prosperity to the country.

The university takes two paths: the path to hell and the path to prosperity; the path to ignominy, poverty and servitude, etc. and the path to glory, honor and magnanimity. The university that we have is of no use. We have had one for the past fifty years. Whatever corruption there was in this country was because of these people who had been educated in it, and, perhaps, had even specialized. In the days of Reza Khan, that Ahmadi[10] who killed many dignitaries of the country by his injections, had also graduated from the university. He had specialized as well. But he used his specialization to kill by injection those people whom he had been ordered to kill. Do you want such a university, such professors and such specialization? On the other hand, noble people also graduate from the university. We want all of them to be noble.

The need for the seminaries to make efforts in training people to become refined

---

[10] Ahmad Ahmadi known as Dr. Ahmadi (1261-1322 SH) was the special physician of Qasr prison in the time of Reza Shah. He killed several religious activists by injecting air in their body. Ultimately he was publicly hanged at the Toop Khaneh Square of Tehran (now Imam Khomeini Square) in the year 1322 SH.

The knowledge of monotheism will be of no use if there be no refinement in the Faydiyyah. "Knowledge is the greatest hijab." No matter how much knowledge is accumulated- even that of monotheism which is the highest kind of knowledge- in the hearts and minds of human beings, it will only distance them from God the Blessed and Exalted if there be no edification. Efforts must be made now and also later on, to make these seminaries refined. Together with the teaching of jurisprudence, philosophy, etc., the seminaries ought to be the seats of refinement, that guide people towards God. Do you know who the judge that tried the late Shaykh Fadlullah Nouri[11] was? He was a clergyman from Zanjan.[12] A cleric from Zanjan handled the trial and sentenced him to death. When a clergyman is not an edified person, his corruption will be much more than that of other people. It is mentioned in some of the narrations that those who dwell in hell will be bothered by the smell emanating from some of the clergymen. And such is the case in this world as well.[13]

Unless you purify your souls, unless you begin with edifying yourselves, you will not be able to make other people refined. A person who is not decent himself cannot reform others. It will be of no use no matter how much one insists. The *'ulama* now teaching in the seminaries ought to make efforts to ensure that these youths of sound character who enter any of these Islamic seminaries, do not leave with corrupt natures after ten to twenty years. It is necessary to be refined; whether it be you or the others. Everybody of course; the whole nation and all human beings, ought to be refined in character. If a merchant is not upright, he will overcharge the people. He will indulge in such practices. When such practices increase, so will the corruption. A single (ordinary) person cannot create so much corruption. But if a learned person turns corrupt, he can corrupt a whole city, a whole country. It makes no difference whether he is a scholar from the university or the Faydiyyah.

Date: Before noon, December 18, 1980/Azar 27, 1359 SH/Safar 01, 1401 AH.

Place: Jamaran, Tehran

Subject: The importance of the roles of the seminary and the university; stating the duties of these two institutions of learning

---

[11] Sheikh Fadlullah Nouri (1258-1325 SH) was one of the students of Mirzaye Shirazi and representative of Tehran and was one of the leaders of *Mashrooteh* movement. After sometime, because of opposition to his movement and those who had deviated views and because of false slogan (*Mashrooteh* v/s *Mashroo'eh*), he was hanged by them.

[12] Sheikh Ibrahim Zanjani, representative in the first to fourth rounds of national parliament. In the year 1328 AH, he persecuted and sentenced Sheikh Fadlullah Nouri to death. He died in the Azar, 1313 SH.

[13] *Vide* footnote in previous pages for hadith reference.

Occasion: The day of unity between the seminary and the university

Audience: Teachers and students of Qum Theological Center; the student members of the office for the consolidation of unity between the seminary and the university

Educating and upbringing ought to go together. Upbringing ought to be human and useful to human beings. Education should be directed towards the benefit of the people. The name of God should be present in it, and attention given to Him.

Date: December 27, 1980/Dey 6, 1359 SH/Safar 19, 1401 AH.

Place: Jamaran, Tehran

Subject: The importance of knowledge and learning in Islam, and the need for education to be accompanied by training

Audience: The authorities responsible for the countrywide literacy campaign and those participating in the seminar on the literacy campaign

The issue of training is more important than that of education. In the noble verse in question, God speaks the education and training first. Afterwards He says: "Refine them." From this verse, it can be construed that purification of self and soul is more important than teaching the Book and Wisdom. The purpose of this prelude is that the Book and Wisdom be embedded in his inner being. If man becomes refined and gets trained under the training of the prophets (a), which they brought as a gift to mankind, then after his edification, the Book and Wisdom in their real sense will become imprinted within him and he will attain the pinnacle of perfection. Hence, the Qur'an mentions another verse: The likeness of those who are entrusted of those with the Law of Moses, yet apply it not, is as the *likeness of the ass carrying books*[14] (which he does not understand, nor benefit by them). It wants to point out that knowledge in itself is of no use. Knowledge without training and refinement is useless knowledge. It is similar to an ass or a donkey carrying a load of books of whatever kind- books on monotheism, jurisprudence, anthropology or whatever- on its back. They cannot be of any use to the ass. It will not benefit by them. In the same way, the people who have a store of knowledge of all things- of all the industries, for example- and have all the specializations, but have not been trained and have not undergone refinement, will not benefit by that knowledge. In fact, it is harmful on many occasions. Many a time, the knowledge of the one who is a scholar and knows everything but has not been refined, purified nor received divine training, turns out to be the means of dragging humanity to destruction. How often had scholars brought mankind the gift of destruction. Such people are worse than the ignorant ones. And how often do the experts bring about

---

[14] Qur'an, 62:5.

death and destruction for human beings. They are worse than those that are illiterate. The harm they do is more. They are the same people about whom the Qur'an mentions as being "like a donkey." They are even worse than a donkey because they harm others. You who have embarked upon training teachers and whoever dose likewise, ought to know that the profession is a divine one. The Blessed and Exalted Lord is the Trainer of teachers who are the prophets. So, it is first and foremost a divine profession. Secondly, training and refining people takes precedence over education. Our schools, our teachers' training colleges, our universities and all the institutes of learning, whether of the Islamic sciences or the non-Islamic ones, can render service and bring the gift of prosperity to humanity in case their curriculum includes the nurturing and edification of the students. Man's prosperity and welfare results from learning, faith and edification: "*Lo! Man is in a state of loss.*" (Qur'an, 103:1). Man is basically an animal called "man." He is in a state of loss save one group. It consists of those who believe in the Blessed and Exalted God, who obey His commands and have performed acts of piety, one of the indications of which being: and exhort one another to truth and exhort one another to endurance. They recommend truth and endurance (to one another). Otherwise, if one leaves this state of exclusivity that is, "Save those who believe" he will be in a state of loss. He will sustain loss. Try to acquire training and refinement before getting educated. Try to have training along with studies and learning. In keeping with its status, training takes priority over education, the recitation of the (Qur'anic) verses and teaching the Book and Wisdom. You must train teachers. That is, teachers ought to be trained because, apart from having a knowledge of all the fields of learning that people need, that humanity needs- whether needed in this world or the hereafter- apart from this and preceding this there ought to be refinement and purification of the self. Otherwise, without refinement and self-purification, your training and education will not bring and benefits, even if they do not cause harm. In fact, harm could be done. All these scholars who have various specializations but lack that (necessary) training, are responsible for all the harm man suffers and all the losses that he sustains on this planet. If we possessed refinement and received Islamic training, if God, the Blessed and Exalted, and not *taghout*,[15] had been our Guardian, all these imperfections and all these differences that exist around our country and the world would not have been there. The reason for all differences- except one difference that concerns the struggle between right and wrong- that arise is that we have not become trained or purified. Our greatest enemy lies within us. "Your worst enemy" is your own inner being; that which exists deep in your own breast. Man is his own big enemy. If man is not trained and purified, he will drag himself to destruction and lead himself into darkness, ending up in the "great darkness" that is hell. We can get rid of

---

[15] A despotic irreligious government that doesn't believe in justice. Imam (ra) uses this term for the Pahlavi regime.

all our difficulties by training ourselves. All the problems stem from our not being trained. We have not undergone divine training, nor have we placed ourselves under the banner of Islam. There is only ignorance or knowledge that is more harmful than ignorance to man.

Date/Time: Before noon, January 8, 1981/Dey 18, 1359 SH/Rabi' al-Awwal 1, 1401 AH.

Place: Jamaran, Tehran

Subject: The importance of education and training. Priority of training over education

Audience: A group of students from the Teacher's Training Centers in Shiraz, Isfahan, Arak and Yazd

Those who think that there must be only learning in the schools, that we have nothing to do with these matters and that they should (only) produce experts, are thinking simplistically. It is naive to think that a teacher who has inclined to East or West and who has received either eastern or western training ought to be appointed as a teacher for our children whose souls are like polished mirrors and accept mirrors and accept anything to which they are exposed. It is being naive to think that we should entrust our youths to a teacher who follows the East and will give our children that kind of an outlook, or follows the West and will westernize them. We are viewing the matter naively when we think that learning and specialization are the sole criteria. Even knowledge of divinity and monotheism are not the set standards, and neither that of jurisprudence and philosophy. No scientific knowledge constitutes the criterion. Only that learning is the standard and is conducive to humanity's welfare when it incorporates training that has been inculcated into human beings by a coach, by one who has had divine training. If such a thing is implemented in all our schools, whether those teaching the Islamic sciences or other sciences, and if there be no deviation but determination, it will not take long for our youths, in whom lies the country's hope for the future, to become reformed and be brought up without leaning towards East or West. All of them will take to the straight path. It would be naive of us to think that it is enough for us to have men of learning. There must be people with knowledge and training, or, at least, they must have knowledge but should not be perverted. Supposing that we want to propagate learning and to make use of the knowledge of the *'ulama*. In that case, there should be knowledge but, at least, there should be no truck with the East and the West. It should not be that the teachers and trainers of our youth had received their training in Moscow or Washington. It would be naive of us to feel that all those who have specialized (in various fields) can behave in any way they like and that we must make use of them. We cannot make use of them if a specialist heals a visible illness of ours but causes us some inner illnesses; or causes a small malady of ours to turn into a big one. We should think of everything, This Ba'ath Party that you observe is the source of all our country's troubles and those of the Muslim country of Iraq. It has created more difficulties for Iraq than it has for us. These are the ones that have many specialists among them. Many of them are university graduates. They, however, did not have that training nor purification. Knowledge without purification leads to having regimes like the previous one and Saddam's. If we do not refine ourselves and if there be no refinement to accompany knowledge, our country will also be pushed into such situations and we, too, will become like Saddam. Your training and a teacher's training ought to be Islamic and humane. It should be directed towards the straight path. Moscow's training and Washington's are not acceptable to us.

Date/Time: Before noon, January 8, 1981/Dey 18, 1359 SH/Rabi' al-Awwal 1, 1401 AH.

Place: Jamaran, Tehran

Subject: The importance of education and training. Priority of training over education

Audience: A group of students from the Teacher's Training Centers in Shiraz, Isfahan, Arak and Yazd

You[16] youth all over the country, right from the kindergarten school levels in which children study, up to the universities which should be the centers for education, learning, and morals should stay alert and should protect these centers from corruption. For those who enter these centers and are involved in propagation activities, you should- our youth should, the teachers of these youth should- check out what their backgrounds have been and where they stand today and what was their thinking in the past and what they are actually propagating. Today your nation, your country is the target of conspiracies. This is because your country has caused great damage to the interests of the superpowers and has brought about such humiliation to those big powers and their roots of corruption that they will not rest until they revert it back, or so they think, to its former state and into corruption. And they know that if they manage to mislead our children right from the beginning, this deviation will stay with them for life. And that if they lead our adolescents astray this nation will be led astray. And that if they deviate our secondary schools and our universities this country will be deviated.

The biggest safeguards for Islam are these centers in which you are spending your lives and in which you are gaining education. These are the centers, on the welfare of which depends the welfare of the nation and with the destruction of which the nation will be led to destruction. Our youth and our children should open their eyes and their ears

---

[16] Addressed to school students.

wide and big so that these devils do not mislead them; and so that they are not coerced every day by them into creating chaos and leading protests. No matter where you are studying, wherever all our youth and children all over the country are studying, you should always keep in mind that no matter which educational centers you are attending, education must always be accompanied by ethics, moral commitment, and lofty human values in order to have a life worthy of a human being and to free our country and make us self-reliant. If you youth pursue education simply in order to gain a certificate or a degree to put at the disposal of your material needs, this is exactly the deviation that they are aiming at. And if those of you who are studying in these centers adhere to the right trend of thought and follow a desirable goal and pursue your education in order to attain to this goal and to reach the aim that Allah, the Almighty, wants us to- which is purification of the soul and the sole worship of Allah and warding off all kinds of polytheism, deviations, and atheism from yourselves and from your centers- you will emerge victorious. All the deviation and all the problems that a country faces are because its centers of learning and education are not centers that teach moral virtues. And this applies for both the traditional schools of learning and the modern schools. So long as there is no ethical development and moral commitment and if man has not found his path at the onset, i.e. his Straight Path, and if his education is not abiding by the pure Islamic trend of thought this itself will cause deviation and this is what causes us and the Muslim countries to incline either toward the left or toward the right; either toward communism or toward the commands of America. These trends begin from the schools. They begin from the schools and the universities. They intend that whatever is achieved in our universities, schools, and secondary schools and whatever is achieved by the prolonged struggle of this nation and our youth should be to their benefit.

Date: January 22, 1981/Bahman 2, 1359 SH/Rabi' al-Awwal 15, 1401 AH.

Place: Jamaran, Tehran

Subject: Foreign conspiracies instigating deviation in the scientific-cultural centers of the country

Audience: Various strata of people, revolutionary guards heading for the battlefront, and school students from Tehran

Whenever a training that is worthy of human beings and is conducive to the human disposition- which is the same disposition that is given as a trust to man and is "*the original nature endowed by Allah according to which He originated mankind*" (Qur'an, 30:30) - is imparted also in the universities, then when those youth enter society and when the fate of the society is consequently given into their hands, they succeed in taking their country out of gloom into light and make it worthy enough for human beings to live in and mould it as per the primordial nature and cause it to progress.

If you simply want to impart education to children without bothering to give them ethical training besides their general education, they will pass all the stages of learning, gaining knowledge without any moral training. And knowledge devoid of moral and ethical training will drag most of them toward corruption. It is not as if man is born corrupt into this world. Man first enters into this world with a pure primordial nature; *"All beings are born into this world with a pure nature."*[17] which is the nature of a human being, the nature of the Straight Path, the disposition of Islam, and the disposition toward monotheism (*tawhid*). It is ethical training that causes that disposition to bloom out or then it stands as an obstacle in the blooming of the primordial nature in man. It is this kind of training that can offer the society a desirable perfection, making it a "human" society in its truest sense, and can make it a country based upon Islamic principles. And it is this same learning or gaining knowledge devoid of ethical training that could drag the country to its doom when the fate and the reins of the affairs of the country fall into their hands.

Date: January 03, 1981/Bahman 01, 1359 SH/Rabi' al-Awwal, 23, 1401 AH.

Place: Jamaran, Tehran

Subject: The importance of the teaching profession and the duties of the teachers in training students

Audience: Religious teachers from all over the country

Mere knowledge does not benefit anyone and in fact is very dangerous. When rain, which is divine mercy, falls upon flowers, a fragrance emanates; and when the same rain fall upon filth, a stench arises. Such is also the case for knowledge. If it enters the heart of a virtuous person, its benefits reach the entire world. And if it enters a corrupt heart, it corrupts the entire world. It is said that *"a corrupt scholar corrupts the world."*[18] Conversely, a virtuous scholar emanates peace, goodness, and welfare for mankind.

Date: January 03, 1981/Bahman 01, 1359 SH/Rabi' al-Awwal, 23, 1401 AH.

Place: Jamaran, Tehran

Subject: The importance of the teaching profession and the duties of the teachers in training students

---

[17] *Al-Kafi*, v.2, p.12.
[18] *Vide* previous footnotes for reference to hadith.

Audience: Religious teachers from all over the country

Focus your attention on this aim and keep your mind engrossed in the remembrance of God and do your duty purely for the sake of God Almighty. Make sure to engage yourself seriously in learning as long as you are in this school[19] and keep in mind that what is even more important than learning is the attainment of pure values. Remain true to the message of Islam and adorn your Islamic education with lofty Islam ethics. While you are engaged in a serious study of the Islamic laws and the other fields of learning, make sure to purify yourselves according to the teachings of Islam. All centers of learning as well as the religious schools in the Islamic Republic should ensure that students are trained in values and ethics before everything else. All the Islamic scholars and speakers who have strived on the path of God, each according to his own ability, should go to the various centers of learning all over the country and should form faculties in the areas of ethics, self-purification, and Islamic knowledge in order to supplement regular education with Islamic ethics and Islamic self-purification. If there is no Islamic grooming toward self-purification- whether it is in the theological schools or in the regular universities, which are also Islamic and religious centers of learning- attention should be paid such that the teachers who are engaged in serving in these centers and those who go to teach or speak there, should be people who are purely Islamic and who believe in Islamic laws and teachings so that those who are being trained under them receive Islamic training and education. It is important for you to keep in mind that if any "scholar"- no matter who he is- is not equipped with Islamic ethics and self-purification, he is bound to harm the interests of Islam.

Date: March 1, 1981/Esfand 01, 1359 SH/Rabi' ath-Thani 23, 1401 AH.

Place: Jamaran, Tehran

Subject: The importance of self-purification and its priority over education

Audience: Various strata of the people, employees of Shaheed Mutahhari School, and members of the Islamic Associations of the Girls' Schools of Damghan and Semnan

Try to make use of committed religious experts. We have said time and again that we want experts, albeit committed ones. But the enemies shouted that they are against specialization. Of course, there is no one more dangerous than a deviant expert.

Date/Time: Before noon, October 15, 1981/Mehr 23, 1360 SH/Dhu'l-Hijjah 16, 1401 AH.

---

[19] The audience of Imam (ra) were the employees and faculty of the Shaheed Mutahhari Seminary and the members of the Islamic Students Associations and students of schools from Damghan and Semnan cities.

Place: Jamaran, Tehran

Subject: Striving to achieve cultural independence

Audience: Ali-Akbar Parvaresh (Education Minister) and directors-general of the ministry from all over the country

I think that the thing that has hurt Islam more than anything else is faulty education and training in Islamic morality. If you look at history even that of the prophets, you will obviously find that Islam has been hurt most by unrefined and perverted individuals. The same is true about all other religions. The main blight on the monotheistic schools which had hampered their growth and development was unrefined people. Sometimes these people were learned but unrefined ones, but most of the time they were ignorant and unrefined. Perhaps the damage Islam has sustained from unrefined scholars is much greater than the harm done by the ignorant unrefined people, though the later outnumber the former group. All perverted schools of thought were created by scholars and learned people. These people created new, perverted religious and political schools. All deviations were initiated by this group of people. The harm done to monotheistic schools by this learned people which were versed in many sciences cannot be compared with damage incurred by any other group.

Date/Time: Morning, January 02, 1982/Dey 03, 1360 SH/Rabi' al-Awwal 24, 1402 AH.

Place: Husayniyyah Jamaran, Tehran

Subject: Self-refinement and its significance; explaining the problems of the revolution

Audience: Friday prayer leaders of Isfahan and Chahar Mahal Bakhtiyari provinces

Two great pillars are training and education

Whether at the university or other places in which some sort of training is involved, teaching and education constitute the two important pillars. Islam has greatly recommended these two pillars, laying stress on education. Education is more important and wherever the *ulama* in theological seminaries and professors in universities are engaged in teaching, they are concerned with these two pillars: scientific and moral training or purification of the soul. If we suppose that teaching and educating permeated a nation and all underwent training as much until their needs are fulfilled, purified their selves and edified their ethics, such a nation will be a model nation.

Date: September 19, 1982/Shahrivar 28, 1361 SH/Dhul-Hijjah 1, 1402 AH.

Place: Husayniyyah Jamaran, Tehran

Subject: Two main pillars of education

Audience: Muhammad-Taqi Misbah Yazdi, Muhsin Qara'ati (Imam's representative in the literacy campaign), Ali-Akbar Parvaresh (Education Minister), Muhammad-'Ali Najafi (Minister of Culture and Higher Education), members of the office for coordination of theological seminaries and universities and the educationists

If knowledge were acquired minus spiritual training, this knowledge would many a times serve as a source of corruption. A scientist or scholar who has not undergone self-edification and a university professor not experiencing purification of the self will bring corruption for the country. Such learned people can give rise to corruption in a country. You know that our nation, you and we, have suffered in the course of history. In recent years, the harms had aggravated and the country's dependence had reached its peak. This state of affairs has been the result of domination of knowledge and science minus moral, religious and spiritual education. If the two pillars of knowledge and spiritual training had prevailed in universities from the outset, the products of the universities would have been correct, progressive and constructive, and our country would be in the present state.

Date: September 19, 1982/Shahrivar 28, 1361 SH/Dhul-Hijjah 1, 1402 AH.

Place: Husayniyyah Jamaran, Tehran

Subject: Two main pillars of education

Audience: Muhammad-Taqi Misbah Yazdi, Muhsin Qara'ati (Imam's representative in the literacy campaign), Ali-Akbar Parvaresh (Education Minister), Muhammad-'Ali Najafi (Minister of Culture and Higher Education), members of the office for coordination of theological seminaries and universities and the educationists

If university professors only attempt to teach lessons without regarding spiritual education, those who graduate will spread corruption. The universities in the former regime did not teach properly. If they had done so, we would not lag behind so much in sciences. The same thing is true about theological seminaries. If the seminaries have nothing to do with self-edification, morality and spiritual training and are simply concerned with intellectual teachings and learning, the scholars trained in such seminaries will ruin the world. Therefore, the two pillars of teaching and education are to be inseparable. If the two accompany each other in the society, school or university, then we can benefit from such a university, seminary, other higher or lower centers of learning and everywhere and at all levels.

Therefore, what is important is to nourish the spirit of children from childhood so that they can attain their goals. Wherever they go they should undergo spiritual as well as scientific training. If knowledge enters a corrupt heart and mind, its harm will be greater than that of ignorance. Ignorance is a big defect but it does bring about destruction. However, if knowledge is acquired without any moral insight and spiritual purification, this will perish human beings. The extent to which the Prophets urged people towards edification of the self, they did not encourage people towards seeking knowledge. Self-edification is more useful than knowledge alone. Of course, knowledge is something that all have underscored to acquire, but the two should accompany each other. They can be likened to the two wings enabling one to fly. If a nation wants to fly towards happiness, the two wings are required. If either of them is absent, there will be no flight.

I hope university professors and theological 'ulama preserve their relationship. One of the treasons committed against this country was the separation of university from the theological seminary. Professors avoided the mullahs (clergymen) on the assumption that they were empty-headed and knew nothing. Our seminaries were also scared of universities on the assumption that they were irreligious. If mutual understanding is developed, I guess these cases will disappear. When the 'ulama find their way into university and university professors find their way into seminaries, then they will understand what crime has been committed against this country. When university professors visit Qum and sit together with the 'ulama at the seminary and exchange views, then they will understand that we did not cry out in vain that Islam was a rich culture. Then those things would not be written on the walls of universities. From the beginning, plans were underway to train our children to be hostile to Islam. At university, one could not cite anything concerning Islam and the akhunds (clerics). Such was the case in seminaries. Any one of them who visited the university or seminary felt like a stranger. They assumed to have entered a bad environment. This was because plans had been worked out to keep these two fronts that could protect the country and save the country, hostile to each other. They wanted these two centers to suppress each other so that they could reap the benefits, as they actually did. What was the reason for so much insistence on enmity of the two strata? The reason was that the enemies of Islam feared that if these two got close and understood Islam, they would understand how much affliction we had suffered, particularly in the last 50 years. We were hostile to our brothers. Each tried to weaken the other. Note that this unity between the university and seminary should be established and strengthened so that you can protect your country. If the universities and seminaries strive to be acquainted with each other and develop understanding, our country will not have any defect. All the sufferings are because one corrupt university graduate, examples of whom you know, will ruin a country and if such a graduate is upright, he or she will correct the country. The corruption of a scholar corrupts the world. A scholar corrupts the world. The mass of people cannot corrupt the society.

Date: September 19, 1982/Shahrivar 28, 1361 SH/Dhul-Hijjah 1, 1402 AH.

Place: Husayniyyah Jamaran, Tehran

Subject: Two main pillars of education

Audience: Muhammad-Taqi Misbah Yazdi, Muhsin Qara'ati (Imam's representative in the literacy campaign), Ali-Akbar Parvaresh (Education Minister), Muhammad-'Ali Najafi (Minister of Culture and Higher Education), members of the office for coordination of theological seminaries and universities and the educationists

I am amazed at why the followers of Christ with all the purification of the self and invitation to spirituality have become worse than the Jews. It cannot, of course, be said that anyone is worse than the Jews. I mean the Israeli Jews. What has happened that the followers of Christ, the heads of countries, are eradicating the entire humanity? It is because they have knowledge, the discipline of politics, industries, everything, but they don't have that which they must possess, they don't have that which is useful for humanity. That missing thing is self-edification and spirituality. Christians care not for the spirituality of the Christ; Jews have forgotten the spirituality of Moses, the interlocutor with God; and Muslims have pushed into oblivion the spirituality of Islam. The educative aspect of knowledge is significant but if spiritual education is absent, so these teachings will be harmful for man. All the damages and destructions befalling countries have emanated from scholars. The academicians are the source of these problems. Those who manufacture missiles, jet fighters and other things are the source of all these devastations. Whatever befalls man comes from knowledge- knowledge minus edification.

If we suppose that human beings were morally educated but ignorant, would the world be in peace and quiet? If man did not seek knowledge and simply pursued self-edification, man would lag behind because of failing to acquire knowledge. This state of affairs would be a great defect. Man needs knowledge. If one were to choose between acquiring knowledge and undergoing spiritual training, which would man be predisposed to seek? We have no doubt that if man experienced self-edification with all its prerequisites, so that he would not harm others, would be kind to people, and would consider others to be fellow creatures and people would be in peace and harmony even without knowledge. If knowledge was there but without self-purification and if the Prophets were excluding from humanity and man would be left alone to grow on his own, the entire humanity would perish and live in chaos, and there will not be a single happy face among human beings. If you see that a good number of people are good, it is because of the spiritual teachings of Prophets. It is true that not all people accepted the spiritual teachings of Prophets, yet these teachings have shed so much light on the world that the weaker masses of people are all good.

Corruption is less frequently found among them. But, for example, you who have initiated the literacy campaign and those who want to teach fail to undergo a spiritual education, your good efforts will fall through. Self-edification should accompany learning and knowledge. If you who are in charge of teaching children simply seek to enhance their knowledge without training them in spiritual and moral edification, you will not be successful in your efforts and you have not rendered a positive service to your country.

Date: September 19, 1982/Shahrivar 28, 1361 SH/Dhul-Hijjah 1, 1402 AH.

Place: Husayniyyah Jamaran, Tehran

Subject: Two main pillars of education

Audience: Muhammad-Taqi Misbah Yazdi, Muhsin Qara'ati (Imam's representative in the literacy campaign), Ali-Akbar Parvaresh (Education Minister), Muhammad-'Ali Najafi (Minister of Culture and Higher Education), members of the office for coordination of theological seminaries and universities and the educationists

In any case, the thing that builds nations is proper culture. The thing that enriches the university so that it becomes useful for the nation; becomes useful for the country includes the ingredients that make up the university and it is not the academic lessons. Industry outside the sphere of faith brings corruption; knowledge outside the sphere of faith brings corruption; *"A corrupted intellectual corrupts the whole world."*[20] The greater the knowledge, the greater its corruption. The dwellers of hell are troubled by the stench of the man of learning. The man of learning that has faith is the one whom God praises; whom the Prophet praises; whom Islam praises. If faith is not present beside knowledge, the knowledge will be harmful. If knowledge is present in a country in which there is absence of faith, it will destroy that country and make it to reach a dead-end. We had so many specialists in all fields of study in the former regime; yet what did these specialists do for the nation? Except that they kept on pushing the nation backwards; kept on making it more dependent; everything became dependent; you name it and they would say that we must go to Europe to get it. They knew well how to make pitchers; they would take us in order to teach us; they would not teach us. They would take away our youth and corrupt a group of them and teach them something inadequate. They would leave them to themselves midway.

Date/Time: Morning, December 19, 1982/Azar 28, 1361 SH/Rabi' al-Awwal 3, 1403 AH.

Place: Huseyniyyah Jamaran, Tehran

---

[20] *Ghurar al-Hikam wa Durar al-Kalim*, p.738, hadith #45

Subject: Influence of imported culture on the society

Audience: Muhsin Rezaee (Commander-in-Chief of the Guards Corps), Salik (Head of the Oppressed Mobilization), chiefs of the resistance bases, members of the Guards Corps Mobilization and the instructors of the Basij all over the country

Value in the words of the Prophets and the words of the saints of God and at the top of them the glorious Qur'an and the honorable Prophet of Islam- peace is upon his soul- is value for knowledge and piety. The yardstick is these two qualities, knowledge and piety together. Knowledge alone is not of value or it has low value; piety alone has no value or has a low value.

In a narrative, quoted from the Prophet of God that, *"Two persons broke my back: the man of learning who is unafraid of being disgraced and the man of piety who is ignorant."*[21] The ignorant person that does not know of the Humanitarian-Islamic precepts shall always act in a manner that is contrary to the way of the Prophets however pious he may be. The man of learning that has no piety and is unbridled poses a far greater danger to Islam than anyone else. The value is for knowledge and piety. They accept everything from the men of piety. In the words of the Qur'an, knowledge has been highly acclaimed but with piety beside it. Knowledge alone is useless for a human being unless, it is based on the laws of nature and piety, too, without knowledge does not reach a person to achieve perfection.

Date/Time: Morning, December 26, 1982/Dey 5, 1361 SH/Rabi' al-Awwal 01, 1403 AH.

Place: Husayniyyah Jamaran, Tehran

Subject: Roots of differences of values in the world

Audience: Muhsin Qara'ati (representative of the Imam and head of the Literacy Movement), Ghayouri (representative of the Imam in the Red Crescent Society), teaching staff of the Literacy Movement, employees of the Red Crescent Society from all over the country

If knowledge is separated from piety- even if it is knowledge of monotheism, even if it is knowledge of religions- it has no value in that world. If the loss from unaccompanied knowledge on nations and on Islam would not have been greater than its benefits- which it is- then it must be mentioned that an impious person can destroy a country, destroy human beings and the person who is more learned can corrupt the people better.

---

[21] *Bihar al-Anwar*, v.2, p.111

Date/Time: Morning, December 26, 1982/Dey 5, 1361 SH/Rabi' al-Awwal 01, 1403 AH.

Place: Husayniyyah Jamaran, Tehran

Subject: Roots of differences of values in the world

Audience: Muhsin Qara'ati (representative of the Imam and head of the Literacy Movement), Ghayouri (representative of the Imam in the Red Crescent Society), teaching staff of the Literacy Movement, employees of the Red Crescent Society from all over the country.

The most important of all the efforts are the efforts by the clergy and the university students in the path of self-purification and self-development and the beloved youth in line with education to the level of specialization. This is because their immorality will corrupt the world and it will reform with their reforming. The men of learning and the eminent theologians of the seminaries of the land and the respected and pious professors of the universities should strive to bring the universities and seminaries closer to one another. The respected professors and devoted intellectuals of the universities and the rest of the educational centers that have been affected by the moral corruption of the former regime and the miseries that were inflicted by the corrupt system on the nation and their country, should for the sake of Almighty God, and for safeguarding the independence and freedom of their country, strive in the humanitarian development of the youth together with their education. This is because knowledge and specialization without self-purification and training is a blight that has afflicted humankind today and is on the verge of setting the world on fire. What havoc can the competition and rivalry of the two superpowers and their arming themselves with modern atomic and nuclear weapons that originate from satanic and unrestrained soul wreak upon humankind unless some invisible hand comes out and saves humanity.

Date: April 1, 1983/Farvardin 21, 1361 SH/Jamadi ath-Thani 17, 1403 AH.

Place: Jamaran, Tehran

Subject: Six reminders to the nation, the government, the parliament and the Judiciary

Occasion: Farvardin 21, anniversary of the establishment of the Islamic Republic of Iran system

Addressees: Nation of Iran

If you become a specialist, you must bear in mind to imbibe his piety and devotion because if a faithless specialist does not cause harm to a regime, neither does he have any benefit.

Date: April 26, 1983/Urdibehesht 6, 1362 SH/Rajab 21, 1403 AH.

Place: Jamaran, Tehran

Subject: Hazrat Ali (a) pillar and model

Occasion: Birth anniversary of Hazrat Ali (a)

Audience: Fakir (representative of the Imam in the Guards Corps), personnel of the Air Force division of the Guards Corps

I have repeatedly said that if knowledge minus piety is not harmful, it is not useful either. Islam may have not suffered as much harm from layman as it has from the impious *'ulama*. Piety is the principal factor, but an ignoramus with piety may occasionally cause harm. People with righteous appearance might make mistakes due to lack of acquaintance with principles of Islam but if knowledge and piety come together in one, one will be happy in both this and the next world.

Time: Morning, September 4, 1983/Shahrivar 31, 1362 SH/Dhul-Qa'dah 26, 1403 AH.

Place: Jamaran, Tehran

Subject: The need for seminaries to develop and expand activities in Islamic issues and *fiqh* (Islamic Jurisprudence)

Occasion: Second martyrdom anniversary of Mr. Quddousi

Audience: Martyr Quddousi's Family members and theology students from Quddousi School

We should try hard so that those who raise our children with corrupt mentality would not enter schools and universities. This should not be neglected. They might not do anything at the moment, but they will do their job ten years later. We are opposed to those who are hostile to Islam and stand against them, but we do not bother those who are not hostile to Islam and concerned with their own business. Our concern is Islam and Muslim country. We have offered so many youths for Islam, so we should not let their blood to be wasted. What do we want for the scientist who is harmful to humanity? Today, the world is burning in the fire of the knowledge of pernicious scientists. These destructive weapons, bombs and missiles have been made by these very scientists. Therefore, knowledge should be combined with purification. Basically, purification of the self is prior to knowledge.

Date/Time: Morning, March 19, 1985/Isfand 28, 1363 SH/Jamadi ath-Thani 26, 1405 AH.

Place: Husayniyyah Jamaran, Tehran

Subject: Relation of education and edification

Audience: Akrami (Education Minister), deputies of the ministry and officials in charge of Literacy Movement

Mere knowledge is not useful; knowledge and commitment together can elevate man not to stand in need of others, being proud before God. Of course, this work has its problems and difficulties. Anyone striving to do a positive work will not necessarily be welcomed by others. A right work may be bitter to some groups. But one who seeks right and works for God's gratification should not think that what others tell about him; he should consider God and work for God irrespective of what others may give comments. Good work has also its opponents. You should think of doing good work so as to be proud before God. When you develop such mentality, God will also accompany you and remove your difficulties. If university is improved, country will be improved.

Date/Time: Morning, April 61, 1985/Farvardin 27, 1364 SH/Rajab 25, 1405 AH.

Place: Jamaran, Tehran

Subject: Improvement of university and struggle for liberation from cultural dependence

Audience: Iraj Fadil (Minister of Culture and Higher Education) and deputies

What is important is that the two wings: knowledge and action should go together. Knowledge without action is not useful; in fact, it is harmful. Perhaps many of the disasters befallen man have come about by knowledge. All the devastations visible in the world have been due to knowledge minus edification. Knowledge is there but without purification. If you want to serve Islam and the country, preserve the independence of your country and not be dependent on any country, you should strengthen knowledge, ethical edification and action.

Date: July 03, 1985/Mordad 8, 1364 SH/Dhu'l-Qa'dah 11, 1405 AH.

Place: Jamaran, Tehran

Subject: Need for heeding judgment and duties of ambassadors and representatives of the Islamic Republic in foreign countries

Occasion: Birthday of Hazrat Imam Reza (a)

Audience: Members of Supreme Judicial Council, staff of the Judicial Power, Foreign Minister and representatives of the Islamic Republic in European and American countries

SECTION 2

UNIVERSITIES BEFORE ISLAMIC REVOLUTION

Colonial Culture and Lack of Real Progress

The progress of a nation lies with its universities and look at what you have done to them. For over a hundred years, we have had universities and yet when a king wants to have a tonsillectomy we must bring a doctor here from another country. Foreigners must build the Karaj Dam. Foreigners must come even to build a road. Do international obligations demand this? If you have doctors and engineers, you have education. If you say you have education, you have wealth, you have students, and you have doctors and engineers, so why do you hire them from outside the country? Why do you pay foreigners a hundred thousand tumans a month?! Answer this! If you have no answer, then pity this country! For a hundred years it has had universities but it has no doctors, no engineers.

Date: Before noon, December 2, 1962/Azar 11, 1441 SH/Rajab 4, 1382 AH.

Place: A'zam Mosque, Qum

Subject: The deplorable socio-political conditions and announcement of the Shi'ah clergy services and struggles; the anti-religious policy of the Shah regime

Occasion: The commencement of lessons at the Qum theological center after the conclusion of the Provincial and District Council disturbances

Audience: The *'ulama*, instructors and students of religious sciences and residents of Qum

It's preposterous I know, but they have decided to establish an Islamic university.[22] Apparently they have allocated a budget of a few million tumans for this purpose. Well, those of you responsible for this scheme, if you really are sympathetic toward Islam then why do you demolish our university; yes look, the one standing over there? If you have genuinely reached the conclusion that Islam, Islamic precepts and the *'ulama* of Islam must remain, then although it's true we don't expect any goodwill from you, at least don't subject us to your malevolence.

Date: 8 am, April 15, 1964/Farvardin 26, 1343 SH/Dhu'l-Hijjah 2, 1383 AH.

Place: A'zam Mosque, Qum

Subject: Analysis of the Khordad 15 uprising; performance of the government and the mission of the *'ulama* and the clergy

---

22 Imam (ra) points to the decision by the regime of Reza Shah to establish Islamic University which was in fact project to shut down Islamic Seminaries (*howzeh*) and forcefully employing the *tullab* (*howzeh* students and clergymen) and religious scholars in the government.

Occasion: Imam Khomeini's release from prison

Audience: '*Ulama*', clergymen, merchants, students and people from other sectors of society

Don't be mistaken in thinking that their plan to establish an Islamic university is due to their reconciliation with Islam; this is not at all the case. Instead, it is but a repetition of the time when the Qur'an was raised at the end of the bayonet in the confrontation with Amir al-Mu'minin (the Commander of the Faithful- Imam Ali (a)). Mu'awiyah defeated Amir al-Mu'minin by taking advantage of the power of the Qur'an and using it as a weapon. Yes, by using the Qur'an as a weapon! Otherwise there is no doubt that it would have taken a maximum of a few hours only to wipe the Bani Umayyad off the face of the earth. They drew up a plan, however, whereby the Qur'an was brought forward and they said: "We are Muslims and you too are Muslims. We both bear witness to the same God and quote this Qur'an saying: There is no god but Allah." No matter how much Amir al-Mu'minin insisted on being patient and not rushing into war, arguing no good would come from it, the foolish Kharijites who were the Imam's friends and companions) although they never really came to know him (ignored the Imam's pleas claiming that according to the Qur'an it was incumbent upon them to fight. They thought of an artifice: they fastened copies of the Qur'an onto their lances and raised them up into the air declaring: "The arbitrator between ourselves and yourselves is the Book of Allah; the arbitrator is the Book of Allah." Hazrat Imam (a) sent after those of his companions who were actually engaged in battle, telling them to cease fighting and to return. His companions however, returned a message stating that they needed to fight for a further hour. Thus, the Imam explained to them that the Kharijites, having been deceived by the enemy, had now surrounded him and with swords drawn were about to kill him unless they returned from the battle front. Hence, we see how Islam was defeated by misuse of the Qur'an.

Do you truly believe you can defeat Islam by establishing an Islamic university? Do you imagine we will sit back and permit you to execute your plans? Indeed, we shall anathematize whosoever enters that university. The people themselves will bring it down. Could they conceivably allow the religion, believers and '*ulama* of Islam to be under the auspices of the Ministry of Culture? The Ministry hadn't better make the fatal mistake of interfering with our religion or with Islamic issues, because only if Khomeini or God forbid, all the *maraji'* of Islam actually passed away could they continue to see this program through. Even when we have gone and are thereby relieved of our Islamic duties, the nation of Islam will live on.

Date: 8 am, April 15, 1964/Farvardin 26, 1343 SH/Dhu'l-Hijjah 2, 1383 AH.

Place: A'zam Mosque, Qum

Subject: Analysis of the Khordad 15 uprising; performance of the government and the mission of the *'ulama* and the clergy

Occasion: Imam Khomeini's release from prison

Audience: *'ulama*, clergymen, merchants, students and people from other sectors of society

You ought to reconsider your stand somewhat. Amend your behavior and abandon this reactionary attitude of yours. Try not to behave so savagely. Make efforts to leave these medieval practices behind. Don't be so reactionary; be civilized, be progressive. Allow the country to develop and afford its people respect. Don't subject the people to such hardships. Ensure that university curricula are such that our youth receive good moral and educational instruction. Train them to be combatants so that they refuse to tolerate imperialism.

Date: 8 am, April 15, 1964/Farvardin 26, 1343 SH/Dhu'l-Hijjah 2, 1383 AH.

Place: A'zam Mosque, Qum

Subject: Analysis of the Khordad 15 uprising; performance of the government and the mission of the *'ulama* and the clergy

Occasion: Imam Khomeini's release from prison

Audience: *'Ulama'*, clergymen, merchants, students and people from other sectors of society

I received a letter from one of the students in America. He wrote that unfortunately the students, the university students there (in America) say that all our misfortunes stem from Islam. O you misfortunate students! The Islam that is introduced to you from the radio is not Islam. The Islam that you get from the newspapers is not Islam. That Islam which has been introduced to you is defective, it's something that none of the Muslims accept. I do not accept it, and the other clergymen do not accept it. This is not Islam. They do not let us introduce (true) Islam. In this country, the television is independent and is controlled by an Israeli. He says whatever he wants. The radio too, they produce its programs and its advertisements, and what good use they put it to! Not just in this country, in all Muslim countries; I am talking about all Muslim countries but I keep coming back to our own country.

Date: September 9, 1964/Shahrivar 18, 1343 SH/Jamadi al-Awwal 2, 1384 AH.

Place: A'zam Mosque, Qum

Subject: The danger of the penetration of Israeli influence in Iran and the plots perpetrated by the imperialists in the Muslim countries

Occasion: The beginning of lessons at the theological center

Audience: Religious students, clerics, merchants of the bazaar and other residents in Qum

The way to ameliorate the country is to correct its culture. The correction must start with the culture. The hands of imperialism are very active in our culture. They do not let our youth grow up to be independent; they do not let our youth at the universities develop correctly. They do something to them from childhood so that when they grow up, Islam means nothing to them and they (the West) mean everything. If the culture is put right, the country is put right. For it's the culture which creates the ministers for the ministries; it's the culture which creates the representatives for the Parliament; it's the culture which creates the office workers. Either create an independent culture or give it to us to create. You are afraid of America; you are afraid of others. Give it to us to correct. Give us control of the culture.

Date: September 9, 1964/Shahrivar 18, 1343 SH/Jamadi al-Awwal 2, 1384 AH.

Place: A'zam Mosque, Qum

Subject: The danger of the penetration of Israeli influence in Iran and the plots perpetrated by the imperialists in the Muslim countries

Occasion: The beginning of lessons at the theological center

Audience: Religious students, clerics, merchants of the bazaar and other residents in Qum

The preachers they planted in the religious teaching institution, the agents they employed in the universities, government educational institutions, and publishing houses, and the orientalists who work in the service of the imperialistic states all these people have pooled their energies in an effort to distort the principles of Islam. As a result, many persons, particularly the educated, have formed misguided and incorrect notions of Islam.

Reference: Imam Khomeini (ra), *Wilayate Faqih* (The Governance of the Jurist), p. 23

The agents and hands of imperialism who know that when the nations, especially the young educated generation, become familiar with the lofty principles of Islam, definitely the imperialists will fall and be destroyed and the severance of their hands from the interests of the colonized nations and countries, have resorted to sabotage.

By poisoning and tainting the minds and ideas of the youth, they try to hinder the manifestation of the splendorous countenance of Islam. By means of deceitful titles and colorful schools they mislead our youth. In your research and study of the truths of Islam in the political, economic, social, and other fields, it is necessary for you young Muslims to consider the validities of Islam and not to overlook the distinctions which separate Islam from the other schools of thought. Be careful not to confuse the deliverance-bestowing ordinances of the Holy Qur'an and Islam with the wrong and misleading schools which are mere products of the human mind.

You must bear in mind that so long as the nation of Islam is attached to the imperialist schools of thought or compares the divine laws with them and put them side by side, it will never attain peace and freedom. These different schools of thought offered to the Muslims from the left and right are merely for the purpose of leading them astray; the desire is to keep the Muslims abject, humiliated, backward, and enslaved forever, and to keep them away from the liberating teachings of the Noble Qur'an. The left and right imperialists have agreed to struggle hand in hand to destroy the Islamic nation and Muslim countries, repress nations, and plunder their enormous capital and natural resources.

Date: August 8, 1972/Mordad 17, 1351 SH/Jamadi ath-Thani 28, 1392 AH.

Place: Najaf, Iraq

Subject: Necessity for struggle to advance Islam's lofty goal

Addressees: University Muslim Students residing in America and Canada

Notwithstanding all these troubles, the awakening of the nation is a source of hope. The opposition of the country's universities) to which the Shah himself has admitted (the distinguished spiritual leaders, students and the other strata of society, in spite of all the pressures and the strong-arm tactics, heralds the attainment of liberty and freedom from the clutches of imperialism.

Date: July 11, 1975/Tir 02, 1354 SH/Rajab 1, 1395 AH.

Place: Najaf, Iraq

Subject: Expressing regrets on the suppression of the people, hoping for their awakening

Addressees: The Iranian nation

Culture is the source of a nation's happiness or misfortune. If the culture is not sound then the youth who are trained in this unsound culture will, in the future, create corruption. The imperialist culture produces imperialist youth for the country. A culture which is created by the designs of others- and it is the foreigners who lay their plans for us then hand them over to our society in the form of culture- is an imperialist and parasitic culture. Such a culture is a weapon more lethal than anything else; it is even worse than the arms of these ruffians, for their weapons eventually fall to pieces, as they have done now. But when the culture is corrupt, our youth, who form the foundations of our society, are lost to us; they are trained to become parasites, to become infatuated with the West.

They are trained in this way from the very first day that they enter school and this continues into higher education. If the culture is a correct culture, then our youths will be trained correctly. If the culture is a culture of truth, a divine culture, a culture which is of use to the nation, which is advantageous for the Muslims, then it does not produce such people as those who now exercise authority over us. But our culture is an imperialist culture, our culture does not lie in the hands of suitable people, the just do not administer it.

Date: Circa January 1978/End of Dey 1365 SH/Safar 1398 AH.

Place: Shaykh Ansari Mosque, Najaf, Iraq

Theme: Crimes of the Pahlavi regime

Occasion: Tragedy of the massacre of people of Qum on Dey 19, 1365 SH/January 9, 1978.

Addressees: Clergy, theology students and a group of people

If our universities were correct, independent universities and those who taught there were just and were free to do as they saw fit and what was right to do, then our country would not have got into the state it is in today nor would it reach a potentially worse stage tomorrow, God forbid. Some people have seized control of our universities who are themselves parasites, who are themselves supporters of the imperialists and possess a servile attitude.

Date: Circa January 1978/End of Dey 1365 SH/Safar 1398 AH.

Place: Shaykh Ansari Mosque, Najaf, Iraq

Theme: Crimes of the Pahlavi regime

Occasion: Tragedy of the massacre of people of Qum on Dey 19, 1365 SH/January 9, 1978.

Addressees: Clergy, theology students and a group of people

You have completely ruined the education in Iran. Nowadays, if we need the services of a physician, we have to go to England. Every few days someone heads for England for medical treatment. But if we had doctors of our own then why would we need to go to England? The universities- these too have been destroyed by you. We no longer have universities. On the face of it there are universities, but you won't even allow this semblance of a university system to go unthreatened. What are the poor university students and professors to do about these monstrosities (the Shah and his regime).

Date: May 13, 1978/Khordad 01, 1357 SH/Jamadi ath-Thani 23, 1397 AH.

Place: Shaykh Ansari Mosque, Najaf, Iraq

Subject: Religious duty; to rise up against the Shah

Occasion: The arrival of the anniversary of the bloody uprising of Khordad 15, 1342 SH

Addressees: Religious students, clergy and a group of Iranian residents in Iraq

He has destroyed our education system. He has destroyed our army; our army's honor. And he means to destroy our religious establishment, but, God willing, he will not succeed in this.

Date: May 13, 1978/Khordad 01, 1357 SH/Jamadi ath-Thani 23, 1397 AH.

Place: Shaykh Ansari Mosque, Najaf, Iraq

Subject: Religious duty; to rise up against the Shah

Occasion: The arrival of the anniversary of the bloody uprising of Khordad 15, 1342 SH

Addressees: Religious students, clergy and a group of Iranian residents in Iraq

From the time when Amir Kabir[23] founded Iran's first university some seventy years ago right up to the present, they prevented our youth from receiving adequate education and training, and from being able to perform a job of work competently. They impeded the progress of our youth. They ensured that no one could receive adequate education in our universities. They prevented those in the armed forces from receiving proper military training. American supervisors mislead these servicemen, that is, they instruct them in a way beneficial to themselves! Our culture has become that of the imperialists. We must have our own indigenous culture. These foreign cultures

---

[23] Mirza Taqi Khan Amir Kabir (1220-1268 AH) was the prime minister of the Nasiruddin Shah Qajar and founder of Daroul Funon Technical School. He was assassinated by the orders of Nasiruddin Shah in the bathroom of Fayn Garden in Kashan city.

are ones which prevent our children from being properly educated. Now, even when he) the Shah (needs a tonsillectomy, he has someone brought in from Europe to perform the operation! You are the one who talks of how you took the country to a great civilization and yet even your tonsillectomy is performed by someone from abroad. So evidently you can't do anything for yourselves!

Date: October 11, 1978/Mehr 19, 1357 SH/Dhu'l-Qa'dah 8, 1398 AH.

Place: Neauphle-le-Chateau, Paris, France

Subject: Migration to Paris; the Shah's crimes; objectives of the Revolution

Addressees: A group of Iranians residing in Paris

We have had universities in Iran for some seventy years now. We have had schools from the time of Amir Kabir. We have universities, but they have not been allowed to teach properly. Our educational system is an imperialist system. It is a system which they created for us, which they dictated to us. The imperialists do not let our youth become properly educated. They do not let us progress. If they release their hold on us, then the Iranians will make progress like the rest, they are no less capable than anyone else. But they do not let us progress, because if they were to do this then their interests would be jeopardized.

Date: October 12, 1978/Mehr 29, 1357 SH/Dhu'l-Qa'dah 18, 1398 AH.

Place: Neauphle-le-Chateau, Paris, France

Subject: America's mission for the Shah

Addressees: A group of Iranian students and residents abroad

They reshaped our culture making it into an imperialist one, not one that was independent. Even now our educational system is not the independent one for which the minds of the nation had planned.

Date: October 15, 1978/Mehr 23, 1357 SH/Dhu'l-Qa'dah 21, 1398 AH.

Place: Neauphle-le-Chateau, Paris, France

Subject: The imperialists' study into the customs, mentality and resources of the East; treason against Islam and the clergy; the Americans in Iran

Addressees: A group of Iranian students and residents in Paris

A nation needs education; a nation can have a political existence through its culture and education. Our educational system is not an independent one, it is not one which relates to the people; rather it is planned and controlled by foreigners. Consequently, they do not give us a sound system; they do not give us sound teachers. The university lecturers cannot and have never been able to pursue their tasks as they should. The university students cannot pursue their tasks in a way that they want to. All the institutions must glorify Aryamehr[24]; all must be organs, which support the apparatus of oppression. When the nation looks at its education, it sees a paralyzed system, one which can achieve nothing and which does not have a sound role to play in the society.

Date: October 24, 1978/Aban 2, 1357 SH/Dhu'l-Qa'dah 12, 1398 AH.

Place: Neauphle-le-Chateau, Paris, France

Subject: The roots of the people's opposition to the Shah and the need for propagating Islam

Addressees: A group of students and other Iranians residing abroad

From the very beginning when schools were first established in Iran- schools established with a view to helping the country to develop- this has been the way things were, except they weren't as bad as they now are. From the beginning their intention has been to prevent an educational system in the true sense of the word from materializing; for they knew that if a real educational system and if properly-educated people were to appear in Iran, then they would get in the way of things; they would cause a problem by getting in the way of their goals and interests, interests which lie in plundering the wealth of this nation. From the beginning they planned things so as to hinder the materialization of an educational system which would be capable of developing our youth and of rearing a properly-educated youngster. And so now things have worked out as they wanted them to, whereby our educational system in fact bears no resemblance whatsoever to that which a true educational system should be like, and whereby they are wasting the lives of our youngsters. That is, going to these schools and universities is nothing but a waste of the lives of the teacher and the student. And the teachers know this; the students know this; everyone knows this; but still, that is the way things are. When we say that this page (in history) must be turned back, that all of these schemes which the foreigners have initiated in Iran via these evil agents of theirs must be abandoned, it is because we see that everything we happen to point to is rotten to the core!

Even if we could only be said to have one genuine school and university, how come the wealthy in our country, how come 'His Excellency' himself, on becoming unwell, must either bring doctors into Iran from abroad, or must themselves be taken to another country, to London, to receive treatment?! How come no one ever comes

---

[24] Mohammad Reza Shah Pahlavi

from London to Tehran to be treated, or to any other country for that matter? It is we who have to leave here; these people have to leave Iran and go to London for treatment! The reason for this is that we don't have any proper doctors. Yes, we have doctors, we have doctors who have a license to practice, who have been awarded the appropriate certificates, doctors who have obtained all the necessary qualifications and who are called 'professor', but they are doctors who are not in fact properly qualified. They are not in fact doctors; they only appear to be so. Yet another of those words that has been changed is this word 'professor'. That is to say, they have used this word to mean something that it does not. Hence, when someone becomes ill they say there is nothing else but for him to go abroad, for him to go to London! The doctors also say that he must go to London- yes, even the doctors themselves say this! Even once those doctors who have gone to Iran to treat the patient actually arrive there, they say there is nothing else but for the latter to go abroad, that the patient must go to London for them to treat him! This is the sorry state of our education, the sorry state of our universities, of our colleges. And they want us to be in such a sorry state too.

Date: November 2, 1978/Aban 11, 1357 SH/Dhu'l-Hijjah 1, 1398 AH.

Place: Neauphle-le-Chateau, Paris, France

Subject: The alteration of the meaning of those terms used in the vocabulary of the Shah and of the powers supporting him

Addressees: A group of Iranian students and residents abroad

We have two kinds of resources; all nations have two possible kinds of resources and Iran had them both: one comprised the minerals which lay beneath the ground, and the other was the youth- for they are indeed one of the nation's resources- but both of them have either already been or are presently being destroyed. about our youth who comprise one of our greatest assets. They are not allowed to be educated properly; their intellectual development is not permitted. The foreigners want to keep our youth at a certain level whereby they can do nothing only labor for them, even those Iranians who study abroad are not given a proper education. They will not allow an opposition force to spring from the ranks of the youth, they will not allow our youth to develop intellectually for fear that if they do they will stand up to them and not allow them to plunder us so.

Date: November 8, 1978/Aban 17, 1357 SH/Dhu'l-Hijjah 7, 1398 AH.

Place: Neauphle-le-Chateau, Paris, France

Subject: Fifty years of crimes committed by the Pahlavi (dynasty)

Addressees: A group of Iranian students and residents abroad

If you discern that this is all a ploy to prevent you, the youth (of Iran), from developing your strengths and capabilities, then you should turn your attention to something else. Our universities are just like this, indeed everywhere in Iran the story is the same, they (the foreigners) do not want you to progress; they want to keep you at a certain stage of backwardness so that you will not resist their rule. They keep you at a certain level, bring in experts from abroad and expend our nation's strength on carrying out the orders of the foreign experts, in other words the Iranians labor while the foreigners act like lords, the Iranians labor for a pittance while the foreign consultants sit smoking pipes and drawing up plans against the nation of Iran and receive God knows how much every month for doing so.

Date: November 8, 1978/Aban 17, 1357 SH/Dhu'l-Hijjah 7, 1398 AH.

Place: Neauphle-le-Chateau, Paris, France

Subject: Fifty years of crimes committed by the Pahlavi (dynasty)

Addressees: A group of Iranian students and residents abroad

So now let's take a look at the education. Do we have an independent educational system that others do not interfere in? Do we have universities that are independent, that think for themselves and are run by the university chancellors? We can only dream about such a system. Have we ever had a correct educational system from the constitutional period to the present time? It was always a dependent system, a system that others devised for us! This is why if the tonsils of a viperous prince were to become inflamed and he were to come down with tonsillitis, they would bring doctors from America or Europe to treat him or alternatively take him there for treatment! At one time we did have a proper, independent university, if we had one now, then we would have proper, independent doctors. When we want to tarmac a road, we have to hold out our hands and ask people from other countries to come and do it for us! How shameful! The story of tarmacking roads in Iran is quite an amazing one: with the excuse of tarmacking a road, the nation's wealth is destroyed. The same is true for the very many other jobs which are carried out there. If we need a building put up, if we want to build a hospital, then most certainly someone has to come from abroad to draw up the plans and tell us how to build it! If we had a (proper) educational system... we have had modern schools for over seventy years now, from the time that *Dar al-Funoun*[25] was established, and it has been for many years now that we have had universities; if these universities had been to the benefit of this nation, if they had

---

[25] *Dar ul-Funoun*, established in 1851 by Amir Kabir, was the first modern university and modern institution of higher learning in Iran.

allowed our youth to receive a proper education, if the system had not been an imperialist one, then everything would have been put right by now and our youth would have been people who would have stood up to the government. If we had had one independent university then the country would not have found itself in the state that it is in today where everything is in ruins.

The youth constitute an important force in our country and they (the Shah and his regime) have destroyed this force. They have squandered the energies of the youth. Two groups of young people who came abroad to work in the field of nuclear physics came to see me- the number in one of the groups was quite large- and they said that they were all agreed that what they were doing was quite useless! They said their work was futile because Iran has oil and if we suppose that we have oil for another twenty years, then after that time this kind of nuclear physics in which they are involved will be of no use. The work they are doing is therefore useless, and, more importantly, they told me that they are not allowed to learn anything, that they are kept at a low level beyond which they cannot progress, adding that the training they had received in Iran was more than the small amount they were being given abroad! They said they had been brought over here to be kept at a low level so that they could not progress. Our youth are not allowed to acquire an education.

The story is the same in the Iranian universities; that is the system is such that they are kept at a certain level. The system is an imperialist one. We have an educational system which is in a state of dependence. We do not have an independent system. Through this educational system which is dependent on the imperialist government, they want to keep the youth in a state of backwardness like this. It is at the hands of that man who talks about taking us to "the gates of a great civilization"[26] that our youth are presently being kept at a low level and are not allowed to progress!

So much for our education which is an imperialist education, one kept in a state of backwardness and not allowed to progress. It produces neither competent doctors nor skilled engineers. Nothing comes out of it right. They have paralyzed the country by depriving it of its force of young people. We do not have a force of young people at present.

Date: November 02, 1978/Aban 29, 1357 SH/Dhu'l-Hijjah 19, 1398 AH.

Place: Neauphle-le-Chateau, Paris, France

---

[26] Imam (ra) points to the false claims of Mohammad Reza Shah.

Subject: Clarifying the motives and the aims of the uprising and warning against reconciliatory plans

Addressees: A group of Iranian students and residents abroad

Take for example these centers for learning and education that they have set up, they are all imperialistic, from the universities down. They do not train our children properly; first of all they have a set level above which they do not let the students' progress, secondly, they create numerous obstacles in order to keep them in a state of backwardness; for if these universities were the proper independent ones that we want, they would produce great men, men who would stand up to those who wish to raid our country and take all of our resources. This, however, is not what they (the imperialists and the Shah's regime) want, thus the universities train our youth in a way that suits them, and if they can, they Westernize them, that is they present the West in such a light, they place them under the influence of the West to such a degree that they lose themselves completely and become totally bound to the Western countries. To put it another way, they become agents for the West. Just suppose that this is the method of teaching- as indeed this has been the case until now- then after a while even if the universities did produce great men who wanted to do something for the country, these men would end up doing it for the benefit of the West, not for their own people, because these universities have become so immersed in the foreigners' way of education and training and have created such an overestimated impression of foreigners in the minds of our youth, that they forget all the illustrious deeds carried out by their own people and whatever else concerns their own people. They forget all of these things; pay no attention to themselves and concentrate only on the West and the things related to the West.

Date: December 22, 1978/Dey 1, 1357 SH/Muharram 12, 1399 AH.

Place: Neauphle-le-Chateau, Paris, France

Subject: Helping those on strike and giving shelter to deserter soldiers an incumbency upon the nation; colonial culture of Pahlavi dynasty

Addressees: A group of Iranian students and residents abroad

This is shameful for us; we have had universities for fifty years, or maybe less, yet as they themselves admit, these universities have until now not been able to present us with one proper doctor. People are even sent abroad to be treated; when someone falls ill, he is told to go to England for treatment. Why? Because the education is not right.

They do not give us a proper education. It's not that the people in the East do not have the aptitude, no, this is a mistaken notion. No, it's because these leaders here have had a modicum of suitability, they went after their country's interests. However, their suitability was only good for themselves, they trained their own people properly, but, for us, many of them were harmful. If we had one proper university, abilities would blossom beneath the sun of the East, skills would blossom.

Date: December 13, 1978/Dey 01, 1357 SH/Safar 1, 1399 AH.

Place: Neauphle-le-Chateau, Paris, France

Subject: Unrighteous Pahlavi government; righteous nation needs a righteous ruler

Addressees: A group of Iranian students and residents abroad

You have kept our universities at an inferior level not allowing them to become independent; you do not let the lecturers at the universities get on with their jobs. You have put our education in a state of backwardness. It is an imperialist educational system, one that has been dictated to us by others.

Date: January 7, 1979/Dey 17, 1357 SH/Safar 8, 1399 AH.

Place: Neauphle-le-Chateau, Paris, France

Subject: Deceitful propaganda of the Western press; description of the spiritual universe; signs of Shah's betrayal

Addressees: A group of Iranian students and residents abroad

He made our universities such that they dissipated our human resources; would that were all they did, but they turned our human resources into inhuman resources

Date: January 12, 1979/Bahman 1, 1357 SH/Safar 22, 1399 AH.

Place: Neauphle-Le-Chateau, Paris, France

Subject: Keeping unity and solidarity and rising up for God, the secret behind the victory of the Revolution

Addressees: A group of Iranian students and residents abroad

He destroyed our universities; he destroyed our agriculture; he has exhausted almost all of our oil reserves. He says we will have oil only for another twenty years or so, and at the rate he is giving it away, this will be the case! He has destroyed everything we had. He has destroyed our youth; indeed, the worst of all abominations, the worst crime of them all is his destruction of our human resources. It is the human being who can work and who is valuable. Without man, water and land are of no value. It is the human being who is valuable. He deprived Iran of this humanity; he destroyed that resource of ours which comprises the youth. Ask those young people who are presently in Germany receiving training in the field of atomic energy, they have told me that they are being kept at a certain low level beyond which they are not allowed to progress. You can ask them yourselves. They say their work is useless. These capable forces of ours are prevented from progressing; they are being suppressed and kept at a low level.

Date: January 12, 1979/Bahman 1, 1357 SH/Safar 22, 1399 AH.

Place: Neauphle-Le-Chateau, Paris, France

Subject: Keeping unity and solidarity and rising up for God, the secret behind the victory of the Revolution

Addressees: A group of Iranian students and residents abroad

This Shah had kept our culture so backward that now our youth cannot complete their education here and they have to seek education abroad after partially completing their studies here with all the difficulties and pressure upon them. We have had universities for more than fifty years and approximately thirty or so years that we have had this university, but due to the treachery committed against us this university never grew; it does not have any human development. This man has destroyed all our people and our manpower.

Date: February 1, 1979/Bahman 21, 1357 SH/Rabi' al-Awwal 3, 1399 AH.

Place: Behesht-e Zahra Cemetery, Tehran

Subject: The illegal nature of the Parliament, the government appointed by the Shah, and the regime's seditious elements

Occasion: The return of Imam Khomeini after 15 years in exile

Addressees: Millions of people from Tehran and various cities of Iran

We had never had freedom; it was just recently that we have acquired it. Neither was there a free press, nor did we have an independent judiciary or a lawyers' guild. They had encroached on everything. Neither was there one single decent university, nor could they properly educate the youth whom they had detained in backwardness. The growth of our culture was reversed and our offspring pushed (culturally) backward.

Date: February 7, 1979/Bahman 18, 1357 SH/Rabi' al-Awwal 9, 1399 AH.

Place: Alawi School, Tehran

Subject: Connivance of the discord-mongers and the colonialists

Audience: Three hundred judges and lawyers from the Justice Ministry

During these fifty years of the Pahlavi's dark rule, this dynasty left almost nothing for Iran; that is they have destroyed its human and material resources. They have kept backward the universities that should create human resources for us, and were ordered not to allow one single accomplished and serving human being be produced in them

Date: February 6, 1979/Bahman 17, 1357 SH/Rabi' al-Awwal 8, 1399 AH.

Place: Alawi School, Tehran

Subject: The record of the Pahlavi's rule

Audience: Exporters of agricultural dried fruits and grains

So, with all their might they tried to keep our universities backward. They would not let our professors educate the youths properly or let these young people get correct education. It was because they knew that if our universities functioned properly and became independent, by the time the students left, they would become anti-colonialists.

Date: February 16, 1979/Bahman 27, 1357 SH/Rabi' al-Awwal 18, 1399 AH.

Place: Alawi School, Tehran

Subject: Confronting plots made by small groups to dissolve the army

Occasion: Re-opening of universities after the victory of the Islamic Revolution

Audience: 150 people from university professors and Islamic society of academicians

They have tried to make our culture colonial. They did their best to prevent the emergence of humanity. They feared human beings and they feared learned man. They did their best to prevent the appearance of the elite during their 50 and so years of monarchy. They did such harm to education such that there was neither education nor humanistic growth. They frightened us, they frightened us by their subversive propaganda such that we feared one another and did not trust one another. If someone fell sick, we would send him abroad while we had physicians here in Iran. They frightened us, shook us, and emptied us so hard that if we wanted to asphalt a road we used to send for foreigners.

Date: April 19, 1979/Farvardin 29, 1358 SH/Jamadi al-Awwal 02, 1399 AH.

Place: Qum

Subject: Factors for victory; sabotage of the small groups; importance of culture

Audience: A number of educational staff of the city of Rafsanjan

Children were sent to school. Of course, the schools were also made in a way to teach nothing but depraved ways. Further up and higher (higher education center), they did away with all enlightenment altogether so that there would not be any enlightened in official capacity.

Date: May 23, 1979/Khordad 2, 1358 SH/Jamadi ath-Thani 26, 1399 AH.

Place: Qum

Subject: Role of the Pahlavi dynasty in deterioration of Iran's ideas and morals; sacred mission of motherhood

Audience: Employees of the Wireless Department of Communications Ministry

In the case of the dominance of the West or the East on the Islamic countries, what has been very important is their cultural dominance. They used to train our children in those training centers so as to become supporters of them on their graduation. Therefore when our youths finished their college or university, they were supporters of either the East or the West. As you can see, those youths who are supporting, China or Soviet Union or America in different countries, especially in Iran, are the products of such Universities. In other words, they are educated in such a way as to believe that they are nothing by themselves. All of the agents of the foreigners, from westernized writers through those teaching in our universities, agreed with the notion that we are good for nothing. Therefore, we should be either after the West or after the East. What is considered as a great havoc for Muslims is this sort of culture and civilization influencing our youths and dragging them either this side or that side. They are mostly pro-Americans in Iran, calling themselves as Communists, because some of them who used to call themselves communists or at least just thought they were such.[27]

Date: May 02, 1980/Urdibehesht 03, 1359 SH/Rajab 5, 1400 AH.

Place: Jamaran, Tehran

Subject: Necessity for vigilance of Muslims against arrogant

Audience: Muhammad-Mahdi Shamsuddin (Deputy Chairman of the High Shi'ah Council of Lebanon), Members of the staff of Central Movement of Amal, the military wing of the movement of the deprived ones, Lebanon

Culture can solve all complexes. If the culture is of a kind to rear committed and believing people, if the culture forbids evil and stealing and encourages belief in God

---

[27] Imam (ra) points to the low level of thinking of the opponents

and in the metaphysical, it can protect the nation. A man reared in such a culture will never yield to treachery no matter how much they offer to him. They are like Imam Ali (a) who said in his Nahj al-Balaghah, that *"he would not take a seed from an ant if they gave him the entire world."*[28] Of course, no one can be like him. Those who attack our culture, our old science schools, and universities- openly and secretly- want to prevent the training of man in these schools, because rearing an upright man is contrary to their wishes. If on the contrary, some people are reared that are passive to everything and think of gifts, posts and accumulation of wealth, they colonize then.

Key to salvation and damnation of the nation

Then our jobs, your job and my job, are the jobs of the prophets. If we betray our jobs, we have betrayed the prophets; we have betrayed the Almighty God. And the sign of our betrayal is this that the youth who ought to be reared in our classes go astray. Train the children and the youth towards the right path. If you want to safeguard your country and your religion, the key to this protection will be in your hands. The key to salvation and damnation of a nation is with the teachers. If teachers work well their country will be a good place for living, if not, it will be ruined. Then you are the ones who can work for the spiritual and material development of your country.

Date: May 22, 1979/Khordad 1, 1358 SH/Jamadi ath-Thani 25, 1399 AH.

Place: Qum

Subject: The social standing of the teacher and his rank in Islam and the Qur'an

Audience: Educational staff of Isfahan

These matters constitute the prelude. These are all the preliminaries to creating a humane nation; a nation in which the spirit of humanity is generated and a transformation brought about in the people themselves. What is important to the prophets is humanity itself. It is nothing else; only man is the concern of the prophets. Everything should assume a humane aspect. They wanted to mold man. When man is molded, everything else turns out right. The foreign-dominated regimes did not want people of the countries of the East to be brought up properly. They were afraid of upright people. They did not want any such people around. An upright individual, if found, does not submit to force. An upright person, if found, does not sell the interests of his country to foreigners. An upright person is such. He serves God and exists for His sake. He lives and dies for God. It is not possible for such a one to serve the foreign powers, and to rise against his own country. They did not want our universities to produce upright human beings. They were afraid of such people. They made

---

[28] *Nahjul Balagha*, Sermon # 222.

attempts to prevent the growth of our workforce; to arrest its progress. They tried all this with every means possible and with every plan they had. Their main mission had to do with the people. It was to prevent their development. In a country where the people are not trained properly; where an individual only thinks of material things; when the training is oriented toward materialism, well, such an individual would like to become the owner of a palatial villa in whatever way he can. It makes no difference to him as he is materialistic. Such a person's approach to materialism is like this. He is not concerned from where the material thing, the villa or the car that he has obtained has come from. He wants everything for himself; he is not concerned from where it is. A pious person is one who questions where something is from when it is given to him, what it is, is it right on his part to use it or not. Has the automobile) for example (been obtained legally or not, by honest or by dishonest means? Such questions arise only for human beings and need to be broached as well. We were mistaken when we used to say, or say, that it is enough for us that the regime is not there anymore. It is enough if there is independence; it is enough if there is freedom. Not at all! This is not the issue. We will sacrifice all these for the sake of having proper human beings. We want (upright) human beings. Let everything be sacrificed for the sake of human beings. When people are molded properly, everything will turn out right.

Date: June 6, 1979/Khordad 16, 1358 SH/Rajab 11, 1399 AH.

Place: Qum

Subject: The need for the universities to become Islamic

Addressees: Doctors, professors and students of Shiraz University

As regards the university, since they thought that they could not close down the universities because of the global repercussions, they allowed these to remain open. But these were not universities that could be of use to the nation and solve the people's problems. They adapted the university to turning out people who would be of use to themselves. By means of their extensive propaganda about the West and its advancement, they tried to bring up our youth in that university in a Western way. In that same university, it so happened from the propaganda of some of the professors allied to them (West) that our youth became useful only to the West and not to our country. They brainwashed our youth and made them West-minded instead of Iranian. This made our children and our youth believe- and perhaps, it is the same even now- that everything of ours should be from the West. The propaganda was such that the situation is the same even at present.

Though we have our own doctors, when someone falls ill they say that he has to be taken to Europe! The reason for this is that we have lost our self-confidence; we do not have the freedom of thought anymore. All our attention is focused on the West

Date: June 11, 1979/Khordad 12, 1358 SH/Rajab 16, 1399 AH.

Place: Qum

Subject: The enemy striking a blow against the two poles: the clergy and the university; the danger posed by the West and West-worship

Audience: Students of the Police Academy, Tehran

They did not let our universities to be Islamic ones, humane ones. They did not let us learn our lessons properly in our school. There was pressure and repression, each one in a particular manner, in that period and this.

Date: June 31, 1979/Khordad 23, 1358 SH/Rajab 18, 1399 AH.

Place: Qum

Subject: Explaining "freedom" and its dimensions in an Islamic government

Audience: The pasdars (IRGC guards) and merchants of Tehran

Later on it was not in that manner. It was devilishly worse during the reign of this one. They (Reza Pahlavi) thought that the university would probably stand up to them some day, and so, through various devices, they did not allow it to be a proper university for this country.

Date: July 3, 1979/Tir 21, 1358 SH/Sha'ban 8, 1399 AH.

Place: Qum

Subject: The need to combat the dealers in narcotics

Audience: The employees of the Anti-Drugs Campaign Organization

They would note that well this was an intellectual force that was also young and it was possible that this force would challenge them. Thus, they also repressed the universities through various means. They had different approaches; by means of this same propaganda, they led them astray; they diverted their thoughts. They did some important things in order to preoccupy the youth by whatever means with themselves and prevent them from having a say in the destiny of the country. If they would leave the university alone and there would be no propaganda and sabotage involved, the university would build intellectuals who would think of finding a remedy to the acts of pillage and looting committed by others.

Through diverse tactics they would preoccupy these strata of the youth who were and are capable of doing these things.

Date: July 12, 1979/Tir 03, 1358 SH/Sha'ban 26, 1399 AH.

Place: Qum

Subject: Confrontation of the believers with the arrogant; praising the struggles of the clergy; problems of the youth

Audience: Students of Babol College

They could not act accordingly with universities in those days, because they were afraid of the world community. They could not attack universities in the same light. At that time, they proceeded by restoring to propaganda and teachings that ran counter to the correct religion. They had colonial plans. They were of the opinions that if these two institutions were strengthened, the masses might follow them and frustrate their plans. Consequently, foremost among their plans was to suppress both the clerics and academicians.

Date: September 17, 1979/Shahrivar 26, 1358 SH/Shawwal 25, 1399 AH.

Place: Qum

Subject: All out dependencies in Pahlavi regime and preventing the younger

Occasion: Martyrdom of Imam Ja'far Sadiq (a) and the anniversary of tragic event in Faydiyyah Theological School

Audience: Families of martyrs of Islamic Revolution

Throughout the course of history, particularly in the recent fifty odd years, plans had been charted out to check us from making progress, holding back efforts to produce sound university and high school. The mission aimed to frustrate the growth of centers capable of producing enlightened people.

Date: September 17, 1979/Shahrivar 26, 1358 SH/Shawwal 25, 1399 AH.

Place: Qum

Subject: All out dependencies in Pahlavi regime and preventing the younger

Occasion: Martyrdom of Imam Ja'far Sadiq (a) and the anniversary of tragic event in Faydiyyah Theological School

Audience: Families of martyrs of Islamic Revolution

In universities they sought to appoint teachers to raise the students in a way that they would lag behind. In moral terms, they wanted the students not to undergo Islamic education; they propagated materials to lead our young people to moral degeneration.

67

Date: Before noon, September 19, 1979/Shahrivar 28, 1358 SH/Shawwal 27, 1399 AH.

Place: Qum

Subject: Iranian nation's troubles during the Pahlavi regime

Audience: Tehran education organization officials and staffs

Therefore, they made such a country for us; an overtly westernized one; but not in its real meaning in the west. The things, the sciences, etc. are not the same here in Iran. They want our universities to be advanced to a certain extent and not with a true ethical, religious and scientific form as in their own countries. They do not want a doctor to be trained in Iran to serve the people. They had even made the people pessimistic about them to such an extent that even a person, e. g. with a pain of tonsils goes to England, to the Europe! For medical treatment on the one hand, they publicized that you are nothing and have nothing, and, on the other hand, allowed not our youth to flourish their talents. They made us fully dependent.

As long independence, subject to severance of intellectual independence as we are mentally dependent to the west and as long as we think everything should be brought from the west and should be repaired there; we cannot achieve independence. No independence is obtained unless we know ourselves and know that we have culture, everything and we do not need the west in our affairs, and that what they give us is not a developmental reality but that they want to limit us to a certain extent.

Date: October 6, 1979/Mehr 14, 1358 SH/Dhu'l-Qa'dah 14, 1399 AH.

Place: Qum

Subject: Colonial culture and intellectual dependency- Reforming cultural centers- enemies' plot

Addressees: Professors and Staff of the Sharif University of Technology

They destroyed everything; above all, universities. Fearing that well-educated people might come out of universities and stand against them, they let not universities operate well. They led the universities to control education to meet their desire. Therefore, our manpower was withheld from growth. If we find a chance now, we have to start from the scratch.

Date: October 28, 1979/Aban 6, 1358 SH/Dhu'l-Hijjah 6, 1399 AH.

Place: Qum

Subject: Comparing Iranian revolution with other revolutions- respite and peace for reforming national affairs- Significance of agriculture and Islamic Civilization

Audience: Representatives of Tabriz Students and Firouzabad Reconstruction Jihad

These people in universities, of course some of them, have been injected in their brains a disease or brought up like a westerner by the west for 50 years. They have been prepared so to bring up our youth that way. This is unreasonable expectation to have these ill people cure immediately or replace them with healthy ones. I know all people, particularly educational centers where foreigners favored more their upbringing at a certain level or their distraction, have been affected.

They cared about universities backwardness and distraction much more than other places. Our youth were taken to a different path and you should not be expectant of them to turn away quickly towards the nation's way; nevertheless, be not disappointed. The nation has found its way and you, the youth, have found your way.

Date: October 29, 1979/Aban 7, 1358 SH/Dhu'l-Hijjah 7, 1399 AH.

Place: Qum

Subject: Westernization, a chronic disease in Iran

Audience: Students of Islamic Association of Mufidi High College of Translation

I hope that our youth, teachers and university professors, writers and intellectuals are awakened and notice the negligence. We had been beguiled up to now; our minds had been converted. We should join our hands; writers should contribute to this revolution, speakers should help this revolution, newspapers should back this revolution. I see some newspapers, excluding the leading ones, carrying materials detrimental to the nation. Among these newspapers, some presume that their interests lie in the rule of westerners over our country or coming to power of the like of these treacherous ones. Those newspapers that are not such and the youth who are not without defect because in time of the former regime they were not involved in activities to be brought up like them should think out a way to make real human beings. We have our culture; we can educate our people; we can work to improve the country. It is the beginning of the work that the hands of the criminals have been virtually curtailed from our country. The grip of those who ransacked the country is now curtailed as well. We should think out how to construct our country. First and foremost, our youth should be mended. The youths who should protect the country in future and run it should be raised properly.

Time: November 2, 1979/Aban 11, 1358 SH/Dhu'l-Hijjah 11, 1399 AH.

Place: Qum

Subject: Necessity of cultural-economic independence of the country

Audience: Students of Faculty of Sciences and Faculty of Literature and Foreign Languages

I used to tell those physicians who came over to visit me that it seems their education has not been right since nowadays people go abroad to cure even their weakest kind of diseases. But those physicians replied that they do not know what was going on. What is the reason for this chaotic condition? This is because our brains have washed and something else has been put for it. Our brains have been colonized. We have to replace it now with an independent brain. We will need latter form of brain in managing this country. Our university professors should change the brains of our students. They should develop the independent brains in these students. Our culture and economy, too, should be independent.

Date: December 21, 1979/Azar 12, 1358 SH/Muharram 22, 1400 AH.

Place: Qum

Subject: All-inclusive nature of Islam; reliance on our identity; struggle to be self-sufficient; trial to gain independence

Audience: The craftsmen from Isfahan

One of our so-called scholars[29] in Iran had said that unless everything of us becomes English we will avail nothing and go nowhere. Such intellectuals who believe everything of the West is best have given wind to the propaganda of this like. All these years this propaganda has gone a great length to bring home this belief to us that West is better- as though we ourselves are not human beings. If one got a headache, he sued to go to Europe. If one wants to learn a few words, he saw himself obliged to go to Europe. You can judge by comparing one learned in Europe (in his own conjecture he thinks he has learned) with one studied here itself. The studies here too they had kept too low. Yet, you will see him far better than that one who has learned in Europe. He went there for enjoyment. He returned with a paper of permission to impose himself upon others. In the West, they bestow diploma easily and quickly. But to themselves they don't give such easy and quick diplomas. They want to become scholars. So they

---

[29] Seyyid Hassan Taqizadeh (1256-1349 AH) who was member of the national parliament for several rounds and minister of finance in the cabinet of Hidayat that during his tenure the Iranian oil contract with England was endorsed for next 60 years. He was for a long time Iran's Charge d'Affaires in England.

labor hardly to get a diploma. When our turn comes, they do not want us to become scholars. They keep us at a level to think that we are nothing. Everything is the West.

Date: January 4, 1980/Dey 14, 1358 SH/Safar 15, 1400 AH.

Place: Qum

Subject: Peculiarities of the Islamic Revolution and its distinctions with other revolutions

Audience: Tehran University professors

The imported freedom is one, which has dragged our children to corruption and debauch. Therefore, the centers for this trade multiplied in plenty. All in the name of freedom. All our newspapers were at their service. All this in order to keep our youths away from the university and drag them to corruption. Although our university was not up to the mark or a standard one, but that much too they did not want to render any good to the students.

Date: January 4, 1980/Dey 14, 1358 SH/Safar 15, 1400 AH.

Place: Qum

Subject: Peculiarities of the Islamic Revolution and its distinctions with other revolutions

Audience: Tehran University professors

In the universities by some other way, they tried their mission. They had made the university an imperialist. Our youths when came out they were acting for the interests of foreigners. They talked in their interests more than their own. They used to train in this way.

Date: January 4, 1980/Dey 14, 1358 SH/Safar 15, 1400 AH.

Place: Qum

Subject: Peculiarities of the Islamic Revolution and its distinctions with other revolutions

Audience: Tehran University professors

Had we practiced a principled teaching in the universities, today we would not have had any open-minded elements. In the most fatal moments of Iran, they are in disagreement among themselves. They are isolated from the people. They take sufferings of the people nothing as if they do not live in Iran. We lag behind. The reason is that the open-minded class of the Universities did not grasp the correct knowledge nor were they truly aware of the Islamic society of Iran. Most regrettably they are still so. The fatal blow the society has suffered is the one from the side of those open-minded ones of the universities. They have always looked themselves superior over the others. They only utter what their friends, the open-minded ones, could only understand. The people if do not understand, let them not understand, no matter what. Here people are not counted. They themselves are important. During the period of the ruling of Shah, the annual training brought up the students in such a way that the so-called open-minded ones did not take the oppressed people to account. They are the same even today.

Date: March 12, 1980/Farvardin 1, 1359 SH/Jamadi al-Awwal 4, 1400 AH.

Place: Shemiran, Darband, Tehran

Subject: Thirteen-point recommendations to Muslims

Occasion: The Iranian New Year Eve

Addressees: The Muslim nation of Iran, the Muslims and the oppressed ones worldwide

There has had been no training alongside the education. Therefore, we do not have a man committed to his nation or not prefer and persuade his own selfish motives among the university fellows.

Time/Date: 71: 03 pm, April 12, 1980/Urdibehesht 1, 1359 SH/Jamadi ath-Thani 5, 1400 AH.

Place: Shemiran, Darband, Tehran

Subject: Explanation about the reformation of the country's universities

Audience: From the various classes of the people, students, and Islamic association members of the universities and the institutes of the Muslim students across the country

What we want to say is this: Our universities are affiliated ones. Our universities are those of imperialists. Our universities produce the students fully westernized. The professors mostly are westernized. And they train our youth in the same trend.

Time/Date: 71: 03 pm, April 12, 1980/Urdibehesht 1, 1359 SH/Jamadi ath-Thani 5, 1400 AH.

Place: Shemiran, Darband, Tehran

Subject: Explanation about the reformation of the country's universities

Audience: From the various classes of the people, students, and Islamic association members of the universities and the institutes of the Muslim students across the country

What power was at work, which changed the university to such a form that its products- whoever came out of it- was a seduced, a perverted and a devious one

Date: May 24, 1980/Khordad 3, 1359 SH/Rajab 9, 1400 AH.

Place: Jamaran, Tehran

Subject: Fifty years long plots to create divisions among the various classes of the society

Audience: Teachers, students of the religious institutions, professors, members of the Islamic associations, students of the universities all over the country

We understand through the output what its source is. The plant that produces sugar, we understand by the sugar the nature of the plant. We can understand what and how are the universities by their product that is the students. The gentlemen who claim of having achieved such and such during this period of one gear, we can well know as to really what they have done in this one year. What the product had been during a span of fifty years? In fifty years, one million students should have had served the nation not to others. Has such a thing been ever achieved? Has the university ever produced a mentality in the students to think that they belong to this nation? Therefore, they should be in the service of the nation. They do not belong to foreigners. These communists, from where have they come? These Marxists from they have they come? They have come from this very university. We understand the professors and teachers through the students. We can conceive the inside of the universities. Its product indicates that. A few persons are committed ones- wherever they be. But as for the university, its roll should be a few millions. As such in a period of fifty years, a population of students, one hundred million, should have come out form the university. Indeed, such a figure has come out from the universities. Had this university given birth to a desired type of students, now Iran would have been a paradise. We would have never been on a campaign nor was a war the need. There was no need for a revolution. The product of the universities was an undesired one. Whatever post they occupied, they worked in the interests of the foreigners. Let them tell for whom they worked who had such high posts and stations in the government. Did they work for the nation? They are the products of the same university. They left the university behind and took the high offices, jobs and posts in the government. All of them were in the service of the foreigners. Had they worked for Iran, or had the university been

73

in the service of the country, now we would never have had any dispute nor any controversy. The university would never have been a front of battle. The departments would have taken a different shape and form. The university has had been at a failure to perform its due duty to the nation. It has had been in the service of other. However, so and so have trained our youths. They are still trying to hamper the way for the university to be in the service of the nation. When we say Islamic university, we mean a university based and founded to cater the needs of the nation. It should be for the nation. But in the university, the students are trained against the interests of the country.

Date: May 24, 1980/Khordad 3, 1359 SH/Rajab 9, 1400 AH.

Place: Jamaran, Tehran

Subject: Fifty years long plots to create divisions among the various classes of the society

Audience: Teachers, students of the religious institutions, professors, members of the Islamic associations, students of the universities all over the country

The Muslim fear, God forbid, to lose the opportunity without having done a positive thing. The culture may remain the same as it was during the previous corrupt regime. This important center was kept at the disposal of the colonists, which is quite evident by the output of the university. Few people were at the service of the country and Islam. Others did not do anything except harm, hurt and loss.

Date: June 14, 1980/Khordad 23, 1359 SH/Rajab 29, 1400 AH.

Place: Jamaran, Tehran

Subject: Formation of the Cultural Revolution headquarters

Audience: Appointed members of the Cultural Revolution Headquarters

If the training and education was correct, our country should have been self-sufficient. After so many years' experience and agony for this victimized nation, whose property has gone with the winds, still huge expenses should be charted out! And this nation should still remain hungry! The situation is like a machine. At its one end, Muslims are poured in and from its other end, communists come out. From one side believers go in and come out unbelievers. The good people mingle with them in the plants. In the end, they become corrupt, lewd and licentious too. If it is so, it shows what type of department it has been. We conclude about the nature of the organization from the result of its work. These people who were in the government and in parliament and senate for fifty years, we should see them as who they are. These are the same people who came out from these Universities. Had they had good training and good education, they would not have presented our country by their both hands to the foreigners. There are many difficulties. These difficulties should be lifted out and by your own hands

Time: Morning, July 2, 1980/Tir 01, 1359 SH/Sha'ban 18, 1400 AH.

Place: Jamaran, Tehran

Subject: Education and training from the Qur'an's view, the position of culture in the Pahlavi regime. The need for basic changes there

Audience: The heads of education throughout the country, the Islamic Association members, the Home Ministry workers and the provincial workers

Then what have these colleagues done all these fifty years? Well, let them come and show what they have done. Let them show the people what they have trained. Let them show what coaching they performed. You say training is a subcategory of coaching. So, where is its product, its output? Those whom you have 'trained' and 'coached'-how is their spirit? On their beliefs, their character, their conduct, their manners, what its standard was? What is it and to what extent has it gone that now we clamor and cry to mend it, correct the things, and so forth. This is a cry from far away. The young fellows say that there are such and such women. I know such things are not confined there. Such a thing also exists in ministries too….A college is not a place for debauchery. It should be the center of education.

Time: Morning, July 2, 1980/Tir 01, 1359 SH/Sha'ban 18, 1400 AH.

Place: Jamaran, Tehran

Subject: Education and training from the Qur'an's view, the position of culture in the Pahlavi regime. The need for basic changes there

Audience: The heads of education throughout the country, the Islamic Association members, the Home Ministry workers and the provincial workers

Some of the teachers were in their service. They used to prepare our youths to be available to them.

Time: Morning, July 2, 1980/Tir 01, 1359 SH/Sha'ban 18, 1400 AH.

Place: Jamaran, Tehran

Subject: Education and training from the Qur'an's view, the position of culture in the Pahlavi regime. The need for basic changes there

Audience: The heads of education throughout the country, the Islamic Association members, the Home Ministry workers and the provincial workers

You have seen for fifty years that this tyrannical government had universities and university professors, and that these same universities and university professors dragged our country into the lap of the superpowers. It was tragic for our nation that the tools of knowledge lay in the hands of those that lacked commitment and were unmindful of themselves. It is a tragedy that the instruments of knowledge be possessed by people who are not committed and lack Islamic morality.

Date: Before noon, December 18, 1980/Azar 27, 1359 SH/Safar 01, 1401 AH.

Place: Jamaran, Tehran

Subject: The importance of the roles of the seminary and the university; stating the duties of these two institutions of learning

Occasion: The day of unity between the seminary and the university

Audience: Teachers and students of Qum Theological Center; the student members of the office for the consolidation of unity between the seminary and the university

The university takes two paths: the path to hell and the path to prosperity; the path to ignominy, poverty and servitude, etc. and the path to glory, honor and magnanimity. The university that we have is of no use. We have had one for the past fifty years. Whatever corruption there was in this country was because of these people who had been educated in it, and, perhaps, had even specialized.

Date: Before noon, December 18, 1980/Azar 27, 1359 SH/Safar 01, 1401 AH.

Place: Jamaran, Tehran

Subject: The importance of the roles of the seminary and the university; stating the duties of these two institutions of learning

Occasion: The day of unity between the seminary and the university

Audience: Teachers and students of Qum Theological Center; the student members of the office for the consolidation of unity between the seminary and the university

To corrupt our young children right from the time they entered kindergarten schools up to the time that our talented youth who are the capital of this nation left the universities. Plans were to bring them up in a manner that would leave them totally influenced either by Moscow or by Washington. Such was the case

Date: January 22, 1981/Bahman 2, 1359 SH/Rabi' al-Awwal 15, 1401 AH.

Place: Jamaran, Tehran

Subject: Foreign conspiracies instigating deviation in the scientific-cultural centers of the country

Audience: Various strata of people, revolutionary guards heading for the battlefront, and school students from Tehran

The problem is that in the previous regime they had operated in a manner that had trained us and our youth to see themselves as completely incapable and had turned us into mere consumers who even took pride in the fact! Some people even went to the extent of saying: 'What's wrong in this! The others are our servants and provide for our needs.' Least did they realize that these people had in fact turned into their masters. They carried off everything that belonged to you with the pretext of catering to your needs!

Date: February 15, 1981/Bahman 26, 1359 SH/Rabi' ath-Thani 9, 1401 AH.

Place: Jamaran, Tehran

Subject: Need for self-assurance and using economic sanctions to promote self-sufficiency

Audience: The acting Petroleum Minister and his deputy-ministers, managing directors from the National Oil and Gas Corporation, the petrochemical industries, and other affiliated companies

All the misery that this country has faced has mainly been owing to its teachers who lacked the necessary commitment. And these teachers had churned out students who ruined our society and forced our country to lean either toward the East or toward the West.

Date: March 1, 1981/Esfand 01, 1359 SH/Rabi' ath-Thani 23, 1401 AH.

Place: Jamaran, Tehran

Subject: The importance of self-purification and its priority over education

Audience: Various strata of the people, employees of Shaheed Mutahhari School, and members of the Islamic Associations of the Girls' Schools of Damghan and Semnan

As with the clerics, those same elements also had similar plans for our college-going and other youth to prevent them from getting involved in the political and the other affairs of this country, which is in fact in dire need of their active involvement. They had gone to the extent of employing a large number of school and university teachers who were against Islam and this Islamic nation in order to deviate our youth and to prevent them from working for Islam. They had poisoned the minds of our youth against the clergy and vice versa. They created a rift among the clergy and the university and capitalized on it.

Date: March 5, 1981/Esfand 14, 1359 SH/Rabi' ath-Thani 27, 1401 AH.

Place: Jamaran, Tehran

Subject: Imperialist conspiracies for isolating the clergy; the great responsibility of the clerics; need for unity between the seminaries and the universities

Audience: Clerics from the Bureau of Propagation of the Qum and Mashhad Seminaries and soldiers of the 1974 - 78 service batches

Those who were involved in the upbringing of our children did not care to offer them an Islamic upbringing or to ensure that they developed a greatness of soul which would never allow them to fall under the domination of the foreign powers. Since they did not have any commitment to Islam they were naturally bound to bring up our children like themselves. It is because of this very fact that most of our university graduates had nothing to do with Islam or with an Islamic commitment and ethics.

Date: March 13, 1981/Farvardin 11, 1360 SH/Jamadi al-Awwal 24, 1401 AH.

Place: Jamaran, Tehran

Subject: The mission and the responsibilities of Islamic associations

Audience: Representatives of the school students' Islamic Associations from all over the country

Our issue is that during the fifty long years of the black Pahlavi rule in which the foreigners had managed to establish a firm footing in our country the main focus of their propaganda was to make our nation and our youth believe that Iran and Islam are incapable of developing the knowledge and expertise needed to establish their own industries and that we had no choice but to extend our hands either toward the East and communism or toward the West and the capitalist countries. Their propaganda has been so powerful that there are people who believe that we should either turn completely Eastern or completely Western, from head to toe! When I was in Turkey,

I had seen the Ataturk's[30] statues in some city-squares with his right hand raised in the air. And their explanation was that this symbolically meant that whatever they had was from the West! Similarly, foreign propaganda in other Muslim countries, too, has been so strong that their people have come to believe that they have no choice but to employ either Eastern or Western advisors for everything. They had succeeded in making some people even believe that the Iranian brain is incapable of achieving anything constructive, including agriculture. This was a calculated plan backed by extensive propaganda that had succeeded in making some of our people believe that we cannot have anything of our own and that we should either lean toward the East or toward the West so that they may feel sorry for us and cater to our requirements. Even today there are some people who consider themselves to be great thinkers and yet refuse to believe that we can be self-reliant. Now when we insist that our universities, which are like the think-tanks of the nation, should be freed from any sort of inclination toward the East or the West and that this is only possible provided they are Islamized, it does not mean that our universities should not have departments of medical and engineering sciences and that they should only be confined to teaching Islamic sciences! This is a fallacy. The moment there is any talk of an "Islamic University" and of bringing about a "cultural revolution", the supporters of the East and the West raise a hue and cry about us being against expertise and knowledge. No, that is not true. We are not against expertise and we are not against knowledge! What we are opposed to is becoming enslaved by the foreigners. We believe that the kind of expertise that drags us toward America, Britain, the Soviet Union, or China is more detrimental than constructive.

Our aim is to ensure that the experts that graduate from the universities are at the service of their nation instead of dragging the country toward the East or the West. Our aim is to ensure that our industries grow to high levels of expertise and be at the service of the nation instead of serving alien powers. The kind of know-how seeking that drags us toward America or the Soviet Union is harmful and is hazardous to the nations. Most of those who were educated in the universities of the previous regime, if not harmful, were of no use to this country.

Time/Date: Morning, May 25, 1981/Khordad 4, 1360 SH/Rajab 02, 1401 AH.

Place: Jamaran, Tehran

Subject: Importance of knowledge in Islam; responsibility of the university in an Islamic society; duties of the Islamic associations of the universities

---

[30] Mustafa Kamal Pasha (1299-1357 AH) known as 'Ataturk' by the orders of government of U.K. provoked a revolt against Ottoman Empire and then changed it to Democratic Western style government and named it as 'Turkey'.

Audience: Members of the Islamic Association and the Jihad of the 'Ilm va San'at (Science and Technology) University; members of the Organization for Scientific and Industrial Research; and a group of inventors and innovators

Their magazines were full of deviant and distorted matter, in order to confine the minds of our youth to what they wanted and to prevent them from getting involved in social affairs with free minds and to be able to analyze things for themselves. Children are under the influence of their teachers, right from their primary school years until the end. They were being influenced right from their childhood and when they would get into the universities things would be still worse. If such is the case, the university cannot succeed in training graduates that could prove to be useful for their country. They insisted on bringing deviation into the universities because they did not wish the universities to train people who can think independently for themselves and who can treat the pains of society.

Date: Morning, June 23, 1981/Tir 2, 1360 SH/Sha'ban 02, 1401 AH.

Place: Jamaran Husayniyyah, Tehran

Subject: Freedom from cultural dependence and the impact of the press on the culture of a nation

Audience: Karroubi (The Imam's representative and Head of the Martyr's Foundation), the family of Martyr Ali Mazandarani, and the editorial board and the employees of the monthly, "Shahid"

It is not accidental that all the educational centers of countries including Iran ranging from elementary schools to the universities were invaded by the colonialists, especially Westerners and, lately by Americans and the Soviet Union. The tongue and the pen of the westoxicated and East-oriented people and professors have consciously or unconsciously rendered a great service to the East and West since the establishment of universities, especially over the last few decades. Although among the professors and writers there were some who were aware and committed and who were against this path, unfortunately they were noticeably in minority.

The rush of Iranian students towards the West or occasionally the East after finishing their Western and Eastern oriented studies at schools or universities, which have no fruits except Western and Eastern cultures, was so destructive that unconditionally made all aspects of our social life dependent on the superpowers, to the extent that our society was Islamic Iranian on the surface but brimmed with Western and Eastern cultures.

Date: September 22, 1981/Shahrivar 13, 1360 SH/Dhu'l-Qa'dah 23, 1401 AH.

Place: Jamaran, Tehran

Subject: Effects and consequences of independent versus dependent culture

Occasion: Beginning of academic year

Addressees: High school and university students, the youth, teachers and professors

Of course, our cultural deviation has historical roots, and we still have teachers and professors who have been assimilated into western culture and training which are in no way in conformity with the interests of Islam and our country. All foreign affiliates are by-products of this Western university. Foreigners and their activities emptied our schools and universities of any content.

Date/Time: Before noon, October 15, 1981/Mehr 23, 1360 SH/Dhu'l-Hijjah 16, 1401 AH.

Place: Jamaran, Tehran

Subject: Striving to achieve cultural independence

Audience: Ali-Akbar Parvaresh (Education Minister) and directors-general of the ministry from all over the country

The biggest blow dealt to this country in the last fifty years came from deviant professors who were Western-educated and who governed education centers in the same manner. The harm was much more than what Reza Khan and his son did. Of course, there were committed professors and teachers but the others called the shot. We got rid of the evil of Reza Khan and Muhammad Reza Khan, but we will not rid of the result of Western and Eastern education any time soon. They are the foothold of the domination of the superpowers that cannot be disarmed by any logic. Despite all their failures they have not stopped plotting against the Islamic Republic, and still try to break down this divine edifice

Date: December 28, 1981/Dey 7, 1360 SH/Rabi' al-Awwal 1, 1402 AH.

Place: Jamaran, Tehran

Subject: Attack of superpowers on the culture of the country

Addressees: Academicians, officials and students of teacher training centers

Another place that they fought against, but in a different form, was the universities. If universities were Islamic and national, those who graduated could enter the Majlis and form a government and sap the influence of aliens in this country. They pounded the universities as well though in a different method. They did not storm the universities and close them down; rather, they drew up plans by training instructors and professors who served them to make universities affiliated with foreign powers and with England at one time and the US in the end, training the graduates, excluding a few of them, so as to be at the service of the foreigners. This is, itself, a lengthy chapter of the story which needs a lengthy discussion. They transformed our universities in a way that their products and graduates were at the service of aliens. The graduates who continued their education outside Iran and brought souvenirs were all at the service foreigners. This was how they liked it. Of course, among them were some who were different but were in the minority

Time: Morning, April 01, 1982/Farvardin 12, 1631/Jamadi ath-Thani 15, 1402 AH.

Place: Jamaran, Tehran

Subject: Reviewing the performance of Pahlavi regime

Addressees: Family of martyrs, Majlis deputies, representatives of the tribal people of the country, members of Ahwaz Mustad'afan Basij, members of construction Jihad, medical cadre of dispensary organizations, headquarters for injured ones of the Health Ministry, Red Crescent Society, reporters and photographers and officials of the Islamic Republic News Agency, staff of the Ahwaz and Tehran broadcasting departments, staff of Tavanir Company

Aggressive powers know that this nation cannot be manipulated by coercion and bayonet. Naturally, they formulate a design. They collect their wits and wait in patience.

They work out a design for the next 30 or 50 years from now. They chart out a plan today to reap the fruit 30 years later. If, for instance, a deviation, God forbid, creeps into our universities, they will benefit from this deflection 30 year from now. If non-Islamic and devious persons interlope into our universities, they will gradually undermine them. They are not in a hurry. Even if they cannot do anything now, they take control of the country gradually by propaganda and word of mouth, thus securing the attention of the public through university graduates and command the fate of the nation at the hands of people themselves.

Date: August 29, 1982/Shahrivar 7, 1361 SH/Dhu'l-Qa'dah 9, 1402 AH.

Place: Jamaran, Tehran

Subject: Popularity of officials in the Islamic system and need for them to serve people

Occasion: On the eve of the first anniversary of martyrdom of Messers Raja'i (President) and Bahonar (Prime Minister)- Government Week

Subject: Mir Husayn Mousavi (Prime Minister) and members of the cabinet ministers

At that time, our universities were in the hands of a bunch of people who at one times were English and recently, very American, meaning that they inclined towards America to take orders. There was also a minority of decent people in the parliament or at the university- but they could not speak out and had no following. They would have to suffer in silence and see the crimes being committed in their presence

Date/Time: Morning, December 19, 1982/Azar 28, 1361 SH/Rabi' al-Awwal 3, 1403 AH.

Place: Huseyniyyah Jamaran, Tehran

Subject: Influence of imported culture on the society

Audience: Muhsin Rezaee (Commander-in-Chief of the Guards Corps), Salik (Head of the Oppressed Mobilization), chiefs of the resistance bases, members of the Guards Corps Mobilization and the instructors of the Basij all over the country

All the things that were done during the deviant regime were done by the universities that were deviant.

Date/Time: Morning, June 2, 1983/Khordad 12, 1362 SH/ Sha`ban 22, 1403 AH.

Place: Husayniyyah Jamaran, Tehran

Subject: The parliament and its importance in the Islamic Republic order

Occasion: On the eve of the Day of God of Khordad 15 simultaneous with holding the "Parliament and People" Week

Audience: Akbar Hashemi Rafsanjani (Speaker of the Islamic Consultative Assembly), families of the martyrs of Khordad 15 (June 4), members of parliament and their families, administrative staff of the parliament and the Guardian Council, head and officials of the Khordad 15 Foundation from all over the country

It should be said that our universities were run by a bunch of westernized mercenaries, while committed scientists were in minority and were divested of authority. That westernized majority filled the youth with love of the west and sent them abroad in great numbers. In the west, colonialists did their work and trained the youth in a way that were desired by colonialists and sent them back to the country with westernized, non-Islamic mentality and devoid of patriotism. This was a disaster for Islamic countries in the past century, for which they have to blame. The full story can be deduced from this evidence.

Time: September 3, 1983/Shahrivar 21, 1362 SH/Dhul-Qa'dah 25, 1403 AH.

Place: Jamaran, Tehran

Subject: A Hajj in the manner of Abraham, advices to pilgrims to the House of God

Addressees: Iranian and world Muslims, particularly pilgrims to the House of God

Unfortunately, our universities and seminaries had many shortcomings from one aspect. They could not remedy those shortcomings. If universities had not originally intended to push Iran into the trap of big powers, they were gradually dragged towards this matter. Those in charge trained our dear youth the way they desired and then sent them abroad to be worked upon it. When they returned many of them were entirely opposed to religion and many of them could not do anything even though they were not opposed. At any rate, this was the situation of university.

Time: September 6, 1983/Shahrivar 15, 1362 SH/Dhul-Hijjah 28, 1403 AH.

Place: Husayniyyah Jamaran, Tehran

Subject: Need for educating young theology students for judgment and propagation

Audience: Mahdavi Kani, Imami Kashani, Mousavi Tabrizi; officials, teachers and members of the Jami'ah al-Imam as-Sadiq (a), members of the Cultural Revolution board, teachers and theology students of Martyr Mutahhari School, educational and judicial affairs graduates from Qum, officials of Dar Rahe-Hagh Institute and the staff of Amir Kabir vocational school of Isfahan

He made our university in a way that when students were graduated from university they were enemy of this nation and dependent on other countries particularly on the west. There were few exceptions.

Time: Morning, February 7, 1984/Bahman 18, 1362 SH/Jamadi al-Awwal 4, 1404 AH.

Place: Husayniyyah Jamaran, Tehran

Subject: Disasters befalling the country in time of Pahlavi dynasty; warning the regional countries about supporting Saddam

Audience: Ali-Akbar Velayati (Foreign Minister); ambassadors and charge d'affairs of other countries to Iran

You know that many of those who have been trained in university believe that Iran should be affiliated to foreign countries despite the fact that some of them also say prayer. They argue that Iran cannot manage administration of the country by itself.

Cannot Iran that has preserved its independence despite all pressures and exported its revolution to other countries and awakened other nations administer itself?

Date/Time: Morning, April 16, 1985/Farvardin 27, 1364 SH/Rajab 25, 1405 AH.

Place: Jamaran, Tehran

Subject: Improvement of university and struggle for liberation from cultural dependence

Audience: Iraj Fadil (Minister of Culture and Higher Education) and deputies

The pillaged nation should know that during the past fifty years, all the devastating blows to Iran and Islam have been mainly dealt with universities. If universities and other centers of learning and education were engaged in educating, purifying and training the youth armed with Islamic and patriotic programs for the benefit of the country, our country would have never been swallowed first by England and then by America and Russia. Such ruinous agreements or treaties would not have been imposed on our deprived nation. Nor would foreign advisers have been admitted to the country. Our resources, including the black gold would never go down the pockets of the satanic powers. Similarly, the Pahlavi family and its dependents could not have plundered the people's wealth and build for themselves at home and abroad private parks and villas over the bodies of the oppressed people. Foreign banks could not become rich with the wages of our deprived people and such funds would not have been spent by the *taghout* and his offsprings and kinsmen on carnal whims and debauchery. If the parliament, the government, the judiciary power and other organs had come from Islamic national universities, our nation would have not been facing these ruinous problems today. If chaste personalities, with sound Islamic and nationalistic inclinations, not like that which is offered as Islam today, were dispatched from the universities to the three centers of power: 1) the legislative power, 2) the judiciary power, and 3) the executive power, we would be in different circumstances. We could see different days and our homeland would not be like this. Our deprived people would have been liberated; the cruelty and oppression of the monarchy would have been foiled by people much sooner as would the centers of vice, addiction and pleasure houses, one of which was enough to corrupt a whole generation of our young people. This disastrous legacy would not have been left for our people. If our universities were Islamic, humane and nationalistic, they would have trained, educated and presented to the society hundreds and thousands of teachers and professors. How sad it was that these institutions were administered and our children trained and educated, with a few exceptions, by people who were either Westernized or Easternized. These persons were installed in vital positions with special planning and design. Our dear, oppressed and innocent children were unfortunately trained by such

85

wolves affiliated with the superpowers. They occupied high legislative, executive and judiciary positions and carried out the orders of the tyrannical Pahlavi regime.

Date: Date of writing, February 15, 1983/Bahman 26, 1361 SH/Jamadi al-Awwal 1, 1403 AH.

Date of Editing: Azar 19, 1363 SH

Date of Reciting: Khordad 15, 1368 SH

Place: Jamaran, Tehran

Subject: Politico-divine will (ever-lasting message of Imam Khomeini to the contemporary ones and next generations).

Addressees: Iranian nation, Muslims and peoples of the world and next generations

Suppression and Attacks on Universities

What outcome did you achieve out of putting pressure on the grand *maraji'*, the distinguished *'ulama* and the seminary students, as well as the assault on the universities, but service to the foreigners? Obviously, they do not want to see that the Holy Qur'an and its precepts rule over the Muslim nations as they can plunder the resources without anyone there to raise any objection but instead to grant them immunity. They do not want us to be part of the free people or our speakers to have any freedom. Sadly enough, you are the enforcing agents; the kind of agents who follow blindly and unquestionably. The theological schools have always been and continue to be the corps of literacy, ethics and righteousness in its true sense; this is without exaggeration and devoid of any propaganda. If you are real lovers of learning, why do you attack the centers of learning? Why do you shed innocent bloods at the Faydiyyah Madrasah and the universities? Why don't you leave the students of the theological schools alone? Why do you treat our students in foreign lands as such?

Date: April 15, 1976/Farvardin 26, 1364 SH/Muharram 4, 1387 AH.

Place: Najaf, Iraq

Subject: Details of the corruption and treasons of the Shah and Hoveyda's administration

Addressees: PM 'Amir 'Abbas Hoveyda

Resistance against knowledge and culture more intensely continues. By the order of the imperialists, they want the ill-fated nation to remain backward. With the claim of Islam and pretending to be righteous Muslims, they are set to destroy Islam and one after another obliterate and destroy the sacred laws of the Qur'an. The distinguished *'ulama* and students of the Islamic sciences are struggling under the pressure of the imperialist agents. The imperialists want to take possession of religious schools, mosques and Islamic assemblies and to a certain extent they have carried out this plan. Based on unfounded excuses, they attack the universities. They bring the honorable youth from the universities to the jails and the barracks. The latest incidents of the Iranian universities and the savage and merciless attacks of the tyrannical regime on the students have caused us great regret. This inhumane method is another example of the imperialist agenda to suppress the universities and the students. I strongly condemn these Gengis-Khan methods and Middle Ages acts. I am certain that the zealous and patriotic students will never retreat or surrender.

Date: Circa January-February 1971/Bahman 1349 SH/Dhu'l-Hijjah 1390 AH.

Place: Najaf, Iraq

Subject: Warning to the Muslims of the world in regards to Palestine and the revealing of crimes committed by the Shah's regime

Addressees: The pilgrims to the Sacred House of God

In the name of "Mission for My Country," this nation must remain in desolate and backward state and Islam, which is the only sanctuary of this nation and barrier in the way of the foreigners, must be crushed. It is as if they are commissioned to crackdown down on the enlightened young class whether they are seminary or university graduates; to dishonor the religious schools and imprison and torture the *'ulama*; to offer all the sanctities of the country to Israel and its masters; to give the foreign investors predominance over the country's remaining wealth; to spread the sources of debauchery and violate the sanctity of the Qur'an; to grant immunity to the foreign advisers and their workers while denying the same to the nation, clergymen, scholars, and students.

Date: September 11, 1972/Shahrivar 02, 1351 SH/Sha'ban 2, 1392 AH.

Place: Najaf, Iraq

Subject: Describing the regime's atrocities and tyrannies

Occasion: The dispatching of seminary students and clergy in the military service

Addressees: The Iranian nation, *'ulama* and clergy

It is lamentable, because of the suppression of the oppressed people, and the attacks on the country's universities; lamentable because of the heartbreaking tragedy of the

June 7, 1975/Khordad 17, 1354 SH[31] (that took place in the Faydiyyah Madrasah and the Dar ash-Shafa', events that evoked the massacre of June 5, 1975/Khordad 15, 1342 SH); and the ruthless armed attacks of imperialism's lackeys on the theological centers of learning- whose sole concern is the pursuit of knowledge, Islamic jurisprudence, and the vindication of the Qur'an and constructive Islamic injunctions-smashing doors and windows, breaking people's heads and hands, beating them to the point of death, as well as flinging defenseless youths from roof-tops. All for the 'crimes' of expressing opinions contrary to those of the Shah's party and for holding memorial services for those slain on June 5 (Khordad 15).

Date: July 11, 1975/Tir 02, 1354 SH/Rajab 1, 1395 AH.

Place: Najaf, Iraq

Subject: Expressing regrets on the suppression of the people, hoping for their awakening

Addressees: The Iranian nation

If our universities were proper universities then when the students there try to speak a word of truth, the police would not suppress them so. The things they do to them! They beat the girls, they beat the boys, and they beat our youth and imprison them. This is because our universities are not independent. We don't have universities. Universities which are controlled by one person cannot be called universities. The learning environment should be a free environment.

Date: Circa January 1978/End of Dey 1365 SH/Safar 1398 AH.

Place: Shaykh Ansari Mosque, Najaf, Iraq

Theme: Crimes of the Pahlavi regime

Occasion: Tragedy of the massacre of people of Qum on Dey 19, 1365 SH/January 9, 1978.

Addressees: Clergy, theology students and a group of people

Our universities are shut for half the year and our seminaries and students are beaten up and injured several times a year, and then thrown into prisons.

---

[31] On 15th Khordad 1354 SH, ceremonies and demonstrations were held in Faydiyyah Madrasah and the Dar ash-Shafa' to commemorate the anniversary of uprising of 15th Khordad, 1342. On 17th Khordad (2 days later), the army and forces of Shah's regime attacked Faydiyyah Madrasah and the Dar ash-Shafa'.

Date: April 24, 1978/Urdibehesht 4, 1357 SH/Jamadi al-Awwal 16, 1398 AH.

Place: Najaf, Iraq

Subject: The socio-political affairs of Iran

Interviewer: Lucien George (reporter the French daily, Le Monde)

Do they have any regard for our education system? If they do, then why are the schools in Iran either totally or partially closed? And why do the university lecturers suspend their lectures? It is because the government won't leave the university alone. What have these students done to deserve being deprived of education? What kind of respect does this regime show for education?

Date: May 13, 1978/Khordad 01, 1357 SH/Jamadi ath-Thani 23, 1397 AH.

Place: Shaykh Ansari Mosque, Najaf, Iraq

Subject: Religious duty; to rise up against the Shah

Occasion: The arrival of the anniversary of the bloody uprising of Khordad 15, 1342 SH

Addressees: Religious students, clergy and a group of Iranian residents in Iraq

They have made our universities such that our students cannot study properly. There is so much pressure on them. Nowadays no one can study in our theological schools or universities. The universities are always on strike. It has been over a year now that they have been on strike; they cannot function; the regime does not let them function. Its agents storm the universities, beating and injuring both men and women, or arresting them and taking them off to prison. The same happens in the schools. Every so often they attack the schools and assault the pupils and teachers there. The religious students and university students cannot study in such a tense atmosphere, and now it is the same for the school-children. Nowadays they are beating the school-children, even killing them.

Date: October 12, 1978/Mehr 29, 1357 SH/Dhu'l-Qa'dah 18, 1398 AH.

Place: Neauphle-le-Chateau, Paris, France

Subject: America's mission for the Shah

Addressees: A group of Iranian students and residents abroad

He,[32] who has turned to politicians and the youth of the nation, and seeks their help for the country, is the very same person who used to, and still is executing, torturing and imprisoning them by the groups, has and still is seeping our youth in cold blood and has turned our universities into our youth slaughter-houses (sacrificial altars).

I am grieving over the crimes recently committed to Islam's children in the universities. I thank the precious students who have given lives for Islam and the country, and have stood up against the Shah with clenched fists, and have condemned him.

Date: November 7, 1978/Aban 16, 1357 SH/Dhu'l-Hijjah 6, 1398 AH.

Place: Neauphle-le-Chateau, Paris, France

Occasion: Coming to power of the military cabinet

Addressees: The Iranian nation

All the respectable tribes and clans suffered and not only they alone, but also all strata of the people suffered including all religious people and clerics, and every single person in the nation was under pressure. The situation was aggravated to the point where neither women nor men had any freedom of choice. Neither clergymen nor university people could fulfill their duties. The Pahlavis lost all the luminaries of Iran and had a mission not to leave any source of pride for Iran. Our tribes and clans were a source of pride and they suppressed them.

Date: April 01, 1979/Farvardin 12, 1358 SH/Jamadi al-Awwal 21, 1399 AH.

Place: Qum

Subject: Iran's condition during the Pahlavi Dynasty

Audience: Representatives of the Bakhtiyari tribes from Izeh (township)

If we have a proper university and a clerical order in its full sense, they will not allow the foreigners to ruin the prestige of the country. Therefore, they targeted these two fronts as they had considered them to be dangerous for themselves. But their way of attacking them was different. In Reza Khan's time, which I remember and most of you do not, they would use bayonets to attack this front and smash it. And so they used to attack the seminaries, arresting the people and taking them away. They used to remove the turbans of the clergymen and strip off their cloaks. They used to close down the seminaries and the mosques. They did away altogether with the mourning observances

---

[32] Imam (ra) refers to Mohammad Reza Shah Pahlavi, who in the last months of his government apparently repented for his past atrocities against people.

and preachings. They thought that they would be able to obliterate the clergy in this manner. But they would not employ such methods in the case of the universities as they feared the repercussions abroad. So they used other means to stop the students from developing

Date: June 27, 1979/Tir 6, 1358 SH/Sha'ban 2, 1399 AH.

Place: Qum

Subject: The role of the unity of the seminary and the university; the issue of factionalism and party politics

Audience: Students of the Islamic Association of the Teachers' Training University, Tehran

Their purpose was to purge the country of those people; to crush these people who had the power to jeopardize their interests. What they had realized in the cities was that the clergy constituted a powerful group. They had targeted the clergy before the universities had come into existence. After the number of the universities and the students increase, they, too, became the object of their attention. They suppressed them in a certain way.

Date: Afternoon, July 4, 1979/Tir 31, 1358 SH/Sha'ban 9, 1399 AH.

Place: Qum

Subject: Imperialist plots and the domination of the tribes by Pahlavi

Audience: A group of people from Bouyer-Ahmad tribe

SECTION 3

UNIVERSITY AND CULTURAL REVOLUTION

Universities and Anti-Revolutionary Groups

Yes, my dear ones! Rise together in full awareness in the schools, universities and teachers' colleges, and strive jointly for the salvation of Islam and the country. Before everything else, you must adhere in practice to the invaluable precepts of Islam that have insured the welfare of nations. Alert the groups that- having been duped by foreign propaganda- have accepted or are inclined to certain ideologies, to the ploys of the enemy while exposing the crimes of the deceitful heads of the deviationist doctrines. You must also positively eschew disunity and discord and remind them clearly of our demands that are the demands of the oppressed. Recommend our motto to them which is also that of the oppressed, deprived people. Perhaps they will join you by a proper understanding of the matter. Tell them on my behalf that the Islam that you have heard about from others and those unacquainted with the teachings of the Qur'an, or what the discord- sowing deviationists and the puppets of expansionists have introduced to you, is not Islam. Come, hear about dear Islam from the savants who are well versed in the logic of the Qur'an, and learn the things that are beyond your ken and perception. Do not be deceived by the propagandists of the expansionist powers. A cursory glance at the condition of the heads of such countries is enough to awaken you.

Very recently you saw the Chinese leader[33] without any regard for our dear departed-slain by the Shah's henchmen for the "crime" of demanding freedom- officially backing the Shah with the utmost impudence. The same is the case of the Soviet Union and the leaders in the Kremlin who supported and are supporting the Shah over the massacres of Khordad 15 and those of recent days. All the communist powers are making deadly weapons out of the lifeblood of the meek nations to destroy mankind. Then there is America- the great world-devourer- whose real self is clear for all to see.

Date: October 8, 1978/Mehr 16, 1357 SH/Dhu'l-Qa'dah 1398 AH.

Place: Neauphle-le-Chateau, Paris

Subject: Commencement of the academic year

Addressees: The public

Occasionally, some slogans are used in the universities that are being taken advantage of by the regime. Our youth should know that China and Russia feed on our blood just as America and Britain do. My request from you is to avoid using the Shah's

---

[33] Imam (ra) points to visit of Hua Guofeng, the ex-leader of Chinese Communist Party who came to Iran on official state visit in the month of Shahrivar, 1357 SH. He praised Mohammad Reza Shah in his speech. After the success of Islamic Revolution of he sought forgiveness for that from Iranian nation.

95

slogans, and to stand on your own feet without having any inclination toward the West or the East. Do not be deceived by international looters. Those pulling you into the direction of these types of slogans are of the regime affiliates; keep away from them and join your other friends, and by using the slogans of monotheism and Islam, cut the hands of Pahlavi dynasty and the gang of oil guzzlers from the country, and return to the arms of Islam. Contrary to other ideologies that have made false claims that their leaders have never acted upon, and have made us poor and dependent by taking away Iran's resources. Islam answers the call of all deprived people. We welcome you with open arms and we are at your service. Islam has come for the salvation of the poor.

Date: October 26, 1978/Aban 4, 1357 SH/Dhu'l-Qa'dah 23, 1398 AH.

Place: Neauphle-le-Chateau, Paris, France

Subject: Warning on the withdrawal of the royal jewels by Muhammad Reza Pahlavi

Occasion: Aban 4, the Shah's birthday

Addressees: The Iranian nation

And you, gentlemen of the university, note that presently a group of those who are affiliated to foreigners and are their agents, cannot tolerate the fact that we intend to build up an independent and free Iran. This group, which is disrupting the peaceful situation, cannot bear to see an independent Iran. They wish to see Iran affiliated to either the USSR or the USA, and it seems to me that they are more related to the US under another name close to the USSR. You must guide these people; guide them if they heed your guidance. Guide our youths. Prevent the turmoil in which the Revolution is being plunged into, an Islamic revolution that has united all people. Now, a group of people is actively trying to contaminate this Revolution. Introduce them to your students, to our youths. Tell the youths that such people are foreign agents disguised as nationalists. They are but foreign lackeys. They wish to take Iran back to its previous state, but in another form. This is now a duty binding upon you. Do not let this contamination find its way into the universities. Do not allow demonstrations, which I heard were held yesterday, escalate at universities. Be aware that these demonstrations are instigated by the remnants of the defunct corrupt regime.

Date: February 16, 1979/Bahman 27, 1357 SH/Rabi' al-Awwal 18, 1399 AH.

Place: Alawi School, Tehran

Subject: Confronting plots made by small groups to dissolve the army

Occasion: Re-opening of universities after the victory of the Islamic Revolution

Audience: 150 people from university professors and Islamic society of academicians

Political convulsions, whether deliberately instigated or not, have, at times, been observed occurring at universities. If they are perpetrated intentionally, I have to say that it is tantamount to a treachery. If it is done unintentionally, then I have to say it is ignorance. Today is not a day that this nation should upset this achieved victory by engendering these convulsions.

Date: February 18, 1979/Bahman 29, 1357 SH/Rabi' al-Awwal 02, 1399 AH.

Place: Alawi School, Tehran

Subject: Sowing seeds of discord between the clergymen and intellectuals

Audience: Representatives of Iran's Writers Association

If they can, they accomplish their mission in the factories, if they can, they do it in agriculture, they do it in the universities and these people; though, they are educated or are pursuing an education, are simple-minded and young, and are easily affected and deceived. They offer a few persuasive and tempting words and deceive them; otherwise, they (students and academics) have no bad intentions.

Time/Date: Morning, 9: 00 am, April 18, 1979/Farvardin 29, 1358 SH/Jamadi al-Awwal 02, 1399 AH.

Place: Qum

Subject: The need for existence of committees and their purification

Audience: Commanders and officials of the 14 committees of the Islamic Revolution in Tehran as well as Messrs. Mahdavi Kani, Maliki, Morvarid, Mufatteh, Muhammadi Golpayegani, Jalali Khomeini, Haqqi, Baqiri Kani, Khosroushahi and Zanjani

Coming now to the university, is it to its good for our youth not to be educated? Should they come into the university every day and do something, hold a meeting and create-I should say- disturbances so that our youth do not study? To whose benefit is it? Is it to our country's benefit? Will it be in our nation's interest or to its detriment if our university is proper and does its work well? Well, they (the splinter groups) are preventing the university from commencing its work; who is going to gain by this? The foreigners will benefit by this as well. The reason is that just as those hands (the ex-regime) did not allow the university to function properly in order to make us need the foreigners in these matters as well and to seek foreign assistance, these people are also doing the same thing so that we remain in need of the foreigners for everything that we want.

Date: June 31, 1979/Khordad 23, 1358 SH/Rajab 18, 1399 AH.

Place: Qum

Subject: The splinter groups creating disorder and hatching plots in the universities, the workplaces and farms, and the need to confront them; the danger of discord and deviation

Audience: A group of students from Tehran University

Sir, are you sitting by to see some communists come and take over the university? Are you inferior to them in any way? You are greater in number; you have better credentials. You can expose their treachery by stating these facts in that place; in the university. You can reveal their treason so that they go away. Stand your ground and speak out. Tell them, Sir. Each one of you should ask them who they are to come into the university and create disturbances. Ask them what they are up to; do they want to teach you? Tell them to first consider as to what they are in this country. Ask them whether they belong to this country or are foreign agents out to trouble you. Stand firm, Sir, and speak out. These people need to have their mouths shut up, Sir! Your numbers are greater, your credentials are better and their treacherous deeds are evident. It is necessary to speak out. Gather together and mention the issues. If you see an official or teacher who is a communist, expel him from the university. I am not telling you to fight them; we do not want a conflict now. But should it lead to that at any time, we will drive them out within a day! But we do not want a fight now; we want it to be done gently; by talking to them. They talk and you, too, should talk. You should not just sit around and let others speak for you. A clergyman should come forward and speak up. You yourselves, each one of you who can, should go and stand in front of them and talk to them. They will say something and you, too, say what you have to say. Then you should point out their actions, one by one, to them and ask them why they are doing so. Ask them whose subjects they are that they are doing such things. Are they Iranians who are doing all this, or are they affiliated to America or the Soviet Union? Are they serving these powers or Iran? In case they are serving them, they have no place here. Let them go to those countries and serve; they are working for them. It is obvious that America stands to gain from the non-existence of cultivation in Iran; everybody is aware of this.

Date: June 31, 1979/Khordad 23, 1358 SH/Rajab 18, 1399 AH.

Place: Qum

Subject: The splinter groups creating disorder and hatching plots in the universities, the workplaces and farms, and the need to confront them; the danger of discord and deviation

Audience: A group of students from Tehran University

Write about these things in the university; have them published. Each one of you should go to those who are against (the country's interests) and tell them that they are saboteurs; ask them what they have to say to us. Ask them how they can take control of a university when they are saboteurs. A mischief-making thief cannot run a university.

Date: June 31, 1979/Khordad 23, 1358 SH/Rajab 18, 1399 AH.

Place: Qum

Subject: The splinter groups creating disorder and hatching plots in the universities, the workplaces and farms, and the need to confront them; the danger of discord and deviation

Audience: A group of students from Tehran University

Our university that ought to be the center of molding human beings, and the students, who are committed to Islam, made sacrifices for it and endeavored for its sake, should now be vigilant about a limited number of people who go into the university premises with the intention of preventing Islam from coming to fruition. It is not that they want the university to be reformed; no. They are afraid of it being reformed.

They (who are Westernized) do not want any proper person to be found in the university. You should make efforts to expel those people who have entered the universities and are engaged in seditious activities. You should not complain that somebody has come and is saying certain things. Well, go and confront him; ask him what he is saying. Ask him whether his heart burns for the nation. If so, why did he oppose the referendum? Why is he not allowing the farmers to reap their harvest? Is it other than to create a market for America? The Shah used to do this, and now the little shahs are doing it! Why is he not allowing the factories to start operating? In case they started working, our requirements from abroad would decrease. They would decrease from the West. They are operatives that want to make us dependent on them (the West). Recognize your friends and your enemies. The intellectuals should ostracize the enemies of Islam from their centers.

Date: June 15, 1979/Khordad 25, 1358 SH/Rajab 02, 1399 AH.

Place: Qum

Subjects: The Constitution of the Islamic Republic and the obstructionism of the West-worshippers; the danger posed by the Westernized pseudo-intellectuals

Audience: Air Force personnel

Our thinkers, intellectuals and all the university students and professors ought to realize that this is the plan, the effects of which we are now witnessing. This splitting into groups is for this very purpose of not allowing the solidarity that has been there to be maintained. They do not want the people to wake up and find their own way; that path of being united that Islam has ordained. God has made it incumbent on the people to: "*Hold fast, all of you together to the cable of Allah, and do not be divided.*" (Qur'an 3:103) Be together and do not be dispersed. All evils result from dispersion, while all blessings and prosperity lie in holding fast to God.

Date: June 27, 1979/Tir 6, 1358 SH/Sha'ban 2, 1399 AH.

Place: Qum

Subject: The role of the unity of the seminary and the university; the issue of factionalism and party politics

Audience: Students of the Islamic Association of the Teachers' Training University, Tehran

These people did not want a human being to be to be found. They make efforts to ensure that the university- which is of special interest to them and is a target of their attacks- does not have the right programs. Even if you assume that they have a correct program, they shall not allow it to be implemented and will create a disturbance every day; they would create disturbances in order to preoccupy our youth.

Date: July 12, 1979/Tir 03, 1358 SH/Sha'ban 26, 1399 AH.

Place: Qum

Subject: Characteristics of an ungodly regime; the educational role of radio and television

Audience: Employees of Darya Radio

And yet another of their plans was, besides several others, not to let them to concentrate on their studies in the university. They created a faction called leftists to pour into the universities and create disturbances and get into fights and so forth; and to wean away the university students and the youth from the classrooms and bring them outside to engage in fights and other things. They would promote leftist ideas in the universities to draw their attention to these matters and such issues. All these were things that were done on the basis of a plan so that we become indifferent to the destiny of our country.

Date: July 12, 1979/Tir 03, 1358 SH/Sha'ban 26, 1399 AH.

Place: Qum

Subject: Confrontation of the believers with the arrogant; praising the struggles of the clergy; problems of the youth

Audience: Students of Babol College

We are affected by tomorrow: universities and the conspiracies that they are supposed to brew in the universities. I am running out of time to talk about them. My time is up. But let me add that our youth themselves the majority of whom are committed, the majority of whom belong to this patriotic nation, and the majority of whom believe in Islam; they should not allow a bunch of people to come there and create a state of chaos and engage in acts of conspiracy. Turn your back on them. Do not read their books. I do not suggest setting their books on fire. No, setting things on fire is wrong. Avoiding their books is more effective than setting them on fire. When you set something on fire, people will imagine it has contained something important which has caused the burning of it. But when you turn your back on them, everything is over. Just do not buy their books; do not allow yourselves to be the customers of their books. No, do not be the customers of theirs. Suppose that they bring tons of books and unload them there. Do not rush on them; do not burn their books; do not tear them up either. Just do not read them and do not buy them. If you do not read or buy them, you will see for yourselves that in a matter of a few days, everything will be over. They bring these books for you to read; they want to (change you) from your Eastern state to becoming a Westerner and yet in its worst forms of dictatorship; they want to impose the worst forms of dictatorship on you. Do not buy those books.

Date: September 8, 1979/Shahrivar 17, 1358 SH/Shawwal 16, 1399 AH.

Place: Faydiyyah Madrasah, Qum

Subject: Liberation from West-struckness; explaining the Ayyam Allah (Days of Allah).

Occasion: The anniversary of the 17th of Shahrivar

Audience: Different strata of the people

At every place where the teaching centers are located, there shall be groups that will create trouble; and from Tehran and other places also they have come here and asked

101

what is to be done. They are thinking of presenting a plan but the important thing is that those that are among the subversive elements are in a minority. The majority is not subversive elements and this majority must shun any differences if at all they exist among themselves and with their gathering without causing a confrontation or physical fights, they should remove them from the scene with their protest gathering so that they are not able to engage in any activity. The important point is that those who are themselves in the universities where the Ministry of Education is present, whether they be professors or whether they be youth who are there, they should themselves thwart them in a reasonable manner because these people have nothing to offer. The subversive elements have nothing to say; they only want to create disturbances. If any of them makes a claim, go to him and ask him what he has to say. Ask him to talk. You will come to know that they have nothing to say. Their only language is to create disturbances and prevent anything from being done and this matter is in the hands of the university students, centers of learning, and the professors and non-academic staff to help in this affair. God willing, we also shall take certain steps and the government also plans to do something about it.

Date: September 15, 1979/Shahrivar 24, 1358 SH/Shawwal 23, 1399 AH.

Place: Qum

Subject: Avoiding conflict; logical confrontation with the subversive elements

Audience: Professors of the University of Shiraz and heads of the Education Ministry in Fars province

That is to say, real human beings are made in universities. In later years, the destiny of our country is in the hands of those who graduate from universities. As you know, since the destiny of the country is in the hands of young people who are graduated from universities and engage in different activities, those struggling to sap the progress of the country are sensitive to university. They do not want our country to have useful universities.

Date: September 02, 1979/Shahrivar 29, 1358 SH/Shawwal 28, 1399 AH.

Place: Qum

Subject: Mission of Islamic associations, Foreigners' intervention in turmoil's, Opponents of *Wilayate Faqih*

Audience: The universities Islamic associations' representatives Nationwide

From now on, you[34] will face these problems when the universities open. You are required to deal vigilantly and wisely with these people. You should consult with one another as to how to deal with them. They come in the name of freedom and they are seeking a weird kind of freedom. They want an absolute one, but the freedom. Everyone defines them from his or her point of view. You will certainly face these problems.

Treat those individuals attentively without any conflict. Conflict is not proper. You should act in a way that strips them of pretending to be in the right. If you get involved in conflicts with them and let us suppose that you will beat them, that you have resorted to force and beating them because you are short of logic. If any of such individuals happen to come in university and raise an issue, go over to them and ask them what exactly they say. Once they might aim to make ado. Most of them are like this. Their leaders provoke them to raise Cane. In such cases, arrange a meeting with them and let them voice their opinions. You will see they have nothing to say. Their sole aim is to create tension the universities open and carry out their programs. Confront them without being engaged in clash with them. If they have a gathering of one hundred people or even a thousand, you should gather ten or twenty thousand people facing them. Raise your own issues without conflict. This is how it must be done. I hope, God willing, dealing with those affairs will never reach that level. Nevertheless, once we come to realize that they are hatching plots against us, there would be another course of action to take.

Date: September 02, 1979/Shahrivar 29, 1358 SH/Shawwal 28, 1399 AH.

Place: Qum

Subject: Mission of Islamic associations, Foreigners' intervention in turmoil's, Opponents of *Wilayate Faqih*

Audience: The universities Islamic associations' representatives Nationwide

With the opening of universities, colleges, high school and elementary school, certain groups may work sabotage in the activity of universities' under alluring names and propaganda, preventing students from attending their classes. Collegians and students should treat them coldly and thwart their plots. People know they are the ones who were separate from the path of the nation and in the path of *taghout* right from the very beginning of the revolution till now. They are the ones who were dissociated from the Islamic revolution and moved against it and who struggled to undermine the referendum. They also disobey the votes of the absolute majority of the people. They are against the nation and interests. They are dependent upon the West, East and the

---

[34] Imam (ra) refers to the members of Islamic Students Associations countrywide.

former regime. Do not pay attention to their propaganda. Stay away from them as you did from *taghout* and the *taghouti* regime.

What I have repeatedly underscored as secret of the victory is the unification of collegiate groups and formation of an Islamic-national group against the deviants who struggle to create discord. They strive to lead astray you the dear youth who are the hope of the nation and on whom the promotion and prosperity of the country depend. They work to prevent you from taking steps towards progress of the country and withholding you from preoccupation in science and literature, contribute to advancement and emancipation from old-age and neo-colonialism. Beware that differences and dissensions are the sources of all miseries and slaveries. Some corrupted agents may find their way to universities and other training centers and start provoking disunity among you by calculated plans. You are required to identify them vigilantly and show their true identity to the young generation, so they might be aware of their intrigues and try to frustrate them…

Islam is a religion supported by cogent argument and logic; it never fears the freedom of expression and the pen. It is not afraid of other schools, which have been proved ineffective and doomed to failure endorsed by their own scholars. You, respected students, should not treat the followers of other religions harshly and severely nor should be engaged in commotion conflict with them. Talk to them and invite the Islamic scholars to discuss the matter with them. One of their plans is to draw you in conflicts and make illegal use of that. We agree with freedom and logic. However, if we face intrigue and sabotage, we have another duty to fulfill.

I beseech the Almighty God not to allow this happen at all.

Date: September 22, 1979/Shahrivar 13, 1358 SH/Shawwal 03, 1399 AH.

Place: Qum

Subject: Foreigners' attempts to sweep the Islamic content of the scientific and cultural programs

Occasion: Opening of academic year

Addressees: Professors, collegians and students

One of the important issues, which are a prerequisite to reforms, is to refine all centers particularly cultural and scientific ones. Councils composed of learned and faithful individuals committed to revolution and with the support of chiefs, professors, collegians and teachers, must help purge the cultural-educational centers from corrupt elements and agents of the former regime. As long as these agents, who are at the service of aliens at a wide scale, particularly scientific and educational centers, are not purged, we will not be unable to gain intellectual dependence and will be unable to stand on our own feet.

Date: September 22, 1979/Shahrivar 13, 1358 SH/Shawwal 03, 1399 AH.

Place: Qum

Subject: Foreigners' attempts to sweep the Islamic content of the scientific and cultural programs

Occasion: Opening of academic year

Addressees: Professors, collegians and students

I would like to remark that the perverse and deviated groups in Kurdistan, which are anti-Islam, committed the troubles. In the colleges, the leftist groups, pro-America, did all that turbulence and tumult in the sacred places. The disturbances and clashes that the illegitimate government of Iraq is doing at the borders; it appears that all these are linked with tangible proof to the assault of Carter and his military intervention. At this sensitive time, if these perverted and devious groups go on with their mischievous, the nation will conclude that the mischief-mongers have a close contact and connection directly with America- the world-hungry. As such it will decide its obligation towards them. To ignore or to forget or to forego or to pardon will not be our polity then.

Date: April 25, 1980/Urdibehesht 5, 1359 SH/Jamadi ath-Thani 9, 1400 AH.

Place: Shemiran, Darband, Tehran

Subject: The mistake of Carter and its consequences

Occasion: The American military assault on Iran (the Tabas incident)

Addressees: The Muslim nation of Iran

The entire nation and you the respected students long for Islam. You want an Islamic culture. You do not want to see the persons like those we had in the past regime, and the persons of their ilk that come from abroad. Now they do not want the universities and even the high schools to remain in their healthy and pristine position. On the other hand, you are determined to make the base of the culture an Islamic one to obtain an Islamic output. You want to make the culture to be like a frame that the persons therein be so developed to be beneficial to the society, to Islam and to the Islamic county. The efforts of these people are to stop you making progress in what you want and holding you from attaining the end you have. Now it is essential that you be vigilant of their plans and plots. It would not be surprising that they will infiltrate into the universities, colleges and schools, and whisper their satanic aims to deviate you from.

Date: June 5, 1980/Khordad 14, 1359 SH/Rajab 02, 1400 AH.

Place: Jamaran Husayniyyah Tehran

Subject: Internal change of a nation is the source of victory, unity between religious institute and the university; Importance of Friday prayers

Audience: Professors and students of Divinity and the Islamic Sciences College, Tehran University

What was the purpose of these fortifications that took place in the universities; and who did that? Those who wanted to make the westernized university an Islamic one, should be both Muslims and very committed to Islam. Were they in that fortification, or the pens and the same endeavors, which were active in the days of Reza Khan seeking an opportunity to break Islam and its power?

Date: May 24, 1980/Khordad 3, 1359 SH/Rajab 9, 1400 AH.

Place: Jamaran, Tehran

Subject: Fifty years long plots to create divisions among the various classes of the society

Audience: Teachers, students of the religious institutions, professors, members of the Islamic associations, students of the universities all over the country

The university has served as a war (operations) room for the Kurdistan issue. That is, there is a room in the university where from they have been directing the war in Kurdistan; the democrat party's war, and that of other malevolent elements. Do you want such a university?

Do you who raised that clamor about the university being closed, want such a university to be reopened? Should the war room be opened for the guidance of Democrats and their like for them to ruin Iran? Do you want to feel sorry about this university? Isn't it better for it to be closed rather than remain open?

The people who have been assigned to carry out the Cultural Revolution in the universities, should, of course, make haste in the first place to get the opportunity for them to act so that the university becomes Islamic and exists for the nation. Otherwise, if it is reopened, anybody who wants to enter it will do so. Did you not see what mischief there was when it was open? It was the stronghold and the war (operations) headquarters of the communists. You are sorry that it is closed. Do you realize what you are saying? Are you saying this understandingly? If so, your position ought to be made known. But if you are talking out of ignorance, on what grounds do you want it to be reopened now when, a few months or a year or so ago, it had been turned into a center of all kinds of mischief, and was in the clutches of the communists, the guerrillas and all the other hypocrite organizations? Do you want them to come back?

Date: Before noon, December 18, 1980/Azar 27, 1359 SH/Safar 01, 1401 AH.

Place: Jamaran, Tehran

Subject: The importance of the roles of the seminary and the university; stating the duties of these two institutions of learning.

Occasion: The day of unity between the seminary and the university

Audience: Teachers and students of Qum Theological Center; the student members of the office for the consolidation of unity between the seminary and the university

My dear ones! Those who have gone astray and those who want this religion to fail in its mission and those who have faced humiliation at the hands of the school of Islam and those who see the religion of Islam as being against their personal interests as well as the interests of their lords and masters are first aiming to bring about deviation within the schools in which our children, our youth, as well as our adolescents are seeking to gain perfection. They are lurking for the opportunity to bring about deviation in schools which are the fountainheads of all progress and to lead astray our adolescent youth who should be carrying this country toward its optimum growth and who should rescue it from the clutches of strangers. And that is why you can see that the primary schools right up to the university have become their centers of conspiracy and you are their targets and they want to lead you astray from the precious path of Islam; and to turn the universities and the secondary schools and the primary schools and all the centers of education and moral training into centers in which, if education is offered, it would only be for the benefit of the superpowers. And that whatever is gained in those places and in those sacred centers is to the benefit of the superpowers. They begin right from the kindergarten and as our youth and our children move forward they have plans to chase them there. The kindergarten schools, right up to the universities, are under the detestable sway of imperialism and they know very well that if they manage to lead these youths away from the straight path and from the Path of Allah, they will attain to their wicked goals. And that is why their attempts and their targets begin with the kindergartens and continue up to the universities. And those centers which should be used exclusively for social welfare- for spiritual welfare in society and for material welfare in society and to secure the future of our beloved country- are dragged by them into corruption and then they stand aside and watch our youth because these misled ones have done their job and want to spread corruption at your hands.

Those who step into schools, and with their misleading propaganda compel our youth to act against what they learn through education and do not want them to get educated and do not want them to grow up into youth who are assets for their own country, find various excuses to drag them into staging protests and into differences and then stand aside and laugh at you and at us. Their attempts to re-open the universities before any proper planning was done were because they wanted to tender our society the same former conditions that prevailed when people like them were in power in those days. That is what they wanted. And they enter the kindergartens and the secondary schools with their own propaganda and their own instigation in order to compel our youth and our children to involve themselves in violence and fights instead of seeking education and instead of involving themselves in the purification of the soul, and instead of imparting Islamic ethics, leave them to face corruption, which is nothing but their former strategy. Our children, our youth, all of them, boys as well as girls, should put in all their efforts to recognize them and to understand what their aims are. They should recognize who those people were in the former days. They should know that they are busy causing corruption behind the scenes while our youth from the army and the revolutionary guards and the gendarmerie and all strata of people, tribes, and others are busy sacrificing themselves in the war centers and at the battlefronts. They are busy helping their lords and masters. They should know that they are supported by the foreign radio stations and by all the corrupt radio stations while the Islamic Republic is condemned by them. And they want to eliminate the Islamic Republic. In the same manner that Saddam and other such deviants have attacked our country and have started war. They are also waging the same war although in a different form in the schools, the colleges, and the universities. They are all foreign agents and you should stay very alert, wherever you are, on these matters lest you suddenly open your eyes and find that you have been deceived.

Date: January 22, 1981/Bahman 2, 1359 SH/Rabi' al-Awwal 15, 1401 AH.

Place: Jamaran, Tehran

Subject: Foreign conspiracies instigating deviation in the scientific-cultural centers of the country

Audience: Various strata of people, revolutionary guards heading for the battlefront, and school students from Tehran

Unfortunately, though three years have elapsed since the victory of the Islamic revolution and since the resistance of the Islamic Republic against the East and West and their perverted schools of thought and the loyalty of the Islamic Republic to Islam as a negation of all dependence and perversion, we are troubled by the dependence of groups on either of the two poles and the allegiance of perverted schools of thought and their dependence on either of them. We are also up against those perverted ones who have infiltrated educational centers and by giving them leeway, we were at risk of leading astray the youth. God forbid, when our children go astray and feel inclined to the Western to Eastern countries, all aspects of the society will become dependent on either the West or East, and all efforts of the nation and the blood of the dear youth will go to waste.

Date: September 22, 1981/Shahrivar 13, 1360 SH/Dhu'l-Qa'dah 23, 1401 AH.

Place: Jamaran, Tehran

Subject: Effects and consequences of independent versus dependent culture

Occasion: Beginning of academic year

Addressees: High school and university students, the youth, teachers and professors

….Great Islamic Jihad to confront them and not allow their negative propaganda to corrupt our youth. At the universities and colleges and high schools and academic centers, the teachers and students- the professors and the students- take care not to allow those corrupt elements and the hypocrites and the non-hypocrite elements that are all corrupt gain influence and God forbid, revert the university to the situation it was in before.

Date: April 24, 1983/Urdibehesht 4, 1362 SH/Rajab 01, 1403 AH.

Place: Jamaran, Tehran

Subject: Era of decline of human values and dominance of satanic values

Occasion: Birth anniversary of Imam Muhammad-Taqi (a)

Audience: Ali-Akbar Parvaresh (Minister of Education), Ahmad Tawakkuli (Minister of Labor and Social Affairs), workers from all over the country, teachers and trainers in education, members of the Martyr Professor Murtada Mutahhari honoring committee

University is so important that corrupt views seek to find a wrong in it. They are in search of excuse. God willing they will not be successful. One should always be sensitive lest the bunker that can correct or destroy everything should be taken from you or harmed.

Date/Time: Morning, December 01, 1985/Azar 19, 1364 SH/Rabi' al-Awwal 27, 1406 AH.

Place: Jamaran, Tehran

Subject: University and the Cultural Revolution

Occasion: Anniversary of formation of the Supreme Cultural Revolution Council

Audience: Sayyid Ali Khamenei (President and chairman of the Supreme Cultural Revolution Council), members of the Cultural Revolution Council

The Need for Cultural Revolution

They are wasting the lives of our youngsters. That is, going to these colleges and universities is nothing but a waste of the lives of the teacher and the student. And the teachers know this; the students know this; everyone knows this; but still, that is the way things are. When we say that this page (in history) must be turned back, that all of these schemes which the foreigners have initiated in Iran via these evil agents of theirs must be abandoned, it is because we see that everything we happen to point to is rotten to the core!

Date: November 2, 1978/Aban 11, 1357 SH/Dhu'l-Hijjah 1, 1398 AH.

Place: Neauphle-le-Chateau, Paris, France

Subject: The alteration of the meaning of those terms used in the vocabulary of the Shah and of the powers supporting him.

Addressees: A group of Iranian students and residents abroad

The educational system we now have should be revised. The colonial educational system should be transformed into an independent educational system. Teachers in this educational system or the entire class of professors should be chosen with carefulness and they should be righteous and virtuous individuals. They should be ones to bring up our youth as righteous and not parasitic citizens. In the past, our youth had been brought up in a western way to make them west intoxicated. You should be independent; you should be unaffected by what is happening in the West! Do not think that many (wonderful) things happen in the West. They themselves (western people) are saying, "Nothing exciting is going on in the West!" Events do take place, but events regarding intellectual and human growth are very few. You must be independent and enhance your human growth. You must raise the children and youth with a humane upbringing. Headmasters and teachers that the government chooses for universities and schools to teach will have to be purged of any previous (Western) inclinations.

Teachers and instructors who were previously at the service of foreign individuals and the *taghout* must not be allowed to join (the teaching force) for the second time lest they push our children (educationally) backward once again. This is an issue of great significance in our educational system. Eventually, the educational system has to be transformed into a healthy, independent and humane system.

Date: March 02, 1979/Esfand 29, 1357 SH/Rabi' ath-Thani 12, 1399 AH.

Place: Qum

Subject: Causes of victory; endeavor to reach the final victory; advice to the nation and government

Occasion: Advent of the (Iranian) New Year

Audience: Provisional government's cabinet

All affairs must undergo transformation in an Islamic republic. In an Islamic republic, universities must become independent ones. Our educational system must be changed; colonial education must be an education of independence.

Date: April 1, 1979/Farvardin 21, 1358 SH/Jamadi al-Awwal 3, 1399 AH.

Place: Qum

Subject: The nation's decisive vote for the Islamic Republic

Occasion: Conclusion of the referendum and announcement of the vote

Addressees: The Iranian nation

God willing, when the Islamic government is established, we must join hands to remove the shortcomings, the most important of which is culture. Culture is the cornerstone of the nation; it is the basis of the identity of a nation, the basis of the independence of a nation. However, they have tried to make our culture colonial. They did their best to prevent the emergence of humanity. They feared human beings and they feared learned man. They did their best to prevent the appearance of the elite during their 50 and so years of monarchy. They did such harm to education such that there was neither education nor humanistic growth. They frightened us, they frightened us by their subversive propaganda such that we feared one another and did not trust one another. If someone fell sick, we would send him abroad while we had physicians here in Iran. They frightened us, shook us, and emptied us so hard that if we wanted to asphalt a road we used to send for foreigners. We had everything but the foreigners were the ones to manage the affairs of our army. The foreigners were the ones to exploit our oil, at a time that we had everything at our disposal. This was because they emptied us from what we were, they brainwashed us, and destroyed our self-reliance. Brothers! Bring up your youth by self-trust and by spiritual independence. Teachers! Train the youth to be independent and free. Make them self-reliant. We have everything but they made us to make believe we have nothing.

Date: April 19, 1979/Farvardin 29, 1358 SH/Jamadi al-Awwal 02, 1399 AH.

Place: Qum

Subject: Factors for victory; sabotage of the small groups; importance of culture

Audience: A number of educational staff of the city of Rafsanjan

The greatest development that must be brought about must take place in the culture. That is because culture is the single most important item that may send a nation to its doom, or yet may give rise to its ever greatness and power. Cultural programs are in need of development. Our culture must go through a great change. This is apart from government offices as culture has some other connotations. In this regard, we know there are many obstacles ahead of us. All the same, I appreciate the fact that you are prepared to do anything in the service of the destitute. This latter, of course, is very valuable. It is valuable both in the eyes of the Almighty God and the people. However, your real and fundamental responsibility is in the cultural area, people's poverty is worldly in nature and such deprivation is a mundane impoverishment, and your assistance to rectify this shortcoming is of great spiritual and moral value. However, those spiritual responsibilities that you have boil down to somehow rectifying the cultural poverty of our people and are of foremost priority; rectifying it in such a way to make it be of great benefit to your nation. This, however, may not be achieved unless there is faith.

Date: May 24, 1979/Khordad 3, 1358 SH/Jamadi ath-Thani 27, 1399 AH.

Place: Qum

Subject: Profession of clerics and academicians; creation of discord between the seminary and university; role of culture in the declination and amelioration of the society

Audience: Ali Shari'atmadari (Minister of Culture and Higher Education), chancellors of universities and institutions of higher education

However, the workforce is important. They ruined it and did not let it grow. They acted in a way in our country as to destroy its human resources. They left behind an outward appearance (of progress) but took the content away. They did all this to make us lose our self-confidence. They deprived us of our intellectual freedom, our spiritual freedom. This was worse than the deprivation of our independence due to which our country was not free. We had lost our morale. Whatever would take place was because of our way of thinking that all our affairs should be directed from abroad. If they wanted to asphalt a road or build one to link two cities, the experts had to come from abroad. They insulted our workforce; they deprived us of our meaningfulness. Anybody falling ill had to be taken to England; even now traces of this are present. The doctors who visit me say that they, themselves, are able to treat these people who are taken abroad; they say that they can cure them. But the people had been brought up in such a way as to be deprived of their self-confidence. Even our freedom to think (for ourselves) was taken away from us. We had become intellectually, mentally and psychologically dependent. Such dependence is really deplorable. We can get rid of military dependence within a day, a month. We can expel them (foreign military advisors). Economic dependence can be countered; and in quick time. But mental and human dependence are difficult matters. Because of propaganda, a child is brought up in a dependent way from his early childhood in his mother's lap up to the time he goes to primary school, to secondary school, to university; wherever he goes. He comes to believe that nothing can be accomplished without depending on foreign sources, and that we ourselves have nothing. The general thinking is that even our mindset is not right. Because of this, rectifying the matter is difficult; it cannot be done so quickly. All of us should join hands to rectify the situation so that this dependence is eliminated, thus leading to a country with a non-dependent economy and education. The people themselves should be intellectually free; free in thought, free in spirit. Even nowadays, wherever you go, in the gatherings convened by our intellectuals, you will find the same obsession with the West in what they say; the same words. They say the same things that they used to say in the days of the *taghout* when they would have their get-togethers. They are saying the same things once again. We have not left behind our dependence and Westernization; nor can we do it so quickly. That spokesman of theirs who is no more- may God bless his soul- had said that all our things should come from England! One of their notables says that all our things should be English. He had so lost his essence; he had become emptied of it; a person outwardly like all others but, in reality, dependent.

We cannot cleanse the minds so quickly of these intellectuals and "liberals" of the things that have been dinned into their heads for fifty, thirty, twenty years leading to their self-estrangement and self-negligence. A new culture is required; a transformative one. Our children, from the very beginning, should be brought up in a culture that is humane, Islamic and independent- a culture that is our very own, and in which our children grow up according to their own genius so that they can take their destiny in their own hands, so that the culture of Europe, of America, etc. is not repeatedly dinned into their ears. It used to be repeatedly dinned into their ears that everything of ours should be from there, all our affairs should be dependent on them (foreigners), even our mentality. Even when we want freedom, it should be of the Western type. We should be westernized. We want a type of freedom that is similar to that of the West

Date: May 03, 1979/Khordad 9, 1358 SH/Rajab 4, 1399 AH.

Place: Qum

Subject: Deprivation of intellectual and spiritual freedom more dangerous than political dependence; Westernization and the intellectual dependence of the intellectuals

Audience: The personnel of the Islamic Revolutionary Committees, Qazvin

The university is the source of all changes. It is from the university- whether of the old sciences or the modern ones- that a nation's prosperity and, in contrast, its adversity originate. The universities must be taken seriously. Every effort should be made to set them right; to make them Islamic.

Date: June 6, 1979/Khordad 16, 1358 SH/Rajab 11, 1399 AH.

Place: Qum

Subject: The need for the universities to become Islamic

Addressees: Doctors, professors and students of Shiraz University

But the issue of the upbringing of a nation lies in its education being of the right kind. You should endeavor to create an educational system of the independent Islamic kind. The youth brought up in such a system are those in whose hands lies the destiny of the country. Their proper upbringing, their serving the nation and their trustworthiness regarding the treasury, will all take effect under Islamic leadership. If a nation is educated like this in a complete system of Islamic education, the country will enjoy peace and progress.

Date: June 11, 1979/Khordad 12, 1358 SH/Rajab 16, 1399 AH.

Place: Qum

Subject: The need for government to learn a lesson from the Shah's fate; the difference between a popular government and a puppet government

Audience: Ibrahim Yazdi (Minister of Foreign Affairs), Gundurz Rukchun (Turkish Minister of Foreign Affairs)

Our university that ought to be the center of molding human beings, and the students, who are committed to Islam, made sacrifices for it and endeavored for its sake, should now be vigilant about a limited number of people who go into the university premises with the intention of preventing Islam from coming to fruition. It is not that they want the university to be reformed; no. They are afraid of it being reformed. May God bless the late Fayd Qummi's[35] soul; may God be pleased with him. During the time of Reza Khan, in this Faydiyyah Madrasah, near the place where there was a pool, he had once said to me: "Well, what does it matter? They want to segregate the pious (clerics) from the impious." They had wanted to subject them to an examination which was meant to do away with the clergy. He had believed that they wanted to set the pious clergymen aside and send the bad ones away. I had told him that they feared those that were upright, the pious clergy. What fear had they of the bad ones? The impious were with them, they were in league with them. They feared those who were pious. The university should also reform itself; the academics, the pious ones, themselves, should do it, those people that have now come here and, as they say, want to reform the university, are actually worried about its being reformed. The fear that somebody (pious) might, at sometimes, arise from the university and strike them in the mouth! Those people (at that time) also used to fear that a pious clergyman might strike them in the mouth! Everybody is afraid of an upright person. Nobody fears a manikin!

They (who are Westernized) do not want any proper person to be found in the university. You should make efforts to expel those people who have entered the universities and are engaged in seditious activities

Date: June 15, 1979/Khordad 25, 1358 SH/Rajab 02, 1399 AH.

Place: Qum

Subjects: The Constitution of the Islamic Republic and the obstructionism of the West-worshippers; the danger posed by the Westernized pseudo-intellectuals

Audience: Air Force personnel

The differences between Western and Islamic universities should lie in the programs that Islam plans for the universities. Whatever status the universities in the West attain, they only understand nature. They do not master it for the sake of spiritualities. Islam

---

[35] Marhum Ayatullah Sheikh Mohammad Fayd Qummi was one of the teachers on the *howzeh* of Qum. He passed away in the year 1328 AH. The assassination of Commander Ali Rizm Ara by Fidaeyane Islam group took place in the gathering in Ark Mosque held after passing away of Sheikh Fayd Qummi.

does not view the natural sciences independently. All the natural sciences, whatever their status, do not meet the requirements of Islam. Islam masters nature to make it meaningful. It leads the natural sciences toward unity and monotheism. All the sciences that you name and the foreign universities that you praise- and they do deserve praise- are just a page of the world, a page smaller than all the other ones. The world, from the time God created it up to the very end, is an entity whose natural pleasures are very insignificant. All the natural sciences together are very insignificant in comparison with the divine sciences as all the natural things that exist are trivial in relation to the divine entities.

Date: Afternoon, July 4, 1979/Tir 31, 1358 SH/Sha'ban 9, 1399 AH.

Place: Qum

Subject: The differences between a Western university and an Islamic one

Audience: Tehran University professors

What is important is that the culture be transformed; a culture in which Westernization is driven out from it. All our things should be in this fashion. It should have independence of thought, inner independence. In addition to having independence- and no one should interfere in culture- it must have independence of thought; it should be independent and free and stand on its own two feet. It should not be such that it focuses on what the West is doing and we too should follow suit; what they say, we too should say likewise.

This great affliction has befallen absolutely on Iran and the countries of the East such that they are all ears to what they do and what they say in the West and what they practice while they have totally forsaken themselves. They have lost their independence of thought; their inner values. This is a loss that is greater than that of crude oil and the likes of it. This must be recompensed by culture so that our culture is such that after, God willing, a few years, the individuals that are born from the culture are individuals that have self-confidence and view their own selves and not follow others; not imitate others and think that whatever they are doing in the West, we too should follow them. They must see their own country and their own selves as being independent and to govern their country on their own. With their independent thinking they should pursue the affairs of the country and look after its interests.

Date: July 14, 1979/Tir 23, 1358 SH/Sha'ban 19, 1399 AH.

Place: Qum

Subject: The need to complement education with training and cultural independence

Audience: Teachers of the town of Shahreza

The first thing that the nation, universities and colleges are required to do is to replace eastern and European minds with Iranian and Islamic ones. In the same way that they changed the minds of our youths; likewise, we should react and brainwash our children, replacing their mind with Islamic one to be relieved of mental and cultural dependence. If we were rid of mental dependence, all dependencies would terminate. Our dependence in economy, culture and other areas is rooted in our mental dependence. The time we give up this dependence, all other dependencies would be over. However, our minds fail to grasp that we have a rich culture and country, a country capable of providing for the needs of 150 million populations. Unfortunately, we are 30- odd million people and live in such wretched conditions. It is because they entangled us in such conditions. They did not want you to benefit from your culture and economy

Date: September 19, 1979/Shahrivar 28, 1358 SH/Shawwal 27, 1399 AH.

Place: Qum

Subject: Factors contributing to victory of the nation- Islam's sovereignty in the country

Audience: East Azarbayjan tribal people, Kerman's Finance Office staff

Those who are going to accomplish such a positive task or render the great service of purging the corrupt people in universities across the country, they encounter an arduous task, but they should bear the difficulty because it is a valuable job. Worthwhile activities may always be associated with more difficulties.

Date: September 02, 1979/Shahrivar 29, 1358 SH/Shawwal 28, 1399 AH.

Place: Qum

Subject: Mission of Islamic associations, Foreigners' intervention in turmoil's, Opponents of *Wilayate Faqih*

Audience: The universities Islamic associations' representatives Nationwide

One of the very important issues in all organizations, especially universities and high schools is to introduce fundamental change on programs particularly educational programs and approach, so that we can save our culture from west-intoxication and colonial trainings. During recent half of the century, foreigners particularly America have been trying to eliminate the national-human content of our culture and scientific programs and replace them with colonial and despotic ones. The culture promulgated in time of *taghout* put our country on the verge of collapse, but the Almighty God came to help this nation. Nevertheless, without correct radical changes and cultural and

117

intellectual, mental and spiritual changes would be impossible. We may approach our destination by hard work and all-out efforts made by governments, university chancellors, teaching staff and collegians. God willing, we will be relieved of dependence and affiliation and we will save our dear homeland.

One of the important issues, which are a prerequisite to reforms, is to refine all centers particularly cultural and scientific ones. Councils composed of learned and faithful individuals committed to revolution and with the support of chiefs, professors, collegians and teachers, must help purge the cultural-educational centers from corrupt elements and agents of the former regime. As long as these agents, who are at the service of aliens at a wide scale, particularly scientific and educational centers, are not purged, we will not be unable to gain intellectual dependence and will be unable to stand on our own feet.

Date: September 22, 1979/Shahrivar 13, 1358 SH/Shawwal 03, 1399 AH.

Place: Qum

Subject: Foreigners' attempts to sweep the Islamic content of the scientific and cultural programs

Occasion: Opening of academic year

Addressees: Professors, collegians and students

Now all of us, all of you and all layers of the society in every place are obliged to do reconstruction and reforms. Above all are the matters of education and the university of which reforms are more needed than other things. Bring together those who are interested in the country and those who are not dependent on the former regime or on the east and west, and who think, consult and make plans based on which we can perform, God willing. Of course, in the longer run not so soon. Make a long terms plan to change this (wrong) culture into a right one. If there is any science, it should be the right one, but not that which they brought here to limit us to a certain extent and not opening their knowledge to us.

Date: October 6, 1979/Mehr 14, 1358 SH/Dhu'l-Qa'dah 14, 1399 AH.

Place: Qum

Subject: Colonial culture and intellectual dependency- Reforming cultural centers-enemies' plot

Addressees: Professors and Staff of the Sharif University of Technology

Universities must be enlightened. From primary schools to universities, the western mentality must be cleansed, so the easterners could stand on their feet.

Date: October 26, 1979/Aban 4, 1358 SH/Dhu'l-Hijjah 4, 1399 AH.

Place: Qum

Subject: Priority of Cultural Reforms- Concept of freedom and suffocation-colonialist link of superpowers

Audience: Islamic Association Member Teachers East Azarbayjan

Save our youths! The states are obligated to spare our youths. The universities are dutiful to rescue the youths

Date: October 26, 1979/Aban 4, 1358 SH/Dhu'l-Hijjah 4, 1399 AH.

Place: Qum

Subject: Priority of Cultural Reforms- Concept of freedom and suffocation-colonialist link of superpowers

Audience: Islamic Association Member Teachers East Azarbayjan

What are up to you, teachers after revolution and all those in charge of education are to spare the brains westernized in the course of 50- or-so-year despotic regime and exotic hegemony. If a nation is to be salvaged, culture and universities must come in the category of salvage. As long as our brains remain reliant upon foreigners, none of the troubles mentioned can be elusive. Above all reforms, stands reform of "culture" and salvage of our youths from westernization. The West owns many helpful things exclusively, a small part of which along with a lot of felonies is exported to the East.

What they export in the name of "knowledge," "culture" and "progress" differs from what they own. They think differently for the easterners. A few days or weeks ago one of the papers or magazines said the so and so drugs have been banned in America, but its third world exportation is no problem! The physicians going abroad for studies and license are given no right of occupation in the country of their education after they are graduated. They are said to practice medicine in their own lands! The education our youths receive, as they imagine it a progression, is not qualitatively proper. What is beneficial to all is never at our discretion. If there is education, it is trivial and, I need to say, a colonialist one. They make us dependent on everything and give us nothing. Now, we are generally assumed to be dependent in one way or another, above which is mental reliance. Much of the mentality of our youths, our aged men, our educated people and our intellectuals is west-oriented. In fact, it is U.S.-oriented. Still, even those with no bad faith and an imagination of serving their country are dependent as they

119

are not shown the right way and believe that we must obtain everything from the West. This dependency is sprung from all our dependencies. Our cultural dependency, if existing, is followed by economic, political and social dependency. All this exists.

You, teachers and all professors, consider the point that the West gives us no helpful things. It owns useful things but gives us naught and exports nothing. What it gives us or exports to us are means of leading our country to decadence

Date: October 26, 1979/Aban 4, 1358 SH/Dhu'l-Hijjah 4, 1399 AH.

Place: Qum

Subject: Priority of Cultural Reforms- Concept of freedom and suffocation- colonialist link of superpowers

Audience: Islamic Association Member Teachers East Azarbayjan

Our universities must be such that we do not need of foreigners whom we implore for medical treatment in their country. They must do something to rid us of at least others. Be it not that if one becomes ill, he has to go abroad for treatment. It may not be such that you say no when a trouble comes up. Let us stand on our feet

Date: October 28, 1979/Aban 6, 1358 SH/Dhu'l-Hijjah 6, 1399 AH.

Place: Qum

Subject: Comparing Iranian revolution with other revolutions- respite and peace for reforming national affairs- Significance of agriculture and Islamic Civilization

Audience: Representatives of Tabriz Students and Firouzabad Reconstruction Jihad

We cannot be independent until we realize our full prestige, what we were in history and what we are and have. Your country will not be independent as long as your thoughts are not free. Go get your thoughts independent. The universities shall take care of our youth's independence and should educate them to understand that they have a culture, a great one. They should realize that the culture is exported to the West from the East. They should find out that we are something in the universe and we want to manage ourselves

Date: October 29, 1979/Aban 7, 1358 SH/Dhu'l-Hijjah 7, 1399 AH.

Place: Qum

Subject: Westernization, a chronic disease in Iran

Audience: Students of Islamic Association of Mufidi High College of Translation

Our universities have to change such attitudes. Let the brains that led our kids to decadence go away, instead good brains come ahead.

Date: October 03, 1979/Aban 8, 1358 SH/Dhu'l-Hijjah 8, 1399 AH.

Place: Qum

Subject: Relying on the youth and the oppressed people purging the offices and reforming the culture

Addressees: Members of the Relief Committee

The greatest development that must be brought about must take place in the culture. That is because culture is the single most important item that may send a nation to its doom, or yet may give rise to its ever greatness and power. Cultural programs are in need of development. Our culture must go through a great change. This is apart from government offices as culture has some other connotations. In this regard, we know there are many obstacles ahead of us.

Date: May 24, 1979/Khordad 3, 1358 SH/Jamadi ath-Thani 27, 1399 AH.

Place: Qum

Subject: Profession of clerics and academicians; creation of discord between the seminary and university; role of culture in the declination and amelioration of the society

Audience: Ali Shari'atmadari (Minister of Culture and Higher Education), chancellors of universities and institutions of higher education

The whole country should engage in mending the things. More important is to correct the people. Reform them. Make the universities the center for training. Training is necessary besides the learning. A scholar without a good training is harmful. He will betray. One with learning and knowledge if betrayed, the danger will be far and wide involving all the people. The students are able to be trained. If they are brought up will and calculated, they will be able to administer the things. Later on you have to give this country to these youths to run it. Do long to be independent. God willing you long so. It is you the men of universities, and the men of teaching. So teach the youths along with training.

Date: January 4, 1980/Dey 14, 1358 SH/Safar 15, 1400 AH.

Place: Qum

Subject: Peculiarities of the Islamic Revolution and its distinctions with other revolutions

Audience: Tehran University professors

The whole country should engage in mending the things. More important is to correct the people. Reform them. Make the universities the center for training. Training is necessary besides the learning. A scholar without a good training is harmful. He will betray. One with learning and knowledge if betrayed, the danger will be far and wide involving all the people. The students are able to be trained. If they are brought up will and calculated, they will be able to administer the things. Later on you have to give this country to these youths to run it. Do long to be independent. God willing you long so. It is you the men of universities, and the men of teaching. So teach the youths along with training.

Date: January 4, 1980/Dey 14, 1358 SH/Safar 15, 1400 AH.

Place: Qum

Subject: Peculiarities of the Islamic Revolution and its distinctions with other revolutions

Audience: Tehran University professors

A fundamental revolutionary spirit should be brought into being in the universities throughout Iran so that the professors having links with East and West to be wiped out. The university should be made as a safe environment befitting for the higher Islamic sciences to be taught. The detrimental coaching and teaching of the past regime should be strictly avoided. All this misfortune and sufferings of the society throughout the length of the rule of father and son is due to the detrimental training and teaching

Date: March 12, 1980/Farvardin 1, 1359 SH/Jamadi al-Awwal 4, 1400 AH.

Place: Shemiran, Darband, Tehran

Subject: Thirteen-point recommendations to Muslims

Occasion: The Iranian New Year Eve

Addressees: The Muslim nation of Iran, the Muslims and the oppressed ones worldwide

It is necessary for me to make a remark to you. You should know what our aim by reformation of the universities is. Some imagined and wrongly presumed that there are two categories of knowledge or science- one Islamic and the other non-Islamic. For example: engineering- Islamic and non-Islamic. Physics- Islamic and non-Islamic. So they objected that the science or the knowledge cannot be Islamic and non-Islamic.

Some wrongly concluded that the propose of making the universities Islamic is to teach only the sciences concerning relation such as jurisprudence, science of principles and the interpretation. In other words, it will become like schools of old days. These are errors they committed in conception and comprehension. Or they indulge themselves into such mistakes. What we want to say is this: Our universities are affiliated ones. Our universities are those of imperialists. Our universities produce the students fully westernized. The professors mostly are westernized. And they train our youth in the same trend. Our point here is that the universities we have are not useful to our students. It is more than fifty years that we are having universities and they run on the budget heavy which is the cost of the hard labor of this nation. In a span of fifty years, we could not become self-sufficient in the sciences that are the product of these universities. After fifty years if a sick is to be cured, the doctors say he should be sent to England. It is fifty years we have universities. But a doctor who could be able to attend a sick or a patient we have none as they themselves admit. In spite of having a university, which is a need of a nation, yet we are in need of the West. We say that the universities should fundamentally be changed. We do not mean that the Islamic sciences to be taught there. Science is of course in two categories- Islamic and non-Islamic. But this is not our point. What we mean is to show us the output or outcome of these Universities running since fifty years or even more. We say that our Universities are the hurdles in way of progress of our youth- the sons of this soil.

We say that our Universities have become a field of battle of propaganda. Our youth, supposing, if at all attain knowledge but they fall short of good breeding and a desired appreciable growth concerning moral and manners. They have no Islamic training at all. They go to college only to obtain a piece of paper (by name of a degree) and to go to be a parasite upon the nation.

The college is not in line with the needs of the nation nor does it respond to the necessities of the country. Generations and our youth who are most dear to us are now a waste. Their vigor and energy goes in vain. During these fifty years, our power has had been a loss or it was utilized to the benefit of the foreigners. Teachers of our schools are not Islamic teachers. There has had been no training alongside the education. Therefore, we do not have a man committed to his nation or not prefer and persuade his own selfish motives among the college fellows. Our Universities should be in the service of the nation. This is what we say. So our Universities should fundamentally undergo a change. The teachers in schools and professors in Universities mostly are at the disposal of the West. Our youth are brainwashed. A corrupt and profligate training they give to the youth we don't say that we oppugn the present new sciences. We don't say that the knowledge is of two kinds which some debate either ignorantly or deliberately. We say that our Universities have no Islamic conduct or manners. Had our Universities Islamic manners, they would have not turned into a battlefield of beliefs which is scatheful to the country. Had the Universities been Islamic, these stramashes which are too heavy for us would have never happened. All this is because they have no knowledge about Islam nor do they know Islam.

Our Universities should undergo fundamental change. They should be rebuilt. They should train our youth in Islamic fashion. As sciences are taught to them, the Islamic couching too they should be fed with. We do not want that a group push them towards West and another group towards East. Or to push them towards persons who are at war with us, or the persons who desire us to remain in economic blockade or those who threaten us with the economic blockade. We do not want any our youth to be a succor to them. We want them (our youth) to stand up against the West if our nation does so. If our nation stood against the communists, our Universities too should do the same. But our youth because of their plain-heartedness have concurred with some of the teachers in taking an inimical stand against us when we want them not to depend upon East or West or on Communism and Marxism. We want them and our Universities to be independent. This is the prod that shows that we do not have Islamic system in our Universities or an Islamic couching to our youth in the Universities. This is the evidence that our youth are not brought up in a correct training. On the other hand, they are not after education. They are wasting their age in slogans only. And they engage themselves in disseminating erroneous propaganda. Sometimes they are the supporters of America and sometimes of the Soviet Union. We want them to be of their and at their own. These ones who have occupied streets and starveling or in the lanes of the Universities creating tumult and trouble for themselves, others and the government, are the supporters of either East or West. In my opinion, they are the supporters of West and America.

Today we are in confrontation with America. We are facing a big power. So we need that our youth too stand against them with us. But they stand against themselves. Those who are in the margin and criticize, presume that the members of the Revolutionary consulting board do not understand that Islamization does not mean that all sciences have two categories. One kind of Islamic engineering and the other non-Islamic. They don't know that there are jurisprudents and doctors among the members of the board. The members don't know that the Islamic sciences have their own place and station that is the old schools. Here it is the place for new sciences. In any case, the Universities must turn Islamic one so that the science taught in the Universities should benefit the nation and in line with the necessities of nation. In our opinion, the programs in the Universities intimately end to push the youth towards Communism or the West. This should not happen. In our opinion, these teachers or professors do not let the students to grasp the knowledge thoroughly and fully. They impede the way. They are in the service of the West. They want us to depend upon the West in our every need. The meaning of Islamization is that we should become independent. We should distance ourselves from the West as well as East. We want to have an independent culture, college, and country. My dear ones! We do not fear economic blockade. We do not fear the military intervention. The thing that is dreadful to us is the dependency of culture. We fear imperialists' college. The Universities that train our youth for the service of the West make us to fear. Likewise, we fear the Universities that produce servants of Communism. We want our Universities to not be like the persons traduce us. They don't conceive the meaning of independence and the Islamization of the Universities. I support the president and the revolution consulting board what they have told me regarding the purging of Universities in order to be independent. I want all the youth to not stymie the work not to be recalcitrant. Do not let us to adopt other means by recalibrating the work. I pray to God for the nation's and the youth's prosperity. I hope that a in accordance with the proposal, the Universities be purged from the elements and the attachments. I hope that a good college be created with the Islamic characteristics.

Time/Date: 71: 03 pm, April 12, 1980/Urdibehesht 1, 1359 SH/Jamadi ath-Thani 5, 1400 AH.

Place: Shemiran, Darband, Tehran

Subject: Explanation about the reformation of the country's Universities

Audience: From the various classes of the people, students, and Islamic association members of the Universities and the institutes of the Muslim students across the country

We say we want Cultural Revolution, of course in everything, but we should not amalgamate the affairs. Those who speak of Cultural Revolution mix up the things. I have heard them. They put up the affairs together. This will make the way rather remote. The university and Faydiyyah school; they should first start with the university. The economics of the nation should not be their concern. If the academics want to go ahead with the Cultural Revolution in the field of economy, they will lose their own job as well. If another class, capable of setting right the revolution in their field, come to set it right in another field, ex-army, they will lose both of them and the thread will get loose from their hands. Therefore, each class should work in its own place or location. They should work only in those fields of which they are a member. You should not go after economic revolution. Those who want to make the economic revolution should not come after the university.

Date: May 24, 1980/Khordad 3, 1359 SH/Rajab 9, 1400 AH.

Place: Jamaran, Tehran

Subject: Fifty years long plots to create divisions among the various classes of the society

Audience: Teachers, students of the religious institutions, professors, members of the Islamic associations, students of the Universities all over the country

Had they worked for Iran, or had the university been in the service of the country, now we would never have had any dispute nor any controversy. The university would never have been a front of battle. The departments would have taken a different shape and form. The university has had been at a failure to perform its due duty to the nation. It has had been in the service of other. However, so and so have trained our youths. They are still trying to hamper the way for the university to be in the service of the nation. When we say Islamic university, we mean a university based and founded to cater the needs of the nation. It should be for the nation. But in the university, the students are trained against the interests of the country

Try to be free yourself. Be in persuasion of this. You, between your two classes, try to have a continued touch and link. The programs should be prepared by the students at the university and the clergies at the religious institutes. Things in accordance with the needs and necessities of the country should be charted out, not what is of any use to us. There are several things, which do not concern to our country. There should be a correct and sanative training.

When they come out from the college, they should be able to think independently and so in their work. The West and East should not influence them. They should be servants to their own country not to others. This is the meaning of the revolution at university. We should conceive the university revolution from its product. God willing, if after a few years, the product be human, Islamic, or one with a responsibility towards their own country, we will understand that a change has taken place. If it remains the same, communists be its product and Muslims from one side and communists from the other side would confront each other. We will be lame forever. Even more worse will be in waiting for us.

Date: May 24, 1980/Khordad 3, 1359 SH/Rajab 9, 1400 AH.

Place: Jamaran, Tehran

Subject: Fifty years long plots to create divisions among the various classes of the society

Audience: Teachers, students of the religious institutions, professors, members of the Islamic associations, students of the Universities all over the country

Let the university undergo changes and reformations so that to be useful for us. If the university was our own, though it is named after the nation, that is "National", but it has not a remote bearing upon the Muslim nation. If we had an Islamic university, the one to be useful to us, there would have had not been so much bloodshed. Our youths would not have been killed in such a vast number across the country. This happened because we have led no university of ours. Whoever came out the university got a job. He used to oppress the people and tell them that whoever completed his college would become a servant to others. It the head is corrupted and is mistaken the whole lot will be the same. The first grade servant enters into understanding with his superiors. Then he easily steals the people. They reach an agreement with the head of a village and then they rob the whole village.

Date: June 5, 1980/Khordad 14, 1359 SH/Rajab 02, 1400 AH.

Place: Jamaran Husayniyyah Tehran

Subject: Internal change of a nation is the source of victory, unity between religious institute and the university; Importance of Friday prayers

Audience: Professors and students of Divinity and the Islamic Sciences College, Tehran University

The need for a Cultural Revolution, which is an Islamic issue, besides the demand of the Muslim nation is already announced since some years ago. But it has not yet been put to effect. As such, the Muslim nation, in particular the faithful and committed students are dragged into anxiety and worry. Moreover they are worried about the malefic and mischievous betrayers. The Muslim fear, God forbid, to lose the opportunity without having done a positive thing. The culture may remain the same as it was during the previous corrupt regime. This important center was kept at the disposal of the colonists, which is quite evident by the output of the university. Few people were at the service of the country and Islam. Others did not do anything except harm, hurt and loss. The continuity of this havoc, which is also the desire of some groups affiliated to foreigners, will be a fatal blow to the Islamic Revolution and the Islamic Republic. Any leniency in this matter can be tantamount to a great betrayal to Islam and the Islamic country.

Date: June 14, 1980/Khordad 23, 1359 SH/Rajab 29, 1400 AH.

Place: Jamaran, Tehran

Subject: Formation of the Cultural Revolution headquarters

Audience: Appointed members of the Cultural Revolution Headquarters

They have appeared there and stood against it. Furthermore, I have even pulled the gun and closed my fist. Well, the Universities, which were at the service of imperialists, were supposed to be reformed. As soon as the plan for the reformation of the Universities was charted out, a fortification was made in the Universities to evict the plan taking place. Now they are sheltered in the same fortifications. This time it was done abroad. They try to prevent the formation of the cultural reformation. They do not want a revolution in the culture. They want the same culture to last and remain so that such fellows may come out of its womb- the people like the past deputies and ministers. These people wanted to destroy the country. They did the same before too.

Date: June 26, 1980/Tir 4, 1359 SH/Sha'ban 21, 1400 AH.

Place: Jamaran, Tehran

Subject: Disturbances created by groups related to foreign countries; vigilance of nation against plots and mischief

Addressees: Members of Islamic Consultant Boards, workers of Iran, the personnel of Military Health Sector

If universities and the culture be set right and becomes Islamic, these people who are adversaries shall be the same because they have grown-up in the lap of foreigners. They fear that they would not be able to steal if the Universities become Islamic. They are afraid that the Universities become Islamic; they will miss and lose the center of corruption.

There are many difficulties. These difficulties should be lifted out and by your own hands. Don't wait for one to come from outside and lift the difficulties for you. If one comes from outside, he would not educate or train you. He wants you to be at the same place where you were in the past regime. You should mend and correct the contents although the training is the same one. You try this much that the education be the correct one. Education will only be useful when the person have been purified. Further, the manners and the spirit should have been rightly coached and directed

Time: Morning, July 2, 1980/Tir 01, 1359 SH/Sha'ban 18, 1400 AH.

Place: Jamaran, Tehran

Subject: Education/training from the Qur'an's view, the position of culture in the Pahlavi regime. The need for basic changes there.

Audience: The heads of education throughout the country, the Islamic Association members, the Home Ministry workers and the provincial workers

inside the college there should be reformations because students come out of there. Inside the college the reformation should take place not the fortification or a front for fighting each other. The people who are committed should bring and create a college- a place of education, knowledge and learning. Such a college is the need of our country. A college, which is the source of corruption and deviation for our youths, is neither necessary nor a need. Many things under the head or title of education are most undesired ones because they seduce the youths and pave the way for their perversion. There must be people to chart out a program, which should contain the extent of catering the needs of the country. The students should be taught what they need. The program must cover the things that reform our country. The things existed previously, which were not to the advantage of the country, must be deleted and rescinded. God willing, the Universities become good. The staff will comprise people who are polite and polished. The youths are good in the beginning. The teachers spoil them by their coaching which is not to the advantage of the country. Each infant born is instinctively good, not perverted, bad or corrupt. Later on at the ladder of growth, it is the environment, if bad, that makes the young bad. The teacher, by his erroneous training drags the young to corruption. So the environment of college must be salubrious. If one enters it, he must enjoy the healthy and purified atmosphere there. All the people in that environment must be committed to manners and Islam and to the country. If a foreigner goes in, he will come out well trained and well taught. If a society turns good, the people too will become good. When all members of a family are good, the children will be brought up good. Yes, they will become corrupt if they live in a corrupt environment. Infants are so plain like a mirror. They soon grasp whatever image falls on their mirror- whether a filthy one or a pure one. You, gentlemen, are in the field of education. You are in schools, institutes, Universities and other centers of education. The people who are there should be trained because the old fashion, and the old method that was a corrupt one, is still running there. The scholars for teaching manners and conduct are needed in Universities, schools and everywhere.

Time: Morning, July 2, 1980/Tir 01, 1359 SH/Sha'ban 18, 1400 AH.

Place: Jamaran, Tehran

Subject: Education/training from the Qur'an's view, the position of culture in the Pahlavi regime. The need for basic changes there.

Audience: The heads of education throughout the country, the Islamic Association members, the Home Ministry workers and the provincial workers

All those who hold Islam, this country and this nation dear ought to combine their resources for reforming the university as, otherwise, it is more dangerous than a cluster bomb, just as the danger arising from (corrupt) theological centers is greater than that of the university. They ought to be cleaned. The committed people in the theological centers and the universities, ought to gird themselves to carry out reforms. Now gentlemen, you have taken the first step. It is a most fortunate step in that you have broken the big wall, that huge barrier which they had put up between you- between the Faydiyyah and the university. This is the first step that you have taken. In your subsequent steps, you must try to be independent in every respect; not dependent.

It is important for the one who graduates from a university to realize that he has received an education and has become a specialist attaining the highest level of knowledge by utilizing the country's budget. He must, accordingly, realize that he must serve the country and strive for its independence. For their part, the university professors must erase those things that had been instilled into the minds of these youths over these long years, particularly the last fifty years or so, and which had led them to believe that we ourselves are nothing and that everything must be obtained from there (abroad). This has caused them not to put their minds to work so as to make something by themselves. Those who have love for this country and this nation; those who are not dependent and do not serve the superpowers, ought to make efforts to turn the university into a center of knowledge and edification so that all the specializations be in the service of the country. It should not be that a person becomes a specialist and then drags us into the lap of America or uses his expertise to harm our country; the higher the specialization, the worse being the result.

Date: Before noon, December 18, 1980/Azar 27, 1359 SH/Safar 01, 1401 AH.

Place: Jamaran, Tehran

Subject: The importance of the roles of the seminary and the university; stating the duties of these two institutions of learning

Occasion: The day of unity between the seminary and the university

Audience: Teachers and students of Qum Theological Center; the student members of the office for the consolidation of unity between the seminary and the university

By saying that the university and education should be reformed, we do not mean that we do not want universities. We want universities that are of service to the nation and exist for our own selves. It is better (for us) that a university which is in the service of America, does not exist at all.

Date: Before noon, December 18, 1980/Azar 27, 1359 SH/Safar 01, 1401 AH.

Place: Jamaran, Tehran

Subject: The importance of the roles of the seminary and the university; stating the duties of these two institutions of learning

Occasion: The day of unity between the seminary and the university

Audience: Teachers and students of Qum Theological Center; the student members of the office for the consolidation of unity between the seminary and the university.

Many people are unhappy about the university being shut. According to what one of the informed persons told me just a few days ago, the university has served as a war (operations) room for the Kurdistan issue. That is, there is a room in the university where from they have been directing the war in Kurdistan; the democrat party's war, and that of other malevolent elements. Do you want such a university?

Do you who raised that clamor about the university being closed, want such a university to be reopened? Should the war room be opened for the guidance of Democrats and their like for them to ruin Iran? Do you want to feel sorry about this university? Isn't it better for it to be closed rather than remain open?

The people who have been assigned to carry out the Cultural Revolution in the universities, should, of course, make haste in the first place to get the opportunity for them to act so that the university becomes Islamic and exists for the nation. Otherwise, if it is reopened, anybody who wants to enter it will do so. Did you not see what mischief there was when it was open? It was the stronghold and the war (operations) headquarters of the communists. You are sorry that it is closed. Do you realize what you are saying? Are you saying this understandingly? If so, your position ought to be made known.

But if you are talking out of ignorance, on what grounds do you want it to be reopened now when, a few months or a year or so ago, it had been turned into a center of all kinds of mischief, and was in the clutches of the communists, the guerrillas and all the other hypocrite organizations? Do you want them to come back? Are you sorry that the hypocrites are not in the university? Are you sorry as to why there is an Islamic presence in the university? A university that is the center of such activities cannot even impart knowledge as education and learning require time; a time of calmness and a tranquil atmosphere. An atmosphere wherein people fall upon and beat one another daily cannot be conducive to learning. You who want the university to reopen with those same conditions obtaining, want to make us dependent as we were before. You wish to take us back to that dependent state. Neither does any academic nor do the people want this to happen. You, who have so much sympathy for the university and are distressed over its closure, should come and participate in the task of changing it

131

into an Islamic one. You should extend your assistance instead of writing about the university being closed. Do you want the kind of university that existed in the days of Reza Khan and Muhammad Reza? Do you want the likes of "Sharif Imami"[36] to graduate from the university? Reform yourselves sirs! You are not heedful of the issues. God forbid (the day) that you pay heed. But the truth is that you are heedless of the issues. You lack the feel for politics. The universities all over the world are- and have been- in the service of the superpowers. We do not want them to be so. There was not much activity in our universities either. Some of them were committed no doubt and had such virtues. But they were in a minority. They could not do anything against the strong fists of the communists. Even now- in case the universities reopen and we have dedicated professors- they will not allow the universities to be real ones. There was neither any knowledge in the universities to impart. In case they did have learning to impart to the students, why, after all these years and these big budgets of billions that have been spent on this nation, is it said that one who is unwell, who is stricken by an ailment that is rather difficult to treat, has to be sent abroad for treatment? Is this not being dependent? Do you want such a university that even after fifty years of its existence; a patient has to go to England to get himself treated? Is this not being dependent? If the university remains in that condition, the corruption in the country will increase with every day that passes. Like it or not, such a university will drag us into America's or the Soviet Union's lap. It cannot be otherwise as it all begins basically from the universities. The bazaar cannot drag us into the lap of America or the Soviet Union. The farmers cannot drag us into the lap of this one or that one. The factory workers cannot do such a thing, even if there is a corrupt person among them. It is the university which can make us dependent on America or the Soviet Union, as everything of ours lies in the university. You must jointly strive to reform it. Just do not keep on writing as to why it does not reopen. Such a university ought not to reopen. The university that educates people like Sharif Imami should not be reopened. The university should take learning and specialization to that lofty level, and reach the heights of commitment, ethics and Islamic manners and behavior.

Date: Before noon, December 18, 1980/Azar 27, 1359 SH/Safar 01, 1401 AH.

Place: Jamaran, Tehran

Subject: The importance of the roles of the seminary and the university; stating the duties of these two institutions of learning.

---

[36] Engineer Ja'far Sharif Imami (son of Mohamamd Hussain Nizam al-Islam) was Head of Iranian senate and was Prime Minister of National Reconciliation Government. He as Prime Minister announced military government (martial law) in 16 major cities of Iran that led to the massacre of people on 17th Shahrivar, 1357 HS (8th September, 1978).

Occasion: The day of unity between the seminary and the university

Audience: Teachers and students of Qum Theological Center; the student members of the office for the consolidation of unity between the seminary and the university

Now when we insist that our universities, which are like the think-tanks of the nation, should be freed from any sort of inclination toward the East or the West and that this is only possible provided they are Islamized, it does not mean that our universities should not have departments of medical and engineering sciences and that they should only be confined to teaching Islamic sciences! This is a fallacy. The moment there is any talk of an "Islamic University" and of bringing about a "cultural revolution", the supporters of the East and the West raise a hue and cry about us being against expertise and knowledge. No, that is not true. We are not against expertise and we are not against knowledge! What we are opposed to is becoming enslaved by the foreigners. We believe that the kind of expertise that drags us toward America, Britain, the Soviet Union, or China is more detrimental than constructive.

Our aim is to ensure that the experts that graduate from the universities are at the service of their nation instead of dragging the country toward the East or the West. Our aim is to ensure that our industries grow to high levels of expertise and be at the service of the nation instead of serving alien powers. The kind of know-how seeking that drags us toward America or the Soviet Union is harmful and is hazardous to the nations. Most of those who were educated in the universities of the previous regime, if not harmful, were of no use to this country.

Time/Date: Morning, May 25, 1981/Khordad 4, 1360 SH/Rajab 02, 1401 AH.

Place: Jamaran, Tehran

Subject: Importance of knowledge in Islam; responsibility of the university in an Islamic society; duties of the Islamic associations of the universities

Audience: Members of the Islamic Association and the Jihad of the 'Ilm va San'at (Science and Technology) University; members of the Organization for Scientific and Industrial Research; and a group of inventors and innovators

Following the Revolution, too, those who cared for their country as well as Islam put their finger on that same Achilles' heel and similarly demanded a cultural and academic revolution. And you saw for yourselves how those people whose Mecca was Moscow or America started opposing the move, calling it a reactionary step. Then they started making accusations like "these people are against knowledge and expertise" and that "these people wish to teach how to perform the dry and wet ablutions in the university", oblivious of the fact that if such kind of propaganda did bear any fruit during the past days, they no longer did so, after the Revolution and awakening of millions of the Iranian masses. The people now know very well that when you use the word "reactionary", what you are implying is for them to leave you all free to be "progressive" and to drag our country into the arms of the West or into the hands of the East or the communist bloc. When they refer to the term "reactionary", they mean the Muslims and the people who care for Islam and their country and by "progressive", they mean those who wish to drag the country toward the East and the West and the only way they can achieve this is by dragging the university toward the East and the West.

Oppositions started from the very first day that the talks of a cultural revolution began. If you only took a look at the groups that had opposed this issue and those who insisted on reopening the university before the necessary reforms, you will find that they are all either the supporters of the West or the East. You were and are aware that right from the beginning of the Revolution, pens and words and groups gradually started working against the Revolution and they opposed every step that the Revolution wished to take in the direction of reform. As and when any talks of the university came up, those very people who had turned the university into a center of corruption and whose Mecca was toward the East or the West, were opposed to any reform in the university. Their fear was lest the university turned Islamic and the hands of the East and the West get severed from the university- or in other words, from the country- forever. Those who wish and wished to give an open hand to the East or the West and found personal advantage for themselves in the same, tried with their pens and words to condemn reform and revolutionary activities in the universities. And if you saw which groups opposed and are still opposing this step insisting on reopening the universities under its same earlier conditions, you will find out what they are up to. We can recognize people from the suggestions they have to make for this country.

Those who opposed the Cultural Revolution busied themselves with spreading propaganda like "these people want to close down the universities forever and do not want any university to function." A group from among them comprised the same people who had turned the university into their fortress and had fought their battles from there. Another group comprised those West-infatuated people who saw the Islamization of our university, our youth, and our scholars as going against their own objectives and, thus, accused them of being "reactionaries." For them, all those who refuse to lean toward the East or the West are "reactionaries" because they considered the East and the West better. They only wish for the elimination of Islam, irrespective of what replaces it. All they want is the elimination of an Islamic upbringing from our universities, no matter what else replaces it.

Date: Morning, June 31, 1981/Khordad 23, 1360 SH/Sha'ban 01, 1401 AH.

Place: Jamaran Husayniyyah, Tehran

Subject: Importance of the role of the university in the independence or lack of independence of a country

Occasion: Anniversary of the establishment of the Ad Hoc Committee for the Cultural Revolution

Addressees: The members of the Ad Hoc Committee for the Cultural Revolution and the Supreme Council of the Jihad of the Universities of Tehran and other cities

Students and academic scholars should join hands and reopen the universities as soon as possible- universities with an Islamic and national identity and universities that truly belong to an Islamic nation- and sever the hands of all those who want to drag the university toward the East or the West. The Islamic teachers and professors should take the destiny of the university into their own hands and should ensure that the university proves to be a national university in service of national interests. It should not be that all the trouble is taken by the nation and all the expenses of the university are borne by the nation while it turns into a university whose graduates emerge worshipping the East or the West. The universities should reopen but with an atmosphere in which its teachings are Islamic, national, and human. We should not simply insist on its reopening without considering everything else. Well, it was open for the past fifty years. What kind of graduates did it churn out?! The same people who ruined this country and are still not sparing this nation. We want our universities to liberate our nation from the domination of the East and the West instead of dragging it toward them- an independent nation, with an independent ideology, with independent universities because it is the independence of the universities that ensures the independence of a country. Universities that hold hands with the seminaries and sidetrack the Eastern and Western blocs and instead work in the interests of their own country and beloved Islam and bring up our children in a way that they no longer need to look toward Moscow, London, or Washington as their Mecca. Let them look toward the *Ka'bah* and focus upon God Almighty and welcome Islam with open arms because only Islam guarantees their independence and dignity.

The importance that Islam gives to knowledge is probably not given by any other school. The importance that Islam gives to scholars is probably not given by any other school. Islam gives the utmost importance to knowledge but not the kind of knowledge that drags us to ruin and not the kind of scholars that drag us into the arms of the East and the West. Islam strives to foster knowledge within independent minds and minds that serve Islam. Such independence can ensure the independence of our country.

Imam Khomeini's Views on Academic Institutions and Academicians

Date: Morning, June 31, 1981/Khordad 23, 1360 SH/Sha'ban 01, 1401 AH.

Place: Jamaran Husayniyyah, Tehran

Subject: Importance of the role of the university in the independence or lack of independence of a country

Occasion: Anniversary of the establishment of the Ad Hoc Committee for the Cultural Revolution

Addressees: The members of the Ad Hoc Committee for the Cultural Revolution and the Supreme Council of the Jihad of the Universities of Tehran and other cities

Another issue that these people have raised and which the "National Front" has mentioned in its leaflets is the reopening of the universities. Do not keep on raising this issue. This university has only produced people like you all. If the universities are not reformed, its graduates will be people like you all, who, in a couple of decades from now will oppose the laws of Islam like you are doing and will call them "inhuman." We want our universities to serve this nation. You all are working against the interests of this nation under the pretext of serving it. This nation belongs to the same people who have been striving for Islam and their country everywhere. We want to have a university whose graduates will not turn out to be like you all. We want our universities to produce people who are committed to Islam. If they are committed to Islam they will neither drag us toward the East and nor the West. And neither will they hold your negative belief that we are incapable.

Date: June 15, 1981/Khordad 25, 1360 SH/Sha'ban 21, 1401 AH.

Place: Jamaran Husayniyyah, Tehran

Subject: Strong warning to the opponents of the Retaliation (*qisas*) Bill; declaring those who oppose the necessary laws of Islam as apostates

Addressees: Various strata of people, clerics from the Mazandaran province, some Sunni clerics, a group of people from Mashhad, and employees of the intercity bus services

You all saw what beasts were churned out from the universities in the previous regime when things were not in our hands. In these very universities, if anyone wanted to say his obligatory prayers, he would have to do so secretly, out of embarrassment. It was evident from the beginning that it was not as if they were deeply concerned about Islam and hence insisted on the reopening of the universities. We should keep our eyes wide open while dealing with people

Date: Morning, June 23, 1981/Tir 2, 1360 SH/Sha'ban 02, 1401 AH.

Place: Jamaran Husayniyyah, Tehran

Subject: Freedom from cultural dependence and the impact of the press on the culture of a nation

Audience: Karroubi (The Imam's representative and Head of the Martyr's Foundation), the family of Martyr Ali Mazandarani, and the editorial board and the employees of the monthly, "Shahid"

The question of culture and education and training is a top priority in the country. If the problems of culture and education are solved in a way compatible with the interests of the country, other problems will be resolved easily. The losses our country has suffered from the culture of the monarchical regime is not comparable to economic and other damages. Unfortunately during the time of this father and son foreigners found their way into the country again and educational centers turned into the enemies of the nation instead of being its mainstay. Of course, our cultural deviation has historical roots, and we still have teachers and professors who have been assimilated into western culture and training which are in no way in conformity with the interests of Islam and our country. All foreign affiliates are by-products of this Western university. Foreigners and their activities emptied our schools and universities of any content. A lot of campaigns were carried out against the clergy. They wanted the clergy to change their principles, and were able to persuade some, but others resisted and did not change.

We must try hard for many years to come so as to strip off our second nature, come onto ourselves and stand on our feet. Then, we will not need the East or West. We should start with children. Our only aim should be turning Western man into an Islamic one. If you manage to do this, you can be sure that no one and no power can deal us any blow. How can they deal us any blow when we are independent in our thinking? They can only hurt us from within; they work on an individual inside the country as they have, and later through him they can do whatever they want.

Date/Time: Before noon, October 15, 1981/Mehr 23, 1360 SH/Dhu'l-Hijjah 16, 1401 AH.

Place: Jamaran, Tehran

Subject: Striving to achieve cultural independence

Audience: Ali-Akbar Parvaresh (Education Minister) and directors-general of the ministry from all over the country

The theological seminaries in Iran whether the old ones or the universities were not in a right position, therefore they should transform themselves with this movement. They were not prepared in advance, and suddenly have shoulder heavy responsibilities, which weighed heavily on all strata of people. But due to the great efforts of all people, we are going ahead with this burden of responsibilities. There is a lot to be desired, though.

Date: December 9, 1981/Azar 18, 1360 SH/Safar 21, 1402 AH.

Place: Jamaran, Tehran

Subject: Explaining the mission and functions of theological seminaries in the Islamic system

Audience: Sayyid Ali Khamenei (President and Friday prayer leader of Tehran), members of the organizing committee of the Tehran Friday Prayers, students of Tarbiyat Mu'allim, some Muslim Philippine graduates, some Muslims from southeast Asia, employees of Iran Radio and TV broadcast, personnel of the air force-Sunni clergies from Afghanistan

If the university in a country is reformed, that country will be reformed. Universities lie on top of the executive affairs. By reforming university, the country's affairs will be reformed; by corrupting the university, the country will be corrupted. Even one corrupt professor might have a big effect on a country, because he or she can influence a group of students in a bad way. In their turn, they will develop into a big evil in the long run....Those who wanted to eliminate countries like ours worked to corrupt the university. They were active everywhere, especially in university, because they knew that if university served the West, the country would follow suit... Universities should be entrusted to committed individuals.

I have to criticize some newspapers that change the course of a subject in their headlines. We believe that the universities must be reopened. When they are opened they should make effort towards Islamization. Clergies and other wings should bring the universities in line with Islamic education. But we sometimes see that the newspapers are saying unless the universities are reformed they should not be reopened. Sometime they quote me as saying so. I say that reforming universities take a long time, but we cannot wait that long to open the universities. Another point I would like to make to the Cultural Revolution Council is that from what I have been told, they are very fussy, no doubt the deviants who want to corrupt the atmosphere of universities must not be let in. Those who made the universities a stronghold and set up a war room and were creating all the corruptions should be identified and pushed aside. However, some of them are girls and boys, who committed small offences in the past and repented should be accepted in universities, as the door to repentance is open and we should not disappoint the youth. The clergies should not argue that since they did something wrong, they should be expelled from the university. No, the door of repentance is open. God has left the door of repentance open for all. Of course, corruption in not sanctioned, but those who repented and those who did something wrong such as girls or boys who are repentant should be given. We should embrace them; God accepts their repentance. They have made it to the university, so do not make them lose hope. The youth are the resources of this country. If they were engaged in corruption, they have now repented. Therefore, the universities should be reopened with seriousness. Eventually, it should be Islamized by including Islamic education.

Date/Time: Before noon, January 24, 1982/Bahman 4, 1360 SH/Rabi' al-Awwal 28, 1402 AH.

Place: Jamaran, Tehran

Subject: Problem of Iran, Muslims and the Islamic countries

Audience: Teachers, members of the board of director and students of Qum Judiciary and educational sciences college, officials of Reconstruction Jihad headquarters, Commanders of the revolutionary guards, officials of the Red Cross, women from Qum, theology students and the people from Kashan and Andimeshk

Finally, purging is necessary in all government, civil and military organizations, and it is even more in the seminaries and universities which enjoy special characteristics and are in unison with each other. With the purging of these two Islamic and national bases, entity of Islamic Republic will continue growing and progressing. With the deviation of these two, the revolution and the republic will deflect from its main course.

Time: February 11, 1982/Bahman 22, 1360 SH/Rabi' ath-Thani 16, 1402 AH.

Place: Jamaran, Tehran

Subject: Stating the situation of Iran and the revolution on the 4th anniversary of the victory

Occasion: Anniversary of the victory of the Islamic Revolution (22 Bahman)

Audience: The Iranian nation

The story of university is among the most important concerns, as it is important for our enemies and those who want to deflect the mind of our youths. University is the center of all developments, even establishment of government. We should pursue the efforts to Islamize universities to be useful for the country. Attempts should be made so that the universities do not tilt towards either one of the powers. This calls for time, energy, and close supervision. You should be cautious lest the deviants may correct our youths with preserve ideas after inauguration of universities, and many people are required to supervise the process.

I hope that we have universities that are useful for the nation. To give reality to this idea, it is necessary to use experts and in case of shortage of committed experts use experts who are not antagonistic to the Islamic Republic. God willing make efforts with ever-greater power in this matter and proceed to achieve the divine purpose.

Time: Morning, October 4, 1983/Mehr 21, 1362 SH/Dhul-Hijjah 26, 1403 AH.

Place: Jamaran, Tehran

Subject: Struggle for Islamization of universities

Audience: New members of the Cultural Revolution Board, Mir Husayn Mousavi (Prime Minister), Sayyid Muhammad Khatami, Sayyid 'Abdul-Karim Soroush, Muhammad Ali Najjafi, Ali Shari'atmadari

After the war, we start from scientific schools and universities which are in fact the beating heart of the nation. We know that these two centers are in fact two branches of a single pure tree and two arms of one spiritual human station. If they tilt towards good and preserve their spiritual commitment and hand in hand rise to serve the right and people, they will elevate the nation to perfection in two spiritual and material dimension, by preserving the freedom and independence in the country, standing like a strong dam in the face of foreign attacks and infiltration of corruption and leading the nation and the country towards progress and upliftment with straight statute and rising flag. If God forbid they deviate in any one of their divinely and national duties, they will impose upon the nation that which the universities in time of the former regime affiliated to alien powers did. Still the country and the Muslim nation are suffering from those sufferings. Undoubtedly, our today's problems in economic, cultural and social dimension and in fact in the imposed war and sedition of the mercenaries dependent on the two domineering blocs are the evil traces of the universities affected by the Western and Eastern mentality that encouraging anti-Islamic and anti-national sentiments.

Date: February 11, 1985/Bahman 22, 1363 SH/Jamadi al-Awwal 02, 1405 AH.

Place: Jamaran, Tehran

Subject: Message on the occasion of Bahman 22 and anniversary of the victory of Islamic Revolution dealing with war, universities, duties of the three branches of government mass media and appreciation of the nation

Addressees: Iranian nation

I hope you have felt that all pains in Iran have begun from university. University had bitter experiences that cannot be removed so soon. It calls for diligence and sacrifice to make the university efficient. The university at that time had no right to speak about the interests of Iran and Islam and saying prayer was a shame in university which is the source of all our problems. You should strive to improve the university. You should come to realize that Islam can improve the university. Improvement of university is easy when we raise children efficiently from school. If our children are brought up correctly from childhood, the university will take less trouble.

Date/Time: Morning, April 16, 1985/Farvardin 27, 1364 SH/Rajab 25, 1405 AH.

Place: Jamaran, Tehran

Subject: Improvement of university and struggle for liberation from cultural dependence

Audience: Iraj Fadil (Minister of Culture and Higher Education) and deputies

You should do something that our universities follow the method of masses of people, as if a nation wants something, its contrast cannot be imposed on them. Notice how our million-strong masses of people have been transformed and noted that they should stand against powers. University should be the center of growth for such mentality, something that has unfortunately not been the case.

Date/Time: Morning, April 16, 1985/Farvardin 27, 1364 SH/Rajab 25, 1405 AH.

Place: Jamaran, Tehran

Subject: Improvement of university and struggle for liberation from cultural dependence

Audience: Iraj Fadil (Minister of Culture and Higher Education) and deputies

Consider the universities and Islamize them. If universities become Islamized, our problems will be settled in the future.

Date/Time: Morning, September 4, 1985/Shahrivar 31, 1364 SH/Dhu'l-Hijjah 18, 1405 AH.

Place: Husayniyyah Jamaran, Tehran

Subject: Duty of government with Muslims public treasury, stability of actions

Occasion: Ghadir Khumm auspicious feast, ceremony for confirmation of presidency of Mr. Khamenei

Audience: Officials of Islamic Republic and civil and military authorities and people from different walks of life

A cultural revolution can be of this nature. A revolution is transformation from one state to another, not advancement of the existing thing.

Date/Time: Morning, December 01, 1985/Azar 19, 1364 SH/Rabi' al-Awwal 27, 1406 AH.

Place: Jamaran, Tehran

Subject: University and the Cultural Revolution

Occasion: Anniversary of formation of the Supreme Cultural Revolution Council

Audience: Sayyid Ali Khamenei (President and chairman of the Supreme Cultural Revolution Council), members of the Cultural Revolution Council

As to university, their plan is to alienate the youth with their own values and cultural identity in order to draw them over to the East or the West and to select the statesmen from among them. These selected individuals were instituted in positions of authority and doing whatever they want to the country. They plundered the country's resources and exploited the people through their internal agents. Nevertheless, the clerics, who had been isolated, despised and defeated, reacted passively to the case. This is the best way to hold a nation in a backward state and to plunder the countries under their domination. It is easy for superpowers and of no cost to them while the whole wealth of nations goes to their pockets smoothly.

Now that due to 'the revolution' we are involved in the act of purging the universities and teacher-training Universities, it is necessary for all of us to help the officials and not ever let these institutions deviate from the right path. Take the necessary action as soon as you notice any deviation. This vital task should be primarily carried out by universities students. To save the university from deviation and perversion is to save the nation and the country.

I hereby urge our youth, their parents and friends as well as statesmen and intellectuals who care for the country to participate in this important task wholeheartedly to maintain the safety of the country and to deliver purified universities to the next generation. I also advice coming generations to guard the universities against tendency to the West or the East, as this is necessary for salvation of themselves, the country and beloved Islam. This humane and Islamic act cuts off the hands of superpowers from the country and makes them lose all hope. May Allah bless and protect you!

Date of Reciting: Khordad 15, 1368

Place: Jamaran, Tehran

Subject: Politico-divine will (ever-lasting message of Imam Khomeini to the contemporary ones and next generations)

Addressees: Iranian nation, Muslims and peoples of the world and next generations

Establishment of Headquarter for Cultural Revolution

In the name of God, the beneficent, the merciful

The need for a Cultural Revolution, which is an Islamic issue, besides the demand of the Muslim nation is already announced since long time ago. But it has not yet been put to effect. As such, the Muslim nation, in particular the faithful and committed students are dragged into anxiety and worry. Moreover they are worried about the malefic and mischievous betrayers. The Muslim fear, God forbid, to lose the opportunity without having done a positive thing. The culture may remain the same as it was during the previous corrupt regime. This important center was kept at the disposal of the colonists, which is quite evident by the output of the university. Few people were at the service of the country and Islam. Others did not do anything except harm, hurt and loss. The continuity of this havoc, which is also the desire of some groups affiliated to foreigners, will be a fatal blow to the Islamic Revolution and the Islamic Republic. Any leniency in this matter can be tantamount to a great betrayal to Islam and the Islamic country. Therefore I have vested Messrs Muhammad-Jawad Bahonar, Mahdi Rabbani Amlashi, Hasan Habibi, 'Abd al-Karim Soroush, Shams Al-e Ahmad, Jalaluddin Farsi and Ali Shari'atmadari with responsibility of forming a squad. They may solicit efficient people having obligation, and some among the professors, Muslims and workers with obligation, and the students with Faith and obligation, and the other educated classes having belief in Islamic Republic to form a consultant council to chart the program in the various subjects and adopt a cultural line of walk for future Universities on the ground of Islamic culture. Moreover, they may select professors already girded and befitting and acquainted with the matters related to revolution and Islamic training. Likewise, the schools and other training centers should be based upon the foresaid ground because they were under the management of seduced and deviated and imperialists' learning and training. By so doing, our dear sons will be protected from deviation. I wish God's success for these gentlemen in this very sensitive issue. I pray for the glory of Islam and the Islamic countries. May God's peace be upon you.

Date: June 14, 1980/Khordad 23, 1359 SH/Rajab 29, 1400 AH.

Place: Jamaran, Tehran

Subject: Formation of the Cultural Revolution headquarters

Audience: Appointed members of the Cultural Revolution Headquarters

Inside the University there should be reformations because students come out of there. Inside the University the reformation should take place not the fortification or a front for fighting each other. The people who are committed should bring and create a University- a place of education, knowledge and learning. Such a University is the need of our country. A University, which is the source of corruption and deviation for our youths, is neither necessary nor a need. Many things under the head or title of education are most undesired ones because they seduce the youths and pave the way for their perversion. There must be people to chart out a program, which should contain the extent of catering the needs of the country. The students should be taught what they need. The program must cover the things that reform our country. The things existed previously, which were not to the advantage of the country, must be deleted and rescinded. God willing, the Universities become good. The staff will comprise people who are polite and polished.

Time: Morning, July 2, 1980/Tir 01, 1359 SH/Sha'ban 18, 1400 AH.

Place: Jamaran, Tehran

Subject: Education/training from the Qur'an's view, the position of culture in the Pahlavi regime. The need for basic changes there

Audience: The heads of education throughout the country, the Islamic Association members, the Home Ministry workers and the provincial workers

O my dear, beloved ones! It is absolutely necessary to remain alert and watchful. Today, they (our enemies) intend to cause dissension and despair among people and in the universities. I have to reiterate that Islam and the Islamic Republic fully support the universities and the academicians and experts who serve Islam and this country. Our only demand is that there should be no conspiracies in the universities. I assure all the university teachers and the academicians who are committed to serving their country and desire to train our youth with their expertise that Iran and Islam supports and protects them and that they should endeavor and cooperate with the commission that has been set up for the cultural revolution in order to turn our universities into peaceful places of real learning and skill.

Date: April 31, 1981/Farvardin 24, 1360 SH/Jamadi ath-Thani 8, 1401 AH.

Place: Jamaran, Tehran

Subject: Need to maintain unity and peace and warning against disruptive elements

Audience: Agriculturists and the inhabitants of Gorgan, the clerics and the inhabitants of Ali-Abad, the inhabitants of Gonbad and Turkman Sahra, and the Basij of Shahreza

Those in charge of the Cultural Revolution should deliver upon their responsibility with the utmost care and should endeavor to find committed people and should expedite their work by consulting them so that, with the grace of God, the universities can gradually reopen. And we shall have universities that will function to benefit our own country rather than dragging us toward the left or the right blocs. I am hopeful that the gentlemen who are in charge of implementing the Cultural Revolution will be supported by those who are concerned about this issue and who believe in Islam and the country and who harbor no Western or Eastern inclinations. At the same time, as I mentioned earlier, those in charge should invite such people to work with them so that, with the grace of God, we can soon have Islamic universities whose concern will be to free this nation from the problems it has been facing thus far.

Time/Date: Morning, May 25, 1981/Khordad 4, 1360 SH/Rajab 02, 1401 AH.

Place: Jamaran, Tehran

Subject: Importance of knowledge in Islam; responsibility of the university in an Islamic society; duties of the Islamic associations of the universities

Audience: Members of the Islamic Association and the Jihad of the 'Ilm va San'at (Science and Technology) University; members of the Organization for Scientific and Industrial Research; and a group of inventors and innovators

In the name of God, the beneficent, the mercifuil

Although I had no plans to speak on Saturday, since you gentlemen are academicians and have spoken on the affairs of the university and the "cultural revolution", I therefore, will say a few words.

The most important thing that the enemies of the oppressed countries and the Muslim countries and the enemies of mankind have pinpointed is the university. This is because they know very well that if they manage to influence the university of a country, the entire country can fall into their hands. It is the university that runs the affairs of a country. And it is the university that trains the present and the future generations and if the university falls into the hands of the plunderers of the East and the West, the country falls into their hands. Nothing else has been their target more than the

145

university. The clergy, too, is like the university in this regard. They wanted to introduce the academicians into society with an Eastern or Western upbringing. And since they could not succeed in gaining control over the clergy, they wanted to eliminate them from the scenes. They were neither interested in the university nor in the seminaries. Their attempts were focused on these two groups in whose hands lies the entire future of a country and they tried to groom one of them under foreign and Western or Eastern training before bringing them on the scenes while they tried to eliminate the other from the scenes because they could not manage access to their grooming and could not influence them even after a thousand years of effort. They tried to do everything to eliminate the clergy from the scenes while they put in all their efforts to gain control over the academicians. One of their main conspiracies was to make these two groups cynical toward each other. During these long years, they tried their best to cause a rift between these two groups and to breed animosity between them. If we were to visit a university, even the mention of a "cleric" would bear the same connotation as a narcotic drug. And within the clergy, the term "academician" meant someone "irreligious." They instigated these two groups to each other's throats so that they could misuse the situation to their advantage. It was not without reason that through these fifty years during which they were in power, they did not allow even a single university that could work for the welfare of the country and that would churn out human beings and scholars to get established in the country. I do not say that they succeeded completely but they surely tried their best to gradually succeed in ensuring that all the graduates either worshipped the East or the West! Once they can succeed in doing this to the university and in severing off the ties between the clergy and the university, they are bound to hold the reins of the destinies of all the countries in their hands.

They pinpointed the universities and tried to gain control over the university with all their might. And to attract individuals that were inclined toward the East and more toward the West. And to convert the academicians to their own advantage while sidetracking the clergy. To make the clergy ineffectual and to bring the academicians under either the Eastern or the Western influence. We and this revolution, too, should tap this same sensitivity. Top priority should be given to the cultural and academic revolution just like they did through these last fifty years. Following the Revolution, too, those who cared for their country as well as Islam put their finger on that same Achilles' heel and similarly demanded a cultural and academic revolution. And you saw for yourselves how those people whose Mecca was Moscow or America started opposing the move, calling it a reactionary step. Then they started making accusations like "these people are against knowledge and expertise" and that "these people wish to teach how to perform the dry and wet ablutions in the university", oblivious of the fact that if such kind of propaganda did bear any fruit during the past days, they no longer

146

did so, after the Revolution and awakening of millions of the Iranian masses. The people now know very well that when you use the word "reactionary", what you are implying is for them to leave you all free to be "progressive" and to drag our country into the arms of the West or into the hands of the East or the communist bloc. When they refer to the term "reactionary", they mean the Muslims and the people who care for Islam and their country and by "progressive", they mean those who wish to drag the country toward the East and the West and the only way they can achieve this is by dragging the university toward the East and the West.

Oppositions started from the very first day that the talks of a cultural revolution began. If you only took a look at the groups that had opposed this issue and those who insisted on reopening the university before the necessary reforms, you will find that they are all either the supporters of the West or the East. You were and are aware that right from the beginning of the Revolution, pens and words and groups gradually started working against the Revolution and they opposed every step that the Revolution wished to take in the direction of reform. As and when any talks of the university came up, those very people who had turned the university into a center of corruption and whose Mecca was toward the East or the West, were opposed to any reform in the university. Their fear was lest the university turned Islamic and the hands of the East and the West get severed from the university- or in other words, from the country- forever. Those who wish and wished to give an open hand to the East or the West and found personal advantage for themselves in the same, tried with their pens and words to condemn reform and revolutionary activities in the universities. And if you saw which groups opposed and are still opposing this step insisting on reopening the universities under its same earlier conditions, you will find out what they are up to. We can recognize people from the suggestions they have to make for this country.

Those who opposed the Cultural Revolution busied themselves with spreading propaganda like "these people want to close down the universities forever and do not want any university to function". A group from among them comprised the same people who had turned the university into their fortress and had fought their battles from there. Another group comprised those West-infatuated people who saw the Islamization of our university, our youth, and our scholars as going against their own objectives and, thus, accused them of being "reactionaries." For them, all those who refuse to lean toward the East or the West are "reactionaries" because they considered the East and the West better. They only wish for the elimination of Islam, irrespective of what replaces it. All they want is the elimination of an Islamic upbringing from our universities, no matter what else replaces it. They do not want the university and the seminaries to ever unite together because this could result in the Islamization of the universities and will eliminate all the bad blood that they had spread over the years between the academicians and the students of Islamic sciences. If this cynicism had to

147

disappear, and once the university had to work actively alongside the seminaries, the hands of all those who look toward the East and the West would be severed. Therefore, they tried and are trying with all the might to cause rifts and bad blood between these two groups. Once these two groups get distanced and cynical toward each other, they can get a free hand to carry on with their activities. They have still not given up their main objectives. Even today, the group that wants the universities to reopen without any amendments and as it is, and as they prefer it to be, and within the same previous conditions, comprises the same people who have lost their souls to the East and the West. They wish to sacrifice their own nation either to the Eastern bloc or the Western bloc.

The university should remain aware and alert about these conspiracies. And our beloved university youth should remain alert over this issue that the university of a country can be the cause of the uplift or destruction of its nation. The university and the academic training can drag our youth either toward the West or the East and alienate them from their own identity and infatuate them with the West and the East until the East gains domination over every aspect of Iran and the land of the Muslims or the West gains domination and robs us of our culture and everything else, replacing it with an Eastern or Western ideology and dragging the country to destruction.

However, our nation has awakened with the grace of God and will never give their consent to matters that will serve the interests of the East and the West. Our nation has now gained awareness on the fact that the university can either make a country independent or rob it of its independence.

Students and academic scholars should join hands and reopen the universities as soon as possible, universities with an Islamic and national identity and universities that truly belong to an Islamic nation and sever the hands of all those who want to drag the university toward the East or the West. The Islamic teachers and professors should take the destiny of the university into their own hands and should ensure that the university proves to be a national university in service of national interests. It should not be that all the trouble is taken by the nation and all the expenses of the university are borne by the nation while it turns into a university whose graduates emerge worshipping the East or the West. The universities should reopen but with an atmosphere in which its teachings are Islamic, national, and human. We should not simply insist on its reopening without considering everything else. Well, it was open for the past fifty years. What kind of graduates did it churn out?! The same people who ruined this country and are still not sparing this nation. We want our universities to liberate our nation from the domination of the East and the West instead of dragging it toward them- an independent nation, with an independent ideology, with independent universities because it is the independence of the universities that ensures the independence of a country. Universities that hold hands with the seminaries and sidetrack the Eastern and Western blocs and instead work in the interests of their own country and beloved Islam and bring up our children in a way that they no longer need to look toward Moscow, London, or Washington as their Mecca. Let them look toward the Ka'bah and focus upon God Almighty and welcome Islam with open arms because only Islam guarantees their independence and dignity.

The importance that Islam gives to knowledge is probably not given by any other school. The importance that Islam gives to scholars is probably not given by any other school. Islam gives the utmost importance to knowledge but not the kind of knowledge that drags us to ruin and not the kind of scholars that drag us into the arms of the East and the West. Islam strives to foster knowledge within independent minds and minds that serve Islam. Such independence can ensure the independence of our country. The independence of our country depends on the independence of the universities and the seminaries. The university and seminaries should join hands and protect the independence of their country. They should cut off all their hopes from both the Islamic universities and the seminaries. They should not pay heed to their objections to fostering harmony between the universities and the clerics. They are fearful even of the shadow of a cleric. Their plans are to keep the universities away from the seminaries.

They had tried for long years to foster a rift and animosity between these two groups that are the think-tanks of a nation and in whose hands lie the welfare, grandeur, and independence of this nation. All of us saw how these two groups had been turned into enemies until the Islamic Revolution following which Islam held out its invitation. Islam invites all groups to unity and especially the universities and the seminaries. And as long as these two groups remain united, your country's independence is guaranteed.

Both the universities as well as the seminaries should open their eyes and know that there are still hands at work trying to cause rifts between these two groups. The imperialists and their followers and all those whose Mecca lies in London, Washington, or Moscow see a unity between these two groups as a threat to their own interests and, thus, try to keep them apart. As you all saw, the fifty years of the ominous Pahlavi rule that had proved its dedication to foreign powers fostered rifts and animosity between these two groups while the ill-wishers of this nation took advantage of the situation. The wealth of this nation during the last fifty years and especially during the times of Muhammad Reza was washed out. And all this happened as a result of the animosity between the universities and the seminaries. And if, God forbid, the earlier animosity between these two groups has to be revived, it will only guarantee the interests of the superpowers.

My dear academicians and my dear clerics! Stay alert since the enemies are trying their best to create rifts between you. And do not forget that if reform is brought about in the universities and the seminaries, the independence of your country will be ensured. The Mecca of all those whose pens and words are trying to cause rifts between you two is either Moscow or Washington. Stay alert not to lose this great blessing of the unity between the universities and the seminaries. I am hopeful that you will succeed in managing the affairs of your country independently and that you will no longer need to stretch your hands toward the East and the West and that the mischief they create in our country, boomerangs back to them. May God Almighty help and support the seminaries, the universities, and the entire nation!

Date: Morning, June 31, 1981/Khordad 23, 1360 SH/Sha'ban 01, 1401 AH.

Place: Jamaran Husayniyyah, Tehran

Subject: Importance of the role of the university in the independence or lack of independence of a country

Occasion: Anniversary of the establishment of the Ad Hoc Committee for the Cultural Revolution

Addressees: The members of the Ad Hoc Committee for the Cultural Revolution and the Supreme Council of the Jihad of the Universities of Tehran and other cities

The Cultural Revolution Council should make efforts to reopen the universities with the help of the oppressed people and the scientists, and to consult the scholars about this vital issue. The honorable nation should be harmonious with those in charge to tackle all the war, military, economic and cultural problems.

Date: November 25, 1981/Azar 4, 1360 SH/Muharram 28, 1402 AH.

Place: Jamaran, Tehran

Subject: Necessity to keep and safeguard Islam and the Islamic country

Occasion: Formation anniversary of Basij

Addressees: Basiji forces and the nation of Iran

Hujjat al-Islam Haj Shaykh Muhammad-Reza Mahdavi Kani- may your graces last, I hereby appoint you for the membership of the Cultural Revolution Committee. It is hoped that in cooperation with the respected members of the committee and esteemed professors, students and officials you will do your utmost to reopen the universities as soon as possible. God willing, the honorable Iranian nation will witness scientific activities at the universities all over the country in the near future. I beseech God to grant success to you, the other members of the committee and whoever making efforts in this sphere.

May God's peace be upon you.

Date: December 23, 1981/Dey 2, 1360 SH/Safar 26, 1402 AH.

Place: Jamaran, Tehran

Subject: Appointing a member of the Cultural Revolution Committee

Audience: Muhammad-Reza Mahdavi Kani

Hujjat al-Islam Haj Shaykh Ahmad, Ahmadi- may your graces last, I hereby appoint you for the membership of the Cultural Revolution Committee. It is hoped that in cooperation with the respected members of the committee and esteemed professors, students and officials you will do your utmost to reopen the universities as soon as possible. God willing, the honorable Iranian nation will witness scientific activities at the universities all over the country in the near future. I beseech God to grant success to you and the other members of the committee and whoever making efforts in this sphere.

May God's peace be upon you.

Date: December 23, 1981/Dey 2, 1360 SH/Safar 26, 1402 AH.

Place: Jamaran, Tehran

Subject: Appointing a member of the Cultural Revolution Committee

Audience: Ahmad Ahmadi

As the time to open universities approaches and as you have always paid attention to university and university people the need for effort to make further preparations for admitting students is felt. While appreciating the sincere efforts of the respected members of the Cultural Revolution Board and all the professors, researchers and students engaged in university affairs, I beg to call for reshuffle and completion of the Cultural Revolution Board and propose the new combination in the following order:

1. Esteemed Prime Minister, 2. Minister of Culture and Higher Education, 3. Minister of Culture and Islamic Guidance, 4. Dr. Shari'atmadari, 5. Dr. Ahmadi, 6. Dr. Soroush, 7. Dr. Mu'in, 8. and 9. (two students selected by University Jihad. It is hoped that with the special attention of the great Imam inauguration of the university will coincide with an Islamic movement and with divine success.

Sayyid Ali Khamenei, President of Islamic Republic of Iran

In His Most Exalted Name

Appreciating the efforts of the respected members of the Cultural Revolution Council and all those who have endeavored for making the university courses and curriculum Islamic and human, I hope that by reshuffling the esteemed board and through the efforts of the dear and committed students, coordination of the esteemed professors, attempt of all believing practitioners and support of the honorable nation, this Islamic-national base, on which the destiny of the country depends in remote and near future, would continue with its service independently and efficiently. Today, when the country enjoys efficient independence and the university has been rid of the bonds of the east and the west and easternized and westernized elements, the dear university students should try ever more to acquire sciences and techniques for prosperity their dear country, decisively prevent devious elements affiliated with the right and the left from infiltrating the university and not allow the sacred university environment to be polluted by selfish motives of deviants affiliated with aliens. If they notice any deviation or inclination to east and west from professors or students, inform the cultural board and render the necessary cooperation with the board for eliminating it.

I ask God Almighty success for all to further independence and prosperity of Islamic country.

Rouhullah al-Mousavi al-Khomeini

Time: August 03, 1983/Shahrivar 8, 1362 SH/Dhul-Qa'dah 12, 1403 AH.

Place: Jamaran, Tehran

Subject: Reshuffling the Cultural Revolution Board

Addressees: Sayyid Ali Khamenei (then President)

The decision was adopted to appoint new members instead of the gentlemen who were absent due to some reasons and did not participate in board meetings. All the gentlemen who are today on the board are my representatives. There is no difference between these gentlemen and the old members. However, the story of university is among the most important concerns, as it is important for our enemies and those who want to deflect the mind of our youths. University is the center of all developments, even establishment of government. We should pursue the efforts to Islamize universities to be useful for the country. Attempts should be made so that the universities do not tilt towards either one of the powers. This calls for time, energy, and close supervision. You should be cautious lest the deviants may correct our youths with preserve ideas after inauguration of universities, and many people are required to supervise the process.

I hope that we have universities that are useful for the nation. To give reality to this idea, it is necessary to use experts and in case of shortage of committed experts use experts who are not antagonistic to the Islamic Republic. God willing make efforts with ever-greater power in this matter and proceed to achieve the divine purpose.

Time: Morning, October 4, 1983/Mehr 21, 1362 SH/Dhul-Hijjah 26, 1403 AH.

Place: Jamaran, Tehran

Subject: Struggle for Islamization of universities

Audience: New members of the Cultural Revolution Board, Mir Husayn Mousavi (Prime Minister), Sayyid Muhammad Khatami, Sayyid 'Abdul-Karim Soroush, Muhammad Ali Najjafi, Ali Shari'atmadari

With God's sanctions and attention and prayer of the Savior (may our souls be sacrificed for him), universities and higher education schools of the country have started their work on a wide scale. Reconstruction work in all its dimensions is in progress in the country and committed minds and experts continue with their valuable activities. By expulsion of treacherous foreign experts and fleeing of Westernized and Easternized experts who had made the country dependent on foreign powers in all aspects, the need for committed experts and Islamologists and thoughtful patriotic minds and dynamic skilled forces and teachers and instructors committed to Islam and independence of the country is urgently felt. This need is more palpable in university sciences and progressive culture. The need for development and improvement of educational centers and Cultural Revolution in the real sense of the word grows more evident. Thank God, the Cultural Revolution headquarters in a short period of time since its creation has rendered valuable services and taken useful and effective steps in this vital matter and should be appreciated. Nevertheless, ridding of decadent Western culture and its replacement by constructive Islamic-national culture calls for Cultural Revolution in all aspects across the country. To accomplish this end, necessitates years of unremitting efforts and fighting against the deep of Western culture. We know that if we carefully study the root of the West's cultural infiltration, what has befallen our nation, even the imposed war originates from Westernized university and non-committed and dependent experts. Nevertheless, the religious revolutionary layers of people including committed professors and patriotic Islamic teachers and revolutionary students are obliged to be vigilant. They should not let the universities and schools, which still cherish the idea of restoring the former regime and develop Eastern cultural procedures, divert from the curriculum and wasting their time by diversion talks. If advice did not work, they should report the case to the Supreme

Council of Cultural Revolution, which has taken shape and is performing its duty. They should know that by negligence in this important matter devious line would gradually interlope into universities and high schools. We are responsible before God Almighty.

Now I thank the efforts of the Cultural Revolution Headquarters and deem it necessary to strengthen this organization for enriching the revolution across the country. To this end, in addition to the presence of the current members of cultural headquarters and the respected heads of the three branches of power, the following will be added to the list: Hujjat al-Islam Messers Khamenei, Ardebili, Rafsanjani, Mahdi Karroubi, Sayyid Kazim Akrami (Education Minister), Sayyid Reza Dawari, Nasrullah Pour Jawadi and Muhammad-Reza Hashemi.

It is hoped that with the grace of God, they will succeed in fructifying this important matter by diligence and decisiveness.

Date: September 01, 1984/Azar 19, 1363 SH/Rabi' al-Awwal 16, 1405 AH.

Place: Jamaran, Tehran

Subject: Appointment of several new members of the Cultural Revolution Headquarters

Addressees: Members of the Cultural Revolution Headquarters

I first thank all the gentlemen for coming here so that I meet them closely. I would like to express my certainty that with the respected members in the council, there is no longer any concern over universities and God willing other things. Nevertheless, since the question is very important and destiny of the revolution hinges on it, we should always display this sensitivity. One should be sensitive to all issues, yet there is difference in that regarding which this sensitivity should persist. There are things that are settled. For example, we are engaged in war. War is not something important; it will be settled. It is not important and thank God the situation is good. The political situation in the world will also be settled. There are things to which one should be sensitive. The issue of university is an extraordinary thing. The individuals graduated from university are either destructive or constructive to country. In our country, they either push it towards Islam or deflect it. This is something that can be accomplished from university. Similarly, theological seminaries can handle this. It is, therefore, very important.

In the revolutions taking place in the world or the riots or coups there are three elements that should be heeded: break out of the riot, revolution and coup, their substance and their incentive. The revolutions are corresponding to one another. They are either riot or coup or revolution. Outwardly, they are like human beings who are similar as far as their form is concerned. Their meaning however differs. Incentives and contents are important. Sometimes, incentive is good, but the content is not good. At times, content is good, but incentive is not correct. One human being might do a good thing in his sight with good incentive, while he is bad. This man is on a correct path, but his work is wrong. Individuals might do a good act with bad incentive. For instance, one may discover something, while his incentive is bad but his works good. In another case, both elements might be good. A cultural revolution can be of this nature. A revolution is transformation from one state to another, not advancement of the thing existing. The revolution launched in the Islamic Republic is generally speaking of this nature. A revolution was accomplished by people. There was the incentive of the revolution and its content. I hope that incentive of the revolution would have been divinely in people. However, in revolutions, we might launch a revolution, remove a government and make a different government for us. We want to succeed in making money or so without being concerned as to see what would happen. This is of no avail to us whether the incentive is good or bad, because he wants to establish a revolution with the incentive of gaining power. He wants to be powerful. Formerly one has been powerful and now we want to take the power from the former and become powerful. Such a thing does not differ from the former in principle. That is to say, a government has gone, being replaced by the other. Both are similar. It is like the other coups taking place in the world. There is not difference between them. Once an uprising is launched, a revolution for a good purpose, but with no divinely intention. Since it plans a good end to serve the people, the effort is good. It might be worthwhile, but it does not seek the purpose deserving of man. The purpose worthy of man is that one seeks divinely intention in establishing government, in Cultural Revolution and in revolution. This is of value in the sight of God. This is like prophets. Prophets' efforts were praiseworthy not for the depth of their work and, let me say, scope of their work. Whether the scope of their government is wide or not, it is all the same. Prophets who have not been able to do anything or who have done great works are equal in terms of incentive. Both wanted to do something for God and receive spiritual reward. God grants them spiritual reward to both of them. One has succeeded and the other not. The latter has not been responsible for not being successful.

In the Cultural Revolution that which is of avail to you is once useful for government, once for students and once for you gentlemen. That which is useful for you is that you should be inspired by the incentive to push forward the university towards Islam and divinize it. There is no objection as to what lesson they want to study, the lessons that are useful. Islam favors all lessons excluding some of them. That which is of avail to us is that we want to divinize the Islamization, to seek divinizing end in our work and struggle for God. This attitude is of avail to you. Whether you succeed or not, it is useful. If this incentive motivates you, you will certainly seek to accomplish a good work. When one moves with divinely incentive, one cannot seek selfish end and find a path for him or what may happen. Whatever happens one is not concerned. This will naturally happen when incentive is God-oriented. One seeks to accomplish the work so as to gratify God. As such, he will be successful in this work. If he did not succeed in accomplishing, he has not enjoyed greater power to do it, but in the sight of God his value is the same as the one commanding power.

Therefore, that which has value for man, human and spiritual value, divinely value is to preserve this incentive to do the work for God. If you want to raise the children of people, do it for God, educate the youth to do it for God, and train the nation, for God, rule, for God. Govern in the same way that prophets did. Right! Moses was a ruler, so were the Prophet of Islam and Ali. On the other side, corrupt individuals are also ruler. The outward aspect is similar, unless in minor things. People share corresponding forms. They are like one another, with one essence. If occasionally there is difference, this difference is concerned with physical and animal aspect. That which differentiates between them is the meaning within them. What counts is the divinely incentive. Everything should return to God. God has sent the prophets. The main purpose has not been to rule. The main purpose has not been to establish a system. The high purpose has not been to establish social justice. These are not the sublime goal. Yet they are purposes- some of them are purposes. Of course, justice and its dispensation is a purpose. If you want to administer divinely justice for God Almighty, it is a purpose. If you want to administer divinely justice in order to gain fame and name, to indicate how good you are and to gain so and so, this is bad for you. The essence is good; it is then good for people. Some things are good for people and for university. Some things are good for you. Some things are good for both. If you succeed in developing divinely incentive, not doing things for yourself but for God and for people, this is for God and if this is the case, you are successful in your effort. If God forbid, you fail due to some impediment, this is not your fault and is beyond your power and God will accept. God does not demand beyond your power. Therefore, we should preserve this incentive. One may study a lesson, even divinely lesson, monotheistic lesson and mysticism and yet go to hell, while others who use the products of his efforts go to paradise. It is because he has had a wrong incentive and thus goes to hell. One may study a lesson to gain so and so position, become master of his district, city or country and the world. One may study to become famous in a village or in a city. All return to the self or God: me or He. If man lays foot on this I and become He, he can correct everything. The works are like this in all stages. One should differentiate between doing a divinely work and other activities. One should think about this. Sometimes one will go wrong, but one should think now that I am doing this work and am so happy because I did it for God, if one is found to be more efficient in doing it than I, am I ready to transfer it to him and become happier because he works for God more efficiently or not. If one realized that he was not ready, he should know that his efforts were not divinely-oriented or if it aimed at divinely purpose, he has not been sincerely involved. That which is useful for us is sincerity in doing work for God. God does not need anything; He does not need our sincerity. God has sent prophets to train people and save them. People will be saved if they follow the prophets and develop divinely incentives. If we cannot to this scale, we act as much as we can. Of course, we cannot have the incentive of the Commander of the Faithful. This is clear that we cannot. However, we can have some incentives corresponding to him. We can go that way.

You should move the university forward towards God and spirituality. All lessons should be studied for God. If you can do so, you will be successful whether you reach the destination or not. If you do things for yourselves, the work may be ordinary but brings profit to others though not for you. At times, the work may be to your detriment but is useful for others. It might be harmful to you or useful for you, but harmful to others. You wanted to do a good work but failed and the work has turned out to be bad, but you wanted to do a good work. We should always bear this in mind so that we can be successful in every business. I do not claim that the like of me are such a thing. Never! We are imperfect people and should acquire education so that we can gain perfection. However, among people there were such individuals. At least we know prophets were such people. Immaculate Imams (a) were such people. Whatever they did was for Him; they did not work for government and so and so. They struggled for government in order to strip the tyrants of it; they exerted pressure to take back the government from tyrants. They did not take it from tyrants in order to rule themselves. They did so in order to administer divinely justice. This work characterizes the prophets who worked to dispense divinely justice for God. Since they acted for God and with sincerity, they were divinely and their work was divinely. We are imperfect. We confess before God that we are imperfect and cannot gain such perfection to the end. However, we should think of this and seek this perfection. We should not turn our back at this sense. We should act for God and I hope you are successful. When there is such an incentive, even in works you could not previously do, you can accomplish with this incentive. With the incentive I explained, you find the power to do. God confirms such an incentive and work. We saw that prophets did big works with empty hands. What was the holy Prophet? Well! He was a shepherd in Mecca. All were opposed to him and harassed him. He was however a believer. This shepherd rose up and did such a big work that has developed the world. So was Jesus Christ. Prophet Moses was also a shepherd. So was prophet Ibrahim. They were of the same nature. They were integrated. Every one of them was a nation; that is, they had everything. What counts is that God was their fulcrum; they struggled for God and moved for Him. They traveled towards God Almighty. Since they journeyed towards

God, everything they did was divinely-oriented. Their eating was divinely-oriented. So was their prayer and war.

I hope that we seek this sense. I hope that you gentlemen are successful in what you are doing. Always show sensitivity in it. Never think the matter is over. University is so important that corrupt views seek to find a wrong in it. They are in search of excuse. God willing they will not be successful. One should always be sensitive lest the bunker that can correct or destroy everything should be taken from you or harmed. I pray for you and hope that you will always be successful, sanctioned and victorious, always working for this nation and for God!

Date/Time: Morning, December 01, 1985/Azar 19, 1364 SH/Rabi' al-Awwal 27, 1406 AH.

Place: Jamaran, Tehran

Subject: University and the Cultural Revolution

Occasion: Anniversary of formation of the Supreme Cultural Revolution Council

Audience: Sayyid Ali Khamenei (President and chairman of the Supreme Cultural Revolution Council), members of the Cultural Revolution Council

SECTION 4

THE MISSION OF UNIVERSITIES

Manufacturing Human Beings

Both of us[37] are to educate the people of our society. We need learned people. Our country requires its citizens to be enlightened. There must be pious and faithful persons in this country. The kind of pious people who have been enlightened by you and us would never give in to the foreign oppression, nor could they be bought into submission. The sorts that are prone to be intimidated or bought are those very ones who lack faith. A faithful and pious person would hardly be liable to selling himself. He can neither be intimidated nor bought, because intimidations are contradictory to what a Muslim is duty bound to do, and he would refuse to be intimidated. You and we should unite to give rise to a monotheistic society, which translates into persuading all people to believe in the Almighty God and make sure that our people are aware of the fact that there would be a day of reckoning. Everybody should be faithful and pious in every way. If we unite and try to bring up pious and religiously faithful young people, the country shall never come to harm and would enjoy everlasting longevity…

There would be no sign of previous practices. We would then have a great and fundamental development in our programs. We should do our best to change those plans, which had been contrived to keep us behind. Of course, we would embark on such programs. But, what you have to do now is to change those schemes contrived to keep us depraved, and we should not give in to such schemes. We must change them and that is a big challenge.

Date: May 24, 1979/Khordad 3, 1358 SH/Jamadi ath-Thani 27, 1399 AH.

Place: Qum

Subject: Profession of clerics and academicians; creation of discord between the seminary and university; role of culture in the declination and amelioration of the society

Audience: Ali Shari'atmadari (Minister of Culture and Higher Education), chancellors of universities and institutions of higher education

Possessions are not important in Islam and neither is materialism. What is important is spirituality that should emanate from the university- whether yours or the clergy's- and permeate all the strata of society. It is these two groups with whom the education of the Islamic community rests. The task of these two groups is nobler and their responsibility greater than all the other groups. Noble in function because the universities are the places where human character is molded. The university- whether yours or the clergy's- must be a center for molding human beings. This mission of

---

[37] Imam (ra) here refers to Universities and Islamic Seminaries (*howzeh*)

building human beings had been entrusted to the prophets (a). The Heavenly Book, in fact all of them, came for the purpose of building man. If human beings are molded properly, everything will assume spirituality, and even material things will turn out as spiritual. On the contrary, if these entities (the two kinds of universities) are Satanic and if they produced deviated people, then spirituality will also assume a material aspect and be annihilated within it.

Date: June 6, 1979/Khordad 16, 1358 SH/Rajab 11, 1399 AH.

Place: Qum

Subject: The need for the universities to become Islamic

Addressees: Doctors, professors and students of Shiraz University

We want to evolve into an enlightened society, a people sparkling with piety. We want to attend universities whose affairs are brilliantly administered and the sciences taught are radiant with knowledge. We want it to be ethically resplendent, and everything else of it to be divine and shining with virtue. The victory is not for us to have gained freedom and independence with all the benefits accruing to us, and that is all. Is this the end of everything? Now that the benefits are ours, do we have nothing more to do?

These matters constitute the prelude. These are all the preliminaries to creating a humane nation; a nation in which the spirit of humanity is generated and a transformation brought about in the people themselves. What is important to the prophets is humanity itself. It is nothing else; only man is the concern of the prophets. Everything should assume a humane aspect. They wanted to mold man. When man is molded, everything else turns out right.

Date: June 6, 1979/Khordad 16, 1358 SH/Rajab 11, 1399 AH.

Place: Qum

Subject: The need for the universities to become Islamic

Addressees: Doctors, professors and students of Shiraz University

You, the university authorities should make efforts to mold human character. By doing so, you will save your country. If you are able to turn out committed and trustworthy individuals who believe in the other world and in God; who are faithful to God, if such people are brought up in your universities and ours, they will deliver your country. Therefore, the task is a very noble one and the responsibility great. This responsibility is now on your shoulders and ours. You, the university authorities and the clergymen, should ensure the nation's well-being by discharging this grave responsibility. You must ensure the nation's welfare. This responsibility has been entrusted to you (by virtue of your profession). You did not take up agriculture. If you were a cultivator, you would still have responsibility but not this one. If you were a merchant, you would have responsibility within your own sphere (of activity). But now this responsibility concerns a nation, a country. It is for the sake of Islam. We are all responsible before God. All of us- the university, the theology universities, your science universities- should strive to mold (upright) human beings. All of us should aim for this: a real human being.

If you were to make exceptions of human beings in that you produced a scientist, or a doctor that was better than all the doctors in the world, and if such a doctor was lacking in human qualities, he would, then be most harmful. When this same doctor wants to treat somebody, he will be after personal gain; he will not be concerned with the treatment (of his patient). He will be interested in knowing how much money he will get from the patient! If you produced a doctor who would develop as a humane person, he would just be after treating the patient. He would not be concerned with how much he would get from him. The issue is not business; it is curing people in a divine, humane way. A doctor's treatment can be divine. It can also be satanic and *taghouti*; *taghouti* treatment in the sense that the doctor is concerned with how much money he will get from his patient. It is the case of the patient's purse prolonging the disease! How much can he extract from the patient; how much can he prolong the treatment to get as much money as he can from him! A God-fearing doctor thinks only of saving the patient, even if he is to get nothing! If your university turns out upright human beings, they will save the nation. They do not think about what they or their position will be. Their only concern is to save the patient. But if they become *taghouti*, they will think only of gain. They are not interested in saving the patient. They want to work for their own personal benefit, and not for the country.

Date: June 6, 1979/Khordad 16, 1358 SH/Rajab 11, 1399 AH.

Place: Qum

Subject: The need for the universities to become Islamic

Addressees: Doctors, professors and students of Shiraz University

The university in every country... has the role of molding human character; its mission is to build man. It is possible for a person to emerge from a university who can save a country. It is also possible for one to emerge who will take the country to ruination. The university has this important role. The destiny of every country lies with the university and those who graduate from it. Hence, the university is the most influential institution in the country and has the greatest responsibility. The reason why the alien powers kept our universities backwards by means of their lackeys, and made them "colonial" so to speak- the curricula were all colonial- was that they feared the university because of this very fact of it having a role to play. This is also true in the case of the clergy which also has a role. There may be a clergyman that can save a country, and there may be one who can ruin it. These two poles consisting of the university in every sense of the world- all the universities- and the clergy hold the destiny of the nation in their hands. Therefore, their task is more important and more honorable than all the other tasks because it is that very same mission of the prophets. All the prophets came for the purpose of building a man. Everything turns out right by producing the right people. The task of these two points which concerns the building of man- with the university being responsible for turning out properly-trained and righteous people, and so is the clergy- is among the noblest of tasks as it is the same as that of the prophets. Their responsibility is also greater than all other responsibilities because everything is developed here (the two poles). The entire attention of the foreigners had been riveted to these two poles. However, they crushed these places in similar way.

Date: June 11, 1979/Khordad 12, 1358 SH/Rajab 16, 1399 AH.

Place: Qum

Subject: The enemy striking a blow against the two poles: the clergy and the university; the danger posed by the West and West-worship

Audience: Students of the Police Academy, Tehran

The university- whether the clergy's or yours- is in a country that entrusted with the task of training people, should be responsible for molding them so that when these youths leave the university, they will do so as (proper) human beings; not Westernized ones but Islamic.

Date: June 11, 1979/Khordad 12, 1358 SH/Rajab 16, 1399 AH.

Place: Qum

Subject: The enemy striking a blow against the two poles: the clergy and the university; the danger posed by the West and West-worship

Audience: Students of the Police Academy, Tehran

What is important about the universities, the teachers' college, and the centers for training teachers and students is that people should be trained to be human beings along with teaching and learning. People have often reached the pinnacle of knowledge but without being trained to be human beings. The harm accruing to the country, the nation and Islam from such persons is more than that from the others. One who has knowledge which is not associated with moral refinement and spiritual training is more detrimental to the nation and the country than the ones who lack knowledge. The knowledge of such a person is like a sword in his hands. And it is possible that he will use that sword of knowledge to cut off the root of the country and so destroy it.

Date: June 27, 1979/Tir 6, 1358 SH/Sha'ban 2, 1399 AH.

Place: Qum

Subject: The role of the unity of the seminary and the university; the issue of factionalism and party politics

Audience: Students of the Islamic Association of the Teachers' Training University, Tehran

If the universities are not improved and our schools are not improved, there is no hope that we will find an Islamic Republic. If these two strata are educated in a way that Islam wants it; if they are educated in a humane way, then on the one hand our country will become safe from the possession of the evils and it will revolve round her own pivot and without being dependent on the foreigners and without the domestic treasons. And progress will result for you as well. The importance about being a university student, an associate professor, a full professor and a pupil- in both education and science- is that there exists a proper way that accompanies the science and education; the learned man who is educated in a humane way which is the same as Islamic teaching. Any step that you take for the sake of knowledge, for an outward deed or the inwardly deeds, to create piety, perseverance and trust in you, so that when you leave the university, be a human being who is both educated and who is a trustee, God willing. As for your education, you should both act as a trustee and have a purified soul; then you have leashed your ego. Human's soul is mutinous and that mutiny will overthrow the man. In the same way that when a person rides an obstinate horse and it is unleashed, such mutinous horse will cause the death of man. Man's ego is worse than any mutinous creature. The mutiny of the ego will cause the death of man. Any step that you take in the course of education, take a parallel step for taming of your ego from this mutiny it has and the freedom from being leashed that it assumes for itself. You leash your ego. Should such a teaching-learning system exists in a country, that country could be independent; it can be free; it can secure its economy; it can rectify its culture; and it can set straight everything else. In such a country, the head of the state cannot be a crooked; its army cannot be a bully; its gendarmerie cannot infringe on the rights of the citizens; its police cannot do wrong. Most important of all it is for these universities- whether the universities of the new sciences or the universities of the old sciences both of which have the destiny of the country in their hands- will produce human beings, not a quadruped with some books laden on its back. It should not be mere acquisition of knowledge where you are on the side of natural sciences and the other group on the side of divine sciences. Scrutinize the sciences. However, stay away from the egoistic mutiny. If you neglect, every step that you take in (acquiring) knowledge, you stay away from humanity; and away yet. Humanity is on a straight course. If someone steps in that path, they are considered crooked and against humanity. Should you step in the other direction, it is the wrong way. And he who chose to be crooked and deviated from the straight path, the farther they go the farther they move away from the path of humanity. It is as if you draw a straight line- two lines like this- the more this line moves forward, the more it is removed from the straight path.

The more you all study and we all study, if we do not follow the straight path and do not control our knowledge and do not leash our ego, and do not kill our ego in this course, the more educated we are the farther we get from humanity and from the human beings. Thus, it gets more difficult for the humankind to restore to his previous quality.

Time/Date: Morning, July 7, 1979/Tir 17, 1358 SH/Sha'ban 31, 1399 AH.

Place: Qum

Subject: The role of reform and self-purification in training and education

Audience: Students of Ahwaz

You and we[38] should chip in our efforts to create faith for those future generations who will be responsible for the fate of this country. You would let pious people graduate from your universities, and we would send pious clerics out of the schools. Neither scholars nor scientists for their own sakes are any good in the absence of faith. As a matter of fact, piety by itself would not be very effective, as there are many pious people around, but when a scholar is pious and he is also faithful, then he will be the source of many blessings and contributions in safeguarding the country. It is in this light that we are burdened with such a great responsibility; both you and we are given such a great responsibility. If we find the right path and act according to what we have been assigned with, we have given strength to faith along with science so that there would be no sign of previous practices.

Date: May 24, 1979/Khordad 3, 1358 SH/Jamadi ath-Thani 27, 1399 AH.

---

[38] Imam (ra) refers to university faculty members and Islamic Seminary (*howzeh*) teachers

Place: Qum

Subject: Profession of clerics and academicians; creation of discord between the seminary and university; role of culture in the declination and amelioration of the society

Audience: Ali Shari'atmadari (Minister of Culture and Higher Education), chancellors of universities and institutions of higher education

The whole country should engage in mending the things. More important is to correct the people. Reform them. Make the universities the center for training. Training is necessary besides the learning. A scholar without a good training is harmful. He will betray. One with learning and knowledge if betrayed, the danger will be far and wide involving all the people. The students are able to be trained. If they are brought up will and calculated, they will be able to administer the things. Later on you have to give this country to these youths to run it. Do long to be independent. God willing you long so. It is you the men of universities, and the men of teaching. So teach the youths along with training.

Date: January 4, 1980/Dey 14, 1358 SH/Safar 15, 1400 AH.

Place: Qum

Subject: Peculiarities of the Islamic Revolution and its distinctions with other revolutions

Audience: Tehran University professors

If universities have love towards Islam, towards their country, towards their nation, they should train our youths rightly and mould them with a good, virtuous, and correct training. We should rescue them from getting Westernized. Everyone among us should be after this aim. The governments regrettably are under the line of this thought to be able to do or have a say in this matter. They should revise their stand. From now onwards they should abstain from doing what they had been doing so far. Again it depends upon love and attachment if they have towards Islam and nation and homeland.

Date: Afternoon, January 01, 1980/Dey 02, 1358 SH/Safar 12, 1400 AH.

Place: Qum

Subject: Reformation and the Oneness of the word of Iranian nation a paragon to the other nations

Audience: Representatives of the Freedom-seeking organizations of the world

All the universities, all the schools, all the old centers of education, where the clergies learn and where the students (not clergies) learn, should be instructors whose self, the inner being, must be purified. As they teach and train, so they should purify the spirit of students.

Time: Morning, July 2, 1980/Tir 01, 1359 SH/Sha'ban 18, 1400 AH.

Place: Jamaran, Tehran

Subject: Education and training from the Qur'an's view, the position of culture in the Pahlavi regime. The need for basic changes there

Audience: The heads of education throughout the country, the Islamic Association members, the Home Ministry workers and the provincial workers

We want an academic not a student or a teacher. The university must produce proper human beings. In such a case, nobody will be prepared to surrender his country to others. He will be ready to undergo suffering and captivity; and such people, they fear.

Date: Before noon, December 18, 1980/Azar 27, 1359 SH/Safar 01, 1401 AH.

Place: Jamaran, Tehran

Subject: The importance of the roles of the seminary and the university; stating the duties of these two institutions of learning

Occasion: The day of unity between the seminary and the university

Audience: Teachers and students of Qum Theological Center; the student members of the office for the consolidation of unity between the seminary and the university

Whenever a training that is worthy of human beings and is conducive to the human disposition- which is the same disposition that is given as a trust to man and is "*the nature made by Allah in which He has made men*" - is imparted also in the universities, then when those youth enter society and when the fate of the society is consequently given into their hands, they succeed in taking their country out of gloom into light and make it worthy enough for human beings to live in and mould it as per the primordial nature and cause it to progress.

If you simply want to impart education to children without bothering to give them ethical training besides their general education, they will pass all the stages of learning, gaining knowledge without any moral training. And knowledge devoid of moral and ethical training will drag most of them toward corruption.

Date: January 03, 1981/Bahman 01, 1359 SH/Rabi' al-Awwal, 23, 1401 AH.

168

Place: Jamaran, Tehran

Subject: The importance of the teaching profession and the duties of the teachers in training students

Audience: Religious teachers from all over the country

We want to have a university whose graduates will not turn out to be like you[39] all. We want our universities to produce people who are committed to Islam. If they are committed to Islam they will neither drag us toward the East and nor the West. And neither will they hold your negative belief that we are incapable

Date: June 15, 1981/Khordad 25, 1360 SH/Sha'ban 21, 1401 AH.

Place: Jamaran Husayniyyah, Tehran

Subject: Strong warning to the opponents of the Retaliation (*qisas*) Bill; declaring those who oppose the necessary laws of Islam as apostates

Addressees: Various strata of people, clerics from the Mazandaran province, some Sunni clerics, a group of people from Mashhad, and employees of the intercity bus services

They must equip the universities so that they can build the youths.

Date/Time: Morning, December 31, 1981/Azar 22, 1360 SH/Safar 16, 1402 AH.

Place: Jamaran, Tehran

Subject: Place and role of university in the country

Audience: Board of trustees of the National University and heads of various faculties and hospitals affiliated to this university

We should educate our youths in a way that the Muslims of other countries come to realize that education in there is useful. Be aware that if the university worked efficiently and presented a good model of itself and the people of the world would understand that the university in Iran works for Iran and not for aliens, Muslims of other countries will naturally come here.

Date/Time: Morning, April 16, 1985/Farvardin 27, 1364 SH/Rajab 25, 1405 AH.

Place: Jamaran, Tehran

---

[39] Imam (ra) here refers to the leaders of National Front

Subject: Improvement of university and struggle for liberation from cultural dependence

Audience: Iraj Fadil (Minister of Culture and Higher Education) and deputies

You should move the university forward towards God and spirituality. All lessons should be studied for God. If you can do so, you will be successful whether you reach the destination or not.

Date/Time: Morning, December 01, 1985/Azar 19, 1364 SH/Rabi' al-Awwal 27, 1406 AH.

Place: Jamaran, Tehran

Subject: University and the Cultural Revolution

Occasion: Anniversary of formation of the Supreme Cultural Revolution Council

Audience: Sayyid Ali Khamenei (President and chairman of the Supreme Cultural Revolution Council), members of the Cultural Revolution Council

Cutting-off Dependence and Independence of Country

If the universities are not improved and our schools are not improved, there is no hope that we will find an Islamic Republic. If these two strata are educated in a way that Islam wants it; if they are educated in a humane way, then on the one hand our country will become safe from the possession of the evils and it will revolve round her own pivot and without being dependent on the foreigners and without the domestic treasons. And progress will result for you[40] as well.

Time/Date: Morning, July 7, 1979/Tir 17, 1358 SH/Sha'ban 31, 1399 AH.

Place: Qum

Subject: The role of reform and self-purification in training and education

Audience: Students of Ahwaz

The universities shall take care of our youth's independence and should educate them to understand that they have a culture, a great one. They should realize that the culture is exported to the West from the East. They should find out that we are something in the universe and we want to manage ourselves.

---

[40] Imam (ra) refers to students here.

Date: October 29, 1979/Aban 7, 1358 SH/Dhu'l-Hijjah 7, 1399 AH.

Place: Qum

Subject: Westernization, a chronic disease in Iran

Audience: Students of Islamic Association of Mufidi High College of Translation

Our universities must endeavor to train and educate students to help the nation to be relieved of foreign need. Our physicians should be domestic; we should not stand in need of foreign doctors or flying overseas for operation of tonsil. In the former regime, the Shah wanted to get the tonsil of his child or a relative and brought physicians from abroad to do it.

Time: November 2, 1979/Aban 11, 1358 SH/Dhu'l-Hijjah 11, 1399 AH.

Place: Qum

Subject: Necessity of cultural-economic independence of the country

Audience: Students of Faculty of Sciences and Faculty of Literature and Foreign Languages

If a country wants to be independent, the first condition is to be free from need to others. If a country stands in need of others, it cannot be independent. Need is itself a political dependence. If once one whom we need supposedly stops meeting our needs, we have to succumb. We should act in a way as to be independent and free from need. This is obtainable provided that university students struggle to fulfill our needs.

Time: November 2, 1979/Aban 11, 1358 SH/Dhu'l-Hijjah 11, 1399 AH.

Place: Qum

Subject: Strife for autonomy and independence

Audience: Political prisoners in the Shah's Regime

The universities should be at their own without the need to depend upon the West.

Date: January 2, 1980/Dey 21, 1358 SH/Safar 31, 1400 AH.

Place: Qum

Audience: Students of Islamic Association, Law College, Learning Center, Ardebil

Subject: The consequences of being intellectually dependent on the west- a sense of loss of direction in the East

The universities should be at their own without the need to depend upon the West.... Our scholars, our professors, nobody should fear West. Our youths too should not fear the West. The East should have the will and movement against the West will take place.

Date: January 2, 1980/Dey 21, 1358 SH/Safar 31, 1400 AH.

Place: Qum

Audience: Students of Islamic Association, Law College, Learning Center, Ardebil

Subject: The consequences of being intellectually dependent on the west- a sense of loss of direction in the East

For the cultural revolution in order to turn our universities into peaceful places of real learning and skill. If there is no peace and tranquility in the university, it cannot accommodate the expertise of the scholars and you respected university teachers will not be able to teach and train your students effectively. In the absence of peace in the universities and the other academic places it would not be possible for the experts to transfer their knowledge to our youth and to turn them into thinkers and experts. What is of utmost importance in this country at present is peace and tranquility everywhere; among the farmers, in the factories, within the industries, and particularly in the universities. Since the universities are the source of knowledge for our youth they need to have peace.

Date: April 31, 1981/Farvardin 24, 1360 SH/Jamadi ath-Thani 8, 1401 AH.

Place: Jamaran, Tehran

Subject: Need to maintain unity and peace and warning against disruptive elements

Audience: Agriculturists and the inhabitants of Gorgan, the clerics and the inhabitants of Ali-Abad, the inhabitants of Gonbad and Turkman Sahra, and the Basij of Shahreza

Our aim is to ensure that the experts that graduate from the universities are at the service of their nation instead of dragging the country toward the East or the West. Our aim is to ensure that our industries grow to high levels of expertise and be at the service of the nation instead of serving alien powers. The kind of know-how seeking that drags us toward America or the Soviet Union is harmful and is hazardous to the nations. Most of those who were educated in the universities of the previous regime, if not harmful, were of no use to this country. Our purpose is to have a university system that is at the service of our nation and at the service of Iran. During the days of the previous regime, the slogans that they raised were that "we want to convert Iran into a flourishing civilization" and that "we should enter the gates of civilization", while you all saw that in reality they had made this country dependent in every way. We categorically oppose a university system that will render us dependent on foreign countries irrespective of which foreign country it is!

We intend to have a university system that can free us from dependence upon others and can make us self-reliant. We need experts and Islam approves of expertise. Islam comes first among all religions that have extolled the value of knowledge and expertise and it has invited people to pursue knowledge. It has asked people to gain knowledge even if it entails going to other places and acquiring it from non-believers. However, Islam emphasizes that knowledge should be at the service of Islam and the Islamic country rather than for use against one's own country. We are looking forward to having a university system that can free us from intellectual dependence, which is the most dangerous form of dependence. We intend to have university teachers that can train our youth to be self-reliant instead of inclining toward the West or the East. We do not want any Ataturks and Taqizadehs. We are looking forward to having a university system that can, after a few years, make us self-reliant in every respect. We are not against expertise. What we oppose is the dependence of the minds of our youth on the West or the East. In the previous regime, our universities, with the exception of a few people, were either indifferent toward this issue or else they worked toward making our youth dependent on foreign powers. What we are seeking out is that if ever our people need treatment for their (complicated) ailments, they should not be asked to go to Britain or America for treatment. What we want is that just as an American or English patient does not need to come to Iran for treatment, our patients, too, do not need to go abroad for their problems. We are looking for the kind of expertise that does not make our youth and their intellects dependent but instead trains them to foster concern for Islam and Iran. We are certainly not against expertise! And the same applies to the Islamic associations. No Islamic association can be against expertise. There is no Islamic association that is against expertise and the self-reliance of our youth in every field. In fact, it is the opposite. And you had seen that the conditions of the universities during the reign of the previous regime were such that even after long years of active work in our universities, when a relative of the deposed Shah- the so called "head of the country"- needed to undergo a simple surgery for appendicitis, a surgeon was brought in from abroad! What prompted this was that the Shah knew very well in his hollow head that he had made Iran so dependent on foreigners that the Iranians were not capable of handling (even simple) things; and even if they were, all efforts should be made to inculcate their minds into believing that they are good-for-nothing! And that they should be made to believe that they are incapable of performing even a simple surgery for appendicitis after spending long years at the university! However, our intention is to free the minds (of our people) from such ill-thoughts.

The aim of the Islamic associations should be to eliminate this wrong belief so that our people can rediscover themselves after centuries of alienation. We want our universities to train people like Avicenna[41] whose book, "The Canon of Medicine", is still being used in Europe rather than having people who, without even knowing the alphabets of Islam, claim that Islam is incompetent! We want our universities to become as independent as our seminaries in which the agents of the foreign powers are easily exposed. We want them to be freed from all kinds of dependence, like they were in the olden days, during which, even if deviants emerged they would immediately be exposed. We are looking for the fulfillment of this ideal.

Time/Date: Morning, May 25, 1981/Khordad 4, 1360 SH/Rajab 02, 1401 AH.

Place: Jamaran, Tehran

Subject: Importance of knowledge in Islam; responsibility of the university in an Islamic society; duties of the Islamic associations of the universities

Audience: Members of the Islamic Association and the Jihad of the 'Ilm va San'at (Science and Technology) University; members of the Organization for Scientific and Industrial Research; and a group of inventors and innovators

The university can either make a country independent or rob it of its independence. Students and academic scholars should join hands and reopen the universities as soon as possible- universities with an Islamic and national identity and universities that truly belong to an Islamic nation- and sever the hands of all those who want to drag the university toward the East or the West. The Islamic teachers and professors should take the destiny of the university into their own hands and should ensure that the university proves to be a national university in service of national interests. It should not be that all the trouble is taken by the nation and all the expenses of the university are borne by the nation while it turns into a university whose graduates emerge worshipping the East or the West. The universities should reopen but with an atmosphere in which its teachings are Islamic, national, and human. We should not simply insist on its reopening without considering everything else. Well, it was open for the past fifty years. What kind of graduates did it churn out?! The same people who ruined this country and are still not sparing this nation. We want our universities to liberate our nation from the domination of the East and the West instead of dragging it toward them- an independent nation, with an independent ideology, with independent universities because it is the independence of the universities that ensures the independence of a country. Universities that hold hands with the seminaries and

---

[41] Hussain bin Abdullah bin Sina (370-428 AH) famous as Abu Ali Sina, the great Persian Physician and Philosopher who wrote several important books including *Isharaat wa al-Tanbihaat*, *Shifa* etc.

sidetrack the Eastern and Western blocs and instead work in the interests of their own country and beloved Islam and bring up our children in a way that they no longer need to look toward Moscow, London, or Washington as their Mecca. Let them look toward the Ka'bah and focus upon God Almighty and welcome Islam with open arms because only Islam guarantees their independence and dignity.

The importance that Islam gives to knowledge is probably not given by any other school. The importance that Islam gives to scholars is probably not given by any other school. Islam gives the utmost importance to knowledge but not the kind of knowledge that drags us to ruin and not the kind of scholars that drag us into the arms of the East and the West. Islam strives to foster knowledge within independent minds and minds that serve Islam. Such independence can ensure the independence of our country. The independence of our country depends on the independence of the universities and the seminaries. The university and seminaries should join hands and protect the independence of their country. They should cut off all their hopes from both the Islamic universities and the seminaries... I am hopeful that you will succeed in managing the affairs of your country independently and that you will no longer need to stretch your hands toward the East and the West and that the mischief they create in our country, boomerangs back to them.

Date: Morning, June 31, 1981/Khordad 23, 1360 SH/Sha'ban 01, 1401 AH.

Place: Jamaran Husayniyyah, Tehran

Subject: Importance of the role of the university in the independence or lack of independence of a country

Occasion: Anniversary of the establishment of the Ad Hoc Committee for the Cultural Revolution

Addressees: The members of the Ad Hoc Committee for the Cultural Revolution and the Supreme Council of the Jihad of the Universities of Tehran and other cities

You know that whatever good and bad befalls a nation, dependence or independence, being subjugated and chained and suppression or freedom are contingent upon the university training. The role that a university plays in a country is an important matter and is a great role so that if it plays this great role in a proper way, the country shall attain its lofty objectives. These two factions of university and Faydiyyah theological school, that praise be to God, have today consolidated their unity and together have become one member of the society, can cause a country to attain true independence and freedom. However, if, God forbid, these two strata deviate, then know for sure that the country and the commandments of Islam shall be drawn towards deviation. For this reason, the task that you the dear students have- which is focusing on Islamic issues of the university- is a very crucial and valuable task and on the other hand, it is also very responsive.

Date/Time: Morning, November 27, 1982/Azar 6, 1361 SH/Safar 11, 1403 AH.

Place: Husayniyyah Jamaran, Tehran

Subject: Importance of the role of Islamic associations, successes of the popular serving government

Audience: Student members of the Office of Consolidation of Unity of the Islamic associations of the universities throughout the country

The scientists must pass on their knowledge to the students. The university, which is at the head of the affairs and the destiny of a country, depends on their existence, must sincerely endeavor to turn its face away from the East and the West and face the straight path. It must turn towards the House of God; it must move towards the Blessed and Almighty God and build the youth for the future of the country.

Date/Time: Morning, January 16, 1983/Dey 26, 1361 SH/Rabi 'al-Thani 1, 1403 AH.

Place: Husayniyyah Jamaran, Tehran

Subject: Termination of excuses in serving Islam and the country

Audience: Salimi (Minister of Defense), Safa'i (Head of the Political-Ideology Department of the Army), employees of the Defense Industries, personnel of the Political-Ideology Section of the Isfahan Center of the Islamic Republic Broadcasting

The story of university is among the most important concerns, as it is important for our enemies and those who want to deflect the mind of our youths. University is the center of all developments, even establishment of government. We should pursue the efforts to Islamize universities to be useful for the country. Attempts should be made so that the universities do not tilt towards either one of the powers. This calls for time, energy, and close supervision... I hope that we have universities that are useful for the nation. To give reality to this idea, it is necessary to use experts and in case of shortage of committed experts use experts who are not antagonistic to the Islamic Republic.

Time: Morning, October 4, 1983/Mehr 21, 1362 SH/Dhul-Hijjah 26, 1403 AH.

Place: Jamaran, Tehran

Subject: Struggle for Islamization of universities

Audience: New members of the Cultural Revolution Board, Mir Husayn Mousavi (Prime Minister), Sayyid Muhammad Khatami, Sayyid 'Abdul-Karim Soroush, Muhammad Ali Najjafi, Ali Shari'atmadari

If we acquire a type of industry from them, we should not become British, Russian or American. We should remain Muslim. Obviously, there is no objection to using the sciences and borrowing it from others, but we should note that we should borrow the sciences from countries, which do not intend to deflect us. In the past if they gave us some of the sciences and expertise, they wanted to deflect us from everything we had and orient us towards consumerism.

Time: Morning, November 15, 1983/Aban 24, 1362 SH/Safar 9, 1404 AH.

Place: Jamaran, Tehran

Subject: Vigilance against cultural schemes of the alliance

Audience: 'Abdullah Jasbi (Superintendent of Azad Islamic University), officials of different branches of the university

I hope this university and all other universities turn to centers that purify our youth and educate them from scholarly aspects to the extent that they are separated from abroad and act independently and serving the cause of Islam and their country.

Date/Time: Morning, July 15, 1985/Tir 24, 1364 SH/Shawwal 26, 1405 AH.

Place: Jamaran, Tehran

Subject: Priority in reforming universities

Audience: Jasbi (dean of Islamic Azad University), deputies and advisors of the university

Prosperity of Nations

The university is the source of all changes. It is from the university- whether of the old sciences or the modern ones- that a nation's prosperity and, in contrast, its adversity originate. The universities must be taken seriously. Every effort should be made to set them right; to make them Islamic.

Date: June 6, 1979/Khordad 16, 1358 SH/Rajab 11, 1399 AH.

Place: Qum

Subject: The need for the universities to become Islamic

Addressees: Doctors, professors and students of Shiraz University

The university is the source of a nation's blessings and paradoxically, the cause of its misfortunes. The university must determine a nation's destiny. While a good university is instrumental in a nation's prosperity, one that is not Islamic and is bad pushes a nation backwards.

Date: June 6, 1979/Khordad 16, 1358 SH/Rajab 11, 1399 AH.

Place: Qum

Subject: The need for the universities to become Islamic

Addressees: Doctors, professors and students of Shiraz University

Our state should be deplorable if our universities are not managed properly. The university holds the key to everything. That is, these two poles, the university and the clergy, hold the country's destiny in their hands. All the problems should be solved by the university students, whether of the new system or the old one. They are the brains of nation. If we are indifferent to the university and are deprived of it, we will then lose everything.

Date: June 31, 1979/Khordad 23, 1358 SH/Rajab 18, 1399 AH.

Place: Qum

Subject: The splinter groups creating disorder and hatching plots in the universities, the workplaces and farms, and the need to confront them; the danger of discord and deviation.

Audience: A group of students from Tehran University

Peace belongs to knowledge, university and students that are the light the path leading the nation towards elevation, prosperity and virtue.

Greeting to the youth endeavor hard for uplifting the dear Islamic country with the weapon of knowledge and its advancement; sparing no efforts in achieving Human-Islamic ends.

Peace belongs to the collegians and professors who have suffered from deprivations, mental and physical tortures during the long years of suffocation, standing bravely and firmly against bullies and tyranny and did not surrender to evil powers.

Greetings to dear ones who defended the deprived people and the oppressed people in the hardest times of the Islamic revolution, never fearing the invasions of troops on cultural-training centers and encountering them selflessly.

Salutations to all students including elementary, high school and university students, scientists and professors throughout the country turning their scientific and sacred places into strong castles and unbeatable redoubts and defending their country's independence and freedom, crushing the devilish bunkers with the support of the great nation and burying the bloodthirsty enemy.

Date: September 22, 1979/Shahrivar 13, 1358 SH/Shawwal 03, 1399 AH.

Place: Qum

Subject: Foreigners' attempts to sweep the Islamic content of the scientific and cultural programs

Occasion: Opening of academic year

Addressees: Professors, collegians and students

The point is that if the said two groups were enlightened, the whole nation would follow their example. The two groups about which has been said, *"A corrupted scholar corrupts the whole world."* The scholar we are talking about does not encompass me alone. It is you,[42] all of us. You, too, are among the scholars. If, God forbid, you were corrupt, you would spread corruptive practices all over the world. On the other hand, if you are morally good, the whole world shall benefit from your goodness. Both the good and the evil in societies are in the hands of those in charge of teaching those societies. You are the teachers, while the clerics are different kinds of teachers, but both of you enlighten the whole society.

Date: May 24, 1979/Khordad 3, 1358 SH/Jamadi ath-Thani 27, 1399 AH.

Place: Qum

Subject: Profession of clerics and academicians; creation of discord between the seminary and university; role of culture in the declination and amelioration of the society

Audience: Ali Shari'atmadari (Minister of Culture and Higher Education), chancellors of universities and institutions of higher education

The universities and the seminaries, together with the clergy, can constitute two centers for the country's progress and development. They can also be two centers of all deviations and perversions. It is from the university that committed intellectuals graduate. If the university be a university, if it is really a university and Islamic in nature; that is; together with the actual education, there is dedication and edification as well,

---

[42] Imam (ra) refers to university faculty members.

then such people (the university graduates) will be able to lead the country to prosperity. Also, if the centers of theology be refined and committed, they will be able to save the country.

Date: Before noon, December 18, 1980/Azar 27, 1359 SH/Safar 01, 1401 AH.

Place: Jamaran, Tehran

Subject: The importance of the roles of the seminary and the university; stating the duties of these two institutions of learning

Occasion: The day of unity between the seminary and the university

Audience: Teachers and students of Qum Theological Center; the student members of the office for the consolidation of unity between the seminary and the university who used to worry about this country in the past- mobilize themselves to ensure that the sons of the soil be committed to serving Iran, the university, then, will be the highest institution that will bring prosperity to the country.

The university takes two paths: the path to hell and the path to prosperity; the path to ignominy, poverty and servitude, etc. and the path to glory, honor and magnanimity. The university that we have is of no use. We have had one for the past fifty years. Whatever corruption there was in this country was because of these people who had been educated in it, and, perhaps, had even specialized.

Date: Before noon, December 18, 1980/Azar 27, 1359 SH/Safar 01, 1401 AH.

Place: Jamaran, Tehran

Subject: The importance of the roles of the seminary and the university; stating the duties of these two institutions of learning

Occasion: The day of unity between the seminary and the university

Audience: Teachers and students of Qum Theological Center; the student members of the office for the consolidation of unity between the seminary and the university.

If the universities are not given direction, they will be the same as the ones existing for the people, and which produce destructive forces. But if they be given (the necessary) direction they will accomplish what the machine guns cannot. They can render service to humanity, which no one can do to that extent.

Date: December 27, 1980/Dey 6, 1359 SH/Safar 19, 1401 AH.

Place: Jamaran, Tehran

Subject: The importance of knowledge and learning in Islam, and the need for education to be accompanied by training

Audience: The authorities responsible for the countrywide literacy campaign and those participating in the seminar on the literacy campaign

The university of a country can be the cause of the uplift or destruction of its nation. The university and the academic training can drag our youth either toward the West or the East and alienate them from their own identity and infatuate them with the West and the East until the East gains domination over every aspect of Iran and the land of the Muslims or the West gains domination and robs us of our culture and everything else, replacing it with an Eastern or Western ideology and dragging the country to destruction.

Date: Morning, June 31, 1981/Khordad 23, 1360 SH/Sha'ban 01, 1401 AH.

Place: Jamaran Husayniyyah, Tehran

Subject: Importance of the role of the university in the independence or lack of independence of a country

Occasion: Anniversary of the establishment of the Ad Hoc Committee for the Cultural Revolution

Addressees: The members of the Ad Hoc Committee for the Cultural Revolution and the Supreme Council of the Jihad of the Universities of Tehran and other cities

The most important thing that the enemies of the oppressed countries and the Muslim countries and the enemies of mankind have pinpointed is the university. This is because they know very well that if they manage to influence the university of a country, the entire country can fall into their hands. It is the university that runs the affairs of a country. And it is the university that trains the present and the future generations and if the university falls into the hands of the plunderers of the East and the West, the country falls into their hands. Nothing else has been their target more than the university.

Date: Morning, June 31, 1981/Khordad 23, 1360 SH/Sha'ban 01, 1401 AH.

Place: Jamaran Husayniyyah, Tehran

Subject: Importance of the role of the university in the independence or lack of independence of a country

Occasion: Anniversary of the establishment of the Ad Hoc Committee for the Cultural Revolution

181

Addressees: The members of the Ad Hoc Committee for the Cultural Revolution and the Supreme Council of the Jihad of the Universities of Tehran and other cities

Committed youths throughout the history and particularly Muslim students of the present generation and future generations are the hope of Islam and Islamic countries. With their commitment, weapons, perseverance and resistance, they can serve as the rescue ship for Islamic nations and their own countries. The independence, freedom and progress of nations depend on their efforts. They are the main target of the colonists and imperialists of the world. Each power pole is intent on entrapping them, because by hunting them, they can drag nations and countries into destruction and poverty.

Date: November 3, 1981/Aban 21, 1360 SH/Muharram 6, 1402 AH.

Place: Jamaran, Tehran

Subject: Explaining the mission of foreign-based Muslim students

Addressees: Islamic Association of Students in America and Canada

Protection and Continuation of Islamic Revolution

The statesmen, the intellectuals and the university authorities should fulfill their Islamic and national obligations, and not allow the movement to be diverted by the clamorous propaganda.

Date: September 18, 1978/Shahrivar 27, 1357 SH/Shawwal 15, 1398 AH.

Place: Najaf, Iraq

Subject: The government deceiving the people and the propaganda machinery of the Shah

Occasion: The earthquake in Tabas

Addressees: The Iranian nation

I hope that our universities will undergo a spiritual change; a transformation…This transformation, because of which the people would look upon martyrdom as a great blessing, and would come into the streets in the hope of perhaps getting martyred, was one that brought about this victory. This transformation ought to be maintained.

What is essential is that you, who are in contact with the youth in the university, remind them that this transformation that was the secret of their victory and brought them up to this stage, and because of which they were able to smash this big satanic barrier, ought to be safeguarded along with this movement so that we could later have our own independent university, our own theological *madrasahs* and our own army.

Date: Afternoon, July 4, 1979/Tir 31, 1358 SH/Sha'ban 9, 1399 AH.

Place: Qum

Subject: The differences between a Western university and an Islamic one

Audience: Tehran University professors

It is necessary for the high school and university students and staff and those learning religious sciences to safeguard their solidarity and further support the Islamic Revolution.

Date: November 1, 1979/Aban 01, 1358 SH/Dhu'l-Hijjah 01, 1399 AH.

Place: Qum

Subject: Pressure actions on America and Israel for extradition of the Shah

Addressees: High school and university students and staff, theological students and clergymen

I implore all the university students and the scholars at the seminaries, all intellectuals, scholars and writers to put aside all sources of disagreement. Rather, I ask them to focus on the enemy. This is my divine and national task to ask you for this feat. I ask God to bestow the unity upon the nation, grant Islam and the distinguished clergy glory and make our Muslim nation victorious.

Date: December 6, 1979/Azar 51 1358 SH/Muharram 16, 1400 AH.

Place: Qum

Subject: The necessity for calmness, tranquility and avoidance of being disrespectful to the clergy

Addressees: The Iranian nation

This Revolution is the result of the struggles of the university youth from among the oppressed strata of the society whose hearts were filled with faith and love for Islam. It was they who propelled this movement and gave martyrs without making any demands in return.

Date: April 5, 1981/Farvardin 16, 1360 SH/Jamadi al-Awwal 29, 1401 AH.

Place: Jamaran, Tehran

Subject: Oppressed people pioneered the Revolution; in appreciation of the sacrifices of the Air Force pilots

Audience: Various strata of people from south Tehran

O dear youths, students, scientists and the present and future hope of the Muslim nation the big trust of independence and freedom obtained by the great Iranian nation from the two power poles of the East and West through their sacrifice and struggle is entrusted to you. You[43] have a big responsibility. All the nations, especially Muslim students, who are the future leaders, are responsible for safeguarding this great divine trust.

The opponents of the Islamic republic and your and our opponents both inside and outside and the two superpowers have stretched their traps for the youths. The great enemies of Islam with their preys and the agents of their schools of thought have launched an all-out propaganda attack against you and against your country here and abroad. We who are here inside and you who are abroad must do our best to free the deceived youths from the trap of these hunters. These uninformed young people who are not aware of having fallen prey to the widespread trap of political players, have totally surrendered to them and wholeheartedly accepted their lies and accusations against the authorities of the Islamic Republic, the revolutionary guards and Muslim devotees in the way of Islam and country. They devote themselves to the chief frauds who destroy them in order to achieve their own inhuman purposes. And unwittingly, these young adults offer the blood of the valiant nation to these godless criminal America.

You, dear alert youths, come together with friends inside the country and guide these uninformed youngsters and release them from the trap of the hunters. One of the religious duties of our nation and yours is to uncover the American and Zionist's propaganda aimed at blemishing the image of the Islamic Republic and isolating our country by spreading lies, libels and rumors. Work to neutralize these sinister attempts. Help our nation as much as you can, a nation whose only fault is their commitment to Islam, independence and freedom. We should be sure that the great nation of Iran has found its way that is the straight path of humanity, is consciously prepared in different arenas and will not let the unbelievers to return to the country. We must fight tooth and nail to defend our dear Islam and country.

Date: November 3, 1981/Aban 21, 1360 SH/Muharram 6, 1402 AH.

---

[43] Imam (ra) refers to Iranian students studying abroad

Place: Jamaran, Tehran

Subject: Explaining the mission of foreign-based Muslim students

Addressees: Islamic Association of Students in America and Canada

Today, one of the most indispensable organizations is the student and seminary Basij. The students of theology and students of universities should exert their utmost efforts in defending the revolution and Islam in their respective centers. My Basiji children in these two centers should be the guards of the unalterable principle of "neither East nor West". Today, the university and the seminary are more in need of unity and solidarity than any other time and place. The children of the revolution should never allow the agents of America and the Soviet Union to penetrate these two places. It is only through the Basij that this important task can be accomplished. Ideological issues of the basijis are on the shoulder of these two academic bastions. The seminary and the university should place the frameworks of the pure Muhammadan (s) Islam at the disposal of all members of the Basij.

Date: November 23, 1988/Azar 2, 1367 SH/Rabi' ath-Thani 21, 1409 AH.

Place: Jamaran, Tehran

Subject: Role and station of the Basij

Occasion: Basij's Week

Addressees: Iranian nation and the combatant Basijis

Now that by the will of Allah, the Exalted, universities have been liberated from the grip of criminals, it behooves the nation and Islamic governments at all times not to permit corrupt elements, who are either the followers of deviant schools of thought or lean toward the West or the East, to influence the colleges, universities or the centers of education. Make guards against such individuals from the beginning and before they have achieved any mischievous plan.

My advice to the students of the teachers training centers, colleges and universities is to rise bravely and oppose all deviation and perversion so that their and the nation's independence and freedom would remain safe and secure.

Date of Reciting: Khordad 15, 1368

Place: Jamaran, Tehran

Subject: Politico-divine will (ever-lasting message of Imam Khomeini to the contemporary ones and next generations)

Addressees: Iranian nation, Muslims and peoples of the world and next generations

Reconstruction and Development

The dear students, specialists, engineers, businessmen, cultivators, and all the ranks of the nation have volunteered to reconstruct an Iran that has come into our hands in a ruined condition. For this reason, we can call it a crusade for reconstruction. We will call this crusade the "Reconstruction Jihad." All the ranks of the people- men and women, young and old, university professors and students, engineers and experts, urban and rural dwellers- should participate in endeavoring to rebuild this ruined country of Iran.

Date: June 16, 1979/Khordad 26, 1358 SH/Rajab 12, 1399 AH.

Place: Qum

Subjects: Formation of the Reconstruction Jihad (Jihad-e Sazandegi)

Addressees: The Iranian nation

A university should create a scholar and not a clerk for an office. This is a simple issue. Now the need is that scholars should come out of the university. It should prepare persons who can run a country, preserving the aspects of culture and knowledge. It should not be this way to get a paper in hand and tomorrow go to an office and sit there. Had there been a work, it was justifiable. But in the offices there is no work. So such a multitude of staff is absorbed there for what? To consume the government budget and nothing else. Ultimately they too become lazy. An active power is congealed into idleness in addition to the government budget having gone in vain. This should be mended and addressed.

> Responsibility of becoming self-sufficient and redressing the environment

I am in the sundown of my life. You are young, you can amend the things. Do amend them. If you want to be independent, you should mend these things.

Date: January 4, 1980/Dey 14, 1358 SH/Safar 15, 1400 AH.

Place: Qum

Subject: Peculiarities of the Islamic Revolution and its distinctions with other revolutions

Audience: Tehran University professors

They must equip the universities so that they can build the youths. You must lay the ground for the future of this country. We should not just think about ourselves, we should think about the future of the country. Islam and the future Islam must be preserved. The future of the country must be preserved. The future generation must understand that preserving Islam and the country has started from here.

Date/Time: Morning, December 31, 1981/Azar 22, 1360 SH/Safar 16, 1402 AH.

Place: Jamaran, Tehran

Subject: Place and role of university in the country

Audience: Board of trustees of the National University and heads of various faculties and hospitals affiliated to this university

The people must get involved in the universities. The people must have university of their own but the government should supervise. The supervision of the government is indispensable.

Date/Time: Morning, June 9, 1986/Khordad 19, 1365 SH/Shawwal 1, 1406 AH.

Place: Jamaran, Tehran

Subject: Manifestations and stages of thanksgiving

Occasion: Auspicious feast of Fitr

Audience: Sayyid Ali Khamenei (President), Mir Husayn Mousavi (Prime Minister), Akbar Hashimi (Speaker of the Islamic Consultative Assembly), Sayyid 'Abdul-Karim Mousavi Ardebili (Chief Justice), ambassadors and charge d'affairs of Islamic countries in Iran, various strata of people

Reconstruction is impossible except through cooperation and collective thinking. This country belongs to Islam and the entire Iranian nation. Just as all were together during the war, they should also be at the side of one another at the time of peace and reconstruction. God willing, academic and university centers will also have a share in this important endeavor.

Date: October 3, 1988/Mehr 11, 1367 SH/Safar 12, 1409 AH.

Place: Jamaran, Tehran

Subject: General policies of the Islamic system in the course of reconstruction of the country

Addressees: The Iranian nation

SECTION 5

UNIVERSITY FACULTY MEMBERS IN THE VIEWS OF IMAM KHOMEINI

Responsibilities of University Faculty Members Towards Society

It is the duty of the university teachers to inform the youth of what is going on behind the curtains of secrecy.

Date: October 26, 1964/Aban 4, 1343 SH/Jamadi ath-Thani 02, 1384 AH.

Place: Qum

Subject: Protesting the Capitulation and inviting the people and *'ulama* to uprising

Addressees: The *'ulama*, clergymen and other classes of the Muslim nation of Iran

Those who are teachers and professors at universities. From the very first day that primary and high schools admit students, the school authorities are duty-bound to educate them in a correct and Islamic way, which embodies all (the right characteristics). That is, if a Muslim grows up the way Islam wants, it is impossible that he will ever betray his country. It is impossible that he commits any treason against his brother, neighbor, his fellow citizen or a stranger. Treachery will be eradicated. We should make an effort to bring up righteous individuals.

Date: April 4, 1979/Farvardin 15, 1358 SH/Jamadi al-Awwal 6, 1399 AH.

Place: Qum

Subject: The discord-sowing danger of colonialism; extraordinary and unique votes of the people for the Islamic Republic; lack of a committed workforce

Audience: Principals and deputy principals of Qum's high schools

Teaching is a general profession for the prophets; from the philosophers and Imams, to the clergies and educational staff, and God Willing, we are among this group. Therefore, it is a very valuable job, making man perfect. Other professions never attain this rank because they deal with other aspects of human life. There is no creature on earth equal to man in status, and no other profession can be equaled to a teacher's job. In this sense, it is a great job, very respectable.

The educational staffs have been burdened with a very important responsibility. The greater the job in importance, the more important will be the liabilities.

Date: May 22, 1979/Khordad 1, 1358 SH/Jamadi ath-Thani 25, 1399 AH.

Place: Qum

Subject: The social standing of the teacher and his rank in Islam and the Qur'an

Audience: Educational staff of Isfahan

You educational staff! You must be the shadow of the prophets.

Teachers have the same job as the Prophet had, and it is quite a heavy responsibility, the same goes for the clergies. This is a heavy responsibility for all. All of us are somehow responsible in the sight of God. You are responsible for rearing those attending your classes.

Date: May 22, 1979/Khordad 1, 1358 SH/Jamadi ath-Thani 25, 1399 AH.

Place: Qum

Subject: The social standing of the teacher and his rank in Islam and the Qur'an

Audience: Educational staff of Isfahan

Then our jobs, your job and my job, are the jobs of the prophets. If we betray our jobs, we have betrayed the prophets; we have betrayed the Almighty God. And the sign of our betrayal is this that the youth who ought to be reared in our classes go astray. Train the children and the youth towards the right path. If you want to safeguard your country and your religion, the key to this protection will be in your hands. The key to salvation and damnation of a nation is with the teachers. If teachers work well their country will be a good place for living, if not, it will be ruined. Then you are the ones who can work for the spiritual and material development of your country. God forbid, you are the ones who can make your country regressive in both areas of spirituality and materiality. Then your job is dignified and your responsibility is heavy. Your job is a Divine blessing, and we are with you in safeguarding this trust. Let us not betray this trust, God willing.

Date: May 22, 1979/Khordad 1, 1358 SH/Jamadi ath-Thani 25, 1399 AH.

Place: Qum

Subject: The social standing of the teacher and his rank in Islam and the Qur'an

Audience: Educational staff of Isfahan

Clergy and the academicians are similarly minded in following the same path. There is no denying the fact that the responsibility of you two groups is greater than that of the rest, since your jobs are more honorable in view of the fact that both the clergy and the academicians are charged with the responsibility of enlightenment, if they perform their duties within the constraints set for the purpose. The fact is that, your job as teachers is one and the same as that of the prophets sent by the Almighty God. It is no secret that the reason for the appointment of prophets was intended to enlighten people and the holy Qur'an is an enlightening book. That is why I stress that your job

192

is honorable but burdened with much responsibility. The reasons are that two universities, that is, the seminary for the clergy and your higher education establishments actually decide the fate and the future of the country.

Date: May 24, 1979/Khordad 3, 1358 SH/Jamadi ath-Thani 27, 1399 AH.

Place: Qum

Subject: Profession of clerics and academicians; creation of discord between the seminary and university; role of culture in the declination and amelioration of the society

Audience: Ali Shari'atmadari (Minister of Culture and Higher Education), chancellors of universities and institutions of higher education

If academicians insist on only instilling sciences into the minds of Iranian children and fill their heads with scientific ways, this will not help the promotion of our people's happiness, in fact it would be detrimental to the people's welfare for that matter. A depraved academician is different from a depraved businessman, or a depraved farmer or laborer for that matter. The latter, if corrupted, will not be promoting evil practices on a mass scale. On the other hand, a morally bad university teacher spreads his evil ways among large groups who will then take charge of running a country. Corruption as such would lead to disaster for a whole nation. In the same breath, the immorality of a cleric does not stay limited to his person and translates into the immorality of the people of a whole country. It is because of such great responsibilities that you two groups must serve and save the country, and if your approaches are not correctly formulated, the fate of the country would suffer the inevitable damages.

Date: May 24, 1979/Khordad 3, 1358 SH/Jamadi ath-Thani 27, 1399 AH.

Place: Qum

Subject: Profession of clerics and academicians; creation of discord between the seminary and university; role of culture in the declination and amelioration of the society.

Audience: Ali Shari'atmadari (Minister of Culture and Higher Education), chancellors of universities and institutions of higher education

The important point is that those who are themselves in the universities where the Ministry of Education is present, whether they be professors or whether they be youth who are there, they should themselves thwart them in a reasonable manner because these people have nothing to offer. The subversive elements have nothing to say; they only want to create disturbances. If any of them makes a claim, go to him and ask him what he has to say. Ask him to talk. You will come to know that they have nothing to say. Their only language is to create disturbances and prevent anything from being done and this matter is in the hands of the university students, centers of learning, and the professors and non-academic staff to help in this affair.

Date: September 15, 1979/Shahrivar 24, 1358 SH/Shawwal 23, 1399 AH.

Place: Qum

Subject: Avoiding conflict; logical confrontation with the subversive elements

Audience: Professors of the University of Shiraz and heads of the Education Ministry in Fars province.

What are up to you, teachers after revolution and all those in charge of education are to spare the brains westernized in the course of 50 or so years despotic regime and exotic hegemony.

Date: October 26, 1979/Aban 4, 1358 SH/Dhu'l-Hijjah 4, 1399 AH.

Place: Qum

Subject: Priority of Cultural Reforms- Concept of freedom and suffocation-colonialist link of superpowers

Audience: Islamic Association Member Teachers East Azarbayjan

The teachers' main task is to educate the youth. If our children are trained properly, our country will be saved. We should train our youth in such a way that they could defend this country. The future belongs to this generation of youth. Later, they will protect this country if they are trained properly.

Date: December 24, 1979/Dey 3, 1358 SH/Safar 4, 1400 AH.

Place: Qum

Subject: The treasons of the Pahlavi regime; the breach of the chains of dependence on others; struggle for self-dependence and sufficiency

Audience: The teachers of the city of Mahallat

You and we[44] should chip in our efforts to create faith for those future generations who will be responsible for the fate of this country. You would let pious people graduate from your universities, and we would send pious clerics out of the schools.

---

[44] University faculty members and Islamic Seminary (*howzeh*) teachers

Neither scholars nor scientists for their own sakes are any good in the absence of faith. As a matter of fact, piety by itself would not be very effective, as there are many pious people around, but when a scholar is pious and he is also faithful, then he will be the source of many blessings and contributions in safeguarding the country. It is in this light that we are burdened with such a great responsibility; both you and we are given such a great responsibility. If we find the right path and act according to what we have been assigned with, we have given strength to faith along with science so that there would be no sign of previous practices.

Date: May 24, 1979/Khordad 3, 1358 SH/Jamadi ath-Thani 27, 1399 AH.

Place: Qum

Subject: Profession of clerics and academicians; creation of discord between the seminary and university; role of culture in the declination and amelioration of the society

Audience: Ali Shari'atmadari (Minister of Culture and Higher Education), chancellors of universities and institutions of higher education

You honorable teachers and the other teachers throughout the country as well as the university teachers are responsible for this trust that has been placed into your hands by Allah Almighty and the parents. Do not look at those five or ten or maybe fifty students who you are teaching and possibly imagine it to be an insignificant number and think that there are "others" who will do the job. It is possible that from among these very ten students who are before you or from among these fifty students whom you are teaching, someone will eventually reach to a very high position and maybe become the president of a country or a prime minister and it is possible that a high position in the country will fall into his hands. Or it could be that this very single student who was placed in your custody and who was later put into the hands of other teachers, finally gains a crooked training- that is he was given knowledge without bothering alongside to train him to become a worthy human being, or if, God forbid, the teacher is himself deviated and that child, from the beginning and then in the later stages, has been under a deviated training, it is possible that this same student may later on lead a country to its doom… You should keep in mind that if your training was, God forbid, against an Islamic and human training, whatever evil that person ends up doing later on, you, too, are his partner in crime. And if your training was a worthy human training based upon the primordial nature in man, you will hold a share in whatever good that person ends up doing.

Date: January 03, 1981/Bahman 01, 1359 SH/Rabi' al-Awwal, 23, 1401 AH.

Place: Jamaran, Tehran

Subject: The importance of the teaching profession and the duties of the teachers in training students

Audience: Religious teachers from all over the country

You are the trustees of such a generation. Your education should go hand in hand with ethical training. This responsibility is not exclusive to religious teachers. This is the duty of each and every school as well as university teacher, no matter what subjects they teach.

In the same way that if a religious teacher who only suffices with academic education without paying attention to ethical or religious training or without paying attention to the overall progress of his students could possibly cause mayhem and bring a country to its ruin, a general teacher could end up doing the same. If, God forbid, in any field of study a deviation occurs or if there happens to be some teachers who cause deviation, not only are they partners in the crimes that are committed at the hands of their students but their own country, too, could be led to destruction.

Date: January 03, 1981/Bahman 01, 1359 SH/Rabi' al-Awwal, 23, 1401 AH.

Place: Jamaran, Tehran

Subject: The importance of the teaching profession and the duties of the teachers in training students

Audience: Religious teachers from all over the country

We intend to have university teachers that can train our youth to be self-reliant instead of inclining toward the West or the East. We do not want any Ataturks and Taqizadehs. We are looking forward to having a university system that can, after a few years, make us self-reliant in every respect. We are not against expertise. What we oppose is the dependence of the minds of our youth on the West or the East. In the previous regime, our universities, with the exception of a few people, were either indifferent toward this issue or else they worked toward making our youth dependent on foreign powers. What we are seeking out is that if ever our people need treatment for their (complicated) ailments, they should not be asked to go to Britain or America for treatment. What we want is that just as an American or English patient does not need to come to Iran for treatment, our patients, too, do not need to go abroad for their problems. We are looking for the kind of expertise that does not make our youth and their intellects dependent but instead trains them to foster concern for Islam and Iran.

Time/Date: Morning, May 25, 1981/Khordad 4, 1360 SH/Rajab 02, 1401 AH.

Place: Jamaran, Tehran

Subject: Importance of knowledge in Islam; responsibility of the university in an Islamic society; duties of the Islamic associations of the universities

Audience: Members of the Islamic Association and the Jihad of the 'Ilm va San'at (Science and Technology) University; members of the Organization for Scientific and Industrial Research; and a group of inventors and innovators

I request writers, speakers, intellectuals, respected professors, teachers and scientists of the country whatever their leaning and affiliations might be, to pay attention to this very important point that if the Islamic Republic, which is the product of the suffering of oppressed masses, is defeated, God forbid, they should not think that in its place a more committed, more sympathetic, more nationalist and more Islamic system will come, and they should know for sure that a regime which is completely Western or American or Eastern communist will take its place with the help of one of the superpowers, which even may look Islamic and nationalist. In such a situation, any act of sabotage or even apathy will bring the country closer to two poles of the superpowers and will render the blood of the youths and the great efforts of the nation useless.

Date: September 24, 1981/Mehr 2, 1360 SH/Dhu'l-Qa'dah 25, 1401 AH.

Place: Jamaran, Tehran

Subject: On the threshold of the presidential elections

Addressees: The Iranian nation

If the university in a country is reformed, that country will be reformed. Universities lie on top of the executive affairs. By reforming university, the country's affairs will be reformed; by corrupting the university, the country will be corrupted. Even one corrupt professor might have a big effect on a country, because he or she can influence a group of students in a bad way. In their turn, they will develop into a big evil in the long run… university, professors, teachers and students and what they were like in the past and what they are like now, and in which ways they have changed? Universities should be entrusted to committed individuals. Of course, universities should be opened, but with these considerations in mind. They should not think that by opening the university every problem would be resolved. Well, university can resolve problems. A bad university is better than no university…

Beyond doubt, in trying to achieve their evil purposes and tyrannizing the oppressed people of the world, the superpowers see no better way than attacking the culture of the oppressed countries. By having Western or Eastern education, teachers or

197

professors prepare the elementary and high schools for Western or Eastern education of the youths who will be the future statesmen. With this kind of education that predisposes the young people toward one of the two poles of power, the way will be paved for dominating the oppressed countries of the world without any trouble and arms. As far as they are concerned, the best way to access the resources and products of the nations and countries is to get hold of one stratum of the native people and educate them. This way, nations will offer what they have to them without making any noise and even with enthusiasm and interest. The biggest blow dealt to this country in the last fifty years came from deviant professors who were Western-educated and who governed education centers in the same manner. The harm was much more than what Reza Khan and his son did. Of course, there were committed professors and teachers but the others called the shot. We got rid of the evil of Reza Khan and Muhammad Reza Khan, but we will not rid of the result of Western and Eastern education any time soon. They are the foothold of the domination of the superpowers that cannot be disarmed by any logic. Despite all their failures they have not stopped plotting against the Islamic Republic, and still try to break down this divine edifice. If the dear nation of Iran and the oppressed countries of the world want to liberate themselves from the trap of the satanic superpowers once and for all, they must reform their culture and make it independent. There is no other way; this road must be taken by committed professors and teachers in high schools and universities.

With education and efforts in various scientific fields and with the right training and refinement of the educational centers and educating the devious elements, the youth who are the hope of the nation, should be reformed. They should be taught in various other fields and be refined through the Islamic teaching, and Islamic sciences that teach morality and refine the self should be taught by experts on Islam so that the youths will get acquainted with this animating and all-inclusive school of thought.

Date: December 28, 1981/Dey 7, 1360 SH/Rabi' al-Awwal 1, 1402 AH.

Place: Jamaran, Tehran

Subject: Attack of superpowers on the culture of the country

Addressees: Academicians, officials and students of teacher training centers

The scientists must pass on their knowledge to the students.

Date/Time: Morning, January 16, 1983/Dey 26, 1361 SH/Rabi 'al-Thani 1, 1403 AH.

Place: Husayniyyah Jamaran, Tehran

Subject: Termination of excuses in serving Islam and the country

Audience: Salimi (Minister of Defense), Safa'i (Head of the Political-Ideology Department of the Army), employees of the Defense Industries, personnel of the Political-Ideology Section of the Isfahan Center of the Islamic Republic Broadcasting

If the clerics, academicians and we are truly interested in keeping this country protected, particularly if university professors actually wish this country not to make a retreat to the former situation, they should be watchful. Academicians and university professors should take care of themselves in terms of education and watch the acts they do in relation to students and young adults. They should preserve the university in a form and reality that is the very development taken place in Iran. University should develop and has obviously undergone development, but needs greater care.

Date/Time: Morning, August 27, 1985/Shahrivar 5, 1364 SH/Dhu'l-Hijjah 01, 1405 AH.

Place: Husayniyyah Jamaran, Tehran

Subject: Comparison between the Islamic Republic and the Pahlavi regime

Occasion: Auspicious Qurban Feast

Audience: Akbar Hashemi Rafsanjani (Majlis Speaker), members of the Society of Teachers of Qum, university professors across the country, officials of the Ministry of Culture and Higher Education, members of the Supreme Council of Cultural Revolution, clerics from Tehran, members of the Office of Islamic Propagation of Qum Theological Seminary and the Tehran Islamic Propagation Organization, ambassadors of Muslim countries

Imam's Expectations from the University Faculty Members

You[45] must, therefore, enlighten the youth who are now with you and talk to them. Make them aware and make them understand that they should oppose this clique, which is now in Iran and is carrying out sabotage. Be sure that this sabotage is serving foreign interests and is perpetrated by foreign agents who show themselves as they are (disguised as Marxists). Like the gentleman[46] who was a foreign lackey donning a nationalist mask but wanted to bring back the Shah here and so on.

I hope that God will grant success to all and support everyone. Today, Iran is in need of your existence and everything. We should all join hands and meet this need. May God keep all of you.

---

45 Imam (ra) here refers to faculty members of Abu Raihan Beiruni University
46 Imam (ra) refers to Shahpur Bakhtiyar, the last Prime Minister of Pahlavi regime

Date: February 16, 1979/Bahman 27, 1357 SH/Rabi' al-Awwal 18, 1399 AH.

Place: Alawi School, Tehran

Subject: Foreign conspiracies and propaganda

Audience: Abu Raihan University professors and a group of Air Force personnel

Educational books, whether primary, secondary or university ones, must have fundamental changes and purged of any materials and pictures which serve the interests of colonialism and exploitation and be replaced by Islamic and revolutionary lessons that will awaken children and bring them up independent and free.

Date: February 19, 1979/Bahman 03, 1357 SH/Rabi' al-Awwal 12, 1399 AH.

Place: Alawi School, Tehran

Subject: Class attendance and the necessity of changes in the educational system

Occasion: Schools' re-opening after the Revolution's victory

Addressees: Education Ministry officials and school students

What is essential is that you, who are in contact with the youth in the university, remind them that this transformation that was the secret of their victory and brought them up to this stage, and because of which they were able to smash this big satanic barrier, ought to be safeguarded along with this movement so that we could later have our own independent university, our own theological *madrasahs* and our own army.

Date: Afternoon, July 4, 1979/Tir 31, 1358 SH/Sha'ban 9, 1399 AH.

Place: Qum

Subject: The differences between a Western university and an Islamic one

Audience: Tehran University professors

The greatest disaster for our nation is the intellectual dependence that makes them believes that everything comes from the West, that we are poor in all aspects and that we should import all our goods from abroad. You, the professors, teachers, university and college students, writers, intellectuals and scholars, should endeavor to wash away your brains from this sort of dependence and save your own country and nation by this great and valuable service.

Date: September 22, 1979/Shahrivar 13, 1358 SH/Shawwal 03, 1399 AH.

Place: Qum

Subject: Foreigners' attempts to sweep the Islamic content of the scientific and cultural programs

Occasion: Opening of academic year

Addressees: Professors, collegians and students

You, young adults, and you who educate the younger generation try to deprogram the mind of the youth that has been filled with western materials. Make them understand that they have their luminaries and everything. Have them understand that they should do their work by themselves? If we have something that is defective, it is better than stretching our hands before our enemies to get a perfect one. I regret that we have to go to our enemies and seek their help to meet our necessities.

Time: November 2, 1979/Aban 11, 1358 SH/Dhu'l-Hijjah 11, 1399 AH.

Place: Qum

Subject: Necessity of cultural-economic independence of the country

Audience: Students of Faculty of Sciences and Faculty of Literature and Foreign Languages

I hope that our youth, teachers and university professors, writers and intellectuals are awakened and notice the negligence. We had been beguiled up to now; our minds had been converted. We should join our hands; writers should contribute to this revolution, speakers should help this revolution, newspapers should back this revolution. I see some newspapers, excluding the leading ones, carrying materials detrimental to the nation. Among these newspapers, some presume that their interests lie in the rule of westerners over our country or coming to power of the like of these treacherous ones. Those newspapers that are not such and the youth who are not without defect because in time of the former regime they were not involved in activities to be brought up like them should think out a way to make real human beings. We have our culture; we can educate our people; we can work to improve the country. It is the beginning of the work that the hands of the criminals have been virtually curtailed from our country. The grip of those who ransacked the country is now curtailed as well. We should think out how to construct our country. First and foremost, our youth should be mended. The youths who should protect the country in future and run it should be raised properly.

Time: November 2, 1979/Aban 11, 1358 SH/Dhu'l-Hijjah 11, 1399 AH.

Place: Qum

Subject: Necessity of cultural-economic independence of the country

Audience: Students of Faculty of Sciences and Faculty of Literature and Foreign Languages

Now we have been liberated from a fifty-year long imprisonment. Now we are encountering another problem and that is our severe reliance on other systems of ideologies. This could be solved only through the endeavors of our teachers at schools and universities.

Date: December 7, 1979/Azar 16, 1358 SH/Muharram 17, 1400 AH.

Place: Qum

Subject: Independent thinking and an independent culture; the role of Islam in the Liberation Organization

Addressees: Mr. Mousa Zargar (the Minister of Health), the deputies and high-ranking personnel of the Ministry of Health

Do not fear the West. Have the will and it will happen. Our scholars, our professors, nobody should fear West. Our youths too should not fear the West. The East should have the will and movement against the West will take place.

Date: January 2, 1980/Dey 21, 1358 SH/Safar 31, 1400 AH.

Place: Qum

Audience: Students of Islamic Association, Law College, Learning Center, Ardebil

Subject: The consequences of being intellectually dependent on the west- a sense of loss of direction in the East

If you, gentlemen,[47] desire and our nation desires- of course, desire, your independence and want freedom- of course, you want, then you should free your thoughts. Our thought is now into fetters. God willingly may it happen that is an appraisal of thought. The appraisal of thought has not taken place. But this appraisal should be pushed ahead to make progress. You are the university elite and you are scholars and thinkers. These youths- they should be brought up in such a way that they should see themselves as somebody.

They should not say that we should rely on West. We should be westernized. No. Be Eastern. If any craft worthy can be availed from the West, try to learn it and obtain it.

---

[47] Imam (ra) is speaking to a gathering of faculty members of Tehran University

But do not become Western. To learn is something. But to make the mind and submit it to the West is something else.

Date: January 4, 1980/Dey 14, 1358 SH/Safar 15, 1400 AH.

Place: Qum

Subject: Peculiarities of the Islamic Revolution and its distinctions with other revolutions

Audience: Tehran University professors

The thinkers, orators, academic personalities, and scholars should exert their abilities to disappoint the enemy totally- particularly our enemy America

Date: April 1, 1980/Farvardin 21, 1359 SH/Jamadi al-Awwal 15, 1400 AH.

Place: Shemiran, Darband, Tehran

Subject: New trends in America and the enemies of Islam and Iran

Occasion: The anniversary of the establishment of the Islamic Republic of Iran

Addressees: The nation of Iran

The people who are there should be trained because the old fashion, and the old method that was a corrupt one, is still running there. The scholars for teaching manners and conduct are needed in Universities, schools and everywhere.

Time: Morning, July 2, 1980/Tir 01, 1359 SH/Sha'ban 18, 1400 AH.

Place: Jamaran, Tehran

Subject: Education/training from the Qur'an's view, the position of culture in the Pahlavi regime. The need for basic changes there.

Audience: The heads of education throughout the country, the Islamic Association members, the Home Ministry workers and the provincial workers

I request those of you who are involved in the fields of education and I request all the judges and the officials of the Judiciary and the Revolutionary Courts to take this major responsibility that they are vested with seriously because any digression among you can drag the culture of the entire nation toward deviation. The children and the youth who are the hope of Islam and this nation are grand and noble trusts placed into your hands and any treachery as regards this trust is like treachery toward Islam and this country. The future of the country lies in the hands of these children and youth and that is why all our schools should seriously impart a good Islamic training to them to insure our country against all damage.

Date: March 02, 1981/Esfand 29, 1359 SH/Jamadi al-Awwal 31, 1401 AH.

Place: Jamaran, Tehran

Subject: Declaration of the Year of Compassion, Brotherhood, Rule of the Law and Confronting Aggressors (including 13 points of reminder to the officials and people)

Occasion: The Iranian New Year and the third year of the victory of the Islamic Revolution

Audience: The Iranian nation and government officials

Study of "humanities" needs to have committed human beings. A person who is not committed to the laws of Islam and its very foundation of monotheism can only cause deviation which is not acceptable. As regards other university courses, the respected teachers are expected to focus on their teachings without getting involved in conspiracies. It is very natural for these teachers to have different motives, but those respected university teachers who wish to serve this country and transfer their knowledge and expertise to others should bear it in mind that a university is a place of learning and should be free from issues that harm the country. They should only engage in the sort of a commitment that a university teacher is expected to have even if they have varying motives. Such university teachers are qualified to serve in the universities and none of us should oppose them, provided it has been determined that they are not deviated and do not intend to make the foundations of this Islamic Republic shaky or to compel our youth to indulge in unbefitting acts.

Date: April 31, 1981/Farvardin 24, 1360 SH/Jamadi ath-Thani 8, 1401 AH.

Place: Jamaran, Tehran

Subject: Need to maintain unity and peace and warning against disruptive elements

Audience: Agriculturists and the inhabitants of Gorgan, the clerics and the inhabitants of Ali-Abad, the inhabitants of Gonbad and Turkman Sahra, and the Basij of Shahreza

It still incumbent upon the dear students and committed teachers and professors to do their utmost to identify the corrupting factors and purge the educational and training atmosphere from their contaminating effects. It should not be thought that this infiltration is just to lead astray the universities, because the perverts and the hypocrites give more importance to influencing high schools and even elementary schools so that they prepare corrupt youths at the universities. They know that if the youth are educated in the right way at the educational centers and they sense the plots and tricks of the colonialist in all their aspects, the agents of the colonialist will have less success at the universities; therefore, they give especial prominence to elementary and high schools so that they gear the youths to Western and Eastern colonial system before they go to universities. For this reason, the educational apparatuses should be committed to and care about saving the country by giving importance to preserving our dear youths because the future of independence and freedom of the country hinges on proper education. For this reason, teachers and professors have the most important role in educating and refining the students. You have all seen how their tendency to East and West brought about tragedies for our country and turned universities into strongholds for serving the East and West. The overwhelming majority of the Western-minded and Eastern-minded graduates of this country changed the society. It is incumbent upon committed and responsible teachers at elementary and high schools to do their best to make the youths change the universities by informing them of the past corruption in universities and make them incline towards the rich and independent Islamic-Iranian culture. With the reopening of the universities, it is incumbent upon the committed professors to enlighten the students on the plots and evil acts of the superpowers whenever they see that youths tend to go for one of the wicked poles. It is incumbent upon those youths who are committed to the interests of the country and are aware of the Islamic objectives, to change the society and be sure that with this service, the complete independence and freedom of their beloved country will be ensured.

Date: September 22, 1981/Shahrivar 13, 1360 SH/Dhu'l-Qa'dah 23, 1401 AH.

Place: Jamaran, Tehran

Subject: Effects and consequences of independent versus dependent culture

Occasion: Beginning of academic year

Addressees: High school and university students, the youth, teachers and professors

The university professors should know that if they build up the universities, they have insured their country for good. Teachers of high schools and primary schools preparing the children for universities know that if they educate these children and nourish them as believers and hand them over to the university as believers and the university delivers them to the nation as believers they have protected their country against all harms.

Date: September 19, 1982/Shahrivar 28, 1361 SH/Dhul-Hijjah 1, 1402 AH.

Place: Husayniyyah Jamaran, Tehran

Subject: Two main pillars of education

Audience: Muhammad-Taqi Misbah Yazdi, Muhsin Qara'ati (Imam's representative in the literacy campaign), Ali-Akbar Parvaresh (Education Minister), Muhammad-'Ali Najafi (Minister of Culture and Higher Education), members of the office for coordination of theological seminaries and universities and the educationists

If university professors only attempt to teach lessons without regarding spiritual education, those who graduate will spread corruption. The universities in the former regime did not teach properly. If they had done so, we would not lag behind so much in sciences

Date: September 19, 1982/Shahrivar 28, 1361 SH/Dhul-Hijjah 1, 1402 AH.

Place: Husayniyyah Jamaran, Tehran

Subject: Two main pillars of education

Audience: Muhammad-Taqi Misbah Yazdi, Muhsin Qara'ati (Imam's representative in the literacy campaign), Ali-Akbar Parvaresh (Education Minister), Muhammad-'Ali Najafi (Minister of Culture and Higher Education), members of the office for coordination of theological seminaries and universities and the educationists

You teachers must give importance to the subject of piety. The students also must give importance to it. The university professors and professors of the seminaries must also give special importance to this aspect that if knowledge is isolated from piety- even if it is knowledge of monotheism, even if it is knowledge of religions- it has no value in that world. If the loss from unaccompanied knowledge on nations and on Islam would not have been greater than its benefits- which it is- then it must be mentioned that an impious person can destroy a country, destroy human beings and the person who is more learned can corrupt the people better. Thus, together with this education, there should also be education of piety. If there are children, teach the children piety to the extent that they can absorb; and likewise the adolescents. The adolescents should not be under the impression that they no longer need or the time is past; the time does pass. It is better for a person in all circumstances to know something than not to know.

Date/Time: Morning, December 26, 1982/Dey 5, 1361 SH/Rabi' al-Awwal 01, 1403 AH.

Place: Husayniyyah Jamaran, Tehran

Subject: Roots of differences of values in the world

Audience: Muhsin Qara'ati (representative of the Imam and head of the Literacy Movement), Ghayouri (representative of the Imam in the Red Crescent Society), teaching staff of the Literacy Movement, employees of the Red Crescent Society from all over the country

I hope that with the efforts of teachers and professors, the situation is so improved that one who completes his education will have emerged a committed individual serving his country, without being concerned to satisfy the alien countries.

Date/Time: Morning, April 16, 1985/Farvardin 27, 1364 SH/Rajab 25, 1405 AH.

Place: Jamaran, Tehran

Subject: Improvement of university and struggle for liberation from cultural dependence

Audience: Iraj Fadil (Minister of Culture and Higher Education) and deputies

If the clerics, academicians and we are truly interested in keeping this country protected, particularly if university professors actually wish this country not to make a retreat to the former situation, they should be watchful. Academicians and university professors should take care of themselves in terms of education and watch the acts they do in relation to students and young adults. They should preserve the university in a form and reality that is the very development taken place in Iran. University should develop and has obviously undergone development, but needs greater care.

Date/Time: Morning, August 27, 1985/Shahrivar 5, 1364 SH/Dhu'l-Hijjah 01, 1405 AH.

Place: Husayniyyah Jamaran, Tehran

Subject: Comparison between the Islamic Republic and the Pahlavi regime

Occasion: Auspicious Qurban Feast

Audience: Akbar Hashemi Rafsanjani (Majlis Speaker), members of the Society of Teachers of Qum, university professors across the country, officials of the Ministry of Culture and Higher Education, members of the Supreme Council of Cultural Revolution, clerics from Tehran, members of the Office of Islamic Propagation of Qum Theological Seminary and the Tehran Islamic Propagation Organization, ambassadors of Muslim countries

SECTION 6

UNIVERSITY STUDENTS IN THE VIEWS OF IMAM KHOMEINI

Responsibilities of University Students Towards Society

It is upon you[48] young intellectuals not to give up so that you could awaken those in lethargy. By exposing the treasons and the crimes of the imperialists and their uncultured followers, awaken the negligent ones and abstain from the difference of expression, discord and carnal desires, which are the chief of all the corruptions. Face Almighty God with your needs and He guides you through that path and helps you with the supernatural army of God. *"And those who struggle in Our path, We will certainly guide them in Our ways. And verily God assists the righteous ones."* (Qur'an, 29:69)

Date: Circa 1976/1364 SH/1378 AH.

Place: Najaf, Iraq

Subject: Glad tidings of a bright future for the oppressed nations

Occasion: The Tenth Annual Meeting of the Islamic Societies of Students to be held in Europe

Addressees: The Union of the Islamic Societies of Students in Europe

It is necessary for you, deserving youth of Islam- who are the hope of the Muslims- to enlighten the nations; to expose the sinister and destructive plans of the imperialists; to be more serious in the study of Islam; to learn and act upon the teachings of the Holy Qur'an; and to struggle with utmost sincerity in the publication, propagation and introduction of Islam to other nations as well as in the promotion of the lofty ideals of Islam. Exert more efforts for the implementation of the Islamic government and the study of its entailing issues. Reform and purify yourselves; be united and organized, and tighten your ranks. Produce more supporters and devotees. Do not neglect exposing the plots of the tyrannical regime[49] of Iran against Islam and the Muslims. Let the world hear the cries of your suffering brothers and Muslims of Iran and be sympathetic with them. Condemn the atrocities, murders, law-violations, and other crimes which are committed unabatedly in Iran.

Date: August 8, 1972/Mordad 17, 1351 SH/Jamadi ath-Thani 28, 1392 AH.

Place: Najaf, Iraq

Subject: Necessity for struggle to advance Islam's lofty goal

Addressees: University Muslim Students residing in America and Canada

---

[48] Response of Imam (ra) to the letter of Associations of Islamic Students of Europe
[49] Imam (ra) refers to despotic Pahlavi regime.

Now, it is for the Muslim educated generation and the enlightened and wary people, with all efforts and in every possible way, to inform the Muslim nations of Islam, the Islamic leaders, and the heavy and gargantuan responsibilities of the *'ulama* of Islam to make the people aware and ostracize the group of deviant pseudo-clergymen who have been directly and indirectly serving the tyrant regime. If only the Islamic nation is aware of the luminous principles of the Qur'an and the heavy responsibilities of the *'ulama* and leaders of Islam, the pseudo-clergymen and court-*akhunds* would be silenced in the society. If the ill-reputed fake turbaned men and pseudo-clergymen who are silenced in the society do not able to deceive the people, the tyrannical regime will not succeed in the execution of the sinister plans of the imperialists.

Date: March 15, 1973/Esfand 24, 1351 SH/Safar 9, 1393 AH.

Place: Najaf, Iraq

Subject: The Shah's regime's new intrigue in uprooting Islam

Addressees: The Union of Islamic Associations of Students residing in Europe, America and Canada

Owing to the internal and external conditions and the repercussions of the regime's crimes among people and in the foreign press, it is now an opportune moment for the scientific and cultural communities, the patriotic dignitaries, the students in Iran and abroad and the Islamic associations, wherever they are, to rise up, at once and vociferously protest the prevailing conditions as also the atrocities of fifty years perpetrated by the illegal, slavish Pahlavi regime. They must also let their voices be heard by the international community and make the US president understand that the Islamic nations attribute the crimes of this dynasty, especially in recent years, to the American leadership.

Date: July 25, 1977/Mordad 3, 1365 SH/Sha'ban 7, 1397 AH.

Place: Najaf, Iraq

Subject: Calling on the cultural circles to expose the crimes of the regime

Addressees: Islamic Association of Students in America and Canada

It is now the duty of all the Muslims, especially the distinguished spiritual leaders, the intellectuals and the university students of the traditional and modern sciences, to avail themselves of this opportunity to say and write what must be said- informing the international authorities and all the communities of people- in defense of dear Islam and its life-sustaining precepts that guarantee freedom and independence, and also in defense of their great country, the cradle of great and freedom-loving people, that is now on the verge of collapse.

Date: November 21, 1977/Aban 12, 1365 SH/Dhu'l-Qa'dah 29, 1397 AH.

Place: Najaf, Iraq

Subject: The duty of the public vis-a-vis the Shah's regime; the Iranian nation's yearning for Islam

Addressees: The distinguished *'ulama* and the Iranian nation

Now that the brave people of Iran, may God always assist them, have become acquainted with his ruses and have risen in full awareness, the learned strata of society, the writers and orators, whatever their garb or occupation, should join hands, and with pen and speech further enlighten the vigilant nation of Iran of the innumerable crimes of the regime. The brave and dear seminarians and students throughout Iran should avail of every opportunity to keep the anti-Shah slogan- which is the slogan of Islam- alive.

The committed and conscientious scholars and students abroad should write and publish to the fullest extent, in Iran and abroad, the crimes of this dangerous element. They should also make the universally-famous, free-minded personalities all over the world aware of the cruelty and oppression to which the Iranians are being subjected, and mobilize them to help save the brave nation of Iran from clutches of world expansionism and exploitation.

Date: August 31, 1978/Mordad 22, 1357 SH/Ramadan 8, 1398 AH.

Place: Najaf, Iraq

Occasion: The savage massacres carried out by the regime in Isfahan and Shiraz

Addressees: The Iranian nation

Our duties and yours, the university, secondary school and theology students, are these:

If you notice any deviation on the part of the professors, teachers and community leaders from the national-religious path, the most important of which is the overthrow of the rotten regime, you must protest vehemently, and invite them to follow the path of the nation which is the path of God. In case they pay no heed, you must ostracize them and report their deviationist aims very clearly to the oppressed nation. Such people are traitors to the religion, nation and country. They want the Shah, his masters and the international plunderers to carry on with their plunder and keep the nation impoverished and backward.

The theology and secular students should have a friendly and working relationship among themselves. They should join all the various categories of the people for the purpose of attaining independence and freedom and for dispossessing the usurpers of everything belonging to the nation by right...

Ponder the current issues with great alertness and do not be deceived by the ruses of the Shah who wants to sow discord through various ploys. According to what is being heard, they want to have the Shah's lackeys and agents to raise communist slogans in the universities in order to alarm the people over its dangers. The Tudeh Party is a despicable party connected to the Shah's apparatus. All its slogans and pretenses are only to weaken the Islamic campaign and to save the Shah from being toppled; to keep the plundering set-up in place and perpetuate exploitation of the oppressed nation's resources. Dear students, it is your duty to neutralize these diabolical plots.

You, dear students, are duty-bound to support the rightful and valiant insurrection of the deprived Muslim workers and employees among whom the strikes are spreading. These are the deprived Muslims who are weary of the Shah's trampling on their rights, and who have risen to uphold these in unison and sympathy with their brothers. Everybody knows that as long as the regime lasts, social justice and redress of the plight of the deprived, hard-working people will never materialize.

The center captured by our young people, as it was informed, had been a center for espionage and conspiracy. The U. S. expects our young adults just to sit and watch while they are busy brewing busy with conspiracy in their base in Iran and in their own country by granting asylum to the Shah... It is expected that they take our number one criminal, protect him, make a center here for concocting plot and I do not know, whatever they crave for our nation, young, adults, university students; and clergymen sit and watch the blood of one hundred thousand being wasted...

Date: November 5, 1979/Aban 14, 1358 SH/Dhu'l-Hijjah 14, 1399 AH.

Place: Qum

Subject: American plots against Iran

Audience: Iranian Central Insurance Office Staff

Some traitors now try to disrupt our movement. Now there are some people who try to defame these pure youth, whom I do not know personally, but who are pious young men. They say these young ones should present the American documents to the Iranian people; but they do not realize that these are not ordinary documents to be presented to the lay people. They are written in codes. They, for instance, would not disclose the fact that a certain political party was with them or not. The American hostages have destroyed some of the significant records within the four or five hours that they had at their disposal. The remaining records are not of high value. However, time is required to decipher them. Unfortunately, now a group of agitators is trying to disgrace these clean young men. Let us be vigilant. Let us not get involved in these rigmaroles. These agitators are the foreigners' agents. Anybody who takes in this way tries to expel these young ones from the Embassy so that they can set the stage for the return of their masters. By leveling accusations against these young ones, these agitators try to divide the Iranian nation and allow this place to remain safe for the Americans and let that man stay in the United States.

Date: November 8, 1979/Aban 17, 1358 SH/Dhu'l-Hijjah 17, 1399 AH.

Place: Qum

Subject: The resolving of hardships and deprivations, the objectives of the enemies and the United States; foreign policies towards other nations

Audience: The personnel of Ahwaz City Hall

I welcome the dear students who will manage this country from now on, and who have attended this session.

Date: December 02, 1979/Azar 29, 1358 SH/Muharram 03, 1400 AH.

Place: Qum

Subject: The necessity of keeping Islamic unity and brotherhood

Audience: The Muslim students of Shiraz University

I welcome the dear students who will manage this country from now on, and who have attended this session.

Date: December 02, 1979/Azar 29, 1358 SH/Muharram 03, 1400 AH

Place: Qum

Subject: The necessity of keeping Islamic unity and brotherhood

Audience: The Muslim students of Shiraz University

Record of the crimes of Shah, and America, in the trial.

The Muslim students, the campaigners, who have occupied the Den of Espionage, have brought down fatal blows on the skeleton of America the world hungry. They have uplifted the honor of the nation.

Date: February 23, 1980/Esfand 4, 1358 SH/Rabi' ath-Thani 6, 1400 AH.

Place: Heart Hospital, Tehran

Subject: Decision about the American spies. Return of the Shah

Addressees: The Nation, the government and the President of Iran

You the teachers and the students: follow this path laid out by the prophets. This is the path of God; the one laid out for humanity by the prophets and the saints of God. This is the divine path along which all of us must proceed. Those who invite the people to a path other than this, are (the followers of) the *taghout*. And those who guide the people to a path contrary to their own natured one; the one that concerns their own essence, are leading them astray. I hope that the teachers, wherever they be; the sisters and brothers who are teachers, the ones who are students or '*alim*s (scholars), consider themselves as students and teachers. The teachers should guide them (the students) to the right way of the prophets, and the others, in turn, follow the straight path shown to them by the prophets.

Date/Time: Morning, August 29, 1980/Shahrivar 9, 1359 SH/Shawwal 02, 1400 AH.

Place: Jamaran Husayniyyah, Tehran

Subject: Training and educating people according to the teachings of the prophets

Addressees: Pakistani students and Iranian teachers

The strata of students especially the university students. It is necessary that they with sagacity and devotion to Islam and service to the country, take care of the circumstances of the students and university students so that God forbid, these great centers of training and education do not fall prey to issues that they were formerly afflicted with.

Date: February 11, 1983/Bahman 22, 1361 SH/Rabi' ath-Thani 27, 1403 AH.

Place: Jamaran, Tehran

Subject: Evaluation of the condition of the Islamic Revolution on the eve of the fifth anniversary of the victory; reminders to the people, combatants and the three armed forces

Occasion: Bahman 22 (fifth anniversary of the victory of the Islamic Revolution)

Addressees: Officials of the Islamic Republic system, the armed forces and other strata of the nation of Iran

The revolutionary students are responsible to be vigilant without any neglectfulness to carefully watch and keep an eye on this important issue that the universities and institutions and those who are still dreaming of previous regime (*taghout*, Reza Shah), and western culture be not allowed to influence young students outside their classes and indulge in deviant conversations. And if they don't take advices, the matter should be reported to High Council for Cultural Revolution. They should know that this matter (deviant path) will slowly penetrate in universities and high schools. They are responsible before God for it (if they fail in their duty).

Date: September 01, 1984/Azar 19, 1363 SH/Rabi` al-Awwal 16, 1405 AH.

Place: Jamaran, Tehran

Subject: Appointment of several new members of the Cultural Revolution Headquarters

Addressee: Members of the Cultural Revolution Headquarters

Imam's Expectations from University Students

This kind of evil propaganda has unfortunately had an effect. Quite apart from the masses, the educated class university students and also many students at the religious teaching institutions have failed to understand Islam correctly and have erroneous notions. Just as people may, in general, be unacquainted with a stranger, so too they are unacquainted with Islam. Islam lives among the people of this world as if it were a stranger.4 If somebody were to present Islam as it truly is, he would find it difficult to make people believe him. In fact, the agents of imperialism in the religious teaching institutions would raise a hue and cry against him.

Reference: Imam Khomeini (ra), *Wilayate Faqih* (The Governance of the Jurist), p. 24

Do your utmost to raise the banner of Islam in the universities, to promote religion, to build mosques, to perform prayers in congregation and to let the act of prayer be seen by others. Religious unity is of the essence. It is religious unity that makes this society so great and firm; if you like Iran to be independent, then be united in religion.

Date: Morning, April 01, 1964/Farvardin 12, 1343 SH/Dhu'l-Qa'dah 26, 1383 AH.

Place: Qum

Subject: The clergy opposes the Shah's White Revolution

Occasion: The Imam's return to Qum after release from prison

Audience: A group of Tehran University students, tullab and people of Qum

It is the duty of the young university-goers to severely oppose this scandalous bill;[50] to announce the opposition of the university to the whole world while being calm and using enlightening slogans. It is the duty of students abroad not to be silent concerning this crucial matter, which has endangered the glory of the religion and nation.

Date: October 26, 1964/Aban 4, 1343 SH/Jamadi ath-Thani 02, 1384 AH.

Place: Qum

Subject: Protesting the Capitulation and inviting the people and *'ulama* to uprising

Addressees: The *'ulama*, clergymen and other classes of the Muslim nation of Iran

While greatly regretting the situation in Iran, I am hopeful of you students in Iran and abroad; hopeful of the day when the country will become purified of the foul presence of the foreigners and their stooges. O you young people do not despair; truth will triumph…Now it is up to you, the young intellectuals and scientists to learn a lesson from the prevailing conditions; to come together and eschew groundless differences; to put aside the empty doctrines of others and turn to the progressive religion of Islam; to tread, hand in hand, the true path of God and wipe out what is false; to inform people of Islam's sublime goals; to expose the atrocities and treacheries of the agents of imperialism and to seek the help of God the Almighty. "May God give you success."

Date: September 26, 1976/Mehr 4, 1355 SH/Shawwal 1, 1369 AH.

Place: Najaf, Iraq

Subject: Exposing the crimes of Iran's ruling administration

Occasion: The auspicious 'Id al-Fitr

Addressees: All Muslims and students in Iran and abroad

It is now the duty of all the Muslims, especially the distinguished spiritual leaders, the intellectuals and the university students of the traditional and modern sciences, to avail themselves of this opportunity to say and write what must be said- informing the international authorities and all the communities of people- in defense of dear Islam and its life-sustaining precepts that guarantee freedom and independence, and also in defense of their great country, the cradle of great and freedom-loving people, that is now on the verge of collapse.

Date: November 21, 1977/Aban 12, 1365 SH/Dhu'l-Qa'dah 29, 1397 AH.

---

[50] Imam (ra) refers to approval of humiliating Capitulation Bill by Pahlavi regime

Place: Najaf, Iraq

Subject: The duty of the public vis-a-vis the Shah's regime; the Iranian nation's yearning for Islam

Addressees: The distinguished *'ulama* and the Iranian nation

The young clergymen and university students must continue with the acquisition of knowledge each in their own sphere. The recent very vexing rumors among some of the youth that there is no use in studying is a deviant matter that surely is either because of ignorance and lack of information, or evil-intentioned arising from devilish suggestions in order to deter the theology students from studying Islamic sciences so that Islamic precepts are consigned to oblivion and the obliteration of religion becomes a reality by our own actions. It is also meant to bring up our university youths as parasites dependent on the expansionists so that everyone be" imported", so to speak, like everything else, and the need for foreigners, in all the spheres and subjects of learning, to keep on increasing. This poses a great danger that will push the country backward to the greatest extent. If Islamic science did not have professionals, the vestiges of religion would have been effaced by now. If it does not have them subsequently, this immense bulwark against the aliens will be destroyed, fully opening the way for the expansionists. If the universities become devoid of the scientists and professionals, foreigners seeking gain will spread like a cancer throughout the country, taking control of our economic and technological affairs, and bringing everything under their supervision. Our youth should fight this erroneous thought on the part of the expansionists, and the best and most effective way of fighting them is to get equipped with the weapons of knowledge of religion and of the world. Vacating this stronghold and asking people to lay down those weapons is treachery to Islam and the Islamic country.

Date: February 31, 1978/Bahman 24, 1365 SH/Rabi' al-Awwal 5, 1398 AH.

Place: Najaf, Iraq

Subject: The duties of Muslim intellectuals

Addressees: The Union of Islamic Students Association in Europe

The young theology and university students should spend some of their time in comprehending the basic principles of Islam, at the top of which is monotheism and justice, and the great prophets- from Abraham Khalil to the Seal of the Prophets (s) who instituted justice and freedom. They must also understand their thoughts from the furthest point of spirituality and monotheism to the organization of society, the type of government, the qualifications of the Imam and the authorities and other ranks including the commanders, provincial governors, judges, teachers who are the *'ulama*,

Islamic taxation officials and their qualifications, the police and the employees of the police force. They should see for themselves what kind of people Islam recognizes as being qualified to be government employees and the kinds that are refused positions in the government and its branches.

You the university students and all the categories of the clergy and others should desist from imposing personal predilections and views in interpreting the holy verses of the Qur'an and in commenting on Islamic writings and their authenticity. You must also be bound to all the aspects of Islamic precepts. Rest assured that Islam fully provides for whatever is good for society in fostering justice, eliminating the instruments of oppression, safeguarding independence, freedom and economic interests, and the judicious, practicable and equitable distribution of wealth, for which illogical explanations are not needed. It is also necessary for you to be wary of those who do not adhere to Islam and to all its aspects- even if they do not agree with you on just one of the principles- and to invite them with the utmost care and tact to the obligations thereof. In case this yields no result, you must not let them participate in Islamic gatherings and associations. Do not imagine that numbers will enable you to approach your goal, and that after having attained your objective, they could be purged. You should know and you do know that non-Muslims and those not committed to Islam will stab you in the back, incapacitating or destroying you before you have reached your goal. You must learn from past experiences.

Date: February 31, 1978/Bahman 24, 1365 SH/Rabi' al-Awwal 5, 1398 AH.

Place: Najaf, Iraq

Subject: The duties of Muslim intellectuals

Addressees: The Union of Islamic Students Association in Europe

O children of Iran! Strengthen your bonds with our great nation that only wants to stand on its own feet and not lean towards East or West for which reason it is being assailed by the leftists and rightists. We are witnessing the daily massacres of our people by the Eastern and Western powers. With the slogan of monotheism, prevent the access of the despots and international plunderers to our rich resources. By securing our huge resources, and by depriving the treacherous ruling circles and officials of their power, you must undertake the task of administering the country's affairs with the support of the great nation. For the interests and the good of the nation and the country, you must utilize the huge assets that are now being destroyed by the plundering, international thieves, the Pahlavis, their relations, the government and others. With the God-given blessing of the Islamic government, you must put an end to the chaos, the profligacy and the lewdness and thus rescue your nation. Rely on the Omnipotent God for He is your protector and supporter... If you notice any deviation on the part of the professors, teachers and community leaders from the national-religious path, the most important of which is the overthrow of the rotten regime, you must protest vehemently, and invite them to follow the path of the nation which is the path of God. In case they pay no heed, you must ostracize them and report their deviationist aims very clearly to the oppressed nation. Such people are traitors to the religion, nation and country. They want the Shah, his masters and the international plunderers to carry on with their plunder and keep the nation impoverished and backward

Our thinkers, intellectuals and all the university students and professors ought to realize that this is the plan, the effects of which we are now witnessing. This splitting into groups is for this very purpose of not allowing the solidarity that has been there to be maintained. They do not want the people to wake up and find their own way; that path of being united that Islam has ordained. God has made it incumbent on the people to: "Hold fast, all of you together to the cable of Allah, and do not separate." Be together and do not be dispersed. All evils result from dispersion, while all blessings and prosperity lie in holding fast to God.

May God awaken us, and all of you and the whole nation. May we move forward in the path of Islam, the path of the country's independence, and the path of truth and freedom, thereby taking this movement to the very end.

Date: June 27, 1979/Tir 6, 1358 SH/Sha'ban 2, 1399 AH.

Place: Qum

Subject: The role of the unity of the seminary and the university; the issue of factionalism and party politics

Audience: Students of the Islamic Association of the Teachers' Training University, Tehran

The importance about being a university student, an associate professor, a full professor and a pupil- in both education and science- is that there exists a proper way that accompanies the science and education; the learned man who is educated in a humane way which is the same as Islamic teaching. Any step that you take for the sake of knowledge, for an outward deed or the inwardly deeds, to create piety, perseverance and trust in you, so that when you leave the university, be a human being who is both educated and who is a trustee, God willing. As for your education, you should both act as a trustee and have a purified soul; then you have leashed your ego. Human's soul is mutinous and that mutiny will overthrow the man. In the same way that when a person rides an obstinate horse and it is unleashed, such mutinous horse will cause the death of man. Man's ego is worse than any mutinous creature. The mutiny of the ego will cause the death of man. Any step that you take in the course of education, take a parallel step for taming of your ego from this mutiny it has and the freedom from being leashed that it assumes for itself. You leash your ego... It should not be mere acquisition of knowledge where you are on the side of natural sciences and the other group on the side of divine sciences. Scrutinize the sciences. However, stay away from the egoistic mutiny. If you neglect, every step that you take in (acquiring) knowledge, you stay away from humanity; and away yet. Humanity is on a straight course. If someone steps in that path, they are considered crooked and against humanity. Should you step in the other direction, it is the wrong way. And he who chose to be crooked and deviated from the straight path, the farther they go the farther they move away from the path of humanity. It is as if you draw a straight line- two lines like this- the more this line moves forward, the more it is removed from the straight path.

The more you all study and we all study, if we do not follow the straight path and do not control our knowledge and do not leash our ego, and do not kill our ego in this course, the more educated we are the farther we get from humanity and from the human beings. Thus, it gets more difficult for the humankind to restore to his previous quality.

You who are now in your youthful years, thanks to God, you possess the youth potency and are not afflicted by the frailty of old age; you are able to quickly improve yourselves. Do not ever think of repentance as belonging to the last years of your life. Repentance is not possible in the last years of one's life. If one does not follow the issue and does not build himself from the beginning of his life; one cannot do this in the last years of his life; Satanic forces are rooted in man and are strengthened while man's (physical) strength is weakened; his will is weakened and not much would come from him.

The youth must be aware of the value of their young age and spend it in the acquisition of knowledge and in piety and in strengthening their own creativity so that they can become trustworthy and pious individuals. The country will be able to stay independent by having trustworthy individuals. The reason we were that dependent on the foreign lands was because we lacked pious statesmen; and if we had any pious statesmen, they were on the sideline- they were put aside. And those who were in the arena were not pious. There were even scientists among them, but were not pious statesmen and were not competent enough to serve the country. It was they who made us dependent on the foreign countries. The foreigners pocketed our country's revenues and they did to us what we see now; we do not have anything left. You are the only resources of this country: you youth, you university students. You are the resources of this country. Act in such a way that these resources become beneficial to your country. Improve yourselves so that, as committed and honest individuals, you run your country, God willing. No one will be able to (make you crooked). Those individuals, who are crooked, are not trustworthy; they are not competent.

Time/Date: Morning, July 7, 1979/Tir 17, 1358 SH/Sha'ban 13, 1399 AH.

Place: Qum

Subject: The role of reform and self-purification in training and education

Audience: Students of Ahwaz

What I have repeatedly underscored as secret of the victory is the unification of collegiate groups and formation of an Islamic-national group against the deviants who struggle to create discord. They strive to lead astray you the dear youth who are the hope of the nation and on whom the promotion and prosperity of the country depend. They work to prevent you from taking steps towards progress of the country and withholding you from preoccupation in science and literature, contribute to advancement and emancipation from old-age and neo-colonialism. Beware that differences and dissensions are the sources of all miseries and slaveries. Some corrupted agents may find their way to universities and other training centers and start provoking disunity among you by calculated plans. You are required to identify them vigilantly and show their true identity to the young generation, so they might be aware of their intrigues and try to frustrate them...

Date: September 22, 1979/Shahrivar 13, 1358 SH/Shawwal 03, 1399 AH.

Place: Qum

Subject: Foreigners' attempts to sweep the Islamic content of the scientific and cultural programs

Occasion: Opening of academic year

Addressees: Professors, collegians and students

You, my dear students! You make yourselves ready and well prepared to come out of this Westernization. Something of you is lost. You should find out that lost one of you. It is you. East has missed itself. East should discover itself. They want to impose themselves upon us in whatever way possible. So, you should fight. It is you who want to be free, independent. It is you who want to stand on the legs that are your own. All classes of the people in this country should determine to be themselves.

Date: January 2, 1980/Dey 21, 1358 SH/Safar 13, 1400 AH.

Place: Qum

Audience: Students of Islamic Association, Law College, Learning Center, Ardebil

Subject: The consequences of being intellectually dependent on the west- a sense of loss of direction in the East

Students of the religious sciences and the college students, you should have your reading and the study based on the fundamentals of Islam. You should refrain from giving the slogans of the seduced and deviated groups. You should replace all the devious and perverted thoughts by the pristine Islam. These two groups must know that Islam is itself a rich school. It does not need anything to be borrowed from other schools and added thereto. All must know that giving any joint of thought (from others to ours) is a great treason and treachery to Islam and the Muslims. The consequence and the fruit of such a conjecture would come to light in future and that will be too sour, too bitter. Sometimes it has been seen that due to wrong comprehension of Islamic issues, some of them are mixed and linked with those of Marxist ones. As such they have brought into being a compound, a mould, a mixture, which is on a way congruous and consistent with high-elevated laws of Islam. Dear students! Don't pace the strayed way of the irresponsible and uncommitted open-minded fellows of the university. Do not distance yourselves from the people.

Date: March 12, 1980/Farvardin 1, 1359 SH/Jamadi al-Awwal 4, 1400 AH.

Place: Shemiran, Darband, Tehran

Subject: Thirteen-point recommendations to Muslims

Occasion: The Iranian New Year Eve

Addressees: The Muslim nation of Iran, the Muslims and the oppressed ones worldwide

Now it is being heard that the anti-Islamic and anti-revolutionary groups are canvassing (anti-Islamic) propaganda to keep our youths from reading the books of this professor. I recommend the students and the class of open-minded ones not to let the books of this scholar be neglected. I wish success for all from God.

Date: March 17, 1980/Esfand 27, 1358 SH/Rabi' ath-Thani 29, 1400 AH.

Place: Shemiran, Darband, Tehran

Subject: An advice to the youth to read the books of Prof. Martyr Mutahhari

Addressees: The nation of Iran

You, the academic students and the religious students, none of you should desert the mosques. Mosques are the fronts. The fronts should be occupied.

Date: June 5, 1980/Khordad 14, 1359 SH/Rajab 02, 1400 AH.

Place: Jamaran Husayniyyah Tehran

Subject: Internal change of a nation is the source of victory, unity between religious institute and the university; Importance of Friday prayers

Audience: Professors and students of Divinity and the Islamic Sciences College, Tehran University

You try to invigorate faith in you when you are in the colleges and universities. Faith will make you honorable here and dear to God. You will arrive in the sacred court of God with reverence and respect.

Time: 10 am, June 6, 1980/Khordad 15, 1359 SH/Rajab 12, 1400 AH.

Place: Jamaran, Tehran

Subject: Explaining the duties of the military in the Islamic system

Occasion: The anniversary of 15th Khordad 1359 SH uprising

Audience: Students of the officers' college

And hence this gathering[51] now is a teachers and students forum. If these two groups are reformed, they will be able to reform a country. If, God forbid, they be anything other than this, the country will be led to rack and ruin.

Teachers and students ought to constitute the country's intelligentsia. Their position is a matter to which great attention must be paid. Their responsibilities must be made clear so that, God willing, they proceed along the path Islam has laid out and the status of humanity demands, and after passing the (various) stages, reach the place where they become (proper) human beings.

Date/Time: Morning, August 29, 1980/Shahrivar 9, 1359 SH/Shawwal 02, 1400 AH.

Place: Jamaran Husayniyyah, Tehran

Subject: Training and educating people according to the teachings of the prophets

Addressees: Pakistani students and Iranian teachers

You young students and all you dear ones who have come here from all corners are the hope of this nation and are expected to complete this mission that has been placed before you. And to continue this movement for which countless sacrifices have been made. This is the Straight Path that the prophets of God (a) have placed before mankind. This is the path that the gracious Prophet of Allah (s), the last of the prophets, and the most noble of them all has placed before mankind and he has invited them to this Straight Path and has guided them to the path of humanity and toward

---

[51] In this gathering with Imam (ra), Pakistani students and Iranian teachers were present

freedom from all kinds of disbelief and atheism and freedom from all forms of darkness to the Absolute Light. You young ones should pursue the same path in order to be the followers of the Noble Prophet (s) as well as the worthy followers of Imam as-Sadiq's (a) school of thought.

Date: January 22, 1981/Bahman 2, 1359 SH/Rabi' al-Awwal 15, 1401 AH.

Place: Jamaran, Tehran

Subject: Foreign conspiracies instigating deviation in the scientific-cultural centers of the country

Audience: Various strata of people, revolutionary guards heading for the battlefront, and school students from Tehran

With the opening of the universities, these youth must be aware that there are certain elements at work to cause you to deviate and project things in a different light. When for the first time you see a professor or a student showing deviant tendencies, you should report them at once in order to nip them in the bud.

Date/Time: Morning, December 19, 1982/Azar 28, 1361 SH/Rabi' al-Awwal 3, 1403 AH.

Place: Huseyniyyah Jamaran, Tehran

Subject: Influence of imported culture on the society

Audience: Muhsin Rezaee (Commander-in-Chief of the Guards Corps), Salik (Head of the Oppressed Mobilization), chiefs of the resistance bases, members of the Guards Corps Mobilization and the instructors of the Basij all over the country

Today, when the country enjoys efficient independence and the university has been rid of the bonds of the east and the west and easternized and westernized elements, the dear university students should try ever more to acquire sciences and techniques for prosperity their dear country, decisively prevent devious elements affiliated with the right and the left from infiltrating the university and not allow the sacred university environment to be polluted by selfish motives of deviants affiliated with aliens. If they notice any deviation or inclination to east and west from professors or students, inform the cultural board and render the necessary cooperation with the board for eliminating it.

Time: August 03, 1983/Shahrivar 8, 1362 SH/Dhul-Qa'dah 12, 1403 AH.

Place: Jamaran, Tehran

Subject: Reshuffling the Cultural Revolution Board

Addressees: Sayyid Ali Khamenei (then President)

As I have heard, some individuals have gone to universities and said that intervention in election amounts to intervention in politics and this is the right of the mujtahids (religious authorities). Up to now, they said mujtahids should not interfere in politics because it was in sharp contrasts to their right. However, they suffered defeat there, and now say the opposite of their previous claims. The same motive gives rise to these statements. Moreover, their claim that election is a political issue and the political issues are the domain of the clerics is wrong. Election determines the fate of a nation. That is, the destiny of the destiny of this nation in both worlds depends on this election. The views of some mujtahids cannot replace the elections. Is it sensible to let a few hundred mujtahids in Qum and other cities decide and ignore the rest of people? This is a plot. For hundred years, they schemed by suggesting that clerics and religion are separate from politics and thus reaped many profits. We suffered greatly. We are still suffering from this mentality. Now they saw that plot was defeated and has concocted another one; that is, election is the right of mujtahids, election or involvement in politics is the right of mujtahids. The universities should know that in the same way that a mujtahid should interfere in his destiny, a young student should also interfere in his destiny. There is no difference between university students and theology students. All are together. This statement at the university is indicative of a plot aimed to disappoint the youths.

Be vigilant! Be attentive! They want to do the job with their plots; they cannot do anything by military intervention; they want to do their work with mischief. At that time, their mischief was to suggest that politics was separate from religion, as a result of which we suffered losses and they reaped much profit. This plot has been defeated. Now they suggest that politics is the right of mujtahids; that is, only 500 people should interfere in the political affairs in Iran, with the rest going after their own business. This implies that people should get preoccupied with their own business and have nothing to do with social issues. Only a number of old mullah (clergymen) should interfere. This plot is worse than the previous one for Iran, because that plot brushed aside a number of the 'ulama though subsequently a large layer are also set aside, but this one brushes aside the entire people. They do not want to get mujtahids involved in politics; they want to destroy the mujtahids at the hands of people. Universities should notice that if there are individuals in universities engaged in mischief, they should not be deceived. The students should interfere in the election. The election determines the destiny of those who are there.

Time: Morning, February 28, 1984/Esfand 9, 1362 SH/Jamadi al-Awwal 25, 1404 AH.

Place: Husayniyyah Jamaran, Tehran

Subject: Mission and role of the radio and television; shattering the flimsy power of superpowers

Audience: Muhammad Hashemi (Managing Director of IRIB), managers and staff of IRIB

Now that by the will of Allah, the Exalted, universities have been liberated from the grip of criminals, it behooves the nation and Islamic governments at all times not to permit corrupt elements, who are either the followers of deviant schools of thought or lean toward the West or the East, to influence the colleges, universities or the centers of education. Make guards against such individuals from the beginning and before they have achieved any mischievous plan.

My advice to the students of the teachers training centers, colleges and universities is to rise bravely and oppose all deviation and perversion so that their and the nation's independence and freedom would remain safe and secure.

Date of Reciting: Khordad 15, 1368

Place: Jamaran, Tehran

Subject: Politico-divine will (ever-lasting message of Imam Khomeini to the contemporary ones and next generations)

Addressees: Iranian nation, Muslims and peoples of the world and next generations

Islamic Students Associations

The Islamic Association of Students in America and Canada

I have received your esteemed letter and would like to say that the points you have mentioned constitute part of the mischief perpetrated by this corrupt, puppet regime and a page of the afflictions of the Muslim nation of Iran. What is going on behind the scenes is much more than we can imagine. The misdeeds of this father and son- two of the stooges of foreigners- are the prelude to other radical things in the offing for the Iranians, if, God forbid, they find the opportunity and the nation loses the opportunities. Owing to the internal and external conditions and the repercussions of the regime's crimes among people and in the foreign press, it is now an opportune moment for the scientific and cultural communities, the patriotic dignitaries, the students in Iran and abroad and the Islamic associations, wherever they are, to rise up, at once and vociferously protest the prevailing conditions as also the atrocities of fifty years perpetrated by the illegal, slavish Pahlavi regime. They must also let their voices be heard by the international community and make the US president understand that the Islamic nations attribute the crimes of this dynasty, especially in recent years, to the American leadership. By supporting this regime, the US government appears to the

Muslims as the head of the tyrants and despots of history. In order to freely exploit the rich resources of the Muslims, the American government has entangled millions of decent people with those dirty and inhuman elements. If the present US president[52] does not revise his policy, if he does not part company with the kernel of impiety, then the responsibility for all the crimes committed by a bunch of godless and inhuman people will lie on him. Ignoring the right of hundreds of millions of Muslims, placing their destinies in the control of a bunch of ruffians, giving the illegal regime of Iran and the bogus government of Israel the opportunity to usurp their rights, and deprive them of their freedom, and also treating them as they have treated people of medieval times, are all crimes that are being recorded in the dossiers of American presidents. It is essential that the incumbent president, in keeping with his promises, refrain from the criminal acts of previous administrations.

We are now waiting to see whether the present American administration will sacrifice its honor and that of its people for the sake of material gain and use the oil of a poor, noble nation to wash away its own prestige, or whether, by eschewing its support for these evil elements, it will restore its reputation and honor. I request all the Islamic Associations to consolidate their relations with one another and to exclude those mysterious people who plan to sow discord and dissension among them. I request them to use Islam and its redeeming tenets as their rules of conduct. I beseech God Almighty to guide all the Muslims and make them successful in observing the enlightening injunctions of the Qur'an and Islam. May God's peace, mercy and blessings be upon you.

Date: July 25, 1977/Mordad 3, 1365 SH/Sha'ban 7, 1397 AH.

Place: Najaf, Iraq

Subject: Calling on the cultural circles to expose the crimes of the regime

Addressees: Islamic Association of Students in America and Canada

In the name of God, the beneficent, the merciful

The Union of Islamic Students Association of Europe

Thank you for your letter. The matter that I had addressed to in all the publications was my particular interest in the unity and harmony among all the Muslims, especially the youth and the dear scholars in Iran and abroad. I thank the Islamic Associations abroad and the youth in Iran and abroad for their loyalty to the ideals of Islam which is the eternal guarantor of mankind's salvation in this world and the hereafter.

The dissension of some of the ruffians and foreign lackeys should not and certainly cannot, weaken the resolve of the gentlemen in the pursuit of their sublime aim. Islam

---

[52] Imam (ra) refers to Jimmy Carter, then US President

has faced such elements in the course of its history. The hypocrites have been a disgrace from the beginning of Islam to the present time. They have always wanted to prevent the true Muslims from following the path of truth by their ruses and Islamic pretensions.

Now, in our own time, pretensions to Islam, in order to consign its progressive tenets to oblivion are a priority in the designs of the Shah and his avaricious accomplices. These Islam-destroying pretensions are, regretfully, excuses for the complacent profiteers who want to evade their responsibilities, little knowing that their deceit is not hidden from Almighty God and His watchful, committed creatures. With his pretensions to Islam, he is violating Islamic principles one by one. He is obfuscating the glorious history of Islam and replacing it with the shameful history of tyrants and despots. He makes a show of Islam in Iran whereas in his interviews with the foreign media he says that religion has no rule in the country's administration. Religion should have no role with this filthy element at the helm of affairs. If it did play a role, it would have brought the palaces of those plunderers crashing down on their heads. If religion did have a role, it would have uprooted this corrupt regime treacherous to Islam and the nation. It is Islam not having a role in your government that has allowed you to place all the resources of the country at the disposal of Islam's enemies for the sake of a dishonorable life of a few days. It is religion not having a role that has given rise to the towering mansions of a bunch of parasites beside which stand the humble hovels of the needy, poor, believers. It is because of religion not having a role that its respected *ulama* spend their days in prison and torture chambers; that the sons of Islam whether the university fraternity or the students of Islamic sciences are harmed and tortured. If religion had a role it would not have given the opportunity to some like your good-for-nothing relations to deprive the girl students of the universities and schools of their liberty. If Islam had a role it would not have given the likes of you the opportunity to start rumors of changing the Friday holiday of the Muslims to the holiday of the Christians on the excuse of gain.

All our woes are due to the fact that religion and Islam have no role in your government. Stripping the country of its freedom and its appearing in the form of a colony, the widespread suppression in the country, the prisons crammed with freemen, the lack of the basic necessities of life, the plunder of the country's resources, the dominance of the market by Israel and its not giving an opportunity to non-Jewish businessmen; all of these are attributed to religion not being given a role by the Shah and his government.

It is now the duty of the intellectuals, the young and the rest of the people of every kind and occupation to strive so that a religion can find a role. We can give religion a role by means of unity of expression, by eschewing periodic differences and by passive resistance which becomes active when the occasion arises, and thereby giving those who talk nonsense a tight slap in the face. I beseech God to set the affairs of the Muslims right and assist those who serve Islam and the Muslims. May God's peace, mercy and blessings be upon you.

Date: July 26, 1977/Mordad 4, 1365 SH/Sha'ban 8, 1397 AH.

Place: Najaf, Iraq

Subject: The lack of a role for Islam in the Shah's regime

Addressees: The Union of Islamic Associations of Students in Europe

Iranian Islamic Students Association of India – May God help you

Your esteemed letter was received at the time when the atrocities of the debased Pahlavi regime had left neither tranquility, nor the time to attend to one's affairs, thereby causing the delay in replying. Our zealous Islamic youths should know that they cannot aspire to victory until and unless they unite and set Islam the sole religion for mankind's salvation and the one and only guardian of the liberty and independence of meek nations as their goal. Now that by the will of the All-Powerful God, our nation comprising all the various classes and categories, has risen bravely with full awareness, making circumstances so difficult for the Shah and his family of scoundrels that they have come to fear their own shadows this is the fright that has been the cause of all their savage and deranged deeds, and made them resort to the massacre of Dey 19,[53] Muharram 24, 1398 AH to enable them to lessen the mounting troubles and repeated anxieties, and obtain temporary relief by means of their Dahhak like bloodthirstiness- it is necessary for you, the young students of the old and new universities to unite and forge the bonds of Islamic brotherhood with the rest of the nation. "And hold fast, all of you together, to the cable of Allah, and do not separate." This is the firm, soul-saving commandment of the Holy Qur'an that we must use as our motto. Avoiding disputes and discord that bring nothing but defeat at the hands of the Devil, we must request God the Almighty to save the nation. I am hopeful that by the Grace of the Almighty God, the hands of those criminals will be cut off and that the country's independence and freedom will be secured.

The news was received of the brave demonstrations held by the dear Iranian students in India against the Shah, this criminal element who, boastfully and exaggeratingly, has announced that the whole nation is supporting him. Although there is a wave of widespread hated and aversion towards him in Iran and abroad, he, maddened by the recent countrywide demonstrations, and has started killing the learned dignitaries of

---

[53] Imam (ra) refers to the massacre of 19th Dey 1356 SH when the guards of Shah, in response to public street protest against an article insulting Imam that was published in *Ittela'at* newspaper, opened fire.

the seminary and the zealous people of Qum in order to compensate for his mental discomfort. However, the brave resistance put up by the great nation has left him more disgraced than ever. He now wants to cover up this ignominious defeat with the ballyhoo that the people of some organizations[54] have started in the provinces, yelling Javid Shah (Long Live the King), by which he will gain nothing but infamy.

I am hopeful of victory and promise you so. By relying on the Exalted Lord, your joining up with the Students Union of Europe was the right thing to do. All the people should knit together tightly and, with one voice, attain their freedom and independence. May God's peace and mercy be upon you.

Date: February 4, 1978/Bahman 15, 1365 SH/Safar 25, 1398 AH.

Place: Najaf, Iraq

Subject: The need to desist from discord; the glad tidings of victory

Occasion: Student demonstrations in India

Addressees: The Iranian students residing in India

In the name of God, the beneficent, the merciful

The Union of Islamic Students Association of Europe – May God the Most High help you

I wish to express my thanks and appreciation for your esteemed letter together with the reports of last year's meeting and the resolutions made for the next year. This year, in the midst of the bloody events and the confrontation of the Iranian nation with the utmost savagery akin to that of the medieval ages on the part of the debased Pahlavi regime, there are obvious signs of the feeble and powerless devilish government being on its last wobbly legs. The unity of the various strata and groups of the alert nation, including the clergy, the university students, orators, writers, merchants, workers and farmers have so caused the regime to tremble, have so jangled that treacherous Shah's nerves and dealt him a blow that he has resorted to savagely attacking the nation whose good lies in Islam, whose refuge is the Glorious Qur'an and whose watchword is monotheism. He has also attacked the Qum Seminary- that solid stronghold of the revolution, of justice and the refuge of the justice-seeking Muslims- and also the honorable Muslim people of Qum who are ever the devoted soldiers of Islam and supporters of the Qur'an. Finally, by attacking the soul-saving Shi'ah teachings, he has sought to mitigate the pressure on himself, and the nervous attacks he has been experiencing.

---

[54] Imam (ra) refers to SAVAK, the Pahlavi regime's notorious secret service

His most scandalous exercises in futility have been the propaganda and the bogus demonstrations carried out by some agents of the security apparatus and the opportunists as well as those who have been compelled to participate therein. According to the radio broadcasts, they explicitly admitted that, in the sixth of Bahman[55] demonstrations, more than one-sixth of those invited did not participate, whereas all are aware that this claim is nothing but talk and exaggeration, and that this Muslim nation does not and cannot have any anybody who approves of him.

The criminal who challenges all the religious and Islamic principles and is against all the manifestations of Islam cannot have anyone amongst the Muslims who are in his favor. How can anyone agree with a criminal who says that religion has no place is in his government? How can this deviant and anachronistic who, on his recent visit to India, showed the Zoroastrians and the Ghebers such fawning admiration while approving of them and their fire-worshipping practices and, for the sake of their reactionary dogma, changed the precious, progressive Islamic calendar, possibly have anyone to agree with him apart from that anachronistic sect? Now it is incumbent on you the youthful intellectuals and all the various categories to:

1. Ensure that the watchword of your goal be Islam and its justice-fostering tenets. Without a justice-seeking Islamic government it is perforce impossible to attain this goal. Avoidance and making friendship are two basic Islamic principles. You must consent to a just government and be attached to a just ruler. You must distance yourself from non-Islamic regimes and those that do not follow Islam, at the top of which is the debased Pahlavi regime. You must very clearly show your opposition to it and strive for its downfall; if not, you will never have liberty and independence.

2. You must invite to the progressive, justice-fostering religion of Islam those non-Islamic groups whose beliefs and practices are contrary to Islam and who are inclined to other religions, whatever these may be. In case they do not accept, you must distance yourselves from, or at least avoid, such people whoever and whatever they may be. Our youth should realize that unless they possess spirituality and belief in monotheism and the hereafter, it will be impossible for them to be devoted to and concerned about the ummah. They should know that the widespread communist propaganda, just like the tumultuous propaganda of global imperialism, is only to deceive and exploit the downtrodden. Such propaganda must be nullified.

3. The young theology and university students should spend some of their time in comprehending the basic principles of Islam, at the top of which is monotheism and justice, and the great prophets- from Abraham Khalil to the Seal of the Prophets (s) who instituted justice and freedom. They must also understand their thoughts from the furthest point of spirituality and monotheism to the organization of society, the

---

[55] Anniversary of fake national referendum by Shah and nation

type of government, the qualifications of the Imam and the authorities and other ranks including the commanders, provincial governors, judges and teachers.

4. Islamic taxation officials and their qualifications, the police and the employees of the police force. They should see for themselves what kind of people Islam recognizes as being qualified to be government employees and the kinds that are refused positions in the government and its branches.

5. You the university students and all the categories of the clergy and others should desist from imposing personal predilections and views in interpreting the holy verses of the Qur'an and in commenting on Islamic writings and their authenticity. You must also be bound to all the aspects of Islamic precepts. Rest assured that Islam fully provides for whatever is good for society in fostering justice, eliminating the instruments of oppression, safeguarding independence, freedom and economic interests, and the judicious, practicable and equitable distribution of wealth, for which illogical explanations are not needed. It is also necessary for you to be wary of those who do not adhere to Islam and to all its aspects- even if they do not agree with you on just one of the principles- and to invite them with the utmost care and tact to the obligations thereof. In case this yields no result, you must not let them participate in Islamic gatherings and associations. Do not imagine that numbers will enable you to approach your goal, and that after having attained your objective, they could be purged. You should know and you do know that non-Muslims and those not committed to Islam will stab you in the back, incapacitating or destroying you before you have reached your goal. You must learn from past experiences.

6. The programs and publications of all the factions should be based, without any ambiguity, on Islam and the Islamic system of government, and at the outset, on overthrowing the devil, in all its forms, which in our country is the puppet Pahlavi regime. You should refrain from demands that necessitate the confirmation of the satanic Pahlavi regime, as is seen in the writings and sayings of certain parties to the effect that the aim is the constitutional framework. Wherever possible, in publications and speeches, you must make it known very clearly, or otherwise insinuatingly, that the core of oppression, atrocities and treacheries is the Shah himself. Attempts at directing attention to the government officials and agents, the need of which is to divert attention from the real culprit, should be strictly avoided. Writers and orators should be accordingly informed.

7. The Shah's anti-Islamic inhuman acts should be emphasized at every opportunity in party and other publications, and in speeches and demonstrations; especially, the changing of the Islamic calendar which constitutes an irreparable act of disrespect to the great personality of the venerable Prophet (s) and to Islam and the Muslims.

8. Mention should also be made of his inclination to Zoroastrianism, and his turning away from Islam and the worship of God. This traitorous element must be disgraced; at no time should there be any neglect in recounting his misdeeds. Khordad 15 and Dey 19 should be kept alive so that the cruelty of the Shah is never forgotten and that future generations may know of the crimes committed by the bloodthirsty kings.

9. I am appreciative of the unity of all Muslim students being an article of the association, as well as their desire to continue with the Islamic and humanitarian activities in coordination and unison, wherever they may be; America, Canada, India, the Philippines and other places. May the Exalted Lord give them success. It is also essential that Islamic centers be set up, wherever possible, in every part of the world for introducing Islam and disseminating its soul-saving truths. These should function under a well-coordinated organization in order to propagate justice and to weed out the hirelings of tyrants and plunderers. It is necessary for you to save our inexperienced, deceived youths by exposing the deviation of the other religions, and to acquaint them with the Islamic system. *"And whose saveth the life of one, it shall be as if he had saved all mankind."* (Qur'an, 5:32)

10. It is necessary that your Islamic activities and publications in Iran, especially in the bustling Qum Seminary and the vigilant universities, be published and circulated so that people in Iran and abroad rise to support and cooperate with one another wholeheartedly and with one voice. It is also necessary for centers to be established in the country, in whatever way possible and feasible, to carry out activities for a common goal. Surely, this would raise the morale of all while making the enemy weak and dispirited.

11. You must, with the utmost wariness and vigilance, persuade all the other unions to be careful about the ways of the union and group members so that suspicious and deviant people, or those liable to deviate, have not infiltrated the groups and unions. In the event of their having done so, they should be ostracized. You must take it for granted that the enemy is very watchful and aware. Do not think that he is negligent and careless enough to become lax in his vigilance.

12. You must positively avoid discord as this, like a spreading, fatal cancer, will engulf the people and bring all activity to a standstill while making people lose sight of their aims. It is also likely that it will change the path to be followed, causing matters to run counter to the aims. Drive away those people from you who sow or exacerbate discord; they are either agents or have evil intentions.

13. Do not oppose groups that supposedly have excuses not to join the unions but are engaged in Islamic and humanitarian activities as this would give rise to differences to the detriment of all. Try to bring about unity, if lacking, by means of friendly advice.

As the goal is the same you must behave like brothers and support one another. Islam is the objective; carnal desires and seeking precedence should be forgotten.

14. It is essential that the venerable clergy and the university students show mutual respect. The enlightened university students should respect the clergy and the clergymen. God, the Exalted, holds them in esteem and the God-inspired Household of the Prophet (a) has recommended them to the people. The clergy is a great source of strength. Losing it would cause the pillars of Islam to collapse, God forbid, thus enabling the cruel might of the enemy to go unchallenged.

Meticulous studies conducted by the alien exploiters in the course of history have led them to the conclusion that this bastion must be demolished. The widespread propaganda that they and their hirelings have been doing over several hundred years have caused some intellectuals to part with the clergy and become pessimistic about them so that the enemy remains unchallenged. In case some unqualified persons pass themselves off as being part of them, but serve and, according to the differences in their rank and service, make the people abide by the main and subsidiary principles of the faith in spite of the foreigners and their agents, this force should be assisted, protected and shown respect. The respected clergy must also respect the young intellectuals, who are serving Islam and the Islamic country and for this reason are the target of the attacks of the foreign agents. They should consider them as their dear children and their esteemed brothers. They should not give up this immense power in whose hand the destiny of the country willy-nilly will fall. They should guard against the malicious propaganda that has been going on against them for hundreds of years, showing them up in a different light to some people in order to benefit further from the disputes. They should ostracize those who either through ignorance or malicious intent have distanced this powerful group from the clergy, and not allow them to sow discord. They should rest assured that with these two great powers joining forces, victory will be attained; divided, they will never gain it.

15. The young clergymen and university students must continue with the acquisition of knowledge each in their own sphere. The recent very vexing rumors among some of the youth that there is no use in studying is a deviant matter that surely is either because of ignorance and lack of information, or evil-intentioned arising from devilish suggestions in order to deter the

16. Theology students from studying Islamic sciences so that Islamic precepts are consigned to oblivion and the obliteration of religion becomes a reality by our own actions. It is also meant to bring up our university youths as parasites dependent on the expansionists so that everyone be" imported", so to speak, like everything else, and the need for foreigners, in all the spheres and subjects of learning, to keep on increasing. This poses a great danger that will push the country backward to the greatest

extent. If Islamic science did not have professionals, the vestiges of religion would have been effaced by now. If it does not have them subsequently, this immense bulwark against the aliens will be destroyed, fully opening the way for the expansionists. If the universities become devoid of the scientists and professionals, foreigners seeking gain will spread like a cancer throughout the country, taking control of our economic and technological affairs, and bringing everything under their supervision. Our youth should fight this erroneous thought on the part of the expansionists, and the best and most effective way of fighting them is to get equipped with the weapons of knowledge of religion and of the world. Vacating this stronghold and asking people to lay down those weapons is treachery to Islam and the Islamic country.

I extend my hand in all humbleness to all the factions who are in the service of Islam, and implore them to strive in unison for the cause of fostering Islamic justice which is the sole path to the nation's prosperity. I also request the groups that are under the influence of the malicious propaganda of foreigners and do not have the correct information regarding all aspects of Islamic laws to reconsider these matters and to appraise and study thoroughly the great, all-embracing religion of Islam. After coming to believe in it, they should give up the other religions and, joining the Muslims, jointly prevent the foreigners and their traitorous, unworthy agents from meddling in the country's affairs, and should drive them out of the country. I beseech the Omnipotent God to grant success to all in serving Islam and the Muslims. May God's peace and mercy be upon you.

Date: February 31, 1978/Bahman 24, 1365 SH/Rabi' al-Awwal 5, 1398 AH.

Place: Najaf, Iraq

Subject: The duties of Muslim intellectuals

Addressees: The Union of Islamic Students Association in Europe

Try to introduce Islam to the people. These Islamic societies should try to introduce this good that we have and no one else has; this Qur'an that we have; this tradition that we have and no one else in the world has. Introduce all this. Take the experts to your place and take advantage of their services and develop this in such a way that Iran will at a time become the Islamic Society of Iran, do not suffice with only an Islamic society in the Air Force or one in the Ground Forces; think of an all-faceted Islamic society.

Date: September 1, 1979/Shahrivar 01, 1358 SH/Shawwal 9, 1399 AH.

Place: Qum

Subject: The necessity of propagating Islam in all its dimensions; liberation from self-defeatism in relation to the West

Audience: Members of the Islamic Association of the Air Force

I am due to point out a few issues when universities are going to be opened. God willing, I will then highlight the details. Now that you gentlemen are members of the Islamic associations, the number of Muslims in universities should be higher than others. The others are in minority; that is, those who are deviant. Now that you represent Islamic universities and Islamic associations, I would like to advise you to perform the Islamic duties. No one will recognize Islamic unless we ourselves act upon the Islamic principles. It is not sufficient to claim we are Islamic. Likewise, Islamic Republic will not be accepted unless its content is also Islamic. It is unacceptable to claim that we are living in an Islamic country, while every part of it is non-Islamic. This will be a meaningless expression. This also applies to Islamic associations no matter where they are. Now, there are many Islamic associations either in universities or in other places. Perhaps many of the offices have these associations as well. The primary duty of those founding the associations is to follow the path of Islam and to act in accordance with the Islamic principles. Their conduct must be Islamic. They should have undergone self-discipline. If they are refined, God willing, they may succeed in being more rectified. If not, they should endeavor to edify their self. I mean they should adapt all their affairs to Islamic precepts and gain insight into Islamic precepts in all its dimensions as much as they can. For what has Islam come? What does it want to say? What kind of ideology is Islam? They should be able to differentiate between Islam and other schools that have their claims but are not real. Then, they can set to work.

Islamic activities in universities are much more delicate than in other places. That is to say, real human beings are made in universities. In later years, the destiny of our country is in the hands of those who graduate from universities. As you know, since the destiny of the country is in the hands of young people who are graduated from universities and engage in different activities, those struggling to sap the progress of the country are sensitive to university. They do not want our country to have useful universities. This is one question that should be given regard so that they will not be able to penetrate into Islamic associations and deviate the associations under the guise of Islamic associations. The foreigners who want to take away all that belong to us so that there would be no university to stand against them are devils. The universities should not be spiritual-oriented to stand against them. Their agents may infiltrate into Islamic associations and deviate them, bringing about other issues in the name of Islam. Members of the associations should be vigilant lest others should penetrate into their rank, exercising their dictates. In many places, this state of affairs has happened. It was the case previously. Under the name of Islam, the Qur'an and the like, they have presented things to society that were irrelevant to Islam and contrary to the path of Islam.

This is an important matter to be taken into consideration. Unless you look into it with all your intelligence, you might face some difficulties. You must look into the record of those who are going to join you. You should give a lot of care to your members. There are so many who are recruited according to their appearance or merely claiming that they are Muslim. They may perform the religious rituals more efficiently than you, but once you look at them more carefully and study their situations, you would find that their way, conduct and manner are completely different from yours. The Islam preached by them is different from what is presented in true Islam. There are such people among them. Therefore, you should be very careful about the individuals you are going to recruit. You should know them like books; you should be well informed of their records and personalities. You should know what objects they seek. Once you have gained insight into these matters, you will be able to establish a true Islamic association, which would be helpful to our society and can purify and refine our universities. Of course, that is a difficult task to accomplish. If we are going to accomplish such a task in all of our universities, it would be much more difficult and burdensome. However, we should tolerate the problems. Those who are going to accomplish such a positive task or render the great service of purging the corrupt people in universities across the country, they encounter an arduous task, but they should bear the difficulty because it is a valuable job.

Date: September 02, 1979/Shahrivar 29, 1358 SH/Shawwal 28, 1399 AH.

Place: Qum

Subject: Mission of Islamic associations, Foreigners' intervention in turmoil's, Opponents of *Wilayate Faqih*

Audience: The universities Islamic associations' representatives Nationwide

If one wants to be the trainer of a society or a place, he should be invited to Islam. In the first place he himself should make himself Islamic. He should invite his inner being to Islam. Then he can invite others to Islam. The teachers, if they have not undergone the teaching, cannot teach others. The origin of every affair starts from the person concerned with self. When the Prophet came, he started the invitation from his own house. He was a perfect person. He invited Khadijah- his wife. She accepted the invitation. Imam Ali- accepted the invitation. He gathered all his kith and kin and relatives and told them the case and kept on his invitation while some didn't accept. When I tell you to do this and don't do that while I happen to be a corrupt man, my saying will not be efficacious. You have the Islamic Association; may God protect you. Those who have established these Islamic Associations should start from themselves. This association should be Islamic in its- moral, conduct, behavior, action, belief and so on- all must be Islamic. In other words, he should be purified. He must have learned the Book and the Wisdom- at least to the extent that the Book invites. Your interest and your loss are hidden there.

I hope all of you will reform yourselves in order to reform the society.

Time: Morning, July 2, 1980/Tir 01, 1359 SH/Sha'ban 18, 1400 AH.

Place: Jamaran, Tehran

Subject: Education/training from the Qur'an's view, the position of culture in the Pahlavi regime. The need for basic changes there

Audience: The heads of education throughout the country, the Islamic Association members, the Home Ministry workers and the provincial workers

I would like to say a few words on the Islamic associations- the ones organized by school students as well as the others- that are, by the grace of God, active throughout the country.

To begin with, the term "Islamic" association signifies a commitment on the part of these associations toward Islam. It is not simply and merely the name for a group of people who have got together. It is a commitment to Islam. In other words, you have made a commitment to act according to (the teachings of) Islam, no matter where you are. Thus, you have the dual responsibilities of living according to Islam and inviting others to it.

As regards your responsibilities toward yourselves, you should stay alert so that deviated elements that are not committed to Islam, and which are in fact the enemies of Islam, do not infiltrate into these associations. Those who have suffered personal material losses at the hands of Islam do not wish for it to prevail in this country and they, thus, try to infiltrate into these associations as well as into the mosques and other Islamic places. It is, therefore, the responsibility of the Islamic associations- school students' and the rest- to be clear about the backgrounds of all those who intend to join the associations as well as to find out about their activities before and during the Revolution and whether their families are committed to Islam or not. You should enquire whether the person who wants to join the association has been committed to Islam before and after the Revolution or not. It may be that the majority of the members of these associations are honest and are committed to Islam and the Revolution, however, even if a couple of deviated elements infiltrate among them they could end up deviating the entire Islamic association. This is one of the important responsibilities of the Islamic associations. I have been informed, perhaps repeatedly, that there are some people in the Islamic associations who are not committed to Islam and who have infiltrated into them, in the name of Islam, in order to cause deviation among them. Thus, your responsibility is to examine the backgrounds of the people before accepting them into the association. Care should be taken not to allow deviated elements and the enemies of Islam to join in, lest they, God forbid, corrupt your Islamic association and the purpose for which these associations have been formed. This is one of your responsibilities to which you should pay the utmost attention.

Another point that I would like to mention concerns the Islamic nature of these associations. Islam is a multi-dimensional religion and due attention would need to be paid to all of its various dimensions by those who really want to be Islamic. One of these dimensions is its belief structure. The Islamic associations should, obviously, uphold the Islamic beliefs. Those who do not believe in and do not abide by Islamic beliefs cannot form Islamic associations. They would never succeed in establishing a real Islamic association and spreading Islam if they did not believe in all the Islamic principles.

Another aspect of Islam is its ethical principles. There may be some people whose beliefs are truly Islamic but they lack Islamic ethics.

Date: March 13, 1981/Farvardin 11, 1360 SH/Jamadi al-Awwal 24, 1401 AH.

Place: Jamaran, Tehran

Subject: The mission and the responsibilities of Islamic associations

Audience: Representatives of the school students' Islamic Associations from all over the country

If God forbid, you deviate or allow deviation into your associations or in the teachings that are being imparted, you will be held responsible. You will be questioned as to why you did not act according to the teachings of Islam. You will be questioned as to why your students were not brought up in an Islamic manner and as to why there was deviation in these Islamic associations.

Date: March 13, 1981/Farvardin 11, 1360 SH/Jamadi al-Awwal 24, 1401 AH.

Place: Jamaran, Tehran

Subject: The mission and the responsibilities of Islamic associations

Audience: Representatives of the school students' Islamic Associations from all over the country

Even those of you[56] who have voluntarily formed the Islamic associations along with your friends and associates throughout the country were not commanded from the top

---

[56] Imam (ra) refers to members of Islamic Association of Teachers of Mazandaran Province

241

to do so. You saw the need for your own selves, for an Islamic country to have Islamic systems for all its affairs, and just like the revolutionary guards who saw the need for guarding the country and took it upon themselves, you too found the need for an Islamic system and tried to provide it in all areas.

The Islamic associations all over the country should know that in these Islamic associations, there are people who are actually enemies and enter into your associations in the guise of friends, wishing to drag your Islamic associations into corruption. All of you should take care to check out the past records of all those who wish to join your associations and you should check out their activities before the Revolution. For all you know they could be SAVAK members who have now sported a beard and are tricking you with prayer beads in the hand. Check out their previous professions and their family backgrounds. Check out their educational backgrounds and their belief systems. The backgrounds of these people, prior to the Revolution, should be inspected. Now everyone can claim to be revolutionaries. You will also find people who worked for the SAVAK now claiming that they were against the previous regime! However, there are some among them who are still loyal to the previous regime and are waiting for conditions to revert back to the previous ones so that they can reach their desires and they, thus, infiltrate among these associations that have been formed by our beloved youth to serve the country. It is quite possible that they creep into these associations without your knowledge, which fact you may realize only after they have already dragged your association into corruption. The Islamic associations should be formed by people who hail from religious families and who themselves hold Islamic beliefs and these people should have been committed Muslims before and after the Revolution. You should not be deceived by people who express interest in joining your associations with claims of being Islamic and revolutionary. You should scrutinize the backgrounds of these people thoroughly so that such people do not end up ruining your associations and denigrate the face of Islam. This is a religious and Islamic obligation on all the groups that wish to form Islamic associations, committees, and Jihad for Reconstruction centers. These people are all committed toward serving this nation and consider this country as their own and are busy serving the nation. However, care should be taken and members should be selected carefully, especially in the case of the Islamic associations which bear the name of Islam. Careful scrutiny should be made and if the past records of certain individuals are not up to mark, do not let them enter into your associations. Not that they should be shunned from society; but there are many other things that they could instead be doing. Since the Islamic associations wish to represent Islam and to establish Islam, people who do not have an Islamic background cannot be trusted for this particular responsibility.

Thus, one of your responsibilities is to be careful in accepting members. Select people with an Islamic background before and during the Revolution and with an Islamic family background. Your other responsibility is taking care of the place in which your Islamic association has been formed. When one claims to be a Muslim it is as if he has made an agreement with God Almighty to remain faithful to Islam and to act according to its teachings. When you claim that yours is an Islamic association- The Teachers' Islamic Association, The Islamic Association of the Armed Forces, etc.- you should take utmost care that the young and inexperienced members do not commit acts that would go against the tenets of Islam. It is good to have Islamic associations everywhere. However, that does not mean that they should try to take power into their hands wherever they go. They should rather take it upon themselves to guide people wherever needed. It is you or the Teachers' Islamic Association that should take on guiding teachers on the ways and methods of teaching. Those of you who are part of the Islamic Association of the Army should disseminate the teachings of Islam and should provide guidance without interfering in official matters.

Date: April 27, 1981/Urdibehesht 7, 1360 SH/Jamadi ath-Thani 22, 1401 AH.

Place: Jamaran, Tehran

Subject: A comparison between the military officials of the Islamic Republic and the *taghouti* regime

Audience: Members of the Islamic Association of the teachers of the Mazandaran province, helicopter and airplane service staff, Directors General of the Tehran Post and Telegraph Office and telephone exchange, staff-members of the Ministry of Education, some people from Larijan

We are certainly not against expertise! And the same applies to the Islamic associations. No Islamic association can be against expertise. There is no Islamic association that is against expertise and the self-reliance of our youth in every field. In fact it is the opposite. And you had seen that the conditions of the universities during the reign of the previous regime were such that even after long years of active work in our universities, when a relative of the deposed Shah- the so called "head of the country"- needed to undergo a simple surgery for appendicitis, a surgeon was brought in from abroad! What prompted this was that the Shah knew very well in his hollow head that he had made Iran so dependent on foreigners that the Iranians were not capable of handling (even simple) things; and even if they were, all efforts should be made to inculcate their minds into believing that they are good-for-nothing! And that they should be made to believe that they are incapable of performing even a simple surgery for appendicitis after spending long years at the university! However, our intention is to free the minds (of our people) from such ill-thoughts. The aim of the Islamic associations should be to eliminate this wrong belief so that our people can rediscover themselves after centuries of alienation. We want our universities to train people like Avicenna whose book, "The Canon of Medicine", is still being used in Europe rather than having people who, without even knowing the alphabets of Islam, claim that Islam is incompetent!

Time/Date: Morning, May 25, 1981/Khordad 4, 1360 SH/Rajab 02, 1401 AH.

Place: Jamaran, Tehran

Subject: Importance of knowledge in Islam; responsibility of the university in an Islamic society; duties of the Islamic associations of the universities

Audience: Members of the Islamic Association and the Jihad of the 'Ilm va San'at (Science and Technology) University; members of the Organization for Scientific and Industrial Research; and a group of inventors and innovators

Let me reiterate what I have repeatedly been reminding the Islamic Associations. Keep your eyes and ears wide open because those who are inclined toward the West or the East can also infiltrate into the Islamic associations and pretend to be perfectly "Islamic". You should take care to check out the past records of all those who wish to join your associations and you should scrutinize their activities before and after the revolution so that, God forbid, things do not go out of hand for you to someday realize all of a sudden that your attention has been deviated from the truth and that your Islamic association has inclined to either of the foreign blocs. I have repeatedly raised this issue for the Islamic associations. However, the significance of what I am saying is even greater as far as the Islamic associations of the universities are concerned. Put in all your efforts to prevent deviant elements from joining your Islamic associations and keep it firmly in mind that since they have failed to attain to their goals by all other means, they now trying to attain them in the name of Islam. Even those sworn opponents who consider Islam to be a stumbling block in their way try to get their work done in the name of Islam. They do not come up and say that we do not believe in Islam, in which case they would not be so dangerous. Those who enter the government offices, the universities, and other government bodies under the disguise of commitment to Islam are more dangerous than those who openly claim that they do not believe in Islam because in the latter case, the people know them and can avoid them. The Islamic associations, in general, and the Islamic associations of the universities, in particular, should bear this point in mind.

Time/Date: Morning, May 25, 1981/Khordad 4, 1360 SH/Rajab 02, 1401 AH.

Place: Jamaran, Tehran

Subject: Importance of knowledge in Islam; responsibility of the university in an Islamic society; duties of the Islamic associations of the universities

Audience: Members of the Islamic Association and the Jihad of the 'Ilm va San'at (Science and Technology) University; members of the Organization for Scientific and Industrial Research; and a group of inventors and innovator

In the name of God, the beneficent, the merciful

Islamic Students Association of United States and Canada

Dear brothers and sisters, your message of total commitment to Islam and human values was received. I know about your activities and I am thankful for it.

Committed youths throughout the history and particularly Muslim students of the present generation and future generations are the hope of Islam and Islamic countries. With their commitment, weapons, perseverance and resistance, they can serve as the rescue ship for Islamic nations and their own countries. The independence, freedom and progress of nations depend on their efforts. They are the main target of the colonists and imperialists of the world. Each power pole is intent on entrapping them, because by hunting them, they can drag nations and countries into destruction and poverty.

And now, O dear youths, students, scientists and the present and future hope of the Muslim nation the big trust of independence and freedom obtained by the great Iranian nation from the two power poles of the East and West through their sacrifice and struggle is entrusted to you. You have a big responsibility. All the nations, especially Muslim students, who are the future leaders, are responsible for safeguarding this great divine trust.

The opponents of the Islamic republic and your and our opponents both inside and outside and the two superpowers have stretched their traps for the youths. The great enemies of Islam with their preys and the agents of their schools of thought have launched an all-out propaganda attack against you and against your country here and abroad. We who are here inside and you who are abroad must do our best to free the deceived youths from the trap of these hunters. These uninformed young people who are not aware of having fallen prey to the widespread trap of political players, have totally surrendered to them and wholeheartedly accepted their lies and accusations against the authorities of the Islamic Republic, the revolutionary guards and Muslim devotees in the way of Islam and country. They devote themselves to the chief frauds who destroy them in order to achieve their own inhuman purposes. And unwittingly, these young adults offer the blood of the valiant nation to these godless criminal America.

You, dear alert youths, come together with friends inside the country and guide these uninformed youngsters and release them from the trap of the hunters. One of the religious duties of our nation and yours is to uncover the American and Zionist's propaganda aimed at blemishing the image of the Islamic Republic and isolating our country by spreading lies, libels and rumors. Work to neutralize these sinister attempts. Help our nation as much as you can, a nation whose only fault is their commitment to Islam, independence and freedom. We should be sure that the great nation of Iran has found its way that is the straight path of humanity, is consciously prepared in different arenas and will not let the unbelievers to return to the country. We must fight tooth and nail to defend our dear Islam and country. Hopefully and with the help of God we will defeat the warmongers, isolate the corrupt criminals, will overcome all problems with effort, will be victorious on all fronts, and thanks to self-confidence and reliance on God we will not fear any power.

The Islamic Revolution of Iran which is supported by God, is spreading all over the world. God willing, with its spread, the satanic powers will be forced to withdraw and the government of the poor will be set up. Thus, the ground will be laid for the universal government of Mahdi at the end of time may God hasten his honorable reappearance and may our souls be sacrificed for him.

Oppressed people of the world, it is high time you rebelled against the arrogant vampires and take your right from them for God is on your side and His promise is sure to be fulfilled. I pray to the exalted God to grant victory to Islam.

Peace be upon the martyrs of the path of Islam and upon all the Muslims of the world and salutations to the dear fighters of the land of Iran and peace be upon you, the young Islamic Association Students in America, Canada and all over the world. Carry out your human-Islamic duties in the heart of satanic and tyrannical states and do not fear their power. Death and damnation to the superpowers of the East and West, especially the criminal America.

Date: November 3, 1981/Aban 21, 1360 SH/Muharram 6, 1402 AH.

Place: Jamaran, Tehran

Subject: Explaining the mission of foreign-based Muslim students

Addressees: Islamic Association of Students in America and Canada

Islamic associations all over the country are highly valuable and should notice two points: the first point is that they must pay attention to the fact that only the committed individuals must be found in their ranks. Beware that if there is one deviant person influential in an Islamic association, he will lead astray association. I have repeatedly said while selecting people for associations, almost care must be taken. Their personal and family background, their ex-friends, and their performance before and after the revolution must be investigated in detail. When you thoroughly investigated their records and found them to be decent people committed to serve the nation and Islam, you can select them. One more advice I would like to give to these clergies is that while you carefully look into the status of the people working in ministries, army and whatever, your job is just to provide guidance. If guidance does not get them anywhere, you should inform those at the top, like the judiciary. If you interfere directly, it will be against the law and religion. Of course, you should not do such a thing. If you see any of them suggesting such a thing, you should know that they want to lead you astray.

Date/Time: Before noon, December 28, 1981/Dey 7, 1360 SH/Rabi' al-Awwal 1, 1402 AH.

Place: Jamaran, Tehran

Subject: The importance of collective cooperation in furthering the goals

Audience: Families of the martyrs of 7th Tir (tragedy of the explosion of the Head Office of the Islamic Republic Party), officials from the illiteracy campaign organization, German-based military college students affiliated with the national defense

These Islamic associations are a good thing, a favorable thing and their members are, God willing, mostly good, but you should note what these associations are and what individuals join them. It is possible to see that an Islamic association has been deflected and defamed. If there are some devious people who intentionally try to defame these Islamic associations, you will see that across the country they say that Islamic associations are composed of dissidents. The persons who have contacts with individuals, wherever they are, should improve the situation and applicants should be accepted only after being identified. If, let us suppose, there is an Islamic association that wants to discredit an office, you should know that this is not an Islamic association. Islamic association should supervise affairs and stay wherever it is. For instance if an Islamic association in a bank wants to expel upright individuals and bring in unfit ones, this association is not Islamic.

Time: April 2, 1983/Farvardin 14, 1361 SH/Jamadi ath-Thani 8, 1402 AH.

Place: Jamaran, Tehran

Subject: Moral deviation, source of degeneration in the world, preventing the influence of deviants; observing religious laws and criteria

Audience: Sayyid Ali Khamenei (President and secretary-general of the Islamic Republic Party), officials and members of the offices of Islamic Republic Party across the country, members of the Islamic Association of Tehran Banks

The matter, which I have stressed to the various strata with whom, I have met and which I advise and emphasize to you the beloved youth is that the Islamic associations must take care that these deviant elements do not penetrate in these associations. Rest assured that these deviant elements and hypocrites and those whose hands have been shortened from this country want to penetrate in all parts of the country and especially in the universities that are the academic centers and centers for all round human perfection. It is possible that individuals that are very pious outwardly, become more pious even than you in your presence and cry out "Oh Islam!" but God forbid, may be of the deviant elements. In the same way that Satan comes in different guises and misleads human beings by means of every trick, these, too, are human devils that take various forms, and guises and God forbid, infiltrate among you. If God forbid, if such an infiltration occurs, then know there is deviation involved and even though it may not be in the short term but in the long term, there will be deviation. Therefore, you must make your utmost efforts and judgment in selection of individuals to these associations and pay attention that the individuals are persons whose past record before the Revolution and within the course of the Revolution is well known and they are admitted to these associations after their credentials have been thoroughly established. The activities of these associations are very valuable but they have such responsibilities, which is also immense. Also the responsibility of paying attention to all aspects of the university and supervision of all aspects of the university in order to ascertain that no deviation occurs; a deviant professor- God forbid- does not enter and the university administration- God forbid- are not of the deviant elements; are also of the crucial tasks that must be looked into carefully. However, attention in the sense that for every minor issue you must not put aside the people because you belong to "Hizbullah" (party of God) dismiss individuals that are pious even if they had made a mistake in the past or committed a wrong that was obligatory. Whatever you do must be appealing and persons that are at present doing a good job and are useful should remain in the universities and continue to educate and to train with the supervision that all the students have in the affairs.

In any case, the task is an important one; and the important task demands an important responsibility. I hope that you the dear brothers and the beloved of the nation succeed in this Islamic-humanitarian task.

Date/Time: Morning, November 27, 1982/Azar 6, 1361 SH/Safar 11, 1403 AH.

Place: Husayniyyah Jamaran, Tehran

Subject: Importance of the role of Islamic associations, successes of the popular serving government

Audience: Student members of the Office of Consolidation of Unity of the Islamic associations of the universities throughout the country

SECTION 7

PURSUING HIGHER EDUCATION ABROAD

Studying Abroad in the Views of Imam Khomeini

We believe that your reform programs are in fact devised by Israel and it is to Israel that you turn for help and advice whenever you want to draw up a plan. You bring military advisers from Israel into this country. You send students from our country to Israel. If only they were sent elsewhere; to America or even to Britain for example. But no, you send them to Israel! These are the kinds of issues we dispute.

Date: 8 am, April 15, 1964/Farvardin 26, 1343 SH/Dhu'l-Hijjah 2, 1383 AH.

Place: A'zam Mosque, Qum

Subject: Analysis of the Khordad 15 uprising, performance of the government and the mission of the *'ulama* and the clergy

Occasion: Imam Khomeini's release from prison

Audience: *'ulama*, clergymen, merchants, students and people from other sectors of society

More importantly, they[57] told me that they are not allowed to learn anything, that they are kept at a low level beyond which they cannot progress, adding that the training they had received in Iran was more than the small amount they were being given abroad! They said they had been brought over here to be kept at a low level so that they could not progress. Our youth are not allowed to acquire an education.

Date: November 02, 1978/Aban 29, 1357 SH/Dhu'l-Hijjah 19, 1398 AH.

Place: Neauphle-le-Chateau, Paris, France

Subject: Clarifying the motives and the aims of the uprising and warning against reconciliatory plans

Addressees: A group of Iranian students and residents abroad

In Europe, we met with many students, four hundred of whom were sent to Germany by the government, and discussed issues including that of atomic energy. A group of these students came to us and brought up their predicament. The first was that they were kept backward and were not allowed to progress scientifically, and second was the fact that this atomic energy is deleterious, not beneficial, to Iran. It is useful until the time there is oil and gas in Iran; once this oil and gas are exhausted then it will outlive its usefulness. Furthermore, it can inflict other material damages as well. Moreover, this act has been done intentionally by the governmental machinery in order

---

[57] Imam (ra) refers to some of the Iranian students living abroad

to retard our youth's progress, destroy our youthful work force, and obstruct the progress of the country. In the name of development, they, in reality, have pushed the country backward.

Date: February 8, 1979/Bahman 19, 1357 SH/Rabi' al-Awwal 01, 1399 AH.

Place: Alawi School, Tehran

Subject: Excellent attributes of the Islamic movement

Audience: Members of the Islamic Society of Physicians, Engineers and Teachers

Those who were around this father and son[58] were from the educated class who were educated in Europe and America; but it was only education. They did not have Islamic training and human development. Therefore, the harm that was inflicted upon our country by the educated ones of this country was not inflicted by others. Even the SAVAK did not inflict as much harm as they did. They corrupted the minds. They corrupted our youth.

Date: July 14, 1979/Tir 23, 1358 SH/Sha'ban 19, 1399 AH.

Place: Qum

Subject: The need to complement education with training and cultural independence

Audience: Teachers of the town of Shahreza

The university cannot be independent unless it puts its Western mind away and has found itself an Eastern mind. What they always say is this: People should go from here to Europe in multitudes for pursuing an education. And if they do not go to Europe, they would not admit them here. The question is this that the nation has turned as such! The people have also turned as such; the government also has turned as such. All are like that. They all have turned as such: unless one goes for some time- let's suppose to France, even though they go there but do not have a job…They will cursorily give them a diploma because they do not want to send a learned person to this country, but they just want to send someone with a diploma in their hand. Actually the plan is for those who go there and get a diploma, a colonial diploma. It is their decision to somehow certify these individuals, otherwise, they will not grant a diploma to their own people that easily. They treat us differently; they give us a diploma very fast. Why? Because they do not want us to reach a point where we have some knowledge to present. We should always be in need of them and always act as a parasite. Until we have come out of that West-struckness, and have not changed our

---

[58] Imam (ra) refers to Reza Shah and Mohammad Reza Shah Pahlavi

minds, and do not know ourselves, we could not gain independence. We cannot have anything.

Date: September 1, 1979/Shahrivar 01, 1358 SH/Shawwal 9, 1399 AH.

Place: Qum

Subject: The necessity of propagating Islam in all its dimensions; liberation from self-defeatism in relation to the West

Audience: Members of the Islamic Association of the Air Force

When I was in Paris, people from all around the world including Germany, which was nearby came to meet me. Those working in the Atomic Energy Center in Germany and the Iranians engaged in this field also came to meet me. The Iranians said that the job they were doing was harmful to Iran. They complained of being denied of mastering the technology! They want to keep us at a level so we cannot understand the relevant technology. Even if it is made, it is harmful for Iran. Such plans were underway as to send the youth abroad and keeping them in the dark. I am not much in the know about today, but in time of the former regime,[59] our youths were sent to America and all around Europe to get diplomas. As I have been told, the diplomas given to our youths were different from those awarded to theirs in terms of quality! Our youths were given the diplomas immediately without mastering the field. However, the certificates were awarded to their own students with great care. I have been quoted time and again about this approach. Why? It is because they did not want us to grow and stop this power to emerge. They feared this empowerment.

Date: September 17, 1979/Shahrivar 26, 1358 SH/Shawwal 25, 1399 AH.

Place: Qum

Subject: All out dependencies in Pahlavi regime and preventing the younger

Occasion: Martyrdom of Imam Ja'far Sadiq (a) and the anniversary of tragic event in Faydiyyah Theological School

Audience: Families of martyrs of Islamic Revolution

Those who pick up their pens and write in favor of the west have grown sick in as much as this idea has been injected in them.

They went abroad since their childhood and brought up in an environment designed for them. Even outside of Iran, things are not the same for us. Even the diplomas they

---

[59] Imam (ra) points to Mohammad Reza Shah

give us are different from theirs. The courses provided for us are different from theirs. They teach us colonialist subjects and grant us colonialist diplomas. The situation provided for us differs from theirs. These helpless people lived in that colonialist environment and had such education. Many of them who failed to complete their education only went swimming in Seine River.[60] We were told the Euphrates! Now, they have come here, sitting in their rooms and writing articles for newspapers to build up a reputation for themselves. They write what they were dictated. They do not leave this nation alone to find its identity and find out that they are integral to this world. This part of the world, the east, was once among progressive countries. However, the west brought about this desperate situation. Avicenna's books are perhaps being taught in their universities now. We brushed aside whatever we had and could not find what we lost. We turned to a "yet mouse"[61], something that is neither eastern, nor western nor Islamic and nor European.

Yes, we are eastern in the sense of "colonized Eastern." We are also westernized in the sense of "colonized by the West." We should come out of this. As long as this disease infects us, no recovery is conceivable; we should be relieved of this disease.

Date: Before noon, September 19, 1979/Shahrivar 28, 1358 SH/Shawwal 27, 1399 AH.

Place: Qum

Subject: Iranian nation's troubles during the Pahlavi regime

Audience: Tehran education organization officials and staffs

Maybe you know that eastern people going abroad to study are awarded a diploma other than their own, i.e. they are awarded certificate sooner than their own students or a person who is awarded on eastern diploma there, is not allowed to have an office. He should return to Iran or other eastern countries to have an office.

Date: October 6, 1979/Mehr 14, 1358 SH/Dhu'l-Qa'dah 14, 1399 AH.

Place: Qum

Subject: Colonial culture and intellectual dependency- Reforming cultural centers-enemies' plot

---

[60] The Seine is a 775-kilometre-long river in northern France.

[61] Imam (ra) points to a story of a student where he recites a couplet: Cat is lion in front of mouse and yet mouse is like cheetah. Means an animal which is neither mouse nor cat, something in the middle.

Addressees: Professors and Staff of the Sharif University of Technology

You, teachers and all professors, consider the point that the West gives us no helpful things. It owns useful things but gives us naught and exports nothing. What it gives us or exports to us are means of leading our country to decadence.

Date: October 26, 1979/Aban 4, 1358 SH/Dhu'l-Hijjah 4, 1399 AH.

Place: Qum

Subject: Priority of Cultural Reforms- Concept of freedom and suffocation-colonialist link of superpowers

Audience: Islamic Association Member Teachers East Azarbayjan

If they offer some know-how, they would give things that would not yield any profit to us. If our youth go there for education, the knowledge they impart to our youth is reserved for colonial schools. Their schools are different from what are offered to Third World. They see the Third World in a different light. Basically, they do not grant anything to the Third World. In fact, they hold no respect for Third World people. The respect they hold for animals there are greater than their treatment towards people living here! The medicine that is banned to use there is authorized to transfer to the Third World. The doctor who is banned to practice medicine there is transmitted to here. It is permissible for such a doctor to practice medicine here! The doctors graduated from there and granted certificates there are not predominantly authorized to practice medicine there; they have to return to their countries to practice. You are not authorized to practice medicine here. This attitude is due to the fact that they maintain no prestige for Third World people or borrowing their words colonized countries. Whatever they desire for themselves is completely different from what they want for us. They give us something different.

I have already said that when we were in Paris, the young students studying in Germany came to us and complained that they were banned from ascending the higher ranks of education. They said they were impeded from reaching a certain level or make progress. Regrettably, they had infiltrated into our universities and blocked the growth of our students could achieve. Some of the university professors were stooges delegated not to let our students make sound progress. If you want to gain independence and real freedom, you should struggle to achieve self-sufficiency in all aspects of life. You should be free from need. Farmers must work such that we no longer wait and be in need of wheat from abroad. University students should struggle so that we would not need foreign doctors. We should not also stand in need of engineering from abroad.

Time: November 2, 1979/Aban 11, 1358 SH/Dhu'l-Hijjah 11, 1399 AH.

Place: Qum

Subject: Necessity of cultural-economic independence of the country

Audience: Students of Faculty of Sciences and Faculty of Literature and Foreign Languages

And these agents insult and treat harshly our university students living abroad. Carter[62] himself who claims to be a "humanitarian" ordered (his security agents) to harass Iranian students who had gone there (the U. S. A) to seek scientific education has issued orders to hurt Iranian university students living in the States. He has ordered his agents to attack them with dogs and commit other crimes against them.

Date: November 17, 1979/Aban 27, 1358 SH/Dhu'l-Hijjah 27, 1399 AH.

Place: Qum

Subject: American hostages, extradition of the Shah and the Iran-American future relations

Interviewer: The reporter of CBS television network of the United States

When our youths go abroad, they are not allowed to learn with English or American students. They are not coached by the same standard and at the same level as they coach their native students. They have different training and coaching for the countries under imperialism. Therefore, the output and outcome of this training comes out like Sharif Imami's and Nasiri's[63]. They have worked abroad. They were educated abroad.

Time: Morning, July 2, 1980/Tir 01, 1359 SH/Sha'ban 18, 1400 AH.

Place: Jamaran, Tehran

Subject: Education/training from the Qur'an's view, the position of culture in the Pahlavi regime. The need for basic changes there

Audience: The heads of education throughout the country, the Islamic Association members, the Home Ministry workers and the provincial workers

Do you realize what the United States and its police are doing to our youth, our boys and girls? Do you know that the United States' Government cooperated with the

---

[62] Then President of the United States

[63] General Nematollah Nasiri, Head of SAVAK, appointed by the Shah. He was among the main culprits behind killings, massacres and torture of Islamic activists from the coup de'tat of 28th Mordad 1332 to the year 1356. After success of Islamic Revolution, he was among the foremost to be tried by the Islamic Revolutionary Court and sentenced to be killed on 26/11/1357.

traitors who held meetings and demonstrations against our oppressed nation, and so did what they wanted to do, but then when our Muslim students who wanted to hold demonstrations so as to let the world know about the oppression that we have been subjected to, the American police confronted them (with hostility)? Does the Pope[64] know that our youth have been chained and shackled; some with broken ribs, others unconscious; that our daughters have also been shackled and chained and some are unconscious? Does he pay any attention to these issues? And how Prophet Jesus (a) treated the people?! And you, who claim to be representing him, do not care about such issues! I wish he (i. e. the Pope) had also sent an emissary[65] to Carter. I wish they would send you with a letter to Carter about what they (the American Police) are doing to the youths who demand justice and want to inform the world that our nation has been a victim of oppression. They (i. e. the United States' police forces) have arrested them (i. e. the students) and have been sending them from one jail to another. They have chained their hands and feet and have broken their teeth (ruthlessly by kicking them) with their boots. They are still being harmed, locked up in chains and brutalized under the crushing boots of Carter's henchmen and American oppressors.

Date: August 3, 1980/Mordad 21, 1359 SH/Ramadan 12, 1400 AH.

Place: Tehran, Jamaran

Subject: Criticizing the stance and Performance of the Christian clergy

Addressees: Archbishop Cappuchi (the representative of Pope John Paul II)

The rush of Iranian students towards the West or occasionally the East after finishing their Western and Eastern oriented studies at schools or universities, which have no fruits except Western and Eastern cultures, was so destructive that unconditionally made all aspects of our social life dependent on the superpowers, to the extent that our society was Islamic - Iranian on the surface but brimmed with Western and Eastern cultures

Date: September 22, 1981/Shahrivar 13, 1360 SH/Dhu'l-Qa'dah 23, 1401 AH.

Place: Jamaran, Tehran

Subject: Effects and consequences of independent versus dependent culture

Occasion: Beginning of academic year

---

[64] Pope John Paul II, then Leader of the World Catholics
[65] Refers to Skoff Cappuchi, Pope's representative sent to Imam (ra) for negotiating the release of American hostages captured from the Den of Spies (US Embassy in Tehran).

Addressees: High school and university students, the youth, teachers and professors

If our university were our own; if the university was not a university to imitate the imported culture; then its output would not have been what it was. Those who at that time graduated from the universities- however, I do not say all; there were exceptions but the exceptions were few- when they graduated, they would line up and flow towards England and France and lately, America. See what they trained in the universities! When they would go abroad and return, what they would turn out and what souvenir would they bring for us! Those who would graduate from the universities and had studied abroad and returned to Iran were the same individuals that would become the ministers and legislators of that time. What would these ministers and legislators of the former regime do in Iran? What souvenir would they bring for Iran? All their efforts would be directed at appeasing at one time England and later America.

Date/Time: Morning, December 19, 1982/Azar 28, 1361 SH/Rabi' al-Awwal 3, 1403 AH.

Place: Huseyniyyah Jamaran, Tehran

Subject: Influence of imported culture on the society

Audience: Muhsin Rezaee (Commander-in-Chief of the Guards Corps), Salik (Head of the Oppressed Mobilization), chiefs of the resistance bases, members of the Guards Corps Mobilization and the instructors of the Basij all over the country

We had so many specialists in all fields of study in the former regime; yet what did these specialists do for the nation? Except that they kept on pushing the nation backwards; kept on making it more dependent; everything became dependent; you name it and they would say that we must go to Europe to get it. They knew well how to make pitchers; they would take us in order to teach us; they would not teach us. They would take away our youth and corrupt a group of them and teach them something inadequate. They would leave them to themselves midway.

Date/Time: Morning, December 19, 1982/Azar 28, 1361 SH/Rabi' al-Awwal 3, 1403 AH.

Place: Huseyniyyah Jamaran, Tehran

Subject: Influence of imported culture on the society

Audience: Muhsin Rezaee (Commander-in-Chief of the Guards Corps), Salik (Head of the Oppressed Mobilization), chiefs of the resistance bases, members of the Guards Corps Mobilization and the instructors of the Basij all over the country

It is the time to realize that we should do things ourselves. The erroneous notion that has been inculcated in the mind of our students, that they cannot reach anywhere without going to the US, France, England and elsewhere thus causing our youth to rush to these countries and become corrupt should be cleared from our mind. We know that the east and the west are not and will not be on good terms with us. The reason is the situation you see. Most political groups of all denominations carry out anti-Iran propagate. It is because they do not want Islam and any country desiring to act according to Islam will be subjected to their attack. We should therefore, provide the ground for our youths to study here. If there is a need to send them abroad, they should go to countries, which have no colonization record and do not want to dominate us. I hope the time will come when we no longer need to send students abroad. This depends on the activity of you gentlemen and other friends in this vital matter. We should use the good youths we have and educate them to serve God and people. We should clean the idea from our mind that everything we need should come from abroad. Sometimes, we have to import something out of necessity, but there is no justification to borrow culture and literature from abroad. We have a rich literature and culture. Is it correct to argue that since they make missiles, we should obey them? They are destroying the world with these industries. We want to have an industry that is not destructive but useful and constructive.

Time: Morning, November 15, 1983/Aban 24, 1362 SH/Safar 9, 1404 AH.

Place: Jamaran, Tehran

Subject: Vigilance against cultural schemes of the alliance

Audience: 'Abdullah Jasbi (Superintendent of Azar Islamic University), officials of different branches of the university

The amount of damage Iran has suffered by Westernized thinkers and modernists has not sustained by any others. It was because they had received education without purification. The basis that was edification had not been cared for. They trained our children from kindergarten to university in a way as to be harmful to the nation and the country and useful for others.

Date/Time: Morning, March 19, 1985/Isfand 28, 1363 SH/Jamadi ath-Thani 26, 1405 AH.

Place: Husayniyyah Jamaran, Tehran

Subject: Relation of education and edification

Audience: Akrami (Education Minister), deputies of the ministry and officials in charge of Literacy Movement

We hope that our youth be educated inside Iran, because outside of Iran our youth are not given opportunity for fundamental education. God willing, a day will come when students from other countries apply to receive education in Iran and when we do not need to send anyone abroad for education. This is something practicable. The attitude that other than abroad no other places are suitable for education is an erroneous notion. By such propaganda, aliens want to take our youth to their countries and send them back to Iran with their own mentality.

I hope this university[66] and all other universities turn to centers that purify our youth and educate them from scholarly aspects to the extent that they are separated from abroad and act independently and serving the cause of Islam and their country.

Date/Time: Morning, July 15, 1985/Tir 24, 1364 SH/Shawwal 26, 1405 AH.

Place: Jamaran, Tehran

Subject: Priority in reforming universities

Audience: Jasbi (dean of Islamic Azad University), deputies and advisors of the university

After such prolonged artificial backwardness, our need for foreign-manufactured goods is an undeniable fact. This, however, does not mean that we should become dependent either of the two poles in advanced sciences. The government and army should send the students who are committed to Islam to countries that command advanced technology but are not colonizers or exploiters. They should not send students to America or Russia or to countries that follow these two poles. Perhaps, by the will of Allah, the day shall come when these powers see their mistakes and fall in the line of philanthropy, humanism and respect for the rights of others. Or, by the will of Allah, the oppressed people, alert nations and devout Muslims make them see their positions. May that day come!

Date of Reciting: Khordad 15, 1368

Place: Jamaran, Tehran

---

[66] Islamic Azad University

Subject: Politico-divine will, ever-lasting message of Imam Khomeini to the contemporary ones and next generations

Addressees: Iranian nation, Muslims and peoples of the world and next generations

Role and Responsibilities of University Students Living Abroad

Experts from Israel are taking care of the arrangements- from Israel, that enemy of Islam and the Qur'an which a few years ago attempted to corrupt the text of the Qur'an and now imputes to the Qur'an unworthy statements. Just recently the Israelis claimed that Sourah five, verse six of the Qur'an says that after easing nature, the Muslim does not have the right to wash his hands with soap only with water, and that this has been the cause of some of the diseases in Germany. This matter created such a hullabaloo in that country. What is verse six of Sourah five? It is a verse which talks about ritual cleanliness. This is what the Israelis are like. They bear so much animosity towards Islam.[67] Our students abroad vigorously protested against this and refuted these statements, may God strengthen and assist them. They wrote to the newspapers, but some of the government-controlled press did not accept their arguments and those which did not really give enough publicity to their counter-arguments. They met with the authorities and told them that this was a lie; they proved its falsehood in articles in their newspapers and magazines. They performed such a great service for Islam. Can the same be said about us? They are the students of the modern sciences, but they are Muslim, they are awake.

The reaction to the uncouthness and injustice of the administration is seen in the traditional schools and universities drawing closer to one another and the old and new fronts, as well as the Unions of Islamic Associations of Students of Europe and America joining forces. It is my hope that these unions of Europe and America consolidate with the rest of the students in other countries such as India, Pakistan, Arab countries, etc. and so expand their activities. They should strive to make Islam and Islamic justice accessible to all so that the misconceptions of the past centuries with which the agents of imperialism have concealed the radiant face of Islam, are removed.

Date: September 12, 1975/Shahrivar 03, 1354 SH/Ramadan 14, 1395 AH.

Place: Najaf, Iraq

Subject: The resistance of the various groups of people; the promise of future successes

---

[67] Imam (ra) points to sinister plot of Zionist regime in distorting the meaning of sixth verse of Surah Maidah that was meant to accuse Muslims of unhygienic lifestyle.

Occasion: The 11th meeting of the Union of Islamic Associations of Students in Europe

Addressees: The Union of the Islamic Associations of Students in Europe

The Islamic Association of Students in America and Canada, may God assist them:

I have received your esteemed letter. I beseech God the Almighty to give guidance and success to you the zealous youth and all the other discerning students who strive for the attainment of Islam's lofty goals, the foremost being social justice and the eradication of oppression and ignorance… The striking point about this that gives me hope in the dusk of my life is the awareness and awakening of the young generation and the movement of the intellectuals which is growing rapidly. With God's help it will culminate in a decisive result: cutting off the hands of foreign powers, on the one hand, and the propagation of Islamic justice, on the other. You, pure-hearted youth, are duty-bound to raise the level of people's awareness to the greatest extent and in every possible manner. You must unmask the various artifices of the regime and introduce Islam, the dispenser of justice to the world.

Date: September 24, 1975/Mehr 2, 1354 SH/Ramadan 17, 1395 AH.

Place: Najaf, Iraq

Subject: The political awakening and maturity of the nation

Occasion: The Seventh Congress of the Union of Islamic Associations of Students in America and Canada

Addressees: The Union of Islamic Associations of Students in America and Canada

Both we here and others who are presently abroad, we are all duty-bound. It is not a question of us having left Iran and therefore having no obligation towards it. We all have an obligation to fulfill- that is to say that reason, the conscience and religious law all tell us that we have a responsibility to meet. Wherever we may be, it is our duty to help this sacred movement of Iran both collectively and individually; both alone and as a member of a group. It is not good enough to say that although they are shedding blood on the battlefield, we are abroad and cannot therefore be with them. No- we too must engage in combat abroad. We too must all fulfill this obligation to the best of our ability- each person, however much or to whatever extent he is able- by speaking out, by writing, by demonstrating.

Date: October 9, 1978/Mehr 17, 1357 SH/Dhu'l-Qa'dah 6, 1398 AH.

Place: Neauphle-le-Chateau, Paris, France

Subject: Monarchial regime the source of all corruptions; glad tidings of victory

Addressees: A group of Iranian students and residents in France and other countries

There is just one more thing that I would like to say to you Iranian gentlemen who are not in Iran, and that is I sometimes hear of there being some trivial differences, some petty grievances between you- I sometimes heard of such things whilst I was in Iran, and I may well have heard of them here too. If this is the case then I believe something is wrong. You are all each other's brothers. Why, and over what do we differ? We must all join hands together to destroy he who is the common enemy. If we are going to be at variance among ourselves he will remain comfortably seated on the throne and our energy and efforts will be wasted. This is yet another of the tricks that they) the imperialists (have always had up their sleeves and that is to create divisions between the different segments of society. They create two parties with two different names, sow discord between the two and thus render the people inert; or, for example, they may build someone up to be the center of attraction and place him in the spotlight, thus causing the people to become preoccupied as they enter into debates with regard to this person. As a result their energies become dissipated whilst the imperialists sit back and take advantage of the situation. You gentlemen who are currently outside the country must be each other's brothers. Resolve your differences. If you have seen a brother doing something which troubles you, then you are to approach him in a brotherly manner and tell him that he has done something to upset you.

Date: October 9, 1978/Mehr 17, 1357 SH/Dhu'l-Qa'dah 6, 1398 AH.

Place: Neauphle-le-Chateau, Paris, France

Subject: Monarchial regime the source of all corruptions; glad tidings of victory

Addressees: A group of Iranian students and residents in France and other countries

Have no doubt that right now, even as we sit here, Iran is in an explosive state. Right now people are being killed, as they were a few days ago in many different Iranian cities when the resultant death toll was extremely high! Even as we sit here I wonder whether such outbursts are occurring in Iran, and I feel sure that they are. But as to whether people are now being killed or not we don't yet know. And why don't we know? Because we are too far away. Such incidents occur on a daily basis. But while they, the people of Iran, are at the battlefield engaged in battle, are we here to remain unconcerned and to carry on living our normal everyday lives?! To do this would be totally unfair and inhuman, and it would be against the canons of Islam… Right now, I am able to speak to you and to urge you to offer your support irrespective of which front you may belong to abroad. I can appeal to you to join hands with your own people who have risen up in the interests of us all, including yourselves. I shall speak

263

as much as I can regardless of the size of the audience present; and I shall write material and have it circulated, again, as much as I am able. You too must play your part and do whatever is within your power- demonstrating whenever it is called for and opportune; writing; speaking; talking to press reporters; doing anything that is within your power. Everyone must contribute as much as he can and help this oppressed nation which is now being trodden underfoot by these merciless beings.

Date: October 11, 1978/Mehr 19, 1357 SH/Dhu'l-Qa'dah 8, 1398 AH.

Place: Neauphle-le-Chateau, Paris, France

Subject: Migration to Paris; the Shah's crimes; objectives of the Revolution

Addressees: A group of Iranians residing in Paris

We are duty-bound. You and I who are now seated here, have a duty to join the Iranian people in their cries of protest; that is we must do what we can to help them. And in doing so we will actually be helping ourselves and not some outsiders, for the people in Iran have risen up in revolt for your sakes. Their blood is now being spilled for your sakes. It is for you that their children are being killed- their youngsters, their sons and their daughters. We must help these people. We mustn't think that because we are here, abroad, then we are not obliged to help them. Our consciences, our religion, and reason, all oblige us to join the people in their struggle, to offer these oppressed people our support- these people who have risen up in revolt with the intention of claiming what is rightly theirs and what is rightly ours also. We can write an article or have something printed in the press. We can tell the people here, abroad, including those in the universities which we attend, as much as possible about what is happening there in Iran. You are to publicize these issues. My good men, no matter where you may be, each and every one of you must make the situation in Iran known to the public. Speak out and do so from the bottom of your hearts. Even though the newspapers here sometimes write about these issues, this is not good enough; it must come from you- you are the ones who must do the talking or the writing. The whole world must be made aware of this agitated state in which Iran now finds itself...

We have a duty to do all we can to serve the people in Iran; to help those helpless souls, to help those who have lost their young. We are human beings and must therefore do all we can to serve them. Yet helping them also means helping ourselves, meaning that we along with other Iranians are all partners and all stand to share whatever assets the country may have. Were our country autonomous, were it independent and in a state of calm, then we too would be able to live in calm and comfort for we too are a part of that country. Those in Iran have risen in revolt and we too must follow suit. It is no use making apologies with the excuse of being in

Europe or America or wherever, while they who have risen are in Iran. This is no excuse. Although you are abroad those of you who are in America are to assist in this struggle as much as you can; those of you who are in Paris are to assist in this struggle as much as you can; I too, who am here in Paris, am to assist as much as I can. Now, as I am holding an audience with you, I can fulfill my duty by speaking to you and by advising you; and this is something which I shall continue to do. You in turn must speak to your friends, with those who are resident here in Paris, with those who live abroad or wherever; and together you must decide how to help this movement which is under way.

Date: October 31, 1978/Mehr 12, 1357 SH/Dhu'l-Qa'dah 01, 1398 AH.

Place: Neauphle-le-Chateau, Paris, France

Subject: The situation in Iran; the Shah's American reforms

Addressees: A group of Iranian students and residents in Paris

I wanted to advise those studying in Europe, may God grant them all success, against categorizing Islam and thereby believing it to be a school of thought like that of communism; believing the issues it covers to resemble those found in the Marxist doctrine; believing it to be a school of thought like other schools of thought; for this is not the case at all. Those who are unacquainted with Islam however, mistakenly believe it to be some such school.

Date: October 14, 1978/Mehr 22, 1357 SH/Dhu'l-Qa'dah 11, 1398 AH.

Place: Neauphle-le-Chateau, Paris, France

Subject: The comprehensive and edifying dimensions of the Islamic school of thought

Addressees: A group of Iranian students and residents in Paris

We should not be neglectful, those of us who are abroad should not be heedless of the situation of our brothers in the country. We have a duty, a moral and a religious duty to help them to the best of our ability. We must propagate their cause in whatever way we can; if we are able to get statements published in the newspapers then we must do so. We must do whatever we can.

Date: October 12, 1978/Mehr 29, 1357 SH/Dhu'l-Qa'dah 18, 1398 AH.

Place: Neauphle-le-Chateau, Paris, France

Subject: America's mission for the Shah

Addressees: A group of Iranian students and residents abroad

At any rate, the duty of those of us here today, and the others who are out of the country is to help the Iranians. They have arisen; they have stood up- actually their movement is fifteen years old now, but it is only over the past year that it has become so strong, that it is proving effective. We are at a very critical stage in our history, perhaps there has never been such a period in Iranian history when the people have demonstrated such emotions… may you all endeavor to be beneficial to your country. God willing, when you return home you will be useful for your country and you will not be like this present ruling body.

Date: October 12, 1978/Mehr 29, 1357 SH/Dhu'l-Qa'dah 18, 1398 AH.

Place: Neauphle-le-Chateau, Paris, France

Subject: America's mission for the Shah

Addressees: A group of Iranian students and residents abroad

Be that as it may, I have told everyone who has come to see me that they have a duty to perform. I, a student of religion, who sits here, you sitting there, all of you, wherever you live and under whatever circumstances, are duty bound to participate with the nation of Iran in their uprising. You who are in Europe, there are no battlefields as such here for you to go to, they lie in Iran, it is there that the battle takes place, that the people are beaten up, killed and shed their blood in combat. It is not like that here. But still you can contribute; you can help the Iranian people by propagating their cause. Each one of you must be acquainted with at least ten or twenty Europeans wherever you are in Europe, they may be your friends, so tell them what the situation is in Iran, tell them why the Iranians are making such an outcry. Adverse propaganda is being disseminated against the movement in Iran and against Islam. You must tell people here that we have not begun this struggle because of the reasons he (Carter) gives, that we are not opposing the Shah and his regime because they have given us freedom and we do not want it. The Iranian people have risen up because they do not have freedom and they want it. The Shah and his regime have betrayed us. They are giving the country's wealth to America. They are giving our oil to America… You who are here today, I, a theologian, who sits here, you sir sitting there, you university student, you high-school pupil, all you men and women, you can propagate the cause of the Iranian nation. Each one of you, wherever you live, explain the problems in Iran to those you are in contact with. If each member of this community of a few thousand Iranians residing abroad, tells ten or twenty people over here about what is happening in Iran, then a wave of public opinion will be created and this in itself will have been a service. People are asking me all the time if they should return to Iran. No, it is not necessary. You can play a role in the movement by propagating its cause wherever you live over here, whether it is in France, Germany, America, or wherever. When you attend your schools or other institutions, tell the people you meet there about the situation of the Iranian people. You know the language; you can speak; so stop and speak to the people where you are. Tell them what is happening in Iran, what the problems of the people are. Tell them that their problems are caused by Mr. Carter[68] and others like him, like Russia. Russia takes our gas and America takes our oil. They are plundering our resources. Tell these people this, and gradually, because of your efforts, these people who have been misled by the propaganda that they are exposed to over here may come to understand your problems. They are human beings too, when they learn of the suffering of the innocent Iranian nation and are told the truth about events in Iran, this large community over here will support your cause and maybe then their leaders will leave us alone.

The Shah has ruined our agriculture; he is exhausting our oil supplies. In a few years' time we will have neither agriculture nor oil, then how will this nation survive? Our nation is now crying out that this traitor must go, they are shouting "death to this monarchy" and, God willing, it will be swept away. When a nation wants something, God willing, it will achieve it. You who are resident over here can help your people, you can propagate their cause and this would prove to be most valuable. You are responsible before God. Do not suppose that because you are over here, you are, thank God, relieved of any responsibility. No, this is not the case. You are responsible before God; each one of you has a duty to speak out wherever you go and to whomever you meet. Do not worry about whether your words will be accepted or not, go ahead and propagate the cause and this will be effective. Gradually, through your efforts, a wave of support for the Iranian nation will be created in Europe and this may force the Western leaders to leave us alone.

Date: October 22, 1978/Mehr 03, 1357 SH/Dhu'l-Qa'dah 17, 1398 AH.

Place: Neauphle-le-Chateau, Paris, France

Subject: Islam, the school of thought of movement and uprising against kings and capitalists

Addressees: A group of Iranian students and residents abroad

Now is the time for us all to join hands together. You who are abroad should do everything within your power to help the country and the people of your country. They are giving their blood; you should give your pen. You should do whatever it is within your power to do, demonstrate, deliver speeches to the people of these countries and

---

[68] Then President of United States

tell them what is happening in Iran, what calamities have befallen the Iranian people so that, God willing, other nations will awaken also.

Date: October 24, 1978/Aban 2, 1357 SH/Dhu'l-Qa'dah 12, 1398 AH.

Place: Neauphle-le-Chateau, Paris, France

Subject: The overthrow of the Pahlavi dynasty as a religious duty and the people's responsibility during this period

Addressees: A group of Iranian students and residents abroad

The country is ours and we have something to say which is right and just and that is that we ourselves want to administer our own country. We have people to administer it, we have suitable men, we have Muslim men, we have educated people: There are so many in Europe and America who cannot return to their country for fear of being harassed, imprisoned or executed, and those things are real but once he has gone they will return to their country there to live and administer it.

Some say if he goes, the communists[69] will take over! This is a mistaken notion. The communists are not involved in this matter; there are no communists in Iran. There may be a few young people who have been misled and sometimes say something- that is if they are not from SAVAK or have been incited by SAVAK- but they are insignificant, they will disappear, they are not going to take over the country if he leaves...You all, we all, are duty bound to help our friends in Iran. Those of us abroad now can help by propagating their cause; each of you should be a speaker for the people. When you go to your schools speak to some of those there with you, tell them the facts, tell them what is really happening in your country and what the people want, tell them what this man (the Shah) has done. You are all informed about the situation in our country now, so you know what to tell them. May God grant you success and protect you. God willing May He protect you. Make ready yourselves for your country. God willing, you will all return to it together and your country will be yours.

Date: October 24, 1978/Aban 2, 1357 SH/Dhu'l-Qa'dah 12, 1398 AH.

Place: Neauphle-le-Chateau, Paris, France

Subject: The overthrow of the Pahlavi dynasty as a religious duty and the people's responsibility during this period

---

[69] Imam (ra) refers to propaganda by Pahlavi regime and western media that if Shah's regime falls, communists will take over Iran.

Addressees: A group of Iranian students and residents abroad

I am surprised at our youth, some of our youth of course, those who have allowed themselves to be led astray by this regime, which has deceived them through various means. Their elders have made them shout slogans at the university, slogans that are anti-Islamic and unpatriotic so that the people will be afraid that if His Imperial Majesty goes the communists will take over! A group of our young people has now become the instruments of some of their elders who make them do such things and who are working for SAVAK and for this regime. These people are not communists; they are communist-makers. They make our young people say and do things, which are for the benefit of the Shah and America and beguile these young people into thinking that what they are doing is for the sake of communism and the Tudeh Party and such things. I find it truly surprising that at a time when such matters are obvious even to the bazaar merchants, the farmers and the young children, some of these young people allow themselves to be deceived so. They are making a mistake and it works to the benefit of the regime, but the Muslims will not let the regime take full advantage of this and only humiliation will be left for these young people. It is indeed surprising for me.

The need to properly introduce Islam abroad

I ask you gentlemen who are studying abroad and who form part of the enlightened classes not to let our youth fall into the trap of these people. Some of our youth have been deceived; they have been deceived by some of their elders. They have made a mistake; they haven't read about Islam; they haven't seen true Islam (in practice); they haven't read about the laws of Islam nor seen them in practice; they are not familiar with the language of the Qur'an; they do not know that the Qur'an is a book designed to create human beings, to stimulate man toward progress and development, toward crushing the oppressors and the apparatus of oppression. They do not know these things. They know nothing about the economics of Islam either. So when they come here, they come almost totally ignorant about Islam, and some people, some groups who themselves have no belief in these matters, mislead these young people and force them to do such acts and our youth are deceived. You are intellectual people; you are Muslim and you preserve your national sentiments; so, I ask you to take care of our children; do not let them fall into these traps. These are the traps of SAVAK, not those of the communists. The SAVAK agents have a mission to make these young people shout slogans which benefit the regime and in this way destroy these youth. If you meet some of these young people here, take them by the hand, do not let them work for the benefit of the Shah or the regime, for America, the Soviet Union and other powers, do not lose them in this way.

Propagate and enlighten all (the people)

Another duty, which we who are residing abroad now have, is to help the Iranian nation. It has a right over all of us who are abroad now for it is giving blood for us, it is sacrificing its youth. Wherever you go in Iran nowadays there are disturbances, a movement has begun, the people are speaking out and are shouting:" We want freedom; we do not want this dynasty because it has deprived us of our freedom and has plundered our resources for its own benefit and that of the foreigners." Those of us here are indebted to them; we are responsible before God, the Blessed and Exalted, and before the nation. We have to help these people and that which you and I can do for them is to propagate their cause. Those of you, who attend the universities and colleges over here, speak to your friends there, whenever and wherever possible sit down and speak about the situation in Iran.

The world's attention is on Iran

Everybody nowadays is watching events in Iran. Tell them what this man is doing to the people; tell them what ails the people and that the cure for their ailment is for him (the Shah) to leave. An even better cure is that Mr. Carter and the leaders of China, the Soviet Union and Britain leave this nation alone and let the people administer their own affairs. What business does that wretch have coming here from the other side of the world, robbing us of our oil, taking it for free or worse than if it were for free. Tell these people, these students that you meet, whether in America or in Europe, about these things. There are about five thousand of you over here, if each one of you tells only ten people, then that will mean that a great number of people have been informed and a wave of support will be created in Europe and America which will prove useful to the Iranian nation's cause. This is a service, which you can do for the Iranian nation, and in this way, you can repay your debt to them. I ask you all to invite the people to support the nation of Iran, ask the American nation to support the Iranian nation, to understand what the American government has done to Iran and why it has the bad reputation that it does in Iran. Gradually, people may come to presume that the American nation supports the policies of their government in Iran, but this is not the case. In the same way, wherever you are living speak to the people about your problems, alert them to the fact that their governments' policies toward Iran are detrimental to your nation, to everything that your nation has, and (in this way) help the Iranians in this movement that they have started.

Date: October 24, 1978/Aban 2, 1357 SH/Dhu'l-Qa'dah 12, 1398 AH.

Place: Neauphle-le-Chateau, Paris, France

Subject: The roots of the people's opposition to the Shah and the need for propagating Islam

Addressees: A group of students and other Iranians residing abroad

We are all duty-bound, all of us. Those of us here all have a duty to perform. Each one of you, if possible, must pass on written material about Iran to the newspapers here, to the journals here, to your fellow students and to the universities here. Pass on information about the situation in Iran. Tell the people about Iran. Their propaganda is widespread.

Even now there may still be certain people who are not aware of what is really going on. Is America right in saying that the people are upset because they have been given freedom, because they have been given too much freedom too quickly? Have the Iranian people got indigestion because of the freedom that has been given to them?! Has the nation raised its voice because it has been given too much freedom?! Indeed, this is how Mr. Carter sees it! And the newspapers- either Kayhan or Ittila'at[70]- have quoted him as saying that a quick democracy has been brought about, a sudden new-found freedom has been given, and that this is why the people are now opposing him (the Shah)! Is this really the case? Is it that he has granted freedom, and because of this the people still cry out:" We want freedom, we want freedom?!" Are they crying out because of the independence and the 'great civilization' that they enjoy?!

Date: October 26, 1978/Aban 4, 1357 SH/Dhu'l-Qa'dah 23, 1398 AH.

Place: Neauphle-le-Chateau, Paris, France

Subject: The Shah himself as the prime culprit behind all of the crimes in Iran

Occasion: Aban 4, the Shah's birthday

Addressees: A group of Iranian students and residents abroad

I beseech God, the Blessed and Exalted, to grant good health to all of those brethren both inside the country and abroad, who are making sacrifices for the sake of Islam. May God grant you all success. May He grant you all good health. Everyone must make an effort to assist this nation which has now risen up and is shedding its blood. Everyone must cooperate seriously with this nation so that, God willing, it may succeed. Right now, in order for you who are abroad to cooperate, you must propagate the nation's message.

Date: October 26, 1978/Aban 4, 1357 SH/Dhu'l-Qa'dah 23, 1398 AH.

Place: Neauphle-le-Chateau, Paris, France

---

[70] Ittela'at Newspaper, 23/7/1357

Subject: The Shah himself as the prime culprit behind all of the crimes in Iran

Occasion: Aban 4, the Shah's birthday

Addressees: A group of Iranian students and residents abroad

So at the same time as you, our dear youth, involve yourselves in the pursuit of the natural sciences or in the jihad which are necessary for you to carry out- indeed a jihad which all of us must carry out now is to assist our Muslim brethren who are suffering in Iran, by at least propagating their cause- you must not neglect the supreme jihad (self-purification), you must not disregard the spiritual aspects of Islam. For you are not a uni-dimensional being, you do not simply possess this dimension, you are not only men of jihad, or men of the natural sciences, you are human beings and a human being possesses both spiritual and material dimensions. Your material dimension is being satisfied by that which you are doing now, but you should struggle to satisfy your spiritual dimension also. You must take heed of all God's commands, a Muslim cannot say that he accepts the aspect of Islam which pertains to jihad, but not its spiritual aspects or vice versa. We should accept it all. A Muslim is he who accepts and acts upon all the teachings of the Most Noble Prophet.

So, although you may find it difficult to understand the relationship that exists between the spirit and the outwardly apparent acts of worship that God commands us to perform in this world, you should not count them as insignificant. They are important for you. They are important for your life in the next world. You should continue with your jihad and your pursuit of the natural sciences and complete your work in these areas, but at the same time pursue spiritual matters so that you will find true happiness.

Our responsibility is to propagate issues relating to the movement to the world

May God grant you all this happiness. May we all act upon our duties, one of which, now that a movement has begun in Iran and the people are relinquishing their lives, their wealth, their children and their dear ones for this cause, is for us who are over here to do our utmost to help them. You gentlemen should speak about the problems of Iran and propagate the Iranian cause among the people of the countries in which you reside at present, be they one of the European countries or America. Speak to your friends and your acquaintances, whenever you get together tell them about the problems in Iran... Tell your American and European friends about this. Speak to your friends at the schools that you attend. God willing, a wave of support will be created among these people and they will help the Iranian nation, and their governments, those which are just, may also help Iran to rid itself of this man. God willing, the evil of this man and the foreigners who assist him will be uprooted from the land and Iran will be yours for you to administer yourselves.

Date: October 28, 1978/Aban 6, 1357 SH/Dhu'l-Qa'dah 25, 1398 AH.

Place: Neauphle-le-Chateau, Paris, France

Subject: Neglect of spiritual matters as dangerous for the continuation of the movement

Addressees: A group of Iranian students and residents abroad

What is the duty of those of you who are sitting here? I am tired and can no longer continue. What is the duty of us all? Our brothers in Iran are presently fulfilling their duty. What I mean to say is that even now as we sit here, have no doubt that some kind of disturbance or other is taking place in Qum or elsewhere. Wherever one goes in Iran, be it Tehran, Zanjan or elsewhere, something or other is happening; some movement or other is under way; screams are being heard; beatings are taking place; murder and plunder are being committed. Those in Iran are now caught up in these affairs, whereas here, you and I are unfortunately not confronted by the same events. Each one of you however is able to propagate the cause, here, abroad. Whoever has some connection with the schools and universities go and talk to ten of the foreigners there. Tell them: the situation in Iran is like this; this is what they (the regime) are doing there; this is how these state leaders are oppressing us.

Date: October 03, 1978/Aban 8, 1357 SH/Dhu'l-Qa'dah 27, 1398 AH.

Place: Neauphle-le-Chateau, Paris, France

Subject: The form of government established by the Holy Prophet (s), and the struggles of the Imams (a) and the Shi'ah clergy against the tyrannical rulers of their day

Addressees: A group of Iranian students and residents abroad

The younger generation must wake up. It must awaken to these devilish conspiracies that they devise. In Europe right now, there are several thousands of you. If these several thousands of people were to fight for the same goal, that is, if those of you who are in France, others of you who are in Germany, and others who are in America, were to set out with one aim in mind, if you were to operate efficiently, if you were well organized, then should you wish to devise a plan of action you would be capable of achieving great things. Regretfully however, this is not the way things now are. Differences still exist. So-and-so has formed one group, and so-and-so has formed another, and these groups are in conflict with each other. X comes and accuses y of something or other and y comes and accuses x of something or other. This is the way things are in Iran. But now that Iran has pulled itself together somewhat, and now that conflict over this ultimate aim is either slight or nonexistent among the popular masses

273

in Iran- those among whom discord is to be expected either being in the minority or having now put their own house in order- it is not the time for us to sit down and argue among ourselves over these trivial matters. For you to do this would be like sitting down together and discussing what such-and-such a story is about; it would be like sitting down somewhere and relating stories to each other while an earthquake is taking place in some city or other which is about to destroy homes and kill everyone.

Date: October 13, 1978/Aban 9, 1357 SH/Dhu'l-Qa'dah 28, 1398 AH.

Place: Neauphle-le-Chateau, Paris, France

Subject: The need for preserving unity and refraining from disunity

Addressees: A group of Iranians students and residents abroad

The duty to be fulfilled is to propagate the cause here as much as possible. Tell those who don't already know, about the issues at stake. Their propaganda has served to introduce us as reactionary people, to introduce the *akhund* as a reactionist. This *akhund* says that we want what is rightly ours; we want freedom; we want independence. Is this being reactionary? Taking away that which belongs to us is not reactionary! Is it then a sign of civilization? Does our wanting not to give what is ours away make us reactionaries? Are you, those who want to keep us in shackles and who want us to remain as captives forever, are you not reactionaries, whereas we who say we want to be free are?! If we abandon our own argument, our own objective, then we will have to bear the burden of this oppression and tyranny forever.

Each person, each individual, now has a duty to perform; he has a sacred duty, a righteous duty, a moral duty to help these Iranians who are now putting up a fight and shouting out. Each person is to help as much as he can. Those in Iran are sacrificing their lives, sacrificing their young for our sakes and for the sake of Islam. They are making sacrifices for the sake of the nation, and we too are a part of that nation so we too must help; whoever is able to must help as much as he can. If you are able to give a press interview, then do so and tell them what you have to say. Or if you are able to talk to those friends that you have in the universities and elsewhere, then when you see a few of them are assembled together, stand and talk to them; tell them that this is the state of affairs in Iran; they are doing this to Iran; this is how much they have oppressed these people. Tell them what it is we want; what this uproar is for. Is it really because they have given us too much freedom that we are shouting out and asking: why do you allow us so much freedom?! Does this uproar stem from the fact that they have given us freedom too quickly and too rapidly, as Mr. Carter says when he argues that the reason these people are crying out is because His Majesty has given freedom too quickly?! When we shout the word 'freedom', are we saying that we have been given indigestion from too much freedom so don't give us any more of it?! Is this what we are saying? Is this the problem? According to Mr. Carter it is! Therefore, we all have a duty to fulfill. All of us must do everything in our power to rescue this Islamic country. Saving a nation is no laughing matter; it concerns the rescue of a nation. We must all join hands together in fraternity. God willing, you will succeed (the **Audience:** "God willing"). May the Lord grant you all success.

Date: November 2, 1978/Aban 11, 1357 SH/Dhu'l-Hijjah 1, 1398 AH.

Place: Neauphle-le-Chateau, Paris, France

Subject: The alteration of the meaning of those terms used in the vocabulary of the Shah and of the powers supporting him

Addressees: A group of Iranian students and residents abroad

You must all help, meaning that all of you who are present here must discard any differences which exist among yourselves; and you can tell these news reporters, these journalists, these people in the universities, these teachers, tell all of them about Iran. What is happening in Iran has been shown in a very bad light over here) (abroad), and so now you must compensate for this and give them your side of the story. This is a service which you are able to do for this nation. You must brush all differences aside, unite with the Iranian people- those who are in Iran that is- whole-heartedly and unanimously, and tell people about Iran, about those things which the general public there are demanding. In the colleges and universities everyone is to shout out the same thing and to chant the same slogan, that being the slogan of unity in Islam. This is what can rescue you. Others cannot come to the rescue; indeed, they will eventually get you hung.

Date: November 4, 1978/Aban 31, 1357 SH/Dhu'l-Hijjah 3, 1398 AH.

Place: Neauphle-le-Chateau, Paris, France

Subject: The need for opposition to the conspiracies of the Shah's regime to maintain sovereignty

Addressees: A group of Iranian students and residents abroad

Each one of us, wherever we are, is duty-bound to help these Iranians to whatever extent we can (the audience replies with "God willing"). I don't know the exact number, but there must be many thousands of Iranians living abroad and if they can tell hundreds of thousands of foreigners what they know then it will neutralize the prevailing propaganda abroad now which speaks of the Iranians as a people who seek anarchy and who are not worthy of being given freedom! This is the nonsense trumpeted over the Shah's propaganda loudspeakers. You must nullify this. The Iranians are people who have stood up and are saying that they want their rights, they want to be free, they no longer want to be under the influence of American military advisers. This nation has progressed such that it no longer wants this situation to remain as it is, and God willing, it will not.

Date: November 7, 1978/Aban 16, 1357 SH/Dhu'l-Hijjah 6, 1398 AH.

Place: Neauphle-le-Chateau, Paris, France

Subject: The negligence of, and mistakes made by, the *ulama* and political figures throughout the Pahlavi rule

Addressees: A group of Iranian students and residents abroad

I hope that you young people will raise one call and will support this movement with unity of purpose and action, shunning all differences, for this movement is of benefit to your country, it is of benefit to you.

Date: November 8, 1978/Aban 17, 1357 SH/Dhu'l-Hijjah 7, 1398 AH.

Place: Neauphle-le-Chateau, Paris, France

Subject: Fifty years of crimes committed by the Pahlavi (dynasty)

Addressees: A group of Iranian students and residents abroad

You (the audience) are all duty bound to tell people about the problems of Iran. Tell these Europeans and Americans and make them understand that this is Iran's situation now. A dissatisfied country has now emerged and this is all because of America, the Soviet Union and the flunkeyism of Muhammad Reza Khan. Anyway, his father was just the same as his son, or perhaps a bit better. Perhaps. You, gentlemen, whomever you meet, inform them of Iran's afflictions. They (the foreign powers) have presented Iran in a bad light. They have propagandized that Iranian people are savages who will not let the country be run properly! You (the foreign powers) are the savages because you did not allow us to run our country ourselves!

Date: November 21, 1978/Aban 12, 1357 SH/Dhu'l-Hijjah 11, 1398 AH.

Place: Neauphle-le-Chateau, Paris, France

Subject: The Islamic government is a government that the people desire and one that earns God's pleasure

Addressees: A group of Iranian students and residents abroad

We are duty bound to help the Muslims in Iran. At least we can help through propagation, by making individuals you meet here understand. For instance, these Europeans you meet, make them understand the facts. It is not true, as the Shah claims, that the people of Iran, may I say, are savages and that the Shah wants to subdue them but they cannot be subdued! You should tell the people that the Iranian people are a nation which wants to be rescued from this oppressor; they want to be free; they want to be independent; they want to lead a humane life and this man will not let them.

Date: November 11, 1978/Aban 02, 1357 SH/Dhu'l-Hijjah 01, 1398 AH.

Place: Neauphle-le-Chateau, Paris, France

Subject: The politico-religious dimensions of Islam

Occasion: The eve of the 'Id al-Qurban

Addressees: A group of Iranian students and residents abroad

We have to help this movement. Even though you are over here you can help by telling the people you are in contact with, your friends and acquaintances, the truth about the situation in Iran and thus counter the propaganda disseminated by the Shah, his regime and the reporters who are in the Shah's pay, which portrays the Iranian people as anarchists and barbarians and so on. You must tell the people over here... You can hold demonstrations, and you must do so. Whenever you are in a gathering of Europeans or Americans, a few of you stand up and tell them they are mistaken in their views on what is happening in Iran. Tell them what the Iranian people are saying. Tell them the Iranian people are not barbarians, they are a progressive people who are saying, "We want freedom; we don't want America to steal our wealth." Put it to them that if someone says America should not take their wealth, does it mean that they are barbaric and have broken the rules? Have these people contravened the rules by saying they want freedom and independence? This is something everyone can accept; whomever you tell will accept that the Iranians are a people who have risen for their independence and their freedom, a people who do not want other countries to hold sway over them. Up until now the Shah and his regime have betrayed the nation and now the nation wants to get rid of these traitors and place the country in the hands of trustworthy individuals, people who at least will not fill up their pockets as is being done now!

Date: November 18, 1978/Aban 27, 1357 SH/Dhu'l-Hijjah 17, 1398 AH.

Place: Neauphle-le-Chateau, Paris, France

Subject: The ultimate aim: the formation of a government of Islamic justice

Addressees: A group of Iranian students and residents abroad

I hope that you young people who are abroad now will unite with the people back home and inform those in the countries where you reside of the situation in Iran. There is much propaganda being put about by the Shah and his family. They present the situation in Iran in a bad cloak and misrepresent the people's demands. Perhaps many foreigners are of the opinion that the Iranians are complaining now because they have been given such extensive freedoms, as indeed Carter would have them believe, and perhaps many of them think that the Iranians are sedition-mongers and barbarians! Whereas in fact they are only after freedom, which every human being desires, and independence, which everybody wants. They want to cut short the arms of the foreigners that are stretched out against their land. They want the economy of their country to be in their own hands. They want to administer their educational system independently. They don't want their army to be administered by others. They don't want American advisers to come to Iran and take possession of the army; they want to get rid of the American bases in their country. They want a free and independent country. The call of the people of Iran is that they want a government of Islamic justice to do away with all the corruption.

I hope that you young people abroad will get the message of the Iranian people across to your American, Italian, British, and French friends and make them understand that it is these things that the Iranian nation wants and the people are not shouting out because they have been given too much freedom! No, this is not the case. They are shouting out because of the repression, which exists in Iran.

Date: November 18, 1978/Aban 27, 1357 SH/Dhu'l-Hijjah 17, 1398 AH.

Place: Neauphle-le-Chateau, Paris, France

Subject: Material and spiritual destructions of the Shah for Iran; the mission of message-conveyance of the Iranians abroad

Addressees: A group of Iranian students and residents abroad

Now that our brothers welter in blood, we have a duty to help them, and the help that each one of you in Europe and other countries can give them is to propagate their cause. In other words, tell the people about the crimes that this dynasty, and in particular this man, the Shah, has committed. Tell your friends in the universities or the factories, wherever you may be, tell these European friends of yours the truth of the matter. Tell them that he (the Shah) has committed crimes and that the people who have risen up want freedom; their call is: "We want freedom, we want independence." Tell them that these people who want freedom and independence are not barbarians, they are civilized for they want freedom and independence. The barbarians are those who have taken their independence and freedom from them, not these people who want freedom and independence. Freedom and independence are two rights to which all of mankind are claimants. They constitute one of the basic rights of human beings. He who deprives the people of these is the barbarian. He who wants this right is civilized.

The nation of Iran is a civilized nation, but it is held captive by barbaric governments. Thus, it is incumbent upon us all to help the nation of Iran, each one of us to the best of our ability. You who are over here should propagate their cause in whatever way you can. You, young people, wherever you may be, in the universities, in the other places you go, enlighten the people there to the facts. They have been exposed to malicious propaganda to such an extent that they cannot believe that this nation is one which has stood up for truth, or that it is a civilized nation which is standing against barbarism. They describe the Iranians as barbaric! But in actual fact, the Iranian people are the civilized ones who have stood up to the barbarians.

Date: November 19, 1978/Aban 28, 1357 SH/Dhu'l-Hijjah 18, 1398 AH.

Place: Neauphle-le-Chateau, Paris, France

Subject: The Iranian nation's uprising is divine and its victory is a certainty

Addressees: A group of Iranian students and residents abroad

You too should serve this movement which concerns Iran, in whatever capacity- those inside the country should serve domestic interests in whatever capacity and those outside the country should do whatever services are feasible such as propagation, press interviews, writing articles in the print media, because Iran and its people have been introduced in a bad light. You are duty bound; all of us are, to clarify the issues for people here, too.

Date: November 12, 1978/Aban 03, 1357 SH/Dhu'l-Hijjah 02, 1398 AH.

Place: Neauphle-le-Chateau, Paris, France

Subject: The establishment of the Pahlavi dynasty and its unconstitutionality

Addressees: A group of (Iranian) university students residing abroad

You who are residing abroad are duty bound, we are all duty bound, it is incumbent upon you to extend a helping hand to Iran in any capacity. Anyone who can, should propagate the cause so that the people here will understand what the Iranian nation wants and what they are crying out for and so that they will not heed the words of some journalists whose palms have been greased: shall I say, some of those propagandists who campaign against the revolution. The nation of Iran is shouting it wants freedom; it is shouting it wants independence. It is screaming for freedom.

Date: November 23, 1978/Azar 2, 1357 SH/Dhu'l-Hijjah 22, 1398 AH.

Place: Neauphle-le-Chateau, Paris, France

Subject: The Shah's perfidy in declaring repentance

Addressees: A group of Iranian students and residents abroad

All of you who are here, from wherever you may have come, are duty bound to serve Iran and help this movement. You can help by propagating the Iranian people's cause over here so that these people in the propaganda business who are receiving stipends from the Shah will shut their mouths. For, indeed, he has people in foreign countries that disseminate propaganda about his rule with the aim of preserving it.

So you too spread the word about the movement, acquaint the people over here with the demands of the Iranian people. It has been for fifteen years now or more that this nation has risen up, and for the past year the people have constantly been shedding their blood, constantly sacrificing their youth. What do they want? This freedom and independence that they seek is so important to them that they are willing to sacrifice their youth for it and still are not afraid. You must help them. You must at least tell the people over here that this is what Iran wants. Tell them not to listen to the propaganda that is spread from some quarters…Please God may He grant you all success and victory and may you return home one day in glory and honor. Today your heads are held high for you have brought alive a nation. You people of Iran, you youth, have brought Iran alive, you have resurrected those who were dead. May God keep you all. May you be successful.

Date: November 25, 1978/Azar 4, 1357 SH/Dhu'l-Hijjah 24, 1398 AH.

Place: Neauphle-le-Chateau, Paris, France

Subject: Confronting America's propaganda and threat

Addressees: A group of Iranian students and residents abroad

All of you are duty bound to counter this propaganda which has been and continues to be put about abroad, and to enlighten the people to the facts. Some of these foreign newspapers get their daily bread from these people and write against the Iranian nation and in favor of Muhammad Reza Khan. Enlighten the people. Tell those you meet the facts about the situation in Iran…We here are duty bound like anyone else. We should follow up these strikes by giving interviews to newspaper reporters, if we can, and by speaking about the problems which afflict Iran. If we are not able to give interviews then we must acquaint the friends we have here, in America, in Britain, wherever we may be, with the facts about Iran. When you see a group of people speaking together at your schools, join them and tell them what the problems facing Iran are, tell them what it is that ails the Iranians who have risen up. Tell them about the treason that this wretch has committed against the people. These newspapers and magazines that are sometimes printed abroad and speak against the Iranian people are not presenting the facts which are that this man has hitherto done nothing but squander Iran's self-respect and its resources and continue to do so.

Date: November 25, 1978/Azar 4, 1357 SH/Dhu'l-Hijjah 24, 1398 AH.

Place: Neauphle-le-Chateau, Paris, France

Subject: The extent of the Shah's crimes and the different dimensions of his treachery

Addressees: A group of Iranian students and residents abroad

I repeat again that those of us who are abroad, who are outside Iran, have a duty to help the Iranians, to help the Iranian nation which has risen up and is now sacrificing everything it has for all our sakes. It is our bounden duty to help them to the best of our ability. While we are here, we can give interviews to the press and if possible write articles for publication in newspapers and magazines. When you speak with the people, enlighten them to the facts, tell them that the people of Iran are not" despicable riffraff," as Mr. Carter describes them, who want to throw an honorable gentleman out of the country. No, they are a people who want their rights, who want the basic right to which a human being is entitled: freedom and independence. They want to throw that person who has encroached upon this right out of Iran and sever the hands of those who have encroached upon their rights. Tell this to the people over here with whom you have relations, repeat it until a wave of support is found abroad (for the Iranian cause) and, God willing, you will achieve your aim that much quicker as indeed I would like you to do, God willing (The audience replies with "God willing"). May God grant you all success.

Date: November 26, 1978/Azar 5, 1357 SH/Dhu'l-Hijjah 25, 1398 AH.

Place: Neauphle-le-Chateau, Paris, France

Subject: Shah's downfall will not end in disintegration of country or dominance of Communism

Addressees: A group of Iranian students and residents abroad

You have risen to save them, not to save your uncle or your cousin, but to save the servants of God.

Assisting the movement for the sake of God

The servants of God are now suffering, they are in danger; you can help them by propagating their cause here. You are able to do this. Give interviews, whichever one of you is able should give press interviews and tell the people over here about the situation in Iran. But your aim should be God; you should turn to God for support. Rise up for God. Even if you are only one person, if your uprising is for God, then it has value, it has divine value. Be it individually or in pairs- "... *rise up for God; it may be in pairs or it may be singly.*" (Qur'an, 34:46). Unite yourself with that endless sea and make your actions divine actions. Pay attention to the laws of God the Blessed and Exalted. These uprisings are to bring into effect the laws of God. All these uprisings that are taking place, that have been taking place for years now, have been in order to bring God's laws into force in the world and to remove Satan's laws from this world. Satan's laws prevail in Iran and the people want the laws of God to prevail. Strive to bring the laws of God into effect within yourselves. Be devout, carry out the actions that God the Blessed and Exalted has told you to perform. Make yourself divine. A servant does not ask for the whys and wherefores, God says do it and I do it. The whys and wherefores are no concern of mine. Why is asked of some ordinary person when one does not know if he is correct or not and thus questions him. When you visit the doctor and he tells you to do something, you don't ask him why. When he prescribes medicine for you, you don't ask him why, even though he is only a doctor and a human being.

You must train yourselves so that you are able to rise up (for God). Train yourselves to obey God's laws; to obey His every command, when He says no, then let it be no; when He says yes, then let it be yes.

Date: December 2, 1978/Azar 11, 1357 SH/Muharram 1, 1399 AH.

Place: Neauphle-le-Chateau, Paris, France

Subject: Any uprising for God's sake is victorious

Occasion: The arrival of the month of Muharram

Addressees: A group of Iranian students and residents abroad

There is no excuse for us today; none of us has an excuse, we who are over here, you gentlemen who are in these countries, are not without a duty to perform…You who are over here must reveal the crimes that this man has committed in whatever way you can; you may be able to give interviews to the press or hold gatherings in which these matters are discussed. Wherever possible you must stand up and speak out on these matters to these friends and acquaintances that you have here abroad and who are of a different denomination or nationality than you, so that the people here will realize that the Iranians who have risen up against him are not just a gang of trouble-makers, but they are people who are speaking the truth and are seeking their rights

Date: December 9, 1978/Azar 18, 1357 SH/Muharram 8, 1399 AH.

Place: Neauphle-le-Chateau, Paris, France

Subject: Campaign against a tyrant king is a divine duty

Addressees: A group of Iranian students and residents abroad

One matter which grieves me deeply and which is spoken of frequently over here, many questions being raised about it, is that occasionally some of our youth living abroad violate the law in shops, government offices, banks or on trains and buses, arguing that because these countries have stolen our wealth, then we may as well steal theirs. This is not right. The position of those of you who are presently living abroad is such that if you are seen to commit a crime, the nation of Iran will be judged by your action. The Iranians will be called a nation of thieves or it will be said that the Muslims in general are thieves! For this reason, you must be very careful about such things. Even if you believe such actions to be permissible- and indeed I say to you that they are not- but even if you believe it is permissible to take money from these organizations, you must not do so. Guard yourselves against doing such things because it is necessary to preserve your own reputation and that of Islam and the nation.

If, for example, when our young people in one of these countries want to travel on a bus or take a plane or train journey they cheat or carry out a fraud when buying the ticket, this constitutes playing with the human dignity of a nation. You should advise your friends against doing such things, tell them that this excuse that because they have stolen our wealth we can steal theirs, is not a justifiable one, it is not right. You should safeguard the dignity of your nation and preserve the high standing of Islam, for suppose that you are arrested by a policeman at the scene of your crime, the onlookers will not say that this man is whatever, they will say that the nation of Iran is like this or Islam is like this. Thus, this is a very important responsibility that you must shoulder.

All Muslims, whether from Iran or other Muslim countries, who are living in Europe or America should preserve their dignity and safeguard their religion and their reputation in these countries; they should never commit crimes which bring dishonor to a nation. Even if you believe this to be permissible, even if someone exploits you, you must not do anything which is classed as a fraud and which the police class as a fraud.

Advise your friends against doing such things. I am repeatedly asked about this matter by people who come here and I have said over and over that they should not do such things, now you too pass this message on. Such actions are damaging to our reputation.

Now as for the problems facing Iran, wherever you may be tell your friends, your American and European friends, about these. Tell them how the Shah has treated the people and that all the people are saying that they don't want him. Make these things known to those over here, so that these foreigners will have no doubts in their minds and they will not think that the people of Iran are barbarians who are acting against a government! No, this is not the case; rather, they want to get rid of a barbaric government. You must speak out about these matters. May you always be successful, victorious and healthy, God willing.

Date: December 11, 1978/Azar 02, 1357 SH/Muharram 01, 1399 AH.

Place: Neauphle-le-Chateau, Paris, France

Subject: Need for observation of the law by Iranians and Muslims abroad

Addressees: A group of Iranian students and residents abroad

But of course those who are thieves, who have stolen the wealth of this nation and have taken it abroad, will be punished. Do not suppose that if they have left Iran then that is an end to the affair! If they come here, these young people are here to deal with them (The audience laughs). If they go to America or Britain it will be the same there too. They should not think that they can stay in Iran until the last moment, steal as much as they can and then fly off to America! Wherever they go, there will be zealous Iranian youth to deal with them.

Date: December 11, 1978/Azar 02, 1357 SH/Muharram 01, 1399 AH.

Place: Neauphle-le-Chateau, Paris, France

Subject: Great referendum of Tasu'a and 'Ashura; necessity for the return of the army to the nation's embrace

Addressees: A group of Iranian students and residents abroad

Only last night, a few people, who had come from somewhere to see me, complained that where there are groupings, all oppose one another; this one speaking badly of that one and vice versa. It is regrettable that you who are a community abroad, who are one of our country's sources of wealth abroad which Islam and your country should be able to use to their advantage, are here today quarrelling with one another when tomorrow, on your return to your country, you should be of use to it and make it flourish. Moreover, according to one of these people who came to see me, every person who comes from Iran is met by a group at the airport as soon as he lands, so that they can take him with them and indoctrinate him with their own ideas while turning him against those of other groups.

Do you know what you are doing? Do you know what harm this kind of thing is doing to yourselves and your country? Don't you see how today in Iran when unity of purpose has come about it has shaken every throne, crown and superpower, how they are all at a loss as to what they should do? Do you see this? Do you not see how, now that the different groups in Iran have come closer together, now that the universities have come closer to the clerical establishment, the clerical establishment to the universities, and the bazaars have become at one with the universities and the clerical establishment, even though differences in some things still exist, which I will speak about later, now that unity of purpose has come about in Iran, it has shaken America and Russia and has made these ruffians within Iran itself flounce. These killings that this man perpetrates and the recourses that he resorts to all stem from the fact that he sees that the people have come together, and he is at a loss as to how to put an end to this union!

You must realize that these things you are doing you have got from the foreigners, you are being subservient to the foreigners and they are making you do such things so that this unity which has been found in Iran and which is possible between these groups abroad will be put to an end. For these groups abroad boast influential people and unity between them would be to the detriment of the foreigners. So they fell to making the groups based in Iran, and likewise those abroad, oppose one another in some way, and to creating some sort of opposition between those groups within Iran and those abroad. Don't you know that you are working to the advantage of others? Don't you realize this? Do you not know what kind of blow this opposition of yours today delivers to the Islamic movement in Iran, coming as it does when the country is in such a sensitive, life-or-death situation? If you merge these different fronts that you have, where ten of you, a hundred of you have joined together and have given yourself a name, if you put aside these names and come together under one name, being unanimous in your aims, then just as you see that Iran has shaken these superpowers, so too this power of yours will add to that in Iran and you will ruffle them even more.

They want to take advantage of you now, and that means setting you against one another. Who is he? He is from the National Front! Who's he? He's from the Freedom Movement! Who's he? He's from such and such a youth association! Who's he? He's from such and such group! Different groups; numerous groups! Whoever you go to will refute the others. Each group is the enemy of the other. What is the meaning of such things among a people who together share a great, common aim which is to extirpate the roots of this oppression and foreshorten the hands of the superpowers from our land?

This present opposition of yours is getting stronger every day. In these past three months that I have been here, I have not been able to solve this problem, and I have become truly disappointed in you all. Do you not realize what a blow you are dealing Islam, what a blow you are dealing your country and the service you are doing to America, Russia or Britain? You do not have to carry their flags around on your shoulders to serve them; you are serving them by belittling yourselves so, by keeping yourselves from your activities so. All your energy is spent on disagreeing with one another, you are arguing with one another from morning till night. You should unite together against others, there will be plenty of time later on for you to go after your personal goals, if indeed, God forbid, you should have any. Why do you bring your personal goals into this affair? Why, in this an Islamic movement, do you have so many selfish desires which stop you from coming together? Put aside these carnal desires a little. This is something that I find very regrettable about you young people abroad, about all of you, not anyone in particular.

Date: December 24, 1978/Dey 3, 1357 SH/Muharram 23, 1399 AH.

Place: Neauphle-le-Chateau, Paris, France

Subject: Need to preserve unity and to avoid disunity

Addressees: A group of Iranian students and residents abroad

I must thank all the young people, the brothers and sisters who are outside the country and whom during this period I have put too much trouble, and also ask their forgiveness. I pray to Almighty God for your health, greatness and happiness. I hope that a suitable environment will be brought into being in Iran so that you can all return and serve your own people and your own country.

Date: January 12, 1979/Bahman 1, 1357 SH/Safar 22, 1399 AH.

Place: Neauphle-le-Chateau, Paris, France

Subject: Keeping unity and solidarity and rising up for God, the secret behind the victory of the Revolution

Addressees: A group of Iranian students and residents abroad

Gentlemen, push aside these divisions and disunity. I ask you all here and all the sections of society in Iran, I beseech you all to make common cause if you want to free your country from the clutches of foreigners.

Date: January 12, 1979/Bahman 1, 1357 SH/Safar 22, 1399 AH.

Place: Neauphle-le-Chateau, Paris, France

Subject: Keeping unity and solidarity and rising up for God, the secret behind the victory of the Revolution

Addressees: A group of Iranian students and residents abroad

His Eminence Hujjat al-Islam Aqa Haj Mirza Husayn Nouri- may his graces last. It is necessary for you to proceed to the European countries in order to get well acquainted with the dear Iranian students and brothers there, and after attending to their needs and looking into their spiritual concerns, you must strive to eliminate their problems within the limits of the authority that has been vested in you. You must familiarize them with the grave duties which they have at this sensitive time and caution them against discord and differences. You must make adequate attempts to strengthen their religious beliefs vis-a-vis the enemies of Islam. Please convey my regards to all of them. I pray to God Almighty for the continued success of all. May God's peace and mercy be upon you.[71]

Date: June 02, 1979/Khordad 03, 1358 SH/Rajab 25, 1399 AH.

Place: Qum

Subject: Looking into the condition of the Iranian students and brothers residing in Europe

Addressees: Husayn Nouri

The youth of that country I thank all our beloved youth who came from all over to ask about our well-being; they gathered and listened to my talks; published my interviews there. Sometimes they would publish them in all places- and this was a path to our victory that was achieved by the grace of God.

Date: July 12, 1979/Tir 03, 1358 SH/Sha'ban 26, 1399 AH.

Place: Qum

Subject: Designs of America against the Islamic Revolution and their failure vis-a-vis the will of the nation

Audience: Members of the Union of Islamic Association of Students in Europe, America and Canada; students from Isfahan

---

[71] It's necessary to point out that similar order was issued on 28/8/58.

....And is a great source of hopefulness. This is a spiritual revolution that has occurred in the nation. A spiritual revolution is superior to this barricade that they smashed. You have come all the way from Europe to help the people. This spiritual revolution is important. This was not done by anyone except God. God is the transformer of the hearts. Among the hands of God, the Exalted, you are the spiritual hand of God, the Blessed and Exalted, that He moves wherever He wishes. At one time you were busy with your own job; in former times I was preoccupied with theological studies; you were busy with your own noble vocation; who was it that brought you over from there to here and made you go and toil in the villages for the sake of your brethren? It was God, it is the hand of God that made your hearts to turn in this manner; be grateful for it. Your hearts are now in the hands of God; He turns it as He wishes; and He has turned it for a good deed. Now it was He that brought you the university-going youth and doctors and engineers and so forth here from there whereas each of you should be engaged somewhere else. The respected ladies and beloved women who must be somewhere else have gone to the villages and are busy harvesting; and doing such jobs. However they are not harvesters in the sense of the peasant laborers but a small action of theirs gives such impetus to the harvesters that if formerly they could harvest one acre now they can harvest two. When the harvesting peasant comes and sees that these ladies who must be sitting down in the shade are harvesting and collecting the barley under the sunlight, this strengthens their spirit. Their deed has such a value that it gives strength to the others and their productivity multiplies; this is very valuable. When they see that you have come all the way from Europe, from America in order to help your brothers- look what a morale it creates in the peasant laborers. This peasant who would be visited every day by a security organization agent breathing down his neck and either whipping him or do so on and so forth now sees that his brothers are coming here from the farthest regions abroad, not from the interior, and say that they have come to help; to help them to harvest; to help them to harvest the produce, you cannot imagine what an honor it is for them and what an effect it has on their hearts; and you do not know how worthy it is to bring happiness to the heart of the weak; we do not know the spiritual value of this deed; it is extremely high however small the deed. And considering that you are not peasant harvesters and perhaps are not able to harvest properly; but a few stalks of wheat that you gather has so much worth and draws the hearts toward you and brings hope to the people and carries our movement forward that only God knows. May God protect all of you and may God bring happiness to all of you; and may He safeguard this spiritual transformation that has come about.

Date: July 12, 1979/Tir 03, 1358 SH/Sha'ban 26, 1399 AH.

Place: Qum

Subject: Designs of America against the Islamic Revolution and their failure vis-a-vis the will of the nation

Audience: Members of the Union of Islamic Association of Students in Europe, America and Canada; students from Isfahan

Today a group of young people from Europe- women and men- came to me and told me that they had arrived in order to go to the villages and serve the people. Young people who previously would be thinking of other issues are today thinking of such issues. They come, they come from Europe, they come from abroad; their women and men come in order to go to the villages and help the rural people. In the same manner, from within the country, from the universities, doctors, engineers, women, all of them are going to these villages to help. This feeling of cooperation is a feeling- is a transformation- that is miraculous; and what is present has been done by God, the Blessed and Exalted.

Date: July 12, 1979/Tir 03, 1358 SH/Sha'ban 26, 1399 AH.

Place: Qum

Subject: Great changes of the nation in the Islamic movement

Audience: The research and propagation department of the Isfahan College of Sciences

You have witnessed how savagely they treated our dear sons, daughters, and our dear university students, and how bravely they held out, holding clenched fists, against the American police and the other security forces. They bore all the blows and the atrocities of the Americans, but did not yield at all on their (principled) stand. Muslims must learn what to do from these youth who are from Iran and are living abroad, whether in Britain, Europe or America.

Date: August 6, 1980/Mordad 15, 1359 SH/Ramadan 24, 1400 AH.

Place: Jamaran, Tehran

Subject: Describing the difficulties that Muslims are faced with: fighting the illegitimate occupiers of Quds

Occasion: International Quds Day

Audience: The Iranian people

Our dear students, wherever they are and whatever groups they are in contact with, must, likewise, make efforts to discuss the issues concerning Islamic Iran. They must examine one by one the articles that appear in foreign magazines and newspapers of whatever place. By so doing, they must prove the falsity of the things, printed therein.

Date: Morning, January 4, 1981/Dey 14, 1359 SH/Safar 27, 1401 AH.

Place: Jamaran, Tehran

Subject: The conduct of the ambassadors and the matters pertaining to the embassies must be in congruity with Islam; exporting the Revolution by the development of Islamic ethics and truths, not by force.

Audience: The Islamic Republic of Iran's ambassadors, and charged affaires; a group of members of Islamic associations of Iranian students overseas

As stated brothers from abroad, including Pakistan, Indonesia and some other countries have come here.[72] I hope during their visit to the country they would appropriately study the issues and problems in Iran and inform their nations of the realities here.

Date/Time: Noon, August 24, 1981/Shahrivar 2, 1360 SH/Shawwal 23, 1401 AH.

Place: Husayniyyah Jamaran

Subject: Injustice of the powers and Iranian people's innocence; unfounded accusations against the Islamic establishment.

Audience: Muwahhidi Kermani (Imam Khomeini's representative in City Police Force) and the police personnel, Members of some Islamic association and Students studying abroad

You, dear ones, who play an important role in foiling the false propaganda and baseless slanders will continue with your path by trusting in God and relying on the favor and assistance of God almighty and since the goal is the establishment of justice and equity, do not be worried above forthcoming events.

My dear sisters and brothers! I feel your numerous problems in that environment, as you do ours. However, both of us know that our path is the path of the truth and we all have stood against falsehood and by patience and perseverance the truth will overcome falsehood. God has promised victory. I hope that the time of victory is near. We endeavor to widen the scope of propaganda and launch activity in this important

---

[72] Imam (ra) addresses the members of Foreign Islamic Students Associations

matter despite all the difficulties. You and we, who seek one and the same purpose and idea, should exert all our efforts to achieve it.

Time: March 19, 1983/Esfand 29, 1360 SH/Jamadi al-Awwal 24, 1402 AH.

Place: Jamaran, Tehran

Subject: Miraculous progress of the Islamic Revolution, victory in battlefields-describe the crimes committed by Munafiqin

Addressees: Union of Islamic Associations of Students in Europe

I thank the dear students who rose in foreign countries in favor of Islam, Islamic Republic and the dear country with those troubles and obstructions. They are also mujahids (strugglers in the cause of God) who serve Islam on the foreign front. I hope that their blessed names will be recorded in Islamic books and that they remain as treasures saving their country from deviation.

Time: Morning, August 23, 1983/Shahrivar 1, 1362 SH/Dhul-Qa'dah 14, 1403 AH.

Place: Husayniyyah Jamaran, Tehran

Subject: Importance of acquaintance with Islamic and patriotic duties

Audience: Commander of the Navy, Commander of Army Aviation, pilots and technical personnel of the air force, personnel from the navy and air forces, students participating in the universal gathering of Islamic movement of students

Unfortunately, many of our physicians live abroad, have left Iran or have been living there, and not returned to the country. One of the points that the physicians living abroad should consider is that their own country needs them.

They have brought up here, received education at the country's expense, and are now living abroad. They are Iranians are indebted to people and Islam. This is the Islamic nation, which is on the receiving end of all sufferings and calamities caused by the superpowers. You physicians, who are living abroad, even if we suppose you live a long life in comfort, what then? Is not it more advisable to be at the service of the destitute and the patients of your own country, and serve this country which has been under oppression for long years? Now that our country wants to free itself from the burdens of the east and the west, all place pressure on it from all directions. Are not these pressures enough for your expatriate physicians to look at your country and see that we lack the likes of you here. Everywhere we have the shortage of specialized physicians. It is fair that you specialized physician of this land, where you and your parents were nurtured, live abroad indifferently and nonchalantly watch the sufferings of our patients and those who were wounded in battlefields. Given this state of affairs, is your conscience clear? I do not think if you contemplate an hour, your conscience permits you to remain there even though living in comfort.

Time: Morning, December 7, 1983/Azar 16, 1362 SH/Rabi' al-Awwal 2, 1404 AH.

Place: Husayniyyah Jamaran, Tehran

Subject: Status of medical profession and duties of doctors and nurses

Audience: Manafi (Health Minister) and staff of the ministry

SECTION 8

SEMINARIES (*Howzeh*) AND UNIVERSITIES

Role of Colonialists in Separation of Seminaries from Universities

Unfortunately, until now the treacherous hands of imperialism have, through different means, created a deep gap between the younger generation and the illustrious issues of the faith as well as the valuable precepts of Islam. They misrepresent the younger generation to the clergy and vice versa. As a result, the unity of thoughts and action was destroyed and it paved the way for wicked intentions. It is further unfortunate that these same mysterious systems prevented the educated class to contemplate on the sacred precepts of Islam- in particular its organizational, social and economic laws. Using various propagandas, they shammed the idea that everything that Islam has to offer is praying precepts and nothing else. Whereas Islam's political and social laws outnumber its praying topics. Now, my days are numbered and I hope that Almighty God will give you, the educated class, the opportunity to endeavor in the course of the Islamic objectives, one of which is the cutting off of the hands of the oppressors, and the uprooting of despotism and imperialism. Try to study the Islamic heavenly laws, which have descended from the very source of the divine revelations, which deal with all aspects of life and are more practical and more beneficial than all other religious duties. Do not fall under the influence of the foreigners' spiteful propaganda.

Date: January 1, 1970/Dey 11, 1348 SH/Shawwal 22, 1389 AH.

Place: Najaf, Iraq

Subject: The treason of the colonial rule in creating a gap between the younger generation and Islamic issues

Addressees: The Persian-speaking Group, Union of Islamic Societies of Students in Europe

It is essential that the venerable clergy and the university students show mutual respect. The enlightened university students should respect the clergy and the clergymen. God, the Exalted, holds them in esteem and the God-inspired Household of the Prophet (a) has recommended them to the people. The clergy is a great source of strength. Losing it would cause the pillars of Islam to collapse, God forbid, thus enabling the cruel might of the enemy to go unchallenged.

Meticulous studies conducted by the alien exploiters in the course of history have led them to the conclusion that this bastion must be demolished. The widespread propaganda that they and their hirelings have been doing over several hundred years have caused some intellectuals to part with the clergy and become pessimistic about them so that the enemy remains unchallenged. In case some unqualified persons pass themselves off as being part of them, but serve and, according to the differences in their rank and service, make the people abide by the main and subsidiary principles of the faith in spite of the foreigners and their agents, this force should be assisted, protected and shown respect. The respected clergy must also respect the young intellectuals, who are serving Islam and the Islamic country and for this reason are the target of the attacks of the foreign agents. They should consider them as their dear children and their esteemed brothers. They should not give up this immense power in whose hand the destiny of the country willy-nilly will fall. They should guard against the malicious propaganda that has been going on against them for hundreds of years, showing them up in a different light to some people in order to benefit further from the disputes. They should ostracize those who either through ignorance or malicious intent have distanced this powerful group from the clergy, and not allow them to sow discord. They should rest assured that with these two great powers joining forces, victory will be attained; divided, they will never gain it.

Date: February 31, 1978/Bahman 24, 1365 SH/Rabi' al-Awwal 5, 1398 AH.

Place: Najaf, Iraq

Subject: The duties of Muslim intellectuals

Addressees: The Union of Islamic Students Association in Europe

Their conspiracy succeeded in one aspect in that they could dissociate the clergy from the university. A clergy was not allowed to speak about the university, even among ourselves. I know of no one who has ever gone to a university. University people would also think of the clergy as pernicious creatures that the British had dumped here! I myself was a witness of an incident. Once I was traveling by bus with two respectable gentlemen from Qum several years ago. There were others riding in the bus with us. One of them was telling the other: "It is ages I have not seen any of these figures." He was referring to us. Then he added, "The British have brought them and have sent some in Najaf in order to deviate the people." From the university people's point of view, the clergy either was a courtier or tied up to the British! From your (clergy's) point of view the academicians were, well, I do not know, (westernized)! They have sowed the seeds of discord among the nation; they separated some people from the others and took advantage of this separation.

Date: February 3, 1979/Bahman 14, 1357 SH/Rabi' al-Awwal 5, 1399 AH.

Place: Alawi School, Tehran

Subject: Enmity of power-mongers toward Islam; the expediency of the coalition of the 'ulama and all the strata of the people

Audience: The clergy

They (the colonial powers) realized that if the entire nation were united, they would not be able to steal the resources they wanted to loot. Hence, they thought they had to sow the seeds of discord among the nation. First, they turned their attention to the clergy. If anyone remembers, all the gentlemen present here remember that during the time of Reza Khan, they beat up the clergy so severely that neither a preacher nor a congregational prayer leader was left for us. They beat up everyone. Nor was there a parliament, that is parliament orators. They had humiliated the clergy in the eyes of the nation in such a manner that drivers sometimes would not give clergy a ride in their automobiles and would repeatedly tell them: "We will not let you sit in our automobiles!" They humiliated the clergy. On the one hand, they caused disparity between parties plunging them into disarray and creating chaos. They segregated the academicians from our universities. The former would ostracize the latter in one way, and vice-versa. There were so many other controversies to expound on and I do not feel very well. The gentlemen themselves should take note that all these were factors that this nation should vouchsafe their nationality under one banner because it was this solidarity that they (colonialists) wanted to snatch away from and divest the nation of and perhaps pit them as foes to one another. This is a great cause for concern. Therefore, prior to the movement we were never confronted by you; we were confronting another "clan."

Date: February 7, 1979/Bahman 18, 1357 SH/Rabi' al-Awwal 9, 1399 AH.

Place: Alawi School, Tehran

Subject: Connivance of the discord-mongers and the colonialists

Audience: Three hundred judges and lawyers from the Justice Ministry

The sufferings we went through and are still undergoing have resulted from being separated from each other. We did not sit together in an assembly to make it known to one another what each side had to say. We (the clerics) were separated from the judges of judiciary system, from universities. They had portrayed the university fraternity in such a way that we formed pessimistic views of them. They portrayed us in a way to make them cynical about us. We were far apart. During Reza Khan's reign, they had presented the clergymen in such a bad light that people would not give them a ride in their cars. A friend of mine told me that once he wanted to get into a car in Arak but the driver told him that they (drivers) had decided not to give rides to two groups of people, namely the prostitutes and the clerics. That was how they humiliated the clergymen. Because Reza Shah knew that it was the clerics, like Mudarris,[73] who

---

[73] Ayatullah Sayyid Hassan Mudarris was born in the year 1287 AH and was member of Iranian Parliament during the years of *Mashrooteh* movement. He was leading figure in struggle against Reza Shah. He was martyred by the orders of Reza Shah in Kashmar city in the 1316 SH.

would impede his way and openly shout at his face "Long live myself, death to Reza Khan!" So, at the time Reza Khan had power, they used to treat us in that manner. They separated us from one another and everyone from everybody else. They made everyone cynical of each other. A nation, in which everyone is suspicious of others, cannot function properly.

Date: February 26, 1979/Esfand 7, 1357 SH/Rabi' al-Awwal 28, 1399 AH.

Place: Alawi School, Tehran

Subject: Colonialists' designs to separate the various strata of the nation from Islam and the clergy

Audience: Members of the Bar Association and lawyers of the judiciary

The idea of separation of politics and religion is an issue that the colonialists had put in people's mouth and through this they wanted to cause a disparity between these two branches. They wanted to cause discord among religious scholars and likewise, among secular groups, segregate politicians from the rest of the people to achieve their vested interests. They embarked upon such factious agitations, firstly, by disseminating the idea that religion and politics were separate, and prior to this (they propagated) that religion was basically the opium of the masses, and that clergymen worked at imperial courts! Because they knew that if these two forces converged, they would not be able to achieve their objectives. They distanced these two and drew a shaky image of the religion before the people's eyes.

Date: February 19, 1979/Bahman 03, 1357 SH/Rabi' al-Awwal 12, 1399 AH.

Place: Alawi School, Tehran

Subject: Illegitimacy of the monarchial regime; the need to educate children on all dimensions of Islam; the peril of one-dimensional Islam

Audience: Alawi School's officials, teachers and workers

Formerly, there were some scientific matters that when the people unite, when a nation gathers, it is impossible to control them. Due to their very knowledge and for their political notions, they prevented proximity of different strata of the people and kept us away from university students. They opened such a wide gap between them and us (clerics) that we used to blame them; they used to call us fools.

Time/Date: Morning, 9: 00 am, April 18, 1979/Farvardin 29, 1358 SH/Jamadi al-Awwal 02, 1399 AH.

Place: Qum

Subject: The need for existence of committees and their purification

Audience: Commanders and officials of the 14 committees of the Islamic Revolution in Tehran as well as Messrs. Mahdavi Kani, Maliki, Morvarid, Mufattih, Muhammadi Golpayegani, Jalali Khomeini, Haqqi, Baqiri Kani, Khosroushahi and Zanjani

Evil hands have unfortunately separated you and the clergy. You are both charged with the same task, which is training the people of the society. A divisive wedge was driven between you, which separated you two from each other. We would never come face to face before. That is to say, you used to keep us at a distance and we too, used to run away from you. You would not take notice of what we said, and we had the same attitude toward you. You used to say something else to us, and we, too, differed from you. When I say you, I mean you individuals in the academic centers, and when I refer to us I am not referring just to myself. Anyway, that was the state of affairs. People of dubious characters would go to the universities and would tell academicians and students and even the non-academicians enticing things and then would tell them these clerics are reactionary people, and they want to push us back to the Stone Age! Muhammad-Reza Khan, in one of his statements before June 3, 1963 (the day when there was a massive civil unrest in Tehran and some other major cities in Iran, against the Shah and was brutally put down by the latter) said these clerics do not even travel by planes! This was the very same day when one of the Religious Reference Authorities had traveled to Mashhad by plane- Muhammad-Reza Khan said that they are even against planes; they are against anything modern. They want to return to those days when they rode donkeys. They want to light candles in darkness as they are against electricity. Anything that smells of civilization, clerics are opposed to. These were the sort of things they used to tell you about the clergy, or worse, they would tell you all the clerics worked for the court and the interests of the monarch, in fact, clerics were created by the monarchs in the first place, and kings gave them their existence through the help of foreign powers. On the other hand, they would come to the clergy and would tell them these people in the universities are divorced from religion and are nothing more than a bunch of western-clothed ascot wearing irreligious people. These were their ways of creating a big division between the academicians and the clergy. Unfortunately, there were some who believed these lies and therefore, both kept drifting away from each other ever more because of mutual suspicions. Now, who were these two groups? They were the ones who were supposed to enlighten the people of the society. Thus, they drove a huge wedge between them.

If the said two groups were on the right path, the whole nation would be on the right path.

Date: May 24, 1979/Khordad 3, 1358 SH/Jamadi ath-Thani 27, 1399 AH.

Place: Qum

Subject: Profession of clerics and academicians; creation of discord between the seminary and university; role of culture in the declination and amelioration of the society

Audience: Ali Shari'atmadari (Minister of Culture and Higher Education), chancellors of universities and institutions of higher education

As it was pointed out, education is at the top of everything. Our opponents had been concentrating on our educational system from the very beginning. They had been concentrating on these schools since the time they came into existence. They did this as they knew that whatever arose was from education. There were two things that, more than anything else, were the objects of the attention of those who opposed us and Islam: one was the clergy, and the other, "education." They realized that these two could bring independence to a country and administer it. They would, therefore, obstruct their affairs. Their educational programs were not exactly suitable for us. As for the clergy they would bash them at every opportunity.

From the time that Reza Khan appeared- except on the few occasions when he would try to beguile the people by showing piety and such things- his main concern, from those days itself, was the clergy whom he tried to do away with, using any excuse that he could. He would see that the mourning ceremonies that are held in every village, borough, town and even the countryside all over Iran were (spiritually) beneficial to the people because of which people and groups could possibly emerge that would prevent the illegal exploitation (of the country). These commemoration meetings, which even if most of you do not remember, perhaps not as we do here, were forbidden to be held throughout Iran. We could not hold meetings. The time was such that we had nothing. They would control the whole country. Their agent would see to it that neither voice be raised anywhere nor any commemoration meeting held. On the other hand, there was the pressure on the clergy to remove their turbans (stop preaching)! And they did remove them. It was the same with education. They could not say that there should be no education; they said that it should be there. But they devised educational programs in such a way as to be unsuitable for the nation.

Date: June 01, 1979/Khordad 02, 1358 SH/Rajab 15, 1399 AH.

Place: Qum

Subject: The enemy's conspiracy against the clergy and education; the moral downfall of the West

Audience: Members of the Central Council of the Iran Statistics Center

The fact that the foreigners, the foreign experts and those who wanted to plunder the country, paid great attention to the fronts- the clergy and the universities- was that they had realized that if these two fronts received the proper training so that, together with knowledge, they had the correct training and conduct, thus becoming what they should, then they, themselves, would not be able to derive benefits (from the country) anymore. If we have a proper university and a clerical order in its full sense, they will not allow the foreigners to ruin the prestige of the country. Therefore, they targeted these two fronts as they had considered them to be dangerous for themselves. But their way of attacking them was different. In Reza Khan's time, which I remember and most of you do not, they would use bayonets to attack this front and smash it. And so they used to attack the seminaries, arresting the people and taking them away. They used to remove the turbans of the clergymen and strip off their cloaks. They used to close down the seminaries and the mosques. They did away altogether with the mourning observances and preachings. They thought that they would be able to obliterate the clergy in this manner. But they would not employ such methods in the case of the universities as they feared the repercussions abroad. So they used other means to stop the students from developing. However, they realized later that it yielded no results, and that the greater the pressure, the worse it would become; worse for themselves. In Reza Shah's time, they changed their (tactic of) attacking the clergy and started propaganda in order to separate the people from them.

As these two forces of Islam, the clergy and the university, were able to stand up to them, that strategy of using force to eliminate the clergy did not work, and so they changed it. They started propaganda against the clergy so as to drive a wedge between the clergy and the university and between them and the people. They wanted to make the university circles, the clergy and clerics so appear to the people as if they were not really religious and were linked to the court, the British, the Americans, etc. The plan was to separate the people from these two classes that were competent. They had even separated these two from each other, making the clergy cynical about the academics and vice-versa. This was the plot to separate these two useful classes from each other and all of them from the nation so that they would not be able to do anything, leaving them (enemies) free to exploit this country.

One of the blessings of this movement was that it brought these classes closer to one another. The university people, the clergy and the young clergymen all became close to one another; they became colleagues. And they developed an affinity with all other classes of the people and became like colleagues. They stated unanimously that the *taghouti* regime must go and a republic of Islamic justice be installed. This was everybody's motive and intention.

Date: June 27, 1979/Tir 6, 1358 SH/Sha'ban 2, 1399 AH.

Place: Qum

Subject: The role of the unity of the seminary and the university; the issue of factionalism and party politics

Audience: Students of the Islamic Association of the Teachers' Training University, Tehran

In the time of this one (the former Shah), when the period of that sort of bullying has passed, or when they did not think it advisable to conduct themselves in this manner, they started carrying out propaganda. They made much propaganda against the *'ulama* and the clergymen. The propaganda was extensive. They started using force, but not with that severity. They did not allow meaningful sermons in the mosques. They set up preachers to oppose Islam; clergymen in appearance, but against Islam. They also made propaganda everywhere, especially in the universities. The extensive propaganda against the clergy in the universities reached a climax such that they totally separated the university from the clergy. They destroyed the university as well as the clergy. I mean they wanted to.

Date: Morning, July 5, 1979/Tir 14, 1358 SH/Sha'ban 01, 1399 AH.

Place: Qum

Subject: The three hundred-year influence of the Westerners in Iran

Audience: The blind of Aba Basir School, Isfahan

On the one hand, belittled Islam in the eyes of the people, and on the other, also belittled the clergy. They took away these two powers from us, enabling them to do whatever they wanted to do.

On the other hand, they came and alienated the universities from the clergy. They made propaganda in the universities against the clergy. Groups of clergymen made propaganda against the university in the mosques, from the pulpits and, I should say, other places. It was not for the sake of Islam that they would come and say that the university professors were, for instance, like this and like that. No, this was not the case; it was a plot. It was a well calculated matter. They wanted to separate these two powers that could work: the university was able to work and the clergymen as well. And they did separate them. You could not mention the name of the clergy in the university- at that time; not nowadays. The clergy could not be mentioned. The university could not be mentioned in the clerical circles. They drove these two powers apart. That is, two energetic powers that, if united, could have put an end to this plunder altogether and cut off foreign hands that had reached out to this spread of booty. They separated these two powers. These were the plots they hatched.

Date: Morning, July 5, 1979/Tir 14, 1358 SH/Sha'ban 01, 1399 AH.

Place: Qum

Subject: The three hundred-year influence of the Westerners in Iran

Audience: The blind of Aba Basir School, Isfahan

During the reign of this son, who was worse than the father in some respects; in this period there was a lot of propaganda such that in the universities also the youth too- who were decent youth- were influenced by these propaganda to the extent that you could not take the name of a cleric in the university! Instead, in the university they would scribble some verses from the Qur'an on the walls and make fun of it. For, those who would lead them astray from the path of the truth their plan was not to allow Islam to become a force in society and in the process, the clergy who are at the service of Islam also become a power and pull the society toward opposition with the governments and opposition to foreigners. In all strata where they assumed the possibility of resistance in them existed, they would in some way infiltrate and would either lead them astray or repress them. The strata of you wrestlers were also not exempt; the strata of sportsmen were not exempt from this plan because they too were a religious-minded population who had affection for Islam and were powerful. These too they would keep them preoccupied by some means; they could not cause them to deviate from Islam; they would not listen to them on this matter; but they would lead them astray from the main issues; they would create some means by which they would keep them busy so that they would be negligent of the main issues of the country. These matters would surface in all strata; they would either directly suppress and if they could not then they would resort to misleading them; and if they considered suppression not to be in their interest or deviation to be the better option, they would mislead them from their path through propaganda; and if even this was not workable then they would keep them busy with other matters. Reza Shah repressed the clergy; and on various pretexts, which perhaps most of you do not remember how it was. After the university was founded, and the university in their view was a force that could challenge them, they started to indulge in misleading propaganda there. They began with extensive propaganda against the basis of religion and on to Islam- the fundamentals and the principles. Later on, they alienated the clergy from the university and sent each of them to obscurity. They even caused many of them to deviate. However, among them there were some who were not very astray, but they could not because the power was in their hands such that they created enmity between the university and the clergy. They saw that it was dangerous to let these two groups become united.

Date: July 14, 1979/Tir 23, 1358 SH/Sha'ban 19, 1399 AH.

Place: Qum

Subject: The imperialists' various ways of repression and misguidance

Audience: Members of the sporting community of Isfahan

In these last few days I heard and read that the university students of Isfahan had a get together with the *'ulama* of Isfahan for which I thank all of you very much and hope that this unity continues. The differences that existed, unfortunately, between the university and the clergy in the former regime was not something accidental; it was a calculated matter of which both the clergy and the students were unaware of.

Agents of the regime, who were commissioned to go to the universities and sow discord between these two groups, would say things about the clergy, which unfortunately, the youth would believe. When they would go to the clergy, they would talk about the university which they too would believe; and both the parties were generally unaware that they were being used. Both the parties were unaware of the fact that they were not intending to build a good university or a good clergyman. They were after creating a rift between these two segments who were the intellectual powers of the nation and who could awaken the nations. Not only did they intend to separate, but to cause them to prepare them for confrontation against each other. They would speak about an issue to this one and then to that one and thus keep them busy and to neglect the primary issues that the nation and the country was going through.

Date: July 15, 1979/Tir 24, 1358 SH/Sha'ban 02, 1399 AH.

Place: Qum

Subject: Review of the constitution; election of the experts; elections of the Majlis and the president

Audience: Clergymen and professors of the University of Isfahan

Yet one bigger plan was to separate the clergy from the university; because all of these do not appear to be accidental; all of these were plans that they had made in order to exploit the resources and that no one should protest.

Separating the clergymen from the university students was echoed with the clergymen in such a way that the university students were treated as a bunch of hip, and so on and so forth. To the students they would say that the *akhunds* were a bunch of courtiers! They would separate these two strata from each other. They would not only divide but also make them enemies; one would say badly about the other; and that one would say something bad about this one. By means of propaganda wars they would separate these two groups from one another. There were plans for this division; it would be put into action at the onset of the month of Ramadan when it is the time for gatherings and at the onset of the month of Muharram when it was the time for gatherings. They would make plans- we the miserable and unaware- that throughout the blessed month of Ramadan the people would quarrel with each other over the plans from the pulpits. The university students would launch an attack on them while they would do the same to the university students. Throughout the blessed month of Ramadan they would keep them busy with issues that were unrelated to the matters of the day and living while they would sit at the side and laugh at us. We were in this way unaware of the daily issues and unaware of their ominous designs. This too was a big issue that they had created; and many issues like this.

Date: July 25, 1979/Mordad 3, 1358 SH/Sha'ban 03, 1399 AH.

Place: Qum

Subject: Aim of the *taghouti* regime: leading the youth astray; elucidation of the characteristic features of the Council of Experts

Audience: Students of Kashan

Now the plot is to separate you from one another. They who felt that their defeat was because of the unity among the people, realized that this unity of expression that had emerged in Iran, and perhaps, brought about by these two groups- the clergy and its preachers, prayer leaders, orators, speakers and such people and you with your lectures and your efforts bringing the people together- resulted in this victory. At one time they may think that "if the people gather together, we will be defeated," though this defeat has not been experienced by them. At another time, your victory and their defeat is actually experienced and (physically) felt. They saw that this defeat and that victory were because of your unity. A plot is now afoot to separate you from one another; to set two brotherly groups against one another and to drive the two groups of thinkers apart. If you do fall apart, neither will the clergy be able to do anything, nor you. You think that the university will be able to succeed without (the help) of this group; no, it cannot. And they think that they are everything and the university, nothing. Not at all; it is erroneous to think so. Unity must be forged between these two strata to confront their malicious propaganda of many years by which they intended to drive you apart from one another, to line you up on one side so that you be their (clergy's) enemy, and to line them up on the other side with them being your enemies as well, and for them to come amidst you and benefit by the situation without anybody being around to question why. Now, they have come to realize that when such a power arises and such unity is formed, it results in their defeat; and they were defeated by such unity and power. The conspiracies nowadays are more and, perhaps, more precisely planned; the plot now is to separate this group from that. Plots are being implemented in Mashhad. Conspiracies have been carried out in Isfahan, and in Tehran also; they may engulf other strata as well.

What are you quarrelling over? Over somebody being very good or very bad? And a group of preachers saying from the pulpit and elsewhere that this person is an unbeliever and another group saying that he is a Muslim and descended from the Imams? What is the result of all this? The result is that you and the clergy will fall apart. You will be confronting one another and lose that unity of expression you had; and all for nothing! Losing your unity of expression for nothing and falling apart from one another will cause all the other classes to become separated from you and to develop differences, which will result in the movement not being able to accomplish its mission. What all the foreigners of East and West want is that you be divided and dispersed.

The purpose of the plots is to divide you, to make enemies and to create various factions and groups, with all of them being enemies of one another so that the outcome would be to their benefit. Should we not wake up? For how long should we be negligent? They made us negligent for many long years and duped us. Should we still not wake up? Should you of the university not wake up? You the clergy, should you not wake up? They robbed us and ruled us by means of this discord that they created. They tortured our youth to a great extent in the prisons and behaved with our clergymen in the way that you saw; and similarly with all other strata of the people. Should we still not wake up? Should we still have differences over petty matters that are nothing and fall upon one another? Should the preachers, the prayer leaders and the academicians all be at loggerheads with one another? Should we not take notice that other hands have come in and are doing all this? Should not this nation be alive to the fact that a hundred factions have announced their formation within the span of two months? This is not by chance. It is that some deliberate hands are at work to drive you of this secret of yours; the key to victory.

Date: July 5, 1979/Tir 14, 1358 SH /Sha'ban 01, 1399 AH.

Place: Qum

Subject: The grave duty and responsibility of the clergy and students

Audience: Students from Mashhad

And they had influenced our youth in such a way that they had other thoughts about you; in the same way that you had other thoughts in relation to them and both the thinking were imported and influenced by propaganda.

The way that the university would think about you all as "a bunch of clerics" and so forth; and also the way you would think about the university students as an "a group of hip and so forth". Both of these were propaganda to divide you. The strata of youth who must hold the destinies of the country in their hands sometimes later should be separated from you. Basically, the plan was to separate you from the active strata of the youth; this meant that the class that is informed and enlightened and are to become the administrators of the affairs were to be separated from you and you also from them so that the two powers who are the two intellectual strengths of one nation were to be in confrontation with each other so that all their work is negated; neither the university student would be able to perform his task properly nor would you be able to work properly. Both of you would be made to confront one another so that they could do as they wished and we would be indifferent to their matters; while we would be busy quarrelling among ourselves. This was a plan which they had in mind in addition to a thousand other plans that they had designed.

Date: September 31, 1979/Shahrivar 22, 1358 SH/Shawwal 12, 1399 AH.

Place: Qum

Subject: Coordination among the forces of the Revolution; the necessity to safeguard the dignity of the clergy

Audience: Clergymen of Tehran

The old and modern scientific and cultural center, the clergy, cultural scholars, theology students, university students constitute two significant poles and two pensive brains of the society. Foreigners have always struggled to separate these two poles and divide these two sensitive and humanizing centers. Separation of these two pillars and pitting them against each other, and thus defusing their activities in the face of colonialists and exploitative powers, would be of the greatest disasters of the present era. This would spoil our country and us altogether and pervert our young generation that is of the most energetic treasure of our country.

Date: September 22, 1979/Shahrivar 13, 1358 SH/Shawwal 03, 1399 AH.

Place: Qum

Subject: Foreigners' attempts to sweep the Islamic content of the scientific and cultural programs

Occasion: Opening of academic year

Addressees: Professors, collegians and students

Plans were underway to separate clergymen from academicians; so they were continually injecting into the minds of clergymen that there is a group of pessimistic dandies in the universities and, inculcated in the minds of the academician that there is a group of English clergyman in theological centers in an attempt to separate you from the clergymen.

One of their numerous plans was to create division between the two layers who were considered as the masterminds of the society; i.e. the clergymen and the collegians. To separate them, or making them stand against each other. All these things, should disappear and we should be awaken and understand that we are all brothers.

Date: October 6, 1979/Mehr 14, 1358 SH/Dhu'l-Qa'dah 14, 1399 AH.

Place: Qum

Subject: Colonial culture and intellectual dependency- Reforming cultural centers- enemies' plot

Addressees: Professors and Staff of the Sharif University of Technology

In the era of Reza Shah they assaulted Islam and the clergymen. They did what should not be done.

There are those who might remember or might have seen. Those who have not seen will read it in history at a later stage because history too was suppressed to record it. The errand was to abolish or weaken Islam. The history of Islam they wanted to destroy. But their endeavor went in vain. They wanted to separate the people form those who need to work for Islam or were Islamic experts. Under the pretext that they had stick-in-the-mud attitudes. They used to approach the university intellectuals and tell them that these clergies are attached to English people. And they used to tell the clergies that these university people have no faith at all. They shave their beards. I myself have heard them saying that English have brought into being these religious institutions of Najaf and Qum. They have made these schools or centers so that we could not progress and remain ignorant and backward.

It was God's will that in a span of time these two classes should be together. Both have one end and one errand. Now they want to repeat the same old thing- to separate the university students from the clergy schools.

Date: January 4, 1980/Dey 14, 1358 SH/Safar 15, 1400 AH.

Place: Qum

Subject: Peculiarities of the Islamic Revolution and its distinctions with other revolutions

Audience: Tehran University professors

What power it must be which separated these two classes from each other and made adversary to each other? What power was at work, which changed the university to such a form that its products- whoever came out of it- was a seduced, a perverted and a devious one. All of them were leaning towards the foreign schools. What hand was at work to change the university into a fortification of battle soon after the victory of the Revolution? Again that power is now busy to crush the clergy class. What had they seen of the clergy? They are disseminating the same thought and the same idea the days of Reza Khan against the clergy. They want to repeat the same past insults, vilifying and defaming the clergy and all those in this spiritual cloak. Why? What have they done to this class of clergy? They have created a gap between the clergy and others. Still they are doing so. But, by the grace of God, they will come close to each other…. Well, why have they created such a division that one cannot utter a name of a clergy in the university? If a student of the university wants to pray, he should do it very secretly. In the religious schools too, they do not look upon an academic fellow favorably. This is also based upon the same research they have carried out for so long. This is quite obvious that these two classes are the thinking minds of the society. Therefore, they can do what they desire only in the event of separation between these two classes. They will not be able to achieve their end in case these two classes are glued with each other. Therefore, the pens, the tongues and the media that were in their service are put in motion. They are separated from each other to the extent of enmity. Now they have witnessed the powers of Islam. They found out that if those two classes become close and united an impregnable power would be formed. With such a power, they succeeded to expel the Satanic power which nobody in the world ever expected to happen. They expelled the traitor while all the powers were behind him.

Date: May 24, 1980/Khordad 3, 1359 SH/Rajab 9, 1400 AH.

Place: Jamaran, Tehran

Subject: Fifty years long plots to create divisions among the various classes of the society.

Audience: Teachers, students of the religious institutions, professors, members of the Islamic associations and students of the Universities all over the country

This is also based upon the same research they have carried out for so long. This is quite obvious that these two classes are the thinking minds of the society. Therefore, they can do what they desire only in the event of separation between these two classes. They will not be able to achieve their end in case these two classes are glued with each other.

Date: May 24, 1980/Khordad 3, 1359 SH/Rajab 9, 1400 AH.

Place: Jamaran, Tehran

Subject: Fifty years long plots to create divisions among the various classes of the society

Audience: Teachers, students of the religious institutions, professors, members of the Islamic associations, students of the Universities all over the country

Now you should know that the best way was what the religious quarters hold. Also the class of students and the university joined them to reach this aim. Now they fear that the students unite with the clergies. They want to come together and form a coalition. They are afraid of this alliance. So this is a dread, a terror, and a fear for them. Alliance between these two classes means the alliance of the whole nation. They labored years long to separate these two classes from each other. It was a plot. It was design. In the university they abused and objurgated clergies. It was a deliberate performance. It was not just an occurrence by chance nor was it an occasional one. Likewise, in the environment of clergies, academics were abused and objurgated. It was an intentional whisper deliberately poured into the ears of both the classes. The public media too gave wind to this. The clergies were openly and publicly scarified. The media as a whole stood against the clergies. Their poets too sang the song that the country cannot be reformed as long as there exists a clergy. One of the verses of this ignoble man was sung by all and disseminated by all the media. The purpose was the separation between the two classes- clergies and the university. They set each other in confrontation. A student would not sit by the side of a clergy. They knew that if these two categories combined, the job for them will become impossible. Even now they are having the same thought. They have not given up the idea. You don't think that their agents have forgone the idea. Now it has been started as it was in the days of Reza Khan. Assaults against the clergies are already in practice. In the north, it is more because of the leftists there. In other places it is a little mild. But it does exist. They have no scuffle with the "ammamah" (turban) holders. They discern the base, the foundation. They see that the nation with its clergy, academy, bazaar and worker- all have become together. They have prepared within a period of one year and a half all the material that a government needs. This thing is unprecedented in the world. It is a thing which others may not be able to accomplish in a period of fifty years. They still do not have. These people have prepared all things within a year and a half. Therefore, they fear from such a gathering or union. They see themselves defeated ones. Since they know that they are defeated by clergies and the academy circle. They know that a clergy can group the people of his locality and his mosque. From the very beginning, their aim is clergy. They want to abolish the clergy class. They lifted the turban from the heads of the clergies. Before, no clergy dared to appear in streets. This was not an occurrence of chance. It was a studied plan. They know that the turban wearers can do many things… Now they see volunteers have become common. People are changed. University students no more spurn a clergy. Likewise, a clergy does not disdain a student. Both sit in an environment of religious institute of Faydiyyah planning how to reform the university. So, now they are terrified. They say that if they separate these two classes, the clergy too will be distanced from the people. Then the job is done. Now these days, wherever you go, the same words that were in winds in the days of Reza Khan are being freshly whispered. All the throats, those of SAVAK's and of "Fada'i-ye Khalq" are emitting and imparting the same past sayings. Every passerby strikes a blow to a clergy. They know the way. They want to burden the youth with their own load of thoughts. Therefore, they try to lower this class in the eyes of the people. This is the same thing done in the era of Reza Khan. At this moment Sayyid is engaged in carrying out this task.

Date: June 5, 1980/Khordad 14, 1359 SH/Rajab 02, 1400 AH.

Place: Jamaran Husayniyyah Tehran

Subject: Internal change of a nation is the source of victory, unity between religious institute and the university; Importance of Friday prayers

Audience: Professors and students of Divinity and the Islamic Sciences College, Tehran University

Now they know that if the clerics, university students and teachers and the other strata unite, they can surely carry out other such great tasks. They are now more persevering in separating the people from this group (the clergy), to separate the university from the (Islamic studies) school, and to make all the different strata of society pessimistic towards one another and to set them against one another.

Date/Time: Before noon, July 11, 1980/Tir 02, 1359 SH/Sha'ban 28, 1400 AH.

Place: Jamaran, Tehran

Subject: Clarifying the duties of the clergy in the Islamic system

Occasion: Before the Holy Month of Ramadhan: The failure of the Nojeh coup d' tat conspiracy

Audience: Clerics and prayer leaders (i. e. those clerics who lead the congregational prayers) and the clergymen who are members of the peoples' voluntary forces (Basij) from Tehran and other cities

There was a time when the university and the centers of theology, being, as they were, separated from one another, had, perhaps, created an inimical atmosphere. The academic could not tolerate a cleric, nor a cleric an academic. The (ex- regime's) basic purpose was to keep these two classes separated, the reason being that if they were united, the whole nation would also be united. They wanted to keep these two groups opposed to each other so as to prevent the people from achieving unity. Thanks be to God that great transformation took place because of this Islamic movement and revolution following which neither of these two classes considers itself as being apart from the other, God willing. The mutual dread that existed between the clergy and the academics has now vanished by the will of God the Blessed and Exalted. You the academic and clergymen brothers have now come together. You stand beside one another in solving the problems and taking the revolution to victory.

Date: Before noon, December 18, 1980/Azar 27, 1359 SH/Safar 01, 1401 AH.

Place: Jamaran, Tehran

Subject: The importance of the roles of the seminary and the university; stating the duties of these two institutions of learning

Occasion: The day of unity between the seminary and the university

Audience: Teachers and students of Qum Theological Center; the student members of the office for the consolidation of unity between the seminary and the university

They had made a wall with you on one side and they (academics) on the other. Both these groups distrusted each other while the enemy derived the benefit. Now you can see that a change has taken place. The academic is favorably disposed towards the clergyman and the clergyman towards the academic. Both of them are together, and both want to take the country forward. The satans now are more keen on crushing the clergy on one side and the academics on the other. They intend to create mischief between the two and tell them what each of them is up to. Keep your eyes wide open. Your eyes and ears must be kept open at this time lest you find one day that they have corrupted and divided you in the university itself and the seminary. They cannot stand your unity. The people who do not want this country to be a safe and sound one, and also their masters who, from the beginning itself, did not want it to be so, cannot bear to see that you have come together and wish to work together. They know what the consequences for them will be in the event of the universities, wherever they be, and the theology centers joining together and planning together for the victory of the revolution. They have studied this matter. They understand it and, therefore, intend to prevent you from attaining unity. Open your eyes and your ears whether you be academics or theology students. If one approaches you and tells you something which concerns this matter, you should realize that there is some selfish motive to it. If at any time they come and tell you something (unsavory) about the clergy or the academics, you should know that the thing that you have accomplished is costing them dearly.

You must make headway, God willing. The persons, whoever and wherever they be, that are able to serve the people, the university and the Faydiyyah, ought to do so. They must make them culturally refined, and also make "'*alim*s," specialists and dedicated individuals out of them.

Date: Before noon, December 18, 1980/Azar 27, 1359 SH/Safar 01, 1401 AH.

Place: Jamaran, Tehran

Subject: The importance of the roles of the seminary and the university; stating the duties of these two institutions of learning

Occasion: The day of unity between the seminary and the university

Audience: Teachers and students of Qum Theological Center; the student members of the office for the consolidation of unity between the seminary and the university

As with the clerics, those same elements also had similar plans for our college-going and other youth to prevent them from getting involved in the political and the other affairs of this country, which is in fact in dire need of their active involvement. They had gone to the extent of employing a large number of school and university teachers who were against Islam and this Islamic nation in order to deviate our youth and to prevent them from working for Islam. They had poisoned the minds of our youth against the clergy and vice versa. They created a rift among the clergy and the university and capitalized on it. By the Grace of God Almighty, this rift has now been eliminated and, today, the clergy and the university people work shoulder to shoulder and are active in socio-political affairs and in defending the country. Both, the clerics as well as the university people should abstain from criticizing each other, keeping in mind that such criticism is in the interest of neither group. It will only serve the interests of the superpowers.

Date: March 5, 1981/Esfand 14, 1359 SH/Rabi' ath-Thani 27, 1401 AH.

Place: Jamaran, Tehran

Subject: Imperialist conspiracies for isolating the clergy; the great responsibility of the clerics; need for unity between the seminaries and the universities

Audience: Clerics from the Bureau of Propagation of the Qum and Mashhad Seminaries and soldiers of the 1974- 78 service batches

The most important thing that the enemies of the oppressed countries and the Muslim countries and the enemies of mankind have pinpointed is the university. This is because they know very well that if they manage to influence the university of a country, the entire country can fall into their hands. It is the university that runs the affairs of a country. And it is the university that trains the present and the future generations and if the university falls into the hands of the plunderers of the East and the West, the country falls into their hands. Nothing else has been their target more than the university. The clergy, too, is like the university in this regard. They wanted to introduce the academicians into society with an Eastern or Western upbringing. And since they could not succeed in gaining control over the clergy, they wanted to eliminate them from the scenes. They were neither interested in the university nor in the seminaries. Their attempts were focused on these two groups in whose hands lies the entire future of a country and they tried to groom one of them under foreign and Western or Eastern training before bringing them on the scenes while they tried to eliminate the other from the scenes because they could not manage access to their grooming and could not influence them even after a thousand years of effort. They tried to do everything to eliminate the clergy from the scenes while they put in all their efforts to gain control over the academicians. One of their main conspiracies was to make these two groups cynical toward each other. During these long years, they tried their best to cause a rift between these two groups and to breed animosity between them. If we were to visit a university, even the mention of a "cleric" would bear the same connotation as a narcotic drug. And within the clergy, the term "academician" meant someone "irreligious." They instigated these two groups to each other's throats so that they could misuse the situation to their advantage. It was not without reason that through these fifty years during which they were in power, they did not allow even a single university that could work for the welfare of the country and that would churn out human beings and scholars to get established in the country. I do not say that they succeeded completely but they surely tried their best to gradually succeed in ensuring that all the graduates either worshipped the East or the West! Once they can succeed in doing this to the university and in severing off the ties between the clergy and the university, they are bound to hold the reins of the destinies of all the countries in their hands.

They pinpointed the universities and tried to gain control over the university with all their might. And to attract individuals that were inclined toward the East and more toward the West. And to convert the academicians to their own advantage while sidetracking the clergy. To make the clergy ineffectual and to bring the academicians under either the Eastern or the Western influence. We and this revolution, too, should tap this same sensitivity. Top priority should be given to the cultural and academic revolution just like they did through these last fifty years.

Date: Morning, June 31, 1981/Khordad 23, 1360 SH/Sha'ban 01, 1401 AH.

Place: Jamaran Husayniyyah, Tehran

Subject: Importance of the role of the university in the independence or lack of independence of a country

Occasion: Anniversary of the establishment of the Ad Hoc Committee for the Cultural Revolution

Addressees: The members of the Ad Hoc Committee for the Cultural Revolution and the Supreme Council of the Jihad of the Universities of Tehran and other cities

They had tried for long years to foster a rift and animosity between these two groups that are the think-tanks of a nation and in whose hands lie the welfare, grandeur, and independence of this nation. All of us saw how these two groups had been turned into enemies until the Islamic Revolution following which Islam held out its invitation. Islam invites all groups to unity and especially the universities and the seminaries. And as long as these two groups remain united, your country's independence is guaranteed.

Both the universities as well as the seminaries should open their eyes and know that there are still hands at work trying to cause rifts between these two groups. The imperialists and their followers and all those whose Mecca lies in London, Washington, or Moscow see a unity between these two groups as a threat to their own interests and, thus, try to keep them apart. As you all saw, the fifty years of the ominous Pahlavi rule that had proved its dedication to foreign powers fostered rifts and animosity between these two groups while the ill-wishers of this nation took advantage of the situation. The wealth of this nation during the last fifty years and especially during the times of Muhammad Reza was washed out. And all this happened as a result of the animosity between the universities and the seminaries. And if, God forbid, the earlier animosity between these two groups has to be revived, it will only guarantee the interests of the superpowers.

My dear academicians and my dear clerics! Stay alert since the enemies are trying their best to create rifts between you. And do not forget that if reform is brought about in the universities and the seminaries, the independence of your country will be ensured. The Mecca of all those whose pens and words are trying to cause rifts between you two is either Moscow or Washington. Stay alert not to lose this great blessing of the unity between the universities and the seminaries. I am hopeful that you will succeed in managing the affairs of your country independently and that you will no longer need to stretch your hands toward the East and the West and that the mischief they create in our country, boomerangs back to them. May God Almighty help and support the seminaries, the universities, and the entire nation!

Date: Morning, June 31, 1981/Khordad 23, 1360 SH/Sha'ban 01, 1401 AH.

Place: Jamaran Husayniyyah, Tehran

Subject: Importance of the role of the university in the independence or lack of independence of a country

Occasion: Anniversary of the establishment of the Ad Hoc Committee for the Cultural Revolution

Addressees: The members of the Ad Hoc Committee for the Cultural Revolution and the Supreme Council of the Jihad of the Universities of Tehran and other cities

When we look at Iran we see that lots of efforts have been made to implant dispute between two wings: the university and the clergy. If these two unite, things will be reformed in the country. How hard have they tried to implant dispute between these two! One could not mention the name of a clergy in university and the reverse was equally true. This was the result of their massive propaganda intensified by our inattentiveness. These problems were due to our inattention, and we received the heaviest blow from disunity. The university ran the country and when it became corrupt, the whole country followed suit.

Date: January 01, 1982/Dey 02, 1360 SH/Rabi' al-Awwal 14, 1402 AH.

Place: Jamaran, Tehran

Subject: Explaining the blessings of the revolution

Occasion: Birth anniversary of the Noble Prophet (s) and Imam Sadiq, Unity Week

Audience: Different strata of people-foreign guests and Sunni clergies taking the unity trip, workers of Housing Foundation, managers of post and telecommunications, participants in the seminar "Seminary and University"- students of the student unit of the Islamic Republic party

I hope university professors and theological *'ulama* preserve their relationship. One of the treasons committed against this country was the separation of university from the theological seminary. Professors avoided the mullahs (clergymen) on the assumption that they were empty-headed and knew nothing. Our seminaries were also scared of universities on the assumption that they were irreligious. If mutual understanding is developed, I guess these cases will disappear. When the *'ulama* find their way into university and university professors find their way into seminaries, then they will understand what crime has been committed against this country. When university professors visit Qum and sit together with the *'ulama* at the seminary and exchange views, then they will understand that we did not cry out in vain that Islam was a rich culture. Then those things would not be written on the walls of universities. From the beginning, plans were underway to train our children to be hostile to Islam. At university, one could not cite anything concerning Islam and the *akhunds* (clerics). Such was the case in seminaries. Any one of them who visited the university or seminary felt like a stranger. They assumed to have entered a bad environment. This was because plans had been worked out to keep these two fronts that could protect the country and save the country, hostile to each other. They wanted these two centers to suppress each other so that they could reap the benefits, as they actually did. What was the reason for so much insistence on enmity of the two strata? The reason was that the enemies of Islam feared that if these two got close and understood Islam, they would understand how much affliction we had suffered, particularly in the last 50 years. We were hostile to our brothers. Each tried to weaken the other.

Date: September 19, 1982/Shahrivar 28, 1361 SH/Dhul-Hijjah 1, 1402 AH.

Place: Husayniyyah Jamaran, Tehran

Subject: Two main pillars of education

Audience: Muhammad-Taqi Misbah Yazdi, Muhsin Qara'ati (Imam's representative in the literacy campaign), Ali-Akbar Parvaresh (Education Minister), Muhammad-'Ali Najafi (Minister of Culture and Higher Education), members of the office for coordination of theological seminaries and universities and the educationists

Presently, the students must gain knowledge of the Islamic Revolution's history, recognize the importance of harmony among themselves and the role of unity between university students and the religious schools. In case of existing mutual understanding between students and religious schools, the Western and Eastern-oriented groups of the hypocrites, leftists and other destructive elements would not set their greedy eyes upon Islamic State. If even they set their greedy eyes in circumstances of your advantage then they would have to face with a decisive defeat.

Additionally, it is worth knowing that it was not without motive that the previous regime used the services of the associated poets, writers, orators' rumormongers and journalists to sow the seeds of discord between these two groups- university and the religious institutions. Unfortunately, they were successful in this regard as these two classes became the sworn enemies of each other and interaction between the two groups in their respective environs was made illegal and each of the group detested the other. Reza Khan and his Son fanned the flames of this discord in order to make this country dependent on the superpowers in all respects. They made their public unknown with their real identity, national and enriched Islamic culture so they become dependent on foreigners and found themselves devoid of values. This tragedy caused to take the country and the great religion of Islam towards the back. Presently, it requires active participation of the nation and the government to compensate the unpleasant occurrences, which took place for our country and nation. It is hoped that we can become totally independent with the help of mutual coordination, guidance of the intellectuals and the devoted religious scholars; and by eliminating despair among ourselves and rediscovering the sense of the self and the great culture of our own.

Date: September 23, 1982/Mehr 1, 1361 SH/Dhul-Hijjah 5, 1402 AH.

Place: Jamaran, Tehran

Subject: Right upbringing is the source of cultural, political, economic and military independence

Occasion: Inaugurating New Academic Year

Addressees: Educational background oriented persons including Chancellors of the universities, teachers, teachers training centers and university students

In the past no such gathering was possible between the *'ulama* of Islam, Theological Seminary of Qum and Tehran and the universities. Never could these two classes sit together in a place replete with empathy and with one idea. Nor could ambassadors of friendly countries and university professors and government organizations sit together to explore our needs and work out solution to fulfillment of the needs. Petty differences had been enlarged and aggravated in our country. The propaganda was made in a way that religious men of letters had been intimidated to express one's words at university milieu. Similarly, the academician did not dare to express his words in academic milieu and educational schools. So were the university professors, civil servants and parliamentarians. They never met to find what their own country needs and what they should do to fulfill these needs. It was because the propaganda plans were of wide scope that suspicion prevailed everywhere. People were afraid of one another and suspected one another. I should say they were hostile to one another. This state of affairs had been created. None of the foreign ambassadors would attend the place where *'ulama* were present. They were not ready to be present in such places because *'ulama* had been introduced as reactionary, backward and intellectually dull. Such ideas were inculcated in former times, particularly in recent time. Obviously, foreign experts, European and American advisors were attentive that if these layers are together, they will be dangerous. That is, they are dangerous to them. And they were right. For this reason, through their domestic agents, their own men and the persons trained in their own milieu, they had made it impossible for such gatherings to be mounted.

Date/Time: Morning, August 27, 1985/Shahrivar 5, 1364 SH/Dhu'l-Hijjah 01, 1405 AH.

Place: Husayniyyah Jamaran, Tehran

Subject: Comparison between the Islamic Republic and the Pahlavi regime

Occasion: Auspicious Qurban Feast

Audience: Akbar Hashemi Rafsanjani (Majlis Speaker), members of the Society of Teachers of Qum, university professors across the country, officials of the Ministry of Culture and Higher Education, members of the Supreme Council of Cultural Revolution, clerics from Tehran, members of the Office of Islamic Propagation of Qum Theological Seminary and the Tehran Islamic Propagation Organization, ambassadors of Muslim countries

Communication between Seminaries (*Howzeh*) and Universities

O God, foreshorten the arms of the oppressors that are stretched out against the lands of the Muslims and root out all traitors to Islam and the Islamic countries. Awaken the heads of the Muslims states from their deep sleep so that they may exert themselves on behalf of their people's interests and renounce divisiveness and the quest for personal gain. Grant that the younger generation studying in the religious colleges and the universities may struggle to reach the sacred aims of Islam and strive together, with ranks united, first, to deliver the Islamic countries from the clutches of imperialism and its vile agents, and then to defend them.

Reference: Imam Khomeini (ra), *Wilayate Faqih* (The Governance of the Jurist), p. 11

Although I am spending the old age of indisposition and have not attained desirably any of the hopes that I had, I firmly believe that through the movement that emerged by the help of God and led to the closeness between the secularly educated and religious scholars, this light will not be extinguished and every day the cleavage that has been brought by the merchant traitors of the East and West with the aim of colonizing the Muslim nations would be removed through a worldly movement and all the classes of the seminary and university graduates. Through information on the sufferings and disruptions, they would look for the remedy and reconstruction.

Date: May 18, 1971/Urdibehesht 28, 1350 SH/Rabi' al-Awwal 22, 1391 AH.

Place: Najaf, in Iraq

Subject: Necessity for confronting the prevalence of the colonial culture

Addressees: Sayyid Sadiq Tabataba'i

While I feel a sense of attachment and fondness toward certain intellectuals-intellectuals who serve Islam, and in particular those who are abroad, those in America, Europe and India for example, with whom I correspond and who are at the service of Islam, who want to serve Islam, who have a love of Islam, and who want to eliminate oppression, on occasion having firmly resolved certain difficulties which have arisen abroad in the past- at the same time, I believe that they should not disregard those services rendered by the *'ulama* of Islam and the *akhunds*, arguing that "We want Islam minus the *akhund*". Don't you see that this is not possible? Islam and the *akhund* are inseparable entities. To say "We want Islam minus the *akhund*", is like saying "We want Islam, but an Islam which does not concern itself with politics". Indeed, this is the extent to which Islam and the *akhund* are intertwined. There is no way that you could have Islam without the *akhund*. The Holy Prophet (s) was also an *akhund*; he was one of the greatest *akhunds* of all time. The Prophet was the *akhund* above all *akhunds*. And Hazrat Ja'far as-Sadiq (a), he too was an *'alim* of Islam. These men were the fuqaha of Islam; they stand supreme among the fuqaha of Islam. So how on earth can you now say "I don't want the *akhund*"?! Indeed, this is why I nurse a grievance against these intellectuals.

However, I also have a complaint to make against the honorable gentlemen of the clergy. They too are guilty of overlooking many factors… if some patent error is to be found in the work of those who are currently striving for the sake of Islam, and who are writing material to this end, then you are to rectify this error. As ones who are learned, you are to rectify this error and are not to ostracize the persons concerned. Do not drive them away. Indeed, today we need the support of as many people as possible. Right now, we are to make the most of every single person. At times like this, when whatever the regime writes is against us; when all its measures and propaganda are aimed against us; when neither the press nor the radio are free to convey our message or to broadcast even one word of our argument; at a time when our hands our bound and we have been placed in a strait-jacket whereby we cannot get our message across and have no means of propagation at our disposal; indeed, we need every single person we can get. Therefore, even supposing that there are a few mistakes to be found in the work of those who are writing to promote Shi'ism, you are to rectify these mistakes. Do not ostracize these people; do not drive them away. Do not reject those from the university. These are the people in whose hands this country's destiny will lie in the future. It is not you who will become a government minister in the future. You and I are not the country's future ministers. We are in a different profession. Tomorrow, this country's destiny will lie in the hands of these people from the university. It is they who will become Members of Parliament, government ministers or whatever. Therefore, you are to be on friendly terms with these people. Do not persist in your rejection of them. Do not continue to mount the pulpit and denounce them. Mount the pulpit and advise them instead of reviling them. Where will reviling people get you? Advise them. Welcome these credit-worthy fronts which are currently active. Like yourselves, their members have also suffered imprisonment and persecution; they too have suffered exile; they too have been forced to live abroad and are afraid to return to their own country. If you ostracize those who are currently writing and publishing material abroad on Islamic and religious issues, then tomorrow, should the country's destiny fall into the hands of some of these people, what will they do with the future generation of *akhunds* having been tormented so by *akhunds* in the past? Everyone must join hands together… To return to my grievance against the honorable gentlemen of the clergy, I ask them not to divorce these other fronts from themselves, but instead to bring all the different fronts together. Moreover, those in the clergy must value this group of people who are striving in the path of Islam and who are writing material to this end. They (the clergy) must make use of these people. My good men of the clergy, extend the right hand of fellowship. Do not talk of a deprave, libertine university and do not continually divorce other fronts from yourselves… And the same goes for the members of other fronts; they too must not divorce the clergy from themselves by saying, for example, that they are reactionaries and old-fashioned. In what way can the *akhund* be said to be reactionary? How can the *akhund* be said to be reactionary when he stands as a forerunner of progress? Thus, we have a situation where one front accuses the clergy of reactionism and so on, while another front makes defamatory statements about those in the university saying so-and-so is an atheist and so on. But this is totally wrong.

Both fronts are to extend a brotherly hand to each other, so go ahead and do this and set out a joint course of action which you can both follow.

Date: November 1, 1977/Aban 01, 1365 SH/Dhu'l-Qa'dah 18, 1397 AH.

Place: Shaykh Ansari Mosque, Najaf, Iraq

Subject: The power of the clergy and the political, intellectual and religious services rendered by the Shi'ah *'ulama*

Addressees: Religious students, clergymen and Iranians residing in Iraq

It is necessary for you, the young students of the old and new universities to unite and forge the bonds of Islamic brotherhood with the rest of the nation. *"And hold fast, all of you together, to the cable of Allah, and do not be divided."* (Qur'an, 3:103) This is the firm, soul-saving commandment of the Holy Qur'an that we must use as our motto. Avoiding disputes and discord that bring nothing but defeat at the hands of the Devil, we must request God the Almighty to save the nation.

Date: February 4, 1978/Bahman 15, 1365 SH/Safar 25, 1398 AH.

Place: Najaf, Iraq

Subject: The need to desist from discord; the glad tidings of victory

Occasion: Student demonstrations in India

Addressees: The Iranian students residing in India

It is essential that the venerable clergy and the university students show mutual respect. The enlightened university students should respect the clergy and the clergymen. God, the Exalted, holds them in esteem and the God-inspired Household of the Prophet (a) has recommended them to the people. The clergy is a great source of strength. Losing it would cause the pillars of Islam to collapse, God forbid, thus enabling the cruel might of the enemy to go unchallenged.

Meticulous studies conducted by the alien exploiters in the course of history have led them to the conclusion that this bastion must be demolished. The widespread propaganda that they and their hirelings have been doing over several hundred years have caused some intellectuals to part with the clergy and become pessimistic about them so that the enemy remains unchallenged. In case some unqualified persons pass themselves off as being part of them, but serve and, according to the differences in their rank and service, make the people abide by the main and subsidiary principles of the faith in spite of the foreigners and their agents, this force should be assisted, protected and shown respect. The respected clergy must also respect the young intellectuals, who are serving Islam and the Islamic country and for this reason are the target of the attacks of the foreign agents. They should consider them as their dear children and their esteemed brothers. They should not give up this immense power in whose hand the destiny of the country willy-nilly will fall. They should guard against the malicious propaganda that has been going on against them for hundreds of years, showing them up in a different light to some people in order to benefit further from the disputes. They should ostracize those who either through ignorance or malicious intent have distanced this powerful group from the clergy, and not allow them to sow discord. They should rest assured that with these two great powers joining forces, victory will be attained; divided, they will never gain it.

Date: February 31, 1978/Bahman 24, 1365 SH/Rabi' al-Awwal 5, 1398 AH.

Place: Najaf, Iraq

Subject: The duties of Muslim intellectuals

Addressees: The Union of Islamic Students Association in Europe

The theological center in Qum has brought Iran back to life; it has performed a service to Islam that will endure for centuries. This service must not be underestimated; we must pray for the theological center in Qum and pray that we will come to emulate it. This center's name will remain inscribed in history for all time. In comparison to Qum, we here in Najaf are dead and buried; it is Qum that has brought Islam back to life. It is the center in Qum and the preaching of its *maraji'* and *'ulama* that have awakened the universities, those same places where we religious scholars used to be accused of being the opium of the people and the agents of the British and other imperialists. No, all that was the propaganda of Britain, Germany, the Soviet Union and others, designed to misrepresent us and make the *'ulama* and their institutions appear to be the opium of the people. They spread such propaganda because they know full well how active the religious scholars are and what a dynamic and militant religion Islam is. They drew up a plan to bring the religious scholars into disrepute, and propagated the notion that religion must be separated from politics.

Date: February 18, 1978/Bahman 29, 1365 SH/Rabi' al-Awwal 01, 1398 AH.

Place: Shaykh Ansari Mosque, Najaf, Iraq

Subject: The crimes of the Shah and of those who claim to support human rights

Occasion: The fortieth day following the martyrdom of those killed in Qum in the tragedy of Dey 19 (January 9)

Addressees: Religious students, clergymen and members of the public

The theology and secular students should have a friendly and working relationship among themselves. They should join all the various categories of the people for the purpose of attaining independence and freedom and for dispossessing the usurpers of everything belonging to the nation by right.

Date: October 8, 1978/Mehr 16, 1357 SH/Dhu'l-Qa'dah 1398 AH.

Place: Neauphle-le-Chateau, Paris

Subject: Commencement of the academic year

Addressees: The public

Don't you see how today in Iran when unity of purpose has come about it has shaken every throne, crown and superpower, how they are all at a loss as to what they should do? Do you see this? Do you not see how, now that the different groups in Iran have come closer together, now that the universities have come closer to the clerical establishment, the clerical establishment to the universities, and the bazaars have become at one with the universities and the clerical establishment- even though differences in some things still exist, which I will speak about later- now that unity of purpose has come about in Iran, it has shaken America and Russia and has made these ruffians within Iran itself flounce. These killings that this man perpetrates and the recourses that he resorts to all stem from the fact that he sees that the people have come together, and he is at a loss as to how to put an end to this union!

Date: December 24, 1978/Dey 3, 1357 SH/Muharram 23, 1399 AH.

Place: Neauphle-le-Chateau, Paris, France

Subject: Need to preserve unity and to avoid disunity

Addressees: A group of Iranian students and residents abroad

For many years now, we have gone to great pains to bring the universities closer to the mullahs, to the schools of the old sciences, and to the students of the old sciences, and to bring the bazaars closer to both of these. Indeed, the bazaars were already close to the clerical establishment in some aspects, but we brought them closer to the universities. We brought these different fronts closer together and always advised them to have unity of purpose so that they could achieve something. For were they each to become factions, one taking one side and the other another, this would first and foremost be of advantage to the foreigners.

Date: December 24, 1978/Dey 3, 1357 SH/Muharram 23, 1399 AH.

Place: Neauphle-le-Chateau, Paris, France

Subject: Need to preserve unity and to avoid disunity

Addressees: A group of Iranian students and residents abroad

If you *akhunds* think that you can reform the country without the help of the universities and the political fronts, then you are mistaken, for reform requires experts and you are Islamic experts, you know the rules of Islam but even you are not able to solve some of the political problems. So you need the other fronts too. You yourselves don't intend to govern, you have another occupation. You need a government, you need office workers, you need offices, a government, an army; all of these will be acquired through these fronts. It is through these universities, through these students at home and abroad that our country should be governed. If you are truly attached to Islam, if those other fronts are truly attached to Islam, then you are not showing it by fighting with one another today! To fight with one another today is the same as committing suicide.

Date: December 24, 1978/Dey 3, 1357 SH/Muharram 23, 1399 AH.

Place: Neauphle-le-Chateau, Paris, France

Subject: Need to preserve unity and to avoid disunity

Addressees: A group of Iranian students and residents abroad

The clerics and the academicians should be alert; all should be brothers and should forget the differences in unity of expression. The Iranian nation should be united to make the movement victorious.

Date: May 19, 1979/Urdibehesht 29, 1358 SH/Jamadi ath-Thani 22, 1399 AH.

Place: Qum

Subject: Treacheries of the period of Reza Khan; the plots of the US and superpowers

Audience: Representatives of the tribes; people of Neyriz of Fars province; representatives of the Air Force Command Headquarters

The academicians and the clergies, both influential members, should pay attention to unity.

Date: May 12, 1979/Urdibehesht 13, 1358 SH/Jamadi ath-Thani 24, 1399 AH.

Place: Qum

Subject: Roots of the Islamic Revolution; heavy responsibility of the university and seminary; SAVAK agents

Audience: Students of the Faculty of Law, University of Tehran

Today all of you should try to be united. The academicians and the clergies, both influential members, should pay attention to unity. The academicians must not try to neglect the clerics, because people are with them. The nation supports the clerics. Wherever they want to take the nation, they will follow the clerics, because people regard them as representatives of the Imam of the Time- may Allah expedite his glorious advent. Do not lose them; they are great potential powers. Do not leave this power. This is not the first time I am recommending this. When I was in Najaf, I used to say we would fail if we forget the clerics. We are not dynamic and energetic today, but the clerics can work effectively. Do not leave this group alone. The clerics, on the other hand, must not understate the academicians. Our administration system is in the hands of the universities. Our tomorrow will be in the hands of the academicians. These two groups must come to new terms with each other. Both groups are among the intellectual, but alas, one group thinks the other is fanatic, and another group considers the other infidel. It was the domineering thought in the past, but today these two groups are united for political growth. You must understand the seeds of discord come from elsewhere, from those who publicize Islam minus clerics. They beguile you from abroad. Clerics should know that academicians are the constructive members of the society and our future salvation will be in the hands of these people, and on the other hand, destroying Iran will be possible by the academicians. These two groups should unite. Do not lose control in the ruckus. Keep united, be colleagues, and advance this movement.

Date: May 12, 1979/Urdibehesht 13, 1358 SH/Jamadi ath-Thani 24, 1399 AH.

Place: Qum

Subject: Roots of the Islamic Revolution; heavy responsibility of the university and seminary; SAVAK agents

Audience: Students of the Faculty of Law, University of Tehran

You the esteemed university professors, and I as a seminarian, each in our respective places, should safeguard this movement and this unity of expression and not split up into groups.

Various groups announcing their formation

You will have noticed that a hundred groups in Tehran have announced their formation! That is, a hundred groups opposed to Islam although they themselves do not understand. Although they themselves say that they are doing it for Islam… If we lose the solidarity we had and if the university and the clergy go their separate ways with both of them getting separated from the people and with the existence of the various, divergent parties that are, unfortunately, ill-disposed toward one another, then we are afraid that in such a case, our movement will not reach the fruitful end that it should. The result will be that neither your university nor our *madrasahs* will attain what you and we have in mind.

The aim that we ought to pursue now and strive to that end is that you in the university, we in the *madrasahs*, the gentlemen in the cities and the others everywhere invite the people to observe unity of expression and to eschew this divergence of paths. All of us, with unity of expression, want to have a just Islamic republic and a just Islamic government; one which allows the freedom to think, to express one's opinion, to act and to have freedom in all things... I am afraid that hands are at work to create discord and to form groups and groups that have been constantly announcing their formation in the newspapers! A hundred groups all hostile to one another!... I hope that everything turns out well, God willing, and that all of us remain together. We should have the correct outlook and should not consider ourselves as being apart from one another. All of us are Muslims and possess Islamic beliefs. We want our country to be independent; to be our very own together with its resources, and the people to enjoy the fruits of their labor. We want the country's spiritual and material aspects to be taken care of; all those matters. If all these things are in place and we remain together, then victory is ours as it has been up to now.

Date: Afternoon, July 4, 1979/Tir 31, 1358 SH/Sha'ban 9, 1399 AH.

Place: Qum

Subject: The differences between a Western university and an Islamic one

Audience: Tehran University professors

Our university brothers; be careful that they do not separate you from the clergy. Our brothers of the clergy; be careful that they do not separate you from the academicians. They (enemies) have been scheming these last few days in Isfahan, Mashhad and Tehran to lay the grounds for discord in order to drive the university and the clergy apart. Some uninformed preachers and academicians intend distancing these two groups from one another. They have made their plans at this time when the Constitution is to be proposed; at a time when results are to be obtained; at a time close to the month of Ramadan when your gatherings pose a threat to the people who wish to destroy Iran and Islam. The auspicious month of Ramadan is the month when people gather; it is the month of unity; the month of God. At this time, just before this month, and the time when the results of all these sacrifices, these troubles, and these pains are materialized, a plan has been made to create bitter discord between the clergy and the academicians. Somebody hands out pamphlets cursing someone else; another hands out pamphlets praising someone! Both of them are offenses; both of them are wrong at this time. Desist from being ignorant! Do not let these people who are the enemies of Islam incite you. Do not be treacherous to Islam! This discord today constitutes treachery to Islam, no matter under what name it is. Having differences today over the succession of the Commander of the Faithful is treachery to Islam. Do not raise these matters now. All of you should see to it that Iran's destiny, which is to be actualized, turns out to be good. Iran should not be forgotten because of your actions. It should not be buried because of your actions. Desist from discord in case your heart burns for Islam. Desist from discord in case your heart burns for the nation. And if your heart burns for your country, you desist from these differences.

Neutralize this satanic plot that has come to light in Isfahan, and also in Mashhad and Tehran. Do not knock one another's heads over a person being an unbeliever or a Muslim! Give the problems your consideration. They want you to fall upon one another so that they can profit by it.

May God awaken us from our negligence. May He preserve our unity. May the Lord guide the ones who sow discord. And may He make Islam victorious

Date: July 6, 1979/Tir 15, 1358 SH/Sha'ban 11, 1399 AH.

Place: Qum

Subject: Faith and unity among the various strata of society as the key to victory

Audience: Various strata of the people; students of the Faculty of Law and Political Science of Tehran University

And I shall say a few words about what our duty is for the sake of those who were not there.

The importance of this duty concerns this class; that is, the clergy, the university professors and students. These two groups constitute the thinkers of society; they are the thinkers. You are the two groups- the university students, whether those who have passed out from university and are now lawyers, legal experts or whatever, or whether of the clerical class who are still studying, or have finished their studies and are engaged in disseminating the faith and in other activities- in society that are the thinkers. And you are the ones that are able to neutralize the plots that are about to be hatched with utmost thoroughness for the purpose of defeating this movement. You two groups have a greater duty than the others, and your responsibility, too, is very great. All the people bear a responsibility, but yours is very great. And now they intend to create discord between you, the two groups that had become united and there was no more talk of the clergy and the university being like this and like that. All of you were together and succeeded, thanks to God, and understood that unity brings success. When you (two groups) the thinkers, came together, the other strata of the people joined you. It is your duty, and also that of the clergy and the university staff, to maintain your unity.

Date: July 5, 1979/Tir 14, 1358 SH/Sha'ban 01, 1399 AH.

Place: Qum

Subject: The grave duty and responsibility of the clergy and students

Audience: Students from Mashhad

You must safeguard this power of the university students and the strata of the youth; do not challenge them; all belong to the same nation; all of us belong to one country and home; both of you should protect this home of yours. The destinies of this country of yours shall after sometime be in the hands of these university students; they shall become its ministers and so forth; protect them. In the same way that I ask them not to lose this power, I ask you also not to lose this power; be brothers; be together. I say to the university students not to divide into so many groups; you have enemies; you must be well-equipped to face the enemy; to be well-equipped is to unite into a single group with unity of expression; if you form into a single group, our devoted Muslim youth who- praise be to Allah- are in the majority in the university, if they repeatedly not divide into groups and sub-groups and join together then a few persons that are corrupt and astray shall either join with them, or get lost and go away. You should not wait for the government to come and prevent them or the nation to come and prevent them; you with your own gathering and without creating any conflict, without any fighting, with your own coming together and your own unity of expression should thwart these plots. Tomorrow the university is reopening; thwart these conspiracies. The plotters are your enemies; they are the enemies of your nation. Both the clergyman must be a friend and brother of the university student and also the university student be such with the clergyman so that these two powers, these two thinking intellectual powers are able to protect their own country.

Date: September 14, 1979/Shahrivar 23, 1358 SH/Shawwal 22, 1399 AH.

Place: Qum

Subject: Description of the dimensions of Mr. Taleqani's personality; the power of Islam and responsibility of the clergy; the necessity to sustain the power of the youth and the university students

Audience: Various strata of people

This evil conspiracy *taghout* to which different strata of people vigilant scholars, must be particularly thwarted with full force and prudence, opening the way leading to understanding and solidarity as soon as possible. Once these two thoughtful poles are united, the country would reach its real growth, development and perfection. The scholars and scientists are required to make efforts to unify these two precious strata. It should be born in mind that neither university excluding theology school would get independence vice versa. My dear ones! If you want Islam, and the country to the order of God and obey *"And obey Allah and His Apostle and do not quarrel then you will be weak in hearts and your power will depart."* (Qur'an, 8:46). Difference and dispute will lead you to defeat power and impacts in humanistic community. *"And cling to the covenant of Allah altogether and be not disunited."* (Qur'an, 3:103)

Date: September 22, 1979/Shahrivar 13, 1358 SH/Shawwal 03, 1399 AH.

Place: Qum

Subject: Foreigners' attempts to sweep the Islamic content of the scientific and cultural programs

Occasion: Opening of academic year

Addressees: Professors, collegians and students

Now, since it is the first anniversary of the attack on Tehran University, it is necessary for the dear *'ulama* of Tehran, Qum and the nearby towns to attend the ceremonies at Tehran University for greater solidarity. Similarly, the *'ulama* throughout the towns and cities of Iran, should participate in the ceremonies being held on this occasion in any university in any part of Iran. Their presence in the universities was throughout Iran. Closing your ranks with high school and university students as well as the esteemed professors would frustrate the plots to create divisions between these two progressive forces.

Date: November 1, 1979/Aban 01, 1358 SH/Dhu'l-Hijjah 01, 1399 AH.

Place: Qum

Subject: Pressure actions on America and Israel for extradition of the Shah

Addressees: High school and university students and staff, theological students and clergymen

Today I have come among you dear students[74] for two purposes: first, commemorating the anniversary of the martyrdom of the young students in university due to savage attack of the agents of the tyrannical regime and second, clergymen-academics unity. I congratulate this union to clergymen and to university students.

---

[74] Students of Hakim Nizami High School of Qum City.

I came here to say to you that I'm your servant in all my life, serving of all Islamic nations, serving the noble Iranians, serving the students and clergymen, serving all groups of people and all Islamic countries and all oppressed citizens of world.

There must be a relationship between these two advanced groups and these two intellectual ones; that is, dear clergymen and university students. It must be a relationship between the enlightened ones, writers, all intellectuals and all sorts of people and the two above-mentioned groups. Our brethren in every place, job and position of knowledge must know that if they are not united and fail to close their ranks in intellectual terms, they cannot serve this oppressed nation, and Islamic country. The burden of this country would reach destination but with difficulty. If these dispersed groups, and votes, and diverse sects protecting the country and Islam we will soon attain our sublime Islamic purposes which is the same as the high aim of nations and the oppressed.

We sacrificed so many young people in the universities, in theological schools, in scientific, Islamic, cultural schools, in streets, markets and alleys in order to achieve our aim which was the one people cried: independence, freedom and Islamic Republic.

My dear brothers, intellectuals, writers, respectable students, honorable clergymen, dear businessmen, respectable employees and noble clerks! Let's join together. Try to employ all pens, step and talks to secure the interest of the oppressed. Do not let the blood of our martyrs be spoiled. Do not let our hovels dwellers still live in hovels. Do not let superpowers covet to swallow us. Do not let superpowers and traitors' develop conspiracies? O' intellectuals and writers! Use up your pens and words in the cause of the oppressed. O' scholars, university students, teachers, professors! Strengthen your gathering to help the downtrodden people. It was you who served, who offered your blood that suffered imprisonment and underwent persecution to be relieved of the yoke of aliens and plundering and plunders. Do not allow all your efforts to come to nothing. Use up pens in the way of serving people, words in the way of the oppressed and deeds in the way of the impoverished people.

O' my friends! O' my brethren! Keep away from disunity. Keep this unity between clergymen and students as before. Intellectuals and writers must join this group. You create an immense historical miracle by your union defeat of all superpowers. Today, they sit at corner and brew schemes keeping you away from unity. They provoke discord among people. Do not contribute to this discord-provoking attempt, as this is lending hand to the enemies of country and Islam.

Do not find fault so much unreasonably. Do not nag unduly because it is to advantage of the enemies.

Date: Before noon, November 4, 1979/Aban 31, 1358 SH/Dhu'l-Hijjah 31, 1399 AH.

Place: Qum, Hakim Nizami High School

Subject: Unity of clerics and university- irrational criticism

Audience: Students of Qum and Tehran

Today any insult and vilification to clergy is in fact, a blow to the independence and freedom and Islam. Today it is a treachery and treason to pace the path of the Shah and call this most reverend class that neither yields to East not to West 'Backward'.

My dear sisters and brothers! You do know that they entail Shah and America who call the clergy 'Backward'. The noble nation of Iran pays back its debt to Islam by giving their support to clergy who are the protectors and a fortification of this native land and its borders. They cut short the greed of the tyrants of history from the country. On the other hand, I remark the respected clergy wherever they are. It is quite likely that the satanic elements would disseminate a vicious propaganda against the youths particularly those of college. The clergy should know that the obligation today is that all the classes of the nation, particularly the two great ones, the thinkers of the nation, should be united, hand in hand, exert their efforts against the Satanic forces and the arrogant and push ahead in one row to safeguard the Islamic campaign as their own life, independence and freedom. It was the design of the world-hungry ones and their stooges to separate these two classes. They succeeded and it resulted in the destruction of the country. The same design is now in effect. A little carelessness will lead us to elimination. I hope that all, particularly these two classes in this New Year be vigilant about the tricks and the treacheries and plots. They should foil the vicious designs by the unity of word.

Date: March 12, 1980/Farvardin 1, 1359 SH/Jamadi al-Awwal 4, 1400 AH.

Place: Shemiran, Darband, Tehran

Subject: Thirteen-point recommendations to Muslims

Occasion: The Iranian New Year Eve

Addressees: The Muslim nation of Iran, the Muslims and the oppressed ones worldwide

The whispers in your ears either in the university or the school, say Faydiyyah, should not get access to the inner most recess of mind. This unity that you have reached is very important to the elements of anti-Islam. Therefore, now their target is you. Their target that are anti-Faydiyyah, anti-university and anti-Islam. To continue a job is more than its creation. You went to Qum Saturday together. Talked together. Reached an understanding and a common ground mutually. Now it's continuity is important. You should repeat your meetings once in a period of certain duration. You should be of one voice.

I am hopeful that this affiliation of your's may be blessed. By this affiliation, you could be able to make your university and the education centers Islamic ones.

Date: May 24, 1980/Khordad 3, 1359 SH/Rajab 9, 1400 AH.

Place: Jamaran, Tehran

Subject: Fifty years long plots to create divisions among the various classes of the society

Audience: Teachers, students of the religious institutions, professors, members of the Islamic associations, students of the Universities all over the country

Save this unity achieved among you. They will assault you to take it away from you. Try to have an independent country for yourself. Try to be free yourself. Be in persuasion of this. You, between your two classes, try to have a continued touch and link. The programs should be prepared by the students at the university and the clergies at the religious institutes. Things in accordance with the needs and necessities of the country should be charted out, not what is of any use to us.

Date: May 24, 1980/Khordad 3, 1359 SH/Rajab 9, 1400 AH.

Place: Jamaran, Tehran

Subject: Fifty years long plots to create divisions among the various classes of the society

Audience: Teachers, students of the religious institutions, professors, members of the Islamic associations, students of the Universities all over the country

The students, academic students, clergies, turban-wearers, scholars- all these classes who are thinking-mind, should enhance their alliance among and amidst themselves. They should be aware that their alliance should not be foiled by the enemy. If they come into the university and say that they have no business with the academics; likewise in the religious schools, you should know that it is chicanery and a trick. They want to separate from each other. They want to open the space for themselves. Be aware. Be awaken. Be vigilant. Now all the eyes are adhered to you.

Date: June 5, 1980/Khordad 14, 1359 SH/Rajab 02, 1400 AH.

Place: Jamaran Husayniyyah Tehran

Subject: Internal change of a nation is the source of victory, unity between religious institute and the university; Importance of Friday prayers

Audience: Professors and students of Divinity and the Islamic Sciences College, Tehran University

Now gentlemen, you have taken the first step. It is a most fortunate step in that you have broken the big wall, that huge barrier which they had put up between you—between the Faydiyyah and the university. This is the first step that you have taken. In your subsequent steps, you must try to be independent in every respect; not dependent. I am telling you all this because I cannot see you again; you who have reached that stage. As for me, it is the last stage. I am saying this so that the others and the generations to come, God willing, be careful about these two centers remaining united. These two centers should consider knowledge and edification, and knowledge and application of knowledge as two wings, and that flying with just one of them is impossible. The next steps are those that have to do with edification.

Date: Before noon, December 18, 1980/Azar 27, 1359 SH/Safar 01, 1401 AH.

Place: Jamaran, Tehran

Subject: The importance of the roles of the seminary and the university; stating the duties of these two institutions of learning

Occasion: The day of unity between the seminary and the university

Audience: Teachers and students of Qum Theological Center; the student members of the office for the consolidation of unity between the seminary and the university

The university teachers as well as the Islamic scholars should share a mutual understanding and should join hands in order to create an Islamic atmosphere in the universities as well as the seminaries. Teachers who are appointed for university jobs as well as the other centers of learning should be committed people who have neither Eastern nor Western leanings.

Date: March 1, 1981/Esfand 01, 1359 SH/Rabi' ath-Thani 23, 1401 AH.

Place: Jamaran, Tehran

Subject: The importance of self-purification and its priority over education

Audience: Various strata of the people, employees of Shaheed Mutahhari School, and members of the Islamic Associations of the Girls' Schools of Damghan and Semnan

Both the seminaries as well as the universities should keep in mind that they need to strengthen their mutual relationship. You are the two vital bodies that have a powerful influence on the health of a society. Your isolation would mean that all those who can do something for the country will, God forbid, get isolated. And all those powers that have had to forfeit their interests in this country will consequently enter the scene and will bring in a seemingly popular government that will lead our country to its doom.

Date: March 5, 1981/Esfand 14, 1359 SH/Rabi' ath-Thani 27, 1401 AH.

Place: Jamaran, Tehran

Subject: Imperialist conspiracies for isolating the clergy; the great responsibility of the clerics; need for unity between the seminaries and the universities

Audience: Clerics from the Bureau of Propagation of the Qum and Mashhad Seminaries and soldiers of the 1974-78 service batches

I forewarn you and all the future generations to come and advise you to keep in mind that the nation, the clergy, and the university should never be disunited because any disunity among them will result in disaster for the entire nation, for Islam, and for the country.

Date: March 5, 1981/Esfand 14, 1359 SH/Rabi' ath-Thani 27, 1401 AH.

Place: Jamaran, Tehran

Subject: Imperialist conspiracies for isolating the clergy; the great responsibility of the clerics; need for unity between the seminaries and the universities

Audience: Clerics from the Bureau of Propagation of the Qum and Mashhad Seminaries and soldiers of the 1974-78 service batches

We want our universities to become as independent as our seminaries in which the agents of the foreign powers are easily exposed. We want them to be freed from all kinds of dependence, like they were in the olden days, during which, even if deviants emerged they would immediately be exposed. We are looking for the fulfillment of this ideal.

Time/Date: Morning, May 25, 1981/Khordad 4, 1360 SH/Rajab 02, 1401 AH.

Place: Jamaran, Tehran

Subject: Importance of knowledge in Islam; responsibility of the university in an Islamic society; duties of the Islamic associations of the universities

Audience: Members of the Islamic Association and the Jihad of the 'Ilm va San'at (Science and Technology) University; members of the Organization for Scientific and Industrial Research; and a group of inventors and innovators

An independent nation, with an independent ideology, with independent universities because it is the independence of the universities that ensures the independence of a country. Universities that hold hands with the seminaries and sidetrack the Eastern and Western blocs and instead work in the interests of their own country and beloved Islam and bring up our children in a way that they no longer need to look toward Moscow, London, or Washington as their Mecca. Let them look toward the Ka'bah and focus upon God Almighty and welcome Islam with open arms because only Islam guarantees their independence and dignity.

The importance that Islam gives to knowledge is probably not given by any other school…the independence of our country depends on the independence of the universities and the seminaries. The university and seminaries should join hands and protect the independence of their country. They should cut off all their hopes from both the Islamic universities and the seminaries. They should not pay heed to their objections to fostering harmony between the universities and the clerics. They are fearful even of the shadow of a cleric. Their plans are to keep the universities away from the seminaries.

They had tried for long years to foster a rift and animosity between these two groups that are the think-tanks of a nation and in whose hands lie the welfare, grandeur, and independence of this nation. All of us saw how these two groups had been turned into enemies until the Islamic Revolution following which Islam held out its invitation. Islam invites all groups to unity and especially the universities and the seminaries. And as long as these two groups remain united, your country's independence is guaranteed.

Date: Morning, June 31, 1981/Khordad 23, 1360 SH/Sha'ban 01, 1401 AH.

Place: Jamaran Husayniyyah, Tehran

Subject: Importance of the role of the university in the independence or lack of independence of a country

Occasion: Anniversary of the establishment of the Ad Hoc Committee for the Cultural Revolution

Addressees: The members of the Ad Hoc Committee for the Cultural Revolution and the Supreme Council of the Jihad of the Universities of Tehran and other cities

Spiritual sciences must be taught at universities just like material sciences. Humanities and educational issues should be taught by those who know what Islamic education is and what Islam is. Some of these people should not think that Islam does not have anything to offer regarding society or education. As far as human issues are concerned, Islam is much deeper than any other school of thought. Islam considers educational issues as having top priority. Islam also deals with economic matters. Today, we cannot be like before when our universities and children were corrupted by things brought from Western educational warehouse as gifts; we cannot just sit and let minds raised in Western education teach our children. Education must be grounded in the Qur'an, the richest book in the world when it comes to education. However, education and training require specialists. It is not like what some people think that they know two Qur'anic verses so they know Qur'an and Islam. People who can hardly recite Qur'an correctly think they are specialists on Islam. Those who have no idea of the Islamic rules, economy, culture and Islamic rational sciences say that Islam does not deal with such things. Well, since you do not know, on what grounds do you say such things? Specialists are necessary and should be produced by theological seminaries. Let them ask the help of the centers where there are such specialists and open the universities but the scholars for the human sciences should be gradually taken from the theological seminaries of the country and especially from those in Qum.

Date: December 9, 1981/Azar 18, 1360 SH/Safar 21, 1402 AH.

Place: Jamaran, Tehran

Subject: Explaining the mission and functions of theological seminaries in the Islamic system

Audience: Sayyid Ali Khamenei (President and Friday prayer leader of Tehran), members of the organizing committee of the Tehran Friday Prayer in; students of Tarbiyat Mu'allim; some Muslim Philippine graduates; some Muslims from southeast Asia; employees of Iran Radio and TV broadcast; personnel of the air force-Sunni clergies from Afghanistan

I hope university professors and theological *'ulama* preserve their relationship. One of the treasons committed against this country was the separation of university from the theological seminary. Professors avoided the mullahs (clergymen) on the assumption that they were empty-headed and knew nothing. Our seminaries were also scared of universities on the assumption that they were irreligious. If mutual understanding is developed, I guess these cases will disappear. When the *'ulama* find their way into university and university professors find their way into seminaries, then they will understand what crime has been committed against this country. When university professors visit Qum and sit together with the *'ulama* at the seminary and exchange views, then they will understand that we did not cry out in vain that Islam was a rich culture. Then those things would not be written on the walls of universities. From the beginning, plans were underway to train our children to be hostile to Islam. At university, one could not cite anything concerning Islam and the *akhunds* (clerics). Such was the case in seminaries. Any one of them who visited the university or seminary felt like a stranger. They assumed to have entered a bad environment. This was because plans had been worked out to keep these two fronts that could protect the country and save the country, hostile to each other. They wanted these two centers to suppress each other so that they could reap the benefits, as they actually did. What was the reason for so much insistence on enmity of the two strata? The reason was that the enemies of Islam feared that if these two got close and understood Islam, they would understand how much affliction we had suffered, particularly in the last 50 years. We were hostile to our brothers. Each tried to weaken the other. Note that this unity between the university and seminary should be established and strengthened so that you can protect your country. If the universities and seminaries strive to be acquainted with each other and develop understanding, our country will not have any defect. All the sufferings are because one corrupt university graduate, examples of whom you know, will ruin a country and if such a graduate is upright, he or she will correct the country. The corruption of a scholar corrupts the world. A scholar corrupts the world. The mass of people cannot corrupt the society.

Date: September 19, 1982/Shahrivar 28, 1361 SH/Dhul-Hijjah 1, 1402 AH.

Place: Husayniyyah Jamaran, Tehran

Subject: Two main pillars of education

Audience: Muhammad-Taqi Misbah Yazdi, Muhsin Qara'ati (Imam's representative in the literacy campaign), Ali-Akbar Parvaresh (Education Minister), Muhammad-'Ali Najafi (Minister of Culture and Higher Education), members of the office for coordination of theological seminaries and universities and the educationists

These two factions of university and Faydiyyah theological school, that praise be to God, have today consolidated their unity and together have become one member of the society, can cause a country to attain true independence and freedom. However, if, God forbid, these two strata deviate, then know for sure that the country and the commandments of Islam shall be drawn towards deviation. For this reason, the task that you the dear students have- which is focusing on Islamic issues of the university- is a very crucial and valuable task and on the other hand, it is also very responsive.

Date/Time: Morning, November 27, 1982/Azar 6, 1361 SH/Safar 11, 1403 AH.

Place: Husayniyyah Jamaran, Tehran

Subject: Importance of the role of Islamic associations, successes of the popular serving government

Audience: Student members of the Office of Consolidation of Unity of the Islamic associations of the universities throughout the country

The men of learning and the eminent theologians of the seminaries of the land and the respected and pious professors of the universities should strive to bring the universities and seminaries closer to one another.

Date: April 1, 1983/Farvardin 21, 1361 SH/Jamadi ath-Thani 17, 1403 AH.

Place: Jamaran, Tehran

Subject: Six reminders to the nation, the government, the parliament and the Judiciary

Occasion: Farvardin 21, anniversary of the establishment of the Islamic Republic of Iran system

Addressees: Nation of Iran

Our seminaries and universities should be ones that can propagate worldwide, in all countries of the world.

Time: September 6, 1983/Shahrivar 15, 1362 SH/Dhul-Hijjah 28, 1403 AH.

Place: Husayniyyah Jamaran, Tehran

Subject: Need for educating young theology students for judgment and propagation

Audience: Mahdavi Kani, Imami Kashani, Mousavi Tabrizi; officials, teachers and members of the Imam as-Sadiq (a) University, members of the Cultural Revolution board, teachers and theology students of Martyr Mutahhari School, educational and judicial affairs graduates from Qum, officials of Dar Rahe-Hagh Institute and the staff of Amir Kabir vocational school of Isfahan

With the relations, you have with seminaries and you can render many services. Perhaps you may not have noticed that during the reign of Reza Khan and his son- I witnessed from beginning to the end- how they exerted pressure on seminaries so that no seminary could exist. On the one hand, they opened the doors and said they would so such and such for every one coming to them. On the other hand, they exerted so much pressure on theology students that they could not stay in their chambers in the mornings. They had to go out prior to the sunrise and return after the sunset. Thanks God, however, they did not succeed. Theological seminaries remained and were preserved in the same pristine form and should be preserved in the same way. Universities should have good relations with theological seminaries and exchange views.

Time: Morning, November 15, 1983/Aban 24, 1362 SH/Safar 9, 1404 AH.

Place: Jamaran, Tehran

Subject: Vigilance against cultural schemes of the alliance

Audience: 'Abdullah Jasbi (Superintendent of Azar Islamic University), officials of different branches of the university

Behold O theological seminaries and universities of the men of research! Stand up and save the Holy Qur'an from the mischief of the pseudo-ascetic ignoramuses and impious scholars who have consciously and deliberately attacked and are attacking the Qur'an and Islam. I am saying seriously, not out of usual compliments, that I feel sorry for my time spent in the path of error and ignorance. O you brave sons of Islam! Let the seminaries and universities pay attention to the stations of the Qur'an and its diverse dimensions. Consider teaching the Qur'an in any of its fields and make it your lofty aim. Because during the autumn of your life when the weakness of old age burdens you, you may regret and feel sorry for what you did during your youthful days, just as this writer does.

Date: August 7, 1986/Mordad 16, 1365 SH/Dhu'l-Hijjah 1, 1406 AH.

Place: Jamaran, Tehran

Subject: Antiquity of the Abrahamic Hajj; disavowal of the polytheists in the grandiose congress of Hajj

Addressees: Muslim nation of Iran and the world and the pilgrims to the Sacred House of God

God willing, the *'ulama* and clerics are familiar with all the dimensions and aspects of their responsibility, but for the sake of reminding and emphasis, I do say that today, many of the youth and intellectuals in the free environment of our Islamic country feel that they can express their own ideas on different Islamic issues and concerns. With a smiling face and open arms, their comments must be listened. If they are going astray, through words full of love and amity you should show the straight path of Islam to them. You should bear in mind that their spiritual and mystical emotions and feelings cannot be overlooked, nor their writings be immediately branded as *iltiqat* (eclectic) and deviant, nor all together subjected to doubt and suspicion. Undoubtedly, the hearts of those who are dealing with an issue like that today are beating for Islam and the guidance of the Muslims. Otherwise, they have no motive behind putting themselves in trouble for designing this issue. They believe that the positions of Islam on various cases are as what they are thinking. Instead of quarreling and sidetracking them, you should fatherly and kindly deal with them. If they do not accept, do not be discouraged. Otherwise, God forbid, they will be snared by the liberals, nationalists or the leftists and hypocrites; the sin of this is not less than that of being "eclectic." We can be hopeful for the future of the country and the future-builders once we give them value in the different issues, forgive their minor lapses and have knowledge of all the means and principles that will lead to their proper training and education. The culture in the universities and non-seminary centers is in such a manner that it is more used to experiencing and feeling of realities than the theoretical and philosophical culture. To blend these two cultures and filling the gaps, the seminary and the university must be fused so that the ground for the spread and expansion of the teachings of Islam be widened.

Date: July 02, 1988/Tir 29, 1367 SH/Dhu'l-Hijjah 5, 1408 AH.

Place: Jamaran, Tehran

Subject: Anniversary of the bloody Mecca Massacre and acceptance of the UN Resolution 895

Addressees: Iranian nation

The most indispensable organizations is the student and seminary Basij. The students of theology and students of universities should exert their utmost efforts in defending the revolution and Islam in their respective centers. My Basiji children in these two centers should be the guards of the unalterable principle of "neither East nor West". Today, the university and the seminary are more in need of unity and solidarity than any other time and place. The children of the revolution should never allow the agents of America and the Soviet Union to penetrate these two places. It is only through the Basij that this important task can be accomplished. Ideological issues of the basijis are on the shoulder of these two academic bastions. The seminary and the university should place the frameworks of the pure Muhammadan (s) Islam at the disposal of all members of the Basij.

Date: November 23, 1988/Azar 2, 1367 SH/Rabi' ath-Thani 21, 1409 AH

Place: Jamaran, Tehran

Subject: Role and station of the Basij

Occasion: Basij's Week

Imam Khomeini's Views on Academic Institutions and Academicians

Addressees: Iranian nation and the combatant Basijis

I would like to advise the present and future generations "not to slacken their efforts". Let the university professors and students strengthen their bonds of friendship and mutual understanding with the clerics and the students of theology. They should never underestimate the plots of the cunning enemy. Whenever they see someone trying to sow the seeds of discord, they should provide counsel and guidance for them. If their advice to such individuals is not effective, they should turn away from them, isolate them and not let their conspiracies take root, for "prevention is better than cure."

Date of Reciting: Khordad 15, 1368

Place: Jamaran, Tehran

Subject: Politico-divine will (ever-lasting message of Imam Khomeini to the contemporary ones and next generations)

Addressees: Iranian nation, Muslims and peoples of the world and next generations

INDEX

A

A'zam Mosque, 58, 59, 60, 61, 286

Aba Basir School, 343, 344

Abdullah Jasbi, 202, 295, 385

absence of faith, 28, 50, 190, 222

absence of purification, 32

Abu Raihan University, 228

academic revolution, 153, 167, 357

academic scholars, 155, 170, 199

academic training, 169, 206

acquisition of knowledge, 7, 16, 25, 30, 189, 248, 252, 268

actual education, 33, 205

Ad Hoc Committee for the Cultural Revolution, 21, 155, 156, 172, 200, 206, 207, 357, 358, 381

Ahmadi, 36, 173

Ahwaz, 31, 97, 190, 194, 244, 253

Akbar Hashemi Rafsanjani, 98, 227, 236, 362

Akrami, 54, 176, 296

Alawi School, 18, 74, 75, 112, 228, 287, 337, 338, 339

Ali Shari'atmadari, 13, 27, 28, 129, 139, 160, 164, 175, 184, 190, 201, 205, 220, 221, 222, 340

Ali-Abad, 166, 196, 233

Ali-Akbar Parvaresh, 22, 45, 46, 47, 48, 50, 96, 126, 158, 235, 360, 383

Ali-Akbar Velayati, 100

alim, 25, 29, 363

America, 32, 35, 42, 60, 61, 63, 66, 69, 76, 94, 98, 100, 105, 110, 111, 114, 115, 121, 131, 135, 137, 143, 149, 150, 152, 153, 168, 197, 207, 209, 210, 211, 224, 231, 232, 241, 245, 259, 260, 266, 278, 279, 286, 287, 288, 294, 296, 297, 298, 301, 302, 303, 305, 306, 307, 308, 310, 311, 314, 315, 319, 322, 323, 324, 325, 327, 328, 329, 363, 367, 374, 376, 387

Amir 'Abbas Hoveyda, 102

Amir al-Mu'minin, 59

Amir Kabir, 65, 66, 70, 99, 385

Andimeshk, 159

anthropology, 14, 38

Arak, 15, 40, 41, 338

Ardebil, 196, 231, 254

Ashura, 323

associate professor, 31, 189, 251

Ataturk, 93

Ataturks and Taqizadehs, 197, 224

Avicenna, 198, 276, 289

Ayatullah Sheikh Mohammad Fayd Qummi, 132

Ayyam Allah, 117

B

Ba'ath Party, 40

Babol College, 80, 117

Bahman 22, 160, 161, 246

Bahonar, 98, 164

Bakhtiyari tribes, 106

Bani Umayyad, 59

Baqiri Kani, 113, 339

Basij, 51, 97, 98, 166, 172, 196, 211, 233, 257, 294, 354, 387

Bouyer-Ahmad tribe, 107

C

Canada, 63, 207, 210, 241, 259, 260, 266, 277, 279, 298, 327, 328

Mashhad, 92, 156, 193, 340, 347, 348, 356, 371, 372, 373, 380

Mazandaran, 156, 193, 274, 276

medical doctor, 27

mental development, 12

Mir Husayn Mousavi, 98, 160, 175, 201, 213

Mission for My Country, 103

modern knowledge, 30

modern schools, 42, 70

molding human beings, 11, 115, 132, 185

Molding human beings, 29

moral and educational instruction, 60

moral and ethical training, 43, 192

moral commitment, 42

moral insight, 47

moral purification, 25

moral training, 43, 46, 124, 192

Morvarid, 113, 339

Moscow, 40, 91, 153, 155, 168, 170, 171, 199, 358, 381

Mousa Zargar, 230

Mousavi Tabrizi, 99, 385

Mu'awiyah, 59

Mufatteh, 113

Mufidi High College, 83, 139, 195

Muhammad Ali Najjafi, 160, 175, 201

Muhammad Hashemi, 258

Muhammad Reza Khan, 96, 226

Muhammad-'Ali Najafi, 22, 46, 47, 49, 50, 235, 360, 383

Muhammadi Golpayegani, 113, 339

Muhammad-Mahdi Shamsuddin, 76

Muhammad-Reza Hashemi, 176

Muhammad-Taqi Misbah Yazdi, 22, 46, 47, 48, 50, 235, 360, 383

Muhsin Qara'ati, 16, 22, 46, 47, 48, 50, 51, 52, 235, 236, 360, 383

Muhsin Rezaee, 51, 98, 257, 294

mujtahids, 257, 258

Muslim intellectuals, 17, 249, 250, 269, 336, 366

Mustafa Kamal Pasha, 93

Muwahhidi Kermani, 330

N

Nahj al-Balaghah, 76

Najaf Religious Seminary, 25

Nasiruddin Shah Qajar, 65

Nasrullah Pour Jawadi, 176

National Front, 156, 193, 325

national university, 155, 170, 199

Neauphle-le-Chateau, 17, 26, 65, 66, 67, 68, 69, 71, 72, 105, 106, 110, 111, 127, 286, 299, 300, 301, 302, 303, 304, 305, 308, 309, 310, 311, 313, 314, 315, 316, 317, 318, 319, 320, 321, 323, 325, 367, 368

Nematollah Nasiri, 292

neo-colonialism, 120, 253

Noble Messenger, 12, 18, 23

Noble Prophet, 11, 256, 309, 359

O

old centers of education, 191

Ottoman Empire, 93

P

Pahlavi, 17, 26, 33, 39, 64, 66, 69, 72, 74, 76, 79, 80, 81, 89, 90, 93, 97, 100, 104, 105, 106, 107, 111, 147, 148, 165, 171, 192, 222, 227, 228, 232, 236, 240, 241, 247, 259, 262, 263, 264, 265, 266, 272, 287, 289, 290, 292, 305, 306, 314, 318, 358, 362

Pahlavi dynasty, 17, 72, 76, 100, 111, 305, 306, 318

Pahlavi government, 26, 72

Pahlavi regime, 33, 39, 64, 80, 81, 89, 90, 97, 101, 104, 147, 148, 165, 192, 222, 227, 228, 232, 236, 240, 241,

Self-edification, 47, 49
self-negligence, 131
self-purification, 7, 31, 39, 44, 45, 49, 52, 92, 190, 194, 253, 309, 379
self-reconstruction, 7
self-reform, 25
seminary and the university, 35, 37, 90, 91, 123, 149, 150, 152, 192, 205, 206, 211, 354, 355, 379, 386, 387
seminary students, 25, 101, 103
Semnan, 44, 45, 92, 379
Seyyid Hassan Taqizadeh, 84
Shah's regime, 71, 103, 241, 242, 248, 262, 305, 313
Shaheed Mutahhari School, 45
Shaheed Mutahhari Seminary, 44
Shahreza, 32, 134, 166, 196, 233, 287
Shams Al-e Ahmad, 164
Sharif University of Technology, 82, 136, 290, 350
Shaykh Fadlullah Nouri, 36
Sheikh Ibrahim Zanjani, 36
Shiraz, 15, 40, 41, 78, 118, 131, 185, 186, 187, 202, 203, 221, 242, 244, 245
sick heart, 33
skilled engineers, 71
Skoff Cappuchi, 293
Soviet Union, 76, 94, 95, 110, 114, 143, 152, 153, 197, 211, 307, 314, 366, 387
spirit of humanity, 77, 185
spiritual and material progress, 34
spiritual and moral edification, 50
spiritual education, 47, 49, 235
spiritual independence, 129
spiritual instruction, 24
spiritual leaders, 63, 242, 248
spiritual purification, 47
spiritual responsibilities, 129
spiritual training, 29, 46, 47, 49, 188
spiritual welfare, 124
spirituality of Islam, 49
students and teachers, 245, 353

Supreme Council of Cultural Revolution, 176
Supreme Judicial Council, 55

T

Tabas, 121, 208
Tabas incident, 121
Tabriz, 82, 138
taghout, 39, 100, 119, 127, 130, 135, 245, 246, 374
Taleqani, 373
tawhid, 11, 43
Teacher's Training Centers, 15, 40, 41
teachers and professors, 18, 95, 96, 101, 126, 155, 157, 170, 199, 218, 233, 234, 236, 293
Teachers' Islamic Association, 275
Teachers' Training University, 30, 107, 116, 188, 251, 343
teacher-training Universities, 163
teaching and learning, 29, 30, 188
teaching centers, 117
teaching-learning system, 189
theological centers, 34, 103, 149, 349
theological seminaries, 22, 46, 47, 49, 50, 158, 177, 235, 360, 382, 383, 385
theology students, 16, 54, 64, 99, 104, 159, 242, 248, 258, 349, 355, 385
think-tanks of society, 20
thoughtful patriotic minds, 175
Torah, 12
traditional knowledge, 30
train human beings, 15
trained and righteous people, 187
training and education, 30, 31, 39, 44, 46, 88, 190, 194, 246, 253, 386
training and teaching, 140
true human beings, 26
Tudeh Party, 243, 306
Turkey, 93
Turkman Sahra, 166, 196, 233

www.ingramcontent.com/pod-product-compliance
Lightning Source LLC
Chambersburg PA
CBHW080509090426
42734CB00015B/3010